Research Methods in Second Language Acquisition

A Practical Guide

Edited by Alison Mackey and Susan M. Gass

WILEY-BLACKWELL

A John Wiley & Sons, Ltd., Publication

Library of Congress Cataloging-in-Publication Data

Research methods in second language acquisition : a practical guide / edited by Alison Mackey and Susan M. Gass. – 1st ed.
    p.   cm. – (Guides to research methods in language and linguistics)
  Includes bibliographical references and index.
  ISBN 978-1-4443-3426-5 (hardcover : alk. paper)
  ISBN 978-1-4443-3427-2 (pbk. : alk. paper)
1. Second language acquisition–Methodology.   2. Language and languages–Study and teaching–Methodology.   I. Mackey, Alison.   II. Gass, Susan M.
  P118.2.R473 2012
  401'.93–dc23
                                        2011021094

A catalogue record for this book is available from the British Library.

This book is published in the following electronic formats: ePDFs 9781444347173; Wiley Online Library 9781444347340; ePub 9781444347326; Mobi 9781444347333

Set in 10/13pt Sabon by SPi Publisher Services, Pondicherry, India
Printed and bound in Malaysia by Vivar Printing Sdn Bhd

1   2012

Contents

List of Contributors

Rebekha Abbuhl, California State University, Long Beach (rabbuhl@csulb.edu)
Melissa Baralt, Florida International University (missybaralt@gmail.com)
Kata Csizér, Eötvös University (weinkata@yahoo.com)
Zoltán Dörnyei, University of Nottingham (zoltan.dornyei@nottingham.ac.uk)
Patricia A. Duff, University of British Columbia (patricia.duff@ubc.ca)
Debra A. Friedman, Michigan State University (fried106@msu.edu)
Susan M. Gass, Michigan State University (gass@msu.edu)
Sylviane Granger, University of Louvain (sylviane.granger@uclouvain.be)
Tania Ionin, University of Illinois (tionin@illinois.edu)
Keiko Koda, Carnegie Mellon University (kkoda@andrew.cmu.edu)
Jenifer Larson-Hall, University of North Texas (jenifer@unt.edu)
Shawn Loewen, Michigan State University (loewens@msu.edu)
Alison Mackey, Georgetown University (mackeya@mac.com)
Kim McDonough, Northern Arizona University (kim.mcdonough@nau.edu)
Frederick L. Oswald, Rice University
Jenefer Philp, University of Auckland (philp@auckland.ac.nz)
Luke Plonsky, Michigan State University (plonskyl@msu.edu)
Charlene Polio, Michigan State University (polio@msu.edu)
Andrea Révész, Lancaster University (a.revesz@lancaster.ac.uk)
Pavel Trofimovich, Concordia University (pavel.trofimovich@concordia.ca)

1 Introduction

Alison Mackey and Susan M. Gass

Second language acquisition (SLA) research draws its research methodology and tools from a number of other fields including education, linguistics, psychology, sociology, and more. Partly for this reason, research methodology in second language studies is frequently evolving in response to developments in other fields as well as to developments in our own field. There is such a diversity of approaches to second language research methodology that a book like this one, where each chapter is authored by a person who is an experienced expert in that particular subarea, is one of the most efficient ways for research to describe and disseminate information about the method in which they have particular expertise.

Designing a research study and determining an appropriate method of investigation is a difficult task. But the task is made easier if one understands that research methods are not determined or decided upon devoid of context; research methods are dependent on the theories that they are designed to investigate. Thus, research questions are intimately tied to the methods used for determining an appropriate dataset.

This volume is intended as a guide for students as they design research projects. Each chapter presents some basic background to the area of research. This is a necessary feature since methodologies, as we noted above, cannot be understood in a vacuum. The book also has a pedagogical focus, with each chapter providing a practical, step-by-step guide to the method it covers, often informed by reference to studies using the method, carried out by the chapter's author. The method is discussed together with the theoretical frameworks within which it is commonly used. This how-to section takes students from beginning to end of a particular area. Finally, project ideas and resources (e.g., analytical tools when appropriate, references to more detailed discussions of a particular area), are also included, together with additional readings, and brief summaries of studies that have used the particular methodology, together with study questions that can be used as a basis for class

Research Methods in Second Language Acquisition: A Practical Guide, First Edition.
Edited by Alison Mackey and Susan M. Gass.
© 2012 Blackwell Publishing Ltd. Published 2012 by Blackwell Publishing Ltd.

discussions. Summary study boxes are given to help readers grasp the main ideas of studies that have used the method in question.

The book is divided into two parts. The first is on data types, which includes representative types of the wide range of data that is commonly studied in SLA, including both newer data types, such as learner corpora, along with more traditionally studied data, such as case studies. The second part is on data coding, analysis, and replication, where we present chapters on topics like meta-analyses. We will briefly summarize the contributions and explain how they fit together. We must also remember, however, that no elicitation instrument or methodology is foolproof; all have their advantages and limitations. And, as we have stressed in our other books dealing with research methods (Mackey & Gass, 2005; Gass & Mackey, 2007), no research project should be undertaken without extensive pilot testing.

In chapter 2, "How to Use Foreign and Second Language Corpora," Sylviane Granger covers learner corpus research, which she describes as originating in the late 1980s and involving the study of computerized databases of written or spoken texts. She focuses on frequency, variation, and co-text, and describes the powerful automatic analysis that can reveal quantitative information on a wide range of language from morphemes to lexical phrases. Tania Ionin's chapter 3, "Formal Theory-Based Methodologies," focuses on methods used in formal, generative SLA research. She describes the collection of empirical data on learners' production and comprehension of the target language, which are used to draw conclusions about the underlying grammar. Methodologies she focuses on include grammaticality judgment tasks and interpretation tasks. In chapter 4, "Instructed Second Language Acquisition," Shawn Loewen and Jenefer Philp focus on an often-studied context in SLA, providing a short review of the ways in which research on instructed SLA has been done, focusing on the practicalities of carrying out each one. Their chapter focuses in general on second language (L2) classroom instruction, and does not specifically address reading and writing research or investigations of individual differences, since those topics are covered in chapters 5, 8, and 9 in this volume.

In chapter 5, "How to Design and Analyze Surveys in Second Language Acquisition Research," Zoltán Dörnyei & Kata Csizér explain how survey studies are carried out in the context of SLA research, including the required steps for designing a survey that can provide valid and reliable data. They also discuss quantitative data analysis in relation to questionnaire data, as well as how to report survey results. In chapter 6, "How to Carry Out Case Study Research," Patricia A. Duff explains the background of one of the earliest methods used to underpin the field, characterizing its focus on a small number of research participants and occasionally just one individual (a focal participant or case) and explaining how behaviors, performance, knowledge, and perspectives are examined closely and intensively, often over an extended period of time. In chapter 7 "How to Use Psycholinguistic Methodologies for Comprehension and Production," Kim McDonough and Pavel Trofimovich explain psycholinguistics as having the twin goals of understanding how people comprehend and produce language. In other words, these authors describe the methodologies used in the attempts to figure out what processes, mechanisms, or procedures underlie language use and learning. In chapter 8, "How to Research Second Language Writing," Charlene Polio classifies empirical studies of L2 writing on the basis of the ways data are collected, coded, analyzed, and interpreted with the goal of understanding L2 learning processes. This chapter on writing is complemented by Keiko Koda's chapter 9, "How to Do Research on Second Language Reading," in which she explains that reading is a multidimensional construct involving a wide range of subskills whose acquisition depends on various learner-internal and learner-external factors. Different approaches to SLA see reading as cognitive or sociocultural and, as she argues, it is important to clarify the theoretical and methodological orientations in relation to the problem motivating the research.

The final chapter in part I, by Debra A. Friedman, focuses on "How to Collect and Analyze Qualitative Data." As she explains, the rise of theoretical and analytical frameworks such as sociocultural theory, L2 socialization, and learner identity has brought important insights to the field. She first provides her perspective on what qualitative research is and what it can contribute to the field, and then takes the reader through the process of designing and conducting a qualitative research project, including theoretical and practical aspects of qualitative methods for data collection and analysis.

In part II, we move away from a focus on data types, and instead the chapters provide input on how to analyze and code data. Complementary to Friedman's chapter is chapter 11 by Andrea Révész, "Coding Second Language Data Validly and Reliably," which brings a welcome perspective on a topic which is critical to all areas of SLA research. Coding, as Révész explains, involves organizing and classifying raw data into categories for the purpose of further analysis and interpretation. She explains the concepts of validity and reliability in relation to coding with a focus on relatively top-down, theory- and instrument-driven coding methods. Qualitative coding which emerges bottom-up from the data is the topic of the preceding chapter, by Friedman, as well as the next chapter, by Baralt. In chapter 12, "Coding Qualitative Data," Melissa Baralt focuses on how to code data using NVivo in qualitative research. NVivo is a type of software that assists researchers in managing data and in carrying out qualitative analysis. As Baralt explains, qualitative data often include text, notes, video files, audio files, photos, and/or other forms of media, and SLA researchers are increasingly using computer-assisted qualitative data analysis software to manage of all these data types, even if the researchers are not doing the kind of corpus work described earlier by Granger. Baralt provides coding examples based on NVivo software, but as she explains, the basic procedures presented in her chapter are also applicable to traditional pen-and-paper methods and other software programs.

Coding in both quantitative and qualitative paradigms having been considered, chapter 13, by Jenifer Larson-Hall, focuses on "How to Run Statistical Analyses." As Larson-Hall explains, inferential statistics let the reader know whether the results that have been found can be generalized to a wider population. She provides a brief survey of how to understand and perform the most basic and frequently used inferential statistical tests in the field of SLA. Chapter 14, by Luke Plonsky and Frederick L. Oswald, "How to Do a Meta-Analysis," defines meta-analyses in both their narrow and broader senses, and focuses primarily on the practical aspects of meta-analysis more broadly conceived. Meta-analyses and research syntheses are becoming more common in the field, representing a coming of age of the field, and also the ability to draw more general conclusions from our increasingly wide body of knowledge. In the final chapter, by Rebekha Abbuhl, "Why, When, and How to Replicate Research," we cover another crucial topic in the field and one which we believe is critically important for the future. If SLA is to continue to go from strength to strength, we need to proceed from a position of confidence in our findings. Replication will be a key part of that. This chapter by Abbuhl (and Porte [in press]) both suggest that replications, when carefully done, represent a cornerstone of our field. A recent UK grant by the Economic and Social Research Council (ESRC) to Emma Marsden (University of York, UK) and Alison Mackey (Georgetown University, US) for the project 'Instruments for Research into Second Languages' (IRIS) will support a database where research instruments can be uploaded and downloaded. This database will be fully searchable by a wide range of parameters including the first and second languages under investigation, the type of instrument, the age of the learner, and so on. The IRIS project aims to make the process of selecting and locating data collection instruments much more streamlined and efficient, which in turn will assist the process of replication in SLA research and, in the longer term, the scope and quality of meta-analyses. IRIS will also facilitate the scrutiny of instruments, so that researchers can more easily evaluate the validity, reliability, and generalizability of tools used for data collection. Replication, along with careful methodological approaches ranging from case studies to surveys to corpus-based studies, represent the past and future of SLA research. An understanding of the topics addressed in this volume is essential for the formation of a solid foundation for doing SLA research.

References

Gass, S. M., & Mackey, A. (2007). *Data elicitation for second and foreign language research*. Mahwah, NJ: Lawrence Erlbaum.

Mackey, A., & Gass, S. M. (2005). *Second language research: Methodology and design*. Mahwah, NJ: Lawrence Erlbaum.

Porte, G. (Ed.). (in press). *Replication studies in applied linguistics and second language acquisition*. Cambridge, England: Cambridge University Press.

Part I   Data Types

2 How to Use Foreign and Second Language Learner Corpora

Sylviane Granger

A New Resource for Second Language Acquisition

Background

Learner corpus research (LCR) originated in the late 1980s within the theoretical and methodological paradigm of corpus linguistics, which studies language use on the basis of corpora, that is, computerized databases of written or spoken texts. Although still relatively young, corpus linguistics has already had a big impact on language theory and description. One of its major contributions is the light it throws on three major facets of language: frequency, variation, and co-text. First, the combined use of large amounts of natural language data and powerful automatic analysis provides unparalleled quantitative information on all types of linguistic units, from morphemes to syntactic structures through single words and lexical phrases. Second, the comparison of corpora representing different varieties of language – geographical (e.g., British English vs. South African English), temporal (nineteenth-century vs. twentieth-century), or stylistic (informal conversation vs. academic writing) – helps uncover the distinguishing features of each variety and generally enhances our appreciation of the multifaceted variation inherent in language. Third, the remarkable ease with which computers identify the immediate context of words, that is, their co-text, has demonstrated the interrelation between lexis and grammar and generally led to a better understanding of the syntagmatic aspects of language.

The idea of compiling learner corpora – computerized databases of foreign or second learner language – and applying corpus linguistic tools and methods to analyze them arose from the wish to bring to the field of second language acquisition (SLA) the same kinds of benefits that corpora were providing to the linguistic field. Several linguists with a keen interest in SLA, often because they were also language teachers, concurrently but independently started to compile and analyze large electronic

Research Methods in Second Language Acquisition: A Practical Guide, First Edition.
Edited by Alison Mackey and Susan M. Gass.
© 2012 Blackwell Publishing Ltd. Published 2012 by Blackwell Publishing Ltd.

collections of second language (L2) data. Their objectives in embarking on this new type of research were theoretical, in that they wanted to gain a better understanding of the process of learning a foreign language or L2, and/or practical, in that they had a view to designing more efficient language teaching tools and methods.

LCR is at the crossroads between corpus linguistics and SLA. So far, it is mainly corpus linguists that have been active in the field. This can be seen as positive, as the first task that needed to be done was to adapt corpus linguistic techniques for learner corpus data and/or design new ones, and this required extended corpus expertise. The downside is that the grounding in SLA theory has been relatively limited to date. However, recent research shows that the LCR community wishes to situate itself firmly within the current SLA debate and, simultaneously, there is a growing - though admittedly still limited - awareness among SLA specialists of the tremendous potential of learner corpora.

The Specificity of Learner Corpus Data

Learner corpus data fall within the more open-ended types of SLA data distinguished by Ellis (1994, pp. 670–672), namely natural language use data and clinical data. Natural language use data is produced by learners who use the L2 for authentic communication purposes. In principle, only this type of data should qualify as bona fide learner corpus data, since corpora are supposed to be "authentic," containing data "gathered from the genuine communications of people going about their normal business" (Sinclair, 1996). However, fully natural learner data is difficult to collect, especially in foreign language settings which give learners few opportunities to use the L2 in authentic everyday situations. Therefore, learner corpus researchers often resort to clinical data, that is, open-ended elicited data such as written compositions or oral interviews. Experimental data, such as fill-in-the-blanks exercises, which force learners to choose between a limited number of options rather than allowing them to select their own wording, clearly falls outside the learner corpus range. Admittedly, in between fully natural data and fully experimental data, there is a wide range of data types which are situated at various points on the scale of naturalness. To reflect this continuum, Nesselhauf (2004, p. 128) suggests distinguishing a category of "peripheral learner corpora," which contain more constrained data such as picture description or translation.

Uncontrolled production data has been relatively neglected in SLA studies in favor of introspection data (especially grammaticality judgment tests) and the more controlled types of production data. The reason is that naturalistic data has been found to suffer from a number of drawbacks, among them (a) the impossibility of studying some language features because of insufficient data, (b) lack of control exerted over the main variables that can influence production, and (c) difficulty in interpreting the data. While fully valid with reference to previous data collections, these three arguments lose some of their validity when applied to learner corpus data, for reasons explained below.

The first argument suggests that unconstrained data collection fails to provide enough occurrences of relatively infrequent linguistic items, therefore making it impossible for researchers to investigate them. Larsen-Freeman and Long (1991, p. 26) provide the following example: "A researcher would have to wait a long time, for example, for subjects to produce enough gerundive complements for the researcher to be able to say anything meaningful about their acquisition." As learner corpora tend to be quite big, often over 1 million words, this oft-cited criticism loses much of its relevance. For a large number of linguistic phenomena, learner corpora provide a wealth of occurrences, to the point that researchers often cannot study the whole set and have to select a representative sample. It remains true, however, that the optimal size of a learner corpus depends on the targeted linguistic phenomenon. Articles, which are very frequent, can be investigated on the basis of a small corpus, while for lexical words – except the high-frequency ones – much larger collections are required. In addition, when assessing the size of an L2 corpus, one should consider not only the total number of words, as is customary in corpus research, but also the number of learners that produced the data. There is no direct relation between the size counted in number of words and representativeness measured in number of learners. For example, while the 80,000-word corpus used by Chen (2006) contains data produced by 10 students, a similar-sized sample from the International Corpus of Learner English (ICLE; see 'Project Ideas and Resources' below) would contain data from c. 130 different learners. The size and representativeness of learner corpora are a major asset of this new resource, which goes some way to meeting a frequent weakness of SLA studies, namely that it is often "difficult to know with any degree of certainty whether the results obtained are applicable only to the one or two learners studied, or whether they are indeed characteristic of a wide range of subjects" (Gass & Selinker, 2001, p. 31).

While previous collections of learner production data have often been criticized for their lack of rigor (e.g., Odlin, 1989, p. 151, for transfer studies, or Ellis, 1994, p. 49, for error analysis studies), this criticism cannot be leveled at learner corpus data, which, like all corpus data, is accompanied by rich ethnographic data. As rightly pointed out by Cobb (2003, p. 396), "It is a common misconception that corpus building means collecting lots of texts from the Internet and pasting them all together." However large it may be, a learner corpus will only be useful if it has been compiled on the basis of strict design criteria. Among the variables that are regularly recorded are learner variables, such as age, gender, mother-tongue background, or knowledge of other foreign languages, and task variables, such as medium, genre, topic, length, or task conditions (timing, use of reference tools, etc.). These variables are used as search criteria by researchers to compile their own tailor-made subcorpora. Admittedly, even in learner corpora that have been very carefully designed, not all variables are recorded. There is rarely any information on the teaching methods, the course material or the first language (L1) or L2 status of the teachers, all crucial factors in foreign language settings. In addition, proficiency level is often assigned on the basis of external criteria (number of years of study), an imperfect measure that has been denounced by a number of researchers (e.g., Pendar & Chapelle, 2008; Wulff & Römer, 2009). One way of overcoming this difficulty is to complement the ethnographic data with additional data obtained, for example, by submitting students to standardized questionnaires (motivation test, aptitude test, general proficiency test, vocabulary test).

The third drawback that has been pointed out in relation to unconstrained production data is that it is difficult to interpret, partly because learners may "avoid the troublesome aspects through circumlocution or some other device (Larsen-Freeman & Long, 1991, p. 26). This criticism also applies to learner corpus data. The absence of a feature in a learner corpus may not be evidence of a lack of knowledge but may result from an avoidance strategy. However, learner corpora provide a much more efficient and reliable basis for investigating avoidance, as they can be analyzed with software tools (see 'Project Ideas and Resources' below) that automatically extract the words or structures that are significantly underused by learners. Reliable measurements of L1 transfer effects are also greatly facilitated by the amount and variety of corpus data available to the researcher (see 'Data analysis' below). However, these advances do not solve all interpretation problems, and learner corpus researchers have recently started to complement learner corpus data with other data types, in particular experimental data (Gilquin, 2007). While in early LCR, learner corpus data and experimental data were seen as incompatible, researchers are now beginning to see the benefit of combining the two. See study box 2.1.

Study Box 2.1

Gilquin, G. (2007). To err is not all: What corpus and elicitation can reveal about the use of collocations by learners. *Zeitschrift für Anglistik und Amerikanistik*, 55(3), 273–91.

Background

Collocations combining a high-frequency verb and a noun phrase are notoriously difficult for learners of English. Previous studies have approached this problem from the perspective of competence (through elicitation tasks) or performance (by using learner corpora), but rarely have the two perspectives been combined.

Research questions

- How well do advanced French-speaking learners of English use *make*-collocations (quantitatively and qualitatively)?
- Do the learners' performance and competence differ in this respect?

Method

- Combination of error analysis, CIA (comparison of learner and native corpus data), and elicitation (fill-in exercise and acceptability judgment test).
- Corpora used: French subcorpus of ICLE and LOCNESS.
- Software tool: WordSmith Tools.

Statistical tools

- Chi-square test and distinctive collexeme analysis.

Results

The corpus study shows that French-speaking learners do not make many errors when using *make*-collocations, but they tend to underuse them and prefer those collocations that have a direct equivalent in French. In the elicited data, on the other hand, the error rate is much higher and learners' judgments are often unreliable. Both performance and competence are characterized by a high degree of L1 influence.

Learner Corpus Typology

Learner corpora have mushroomed in recent years.[1] An exhaustive description is therefore clearly beyond the scope of this chapter (for more details, see Granger, 2008). It is possible, however, to identify a number of dimensions along which they vary, such as time of collection, scope of collection, targeted language (L2), learner's mother tongue (L1), medium, and text type.

Time of collection

Cross-sectional learner corpora contain samples of learner writing or speech gathered from different categories of learners at a single point in time, while *longitudinal* learner corpora track the same learners over a particular time period. The overwhelming majority of learner corpora are cross-sectional. A few are *quasi-longitudinal*, that is, they contain data gathered at a single point in time but from learners of different proficiency levels. Very few are genuinely longitudinal, mainly because of the difficulty of collecting that kind of data in large quantities.

Scope of collection

Global learner corpora are collected on a large scale from a range of learners and used to inform SLA theory and/or generic reference and teaching tools. *Local* learner corpora are much smaller. They are collected by teachers as part of their normal teaching activities and directly used as a basis for classroom materials. Global learner corpora indirectly benefit learners who have the same profile as the students who produced the data (same mother-tongue background, same level of proficiency, etc.), where local learner corpora learners are both producers and users of the data, which can be expected to enhance its relevance and boost learners' motivation. Local learner corpus compilation is still the exception rather than the rule but it is also one of the most promising avenues in LCR.

Targeted language (L2)

Learner corpora can be classified according to the target language they sample. At first, corpora of *L2 English* reigned supreme, but *other L2s* (Dutch, Finnish, French, German, Italian, Korean, Norwegian, Slovene, Spanish, and Swedish, to cite just a few) have progressively joined the learner corpus bandwagon.

Learner's mother tongue (L1)

Mono-L1 learner corpora contain data from learners of one and the same mother-tongue background, while *multi-L1* learner corpora cover learners from several mother-tongue backgrounds. Commercial corpora, such as the Longman Learner Corpus, which are compiled by publishing houses, tend to have a multi-L1 coverage, while academic corpora, collected by researchers in SLA and/or foreign language teaching, tend to be restricted to one mother tongue, although there are some exceptions (see 'Selection and/or Compilation of Learner Corpus' below).

Medium

While the term *written learner corpus* unambiguously refers to corpora of learner writing, the term *spoken learner corpus* may refer to lexical or (much less frequently) phonetic/prosodic transcriptions of oral production data, and may or may not have associated audio files and more recently, with the advent of *multi-media learner corpora*, video recordings. Unsurprisingly, in view of the difficulty of collecting and transcribing spoken data, written corpora dominate the learner corpus scene.

Text type

The two favorite text types represented in LCR to date are *argumentative essays* for writing and *informal interviews* for speech. This preference reflects the wish to sample the least constrained types of production data (see 'The Specificity of Learner Corpus Data' above). It also ensues from the necessity of comparing like with like. Some diversification in terms of textual genres is desirable and indeed has begun to materialize. A good example is the Indiana Business Learner Corpus, which is made up of application letters from native and non-native speakers of English studying in three different undergraduate business classes in Belgium, Finland, and the United States (Connor, Pretch, & Upton, 2002).

Main Stages in Learner Corpus Research

Table 2.1 sums up the seven main stages in LCR. Five of these stages are mandatory, whatever the focus and ultimate objective of the study, while two – data annotation and pedagogical implementation (in italics in the table) – are regular but not required features of LCR.

Choice of Methodological Approach

Any researcher embarking on a corpus project chooses one of two main methodological approaches – corpus-based or corpus-driven – according to his or her research question. The corpus-based approach consists in testing a hypothesis or rule against corpus data. It is therefore essentially a deductive approach, where the corpus does not act as the master but rather as the servant to confirm or refute a pre-existing theoretical construct. The corpus-driven approach exploits the full force of the corpus. It is an inductive approach, which progressively generalizes from the observation of data to build up the theory or rule.

Most studies so far have been of the exploratory type, that is, corpus-driven. This powerful heuristic approach, which is exclusive to learner corpus data, has the advantage of not being limited by the initial hypothesis and is therefore capable of uncovering new features of interlanguage.[2] For example, automatic extraction of recurrent sequences of a particular length (two, three, or more words) has thrown invaluable light on the nature of learners' prefabricated language. The time has come, however, to exploit to the full the other approach, that is, to test SLA theoretical constructs on the basis of learner corpus data. As suggested by Myles (2005, p. 381), "it is now time that corpus linguists and SLA specialists work more closely together in order to advance both their agendas." The few studies that have used learner corpora to test an SLA hypothesis demonstrate the potential of a more SLA-informed approach. For example, Housen (2002) revisits previous morpheme studies on the basis of a longitudinal corpus of annotated oral learner data and native speaker baseline data. While the study generally confirms the general order of emergence of morphemes, it also reveals significant variation at the level of individual

Table 2.1   Main stages in learner corpus research.

1. Choice of methodological approach
2. Selection and/or compilation of learner corpus
3. *Data annotation*
4. Data extraction
5. Data analysis
6. Data interpretation
7. *Pedagogical implementation*

learners and generally highlights a number of benefits that can be gained from investigations of large learner corpora (see also Rankin, 2009, on verb-second structures in advanced L2 English).

Selection and/or Compilation of Learner Corpus

As learner corpus collection is time-consuming and often difficult to undertake, it is advisable to survey the field to find out whether there might be a learner corpus that is available and suitable for the investigation. Unfortunately, although there is a wide range of learner corpora, many are not available outside the team that has compiled them. Some, however, are fully available for research purposes, among them the ICLE (Granger, Dagneaux, Meunier, & Paquot, 2009) and the French Learner Language Oral Corpora (Myles, 2005; see 'Project Ideas and Resources' below).

If no existing learner corpus fits the bill and/or a local corpus is more relevant for the planned study, there remains the possibility of compiling one's own corpus, which in today's electronic world is much less difficult than in the past. A bespoke local corpus also has the invaluable advantage of being fully controllable (Millar & Lehtinen, 2008).

If the corpus analysis stage is planned to include comparison between learner data and a control corpus of native or expert language, it is essential to identify the corpora that best suit the analysis, taking into account important variables such as geographical variety (American English, Indian English, etc.), age, and text type. Failure to ensure full comparability of the data may lead to erroneous results, as demonstrated by De Cock (2002) for prefabricated sequences in speech and by Granger and Tyson (1996) for connectors in writing.

Data Annotation

Whether the learner corpus can be used as-is in raw format or needs to be enriched with linguistic annotations very much depends on the object of study. To analyze the word *clever*, which is a single invariable lexical word which only functions as an adjective, a raw corpus is sufficient and the annotation stage can be skipped. However, this is rarely the case, and as a result, there is often much to be gained from annotating the data. To take a simple example, many words in English can belong to different word categories. This is the case with the word *order*, which can be a verb or a noun and also features in the multiword unit *in order to*. If the research project focuses only on verbs, a raw learner corpus will entail a long process of manual disambiguation to extract all and only the verbal occurrences. Fortunately, some of the most reliable and widely available corpus tools are part-of-speech (POS) taggers, which automatically assign a word category to every word in the corpus with an accuracy rate that can reach 98% (see 'Project Ideas and Resources' below). It is important to bear in mind, however, that corpus linguistic tools were developed on the basis of native corpus data, and the errors present in learner corpora may induce mistaggings (for example, the verb *lose* written *loose* may cause the tagger to assign an adjective tag rather than the correct verb tag). It is therefore essential to start the analysis with a pilot study to check the accuracy of the tagging (see Granger, 1997, for an example of how this can be done, and Van Rooy & Schäfer, 2003, for a description of the impact of spelling errors on the accuracy rate).

There is a danger that analysts may limit themselves to the types of automatic analysis that the computer can provide. It is important to bear in mind, however, that corpus annotation software allows analysts to insert a rich variety of annotations into the text files. Although this work is largely manual and hence time-consuming, the return on investment is high as the annotations can subsequently be used as search criteria to retrieve all the occurrences in the corpus that match a particular query (see 'Data Extraction' and 'Project Ideas and Resources' below). This is the case, for example, with the CHILDES system, which was initially developed for the storage and analysis of L1 data and is particularly well suited for the annotation of spoken data (Myles & Mitchell, 2005). One type of annotation that is particularly relevant for learner corpora is error tagging. In most systems errors are coded for error type (number, gender, tense, etc.), word category (noun, verb, etc.), and/or error domain (spelling, grammar, lexis, etc.). What makes error tagging particularly useful is that the error tags are inserted into the text files and are hence presented in the full context of the text, alongside non-erroneous forms. In some studies all errors are coded (e.g., Chuang & Nesi, 2006), in others the tagging is limited to some specific categories, such as spelling errors in L2 English (Botley & Dillah, 2007) or particle errors in L2 Korean (Lee, Jang, & Seo, 2009; see Díaz-Negrillo & Fernández-Domínguez, 2006, for a survey of error-tagging systems).

Data Extraction

Corpus analysis tools, commonly referred to as concordancers, enable researchers to automatically extract a wealth of information from learner corpora. There are a number of such programs, which differ in their degree of sophistication, user friendliness, and availability (see 'Project Ideas and Resources' below). Most of them include the following functionalities.

Word list

The word list function creates lists of all the word forms in the corpus and displays these alphabetically and by frequency, together with a range of statistics (number of types, number of tokens, type/token ratio, mean sentence length, etc.).

Keyword list

The keyword function compares two previously created word lists and outputs the word forms that are statistically more frequent in one corpus than in the other. This is an extremely useful tool for LCR. Using this function, researchers can

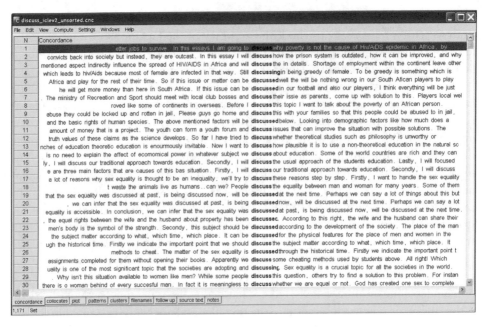

Figure 2.1 Unsorted concordance of the verb *discuss* in the ICLE.

identify the words and word sequences (or word/error categories) that distinguish one learner sample from another, or a learner sample from a comparable native/expert corpus.

Concordancing

The concordancing option presents all the instances of a linguistic item in their immediate linguistic context. Figure 2.1 shows the concordance of the verb *discuss* in the ICLE drawn up with WordSmith Tools (see 'Project Ideas and Resources' below). Sorting the context to the left and/or to the right of the search item allows regular patterns to emerge. As shown in figure 2.2, the sorting brings out occurrences of correct uses of *discuss* (*discuss a topic, a question; discussed above*), but also several occurrences of the erroneous pattern *discuss about*. Clicking on a concordance line shows the item in its wider context. Not only words but word parts and phrases can be searched in this way. In addition, if the corpus has been annotated, it is possible to use the tags or combinations of words and tags as search strings. Any form of the verb *be* followed by a past participle or a present participle will respectively extract passive and progressive verbal forms from the corpus, while a search for forms of the verb *be* followed by the base forms of verbs will extract all morphological passive errors of the type *they were arrest* or *it must be see*. The possibilities are endless.

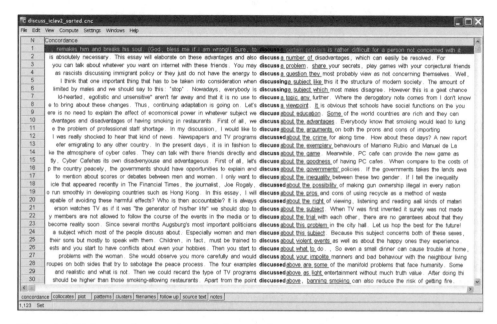

Figure 2.2 Right-sorted concordance of the verb *discuss* in the ICLE.

Distribution/range

This function allows researchers to visualize where the occurrences of the search item are situated in the corpus and hence find out whether the phenomenon under investigation is widespread in the corpus or is found in only a limited number of learner texts.

Collocates

This function retrieves the most common words to the right and/or left of the search items, that is, its collocates. Although useful in that it gives an immediate overview of the preferred company of any given word in a learner text, it cannot compete with the manual scanning of concordance lines, as it will also retrieve non-relevant items which happen to be in the near vicinity of the search item (for illustrations, see Altenberg & Granger, 2001).

Clusters

The clusters option retrieves all repeated sequences of words of a given length (two-word sequences, three-word sequences, etc.) from the concordance lines (e.g., *I will discuss, discuss about, discussed above*, from the concordance of *discuss*).

It is a powerful tool for assessing the rate and quality of prefabricated language in learner texts (De Cock, 2004).

Data Analysis

One of the hallmarks of learner-corpus-based research is the wide range of linguistic phenomena investigated. In addition to those phenomena which have featured prominently in SLA research, such as inflectional morphemes or word order, LCR has scrutinized many phenomena that have been under-researched, if not totally neglected, such as derivational morphemes, collocations, recurrent phrases, lexical richness, hedges, register, spelling, or punctuation, to name but a few.

Some of the analyses have focused exclusively on misuse and have led to the revival of error analysis in the form of *computer-aided error analysis* (CEA; Dagneaux, Denness, & Granger, 1998). The majority of studies, however, have tended to focus on other linguistic features that distinguish learner language from native language, many of which manifest themselves in over- and underuse rather than misuse. This approach, referred to as *contrastive interlanguage analysis* (CIA; see Granger, 1996, and Gilquin, 2000/1), consists in comparing not two different languages, as was the case with contrastive analysis, but two varieties of one and the same language: either two learner varieties (L2 vs. L2) or one learner variety and one native (or expert) variety (L2 vs. L1). Comparing two or more learner varieties is a good method for assessing the influence of the many variables that play a part in SLA, such as task effects, the learner's mother tongue, or level of proficiency. Comparing learner and native varieties makes it possible to uncover typical features of interlanguage, not only errors, but also instances of under- and over-representation of words, phrases, and structures. Two recent studies that illustrate the L2 vs. L2 approach are those by Ädel (2008), who compares the use of involvement markers in timed vs. untimed learner essays, and Groom (2009), who investigates the use of collocations and recurrent sequences by learners who spent less than one month in an English L1 environment compared to those who spent at least one calendar year. Although the number of exclusively L2-focused studies is growing, studies which involve a native or expert control corpus in addition to the L2 data tend to be more popular. Two recent studies representing this approach are those by Luzón (2009), who investigates the use of a rhetorical strategy, namely use of the first person pronoun *we*, by Spanish English as a foreign language (EFL) students and expert writers, and Callies (2008), who compares the use of raising constructions in a native English corpus and two EFL corpora (Polish vs. German learners). See study boxes 2.2 and 2.3.

Both CEA and CIA have been criticized for being guilty of the "comparative fallacy" (Bley-Vroman, 1983), that is, for comparing learner language to a native or expert norm and thus failing to analyze interlanguage in its own right. Several arguments can be offered in defense of the learner corpus position (Granger, 2009). First and foremost, it is important not to confuse theory and method. As rightly pointed out by Tenfjord, Hagen, & Johansen (2006, pp. 93, 102) in relation to CEA, comparisons of interlanguage and native language are methodological aids, which

Study Box 2.2

Cobb, T. (2003) Analyzing late interlanguage with learner corpora: Québec replications of three European studies. *Canadian Modern Language Review/ Revue canadienne des langues vivantes*, 59(3), 393–423.

Background

While the beginning stages of acquisition are well covered in SLA studies, intermediate-advanced interlanguage remains relatively uncharted. One of the main reasons for this neglect is lack of data.

Research question

- Is there a common pattern of interlanguage development across relatively distinct populations of advanced learners?

Method

- Replication of three European studies using comparable learner corpus data collected in Quebec: vocabulary frequency, use of prefabricated sequences, and features of reader/writer visibility in learner argumentative essay writing.
- Corpora used: Quebec teaching English as a second language (TESL) corpus (advanced) and English as a second language (ESL) corpus (intermediate).
- Software tools: WordSmith Tools and VocabProfile.

Statistical tools

Chi-square and t-test.

Results

The study suggests that advanced learners work through identifiable acquisition sequences that are systematic and more or less universal. It also provides avenues for pedagogical implementation of the results.

"can, in principle, service any theory." Errors in CEA are not to be confused with properties of the interlanguage. Rather they are "analytical concepts imposed upon the texts … in order to procure systematic data that any valid theory of SLA should be able to account for." Second, as mentioned above, CIA does not need to include an L1 norm. It is perfectly possible to focus exclusively on L2 data and analyze it in its own right either cross-sectionally or longitudinally. Third, it would seem reasonable to suggest that the comparative fallacy is in fact also present in many non-corpus-based SLA studies but in a hidden, undercover way. For example, all the

Study Box 2.3

Díez-Bedmar, M. B., & Papp, S. (2008). The use of the English article system by Chinese and Spanish learners. In G. Gilquin, S. Papp, & B. Díez-Bedmar (Eds.), *Linking up contrastive and learner corpus research* (pp. 147–175). Amsterdam and New York: Rodopi.

Background

Studies of article use in L1 and L2 acquisition have brought out a number of difficulties of a grammatical and/or pragmatic nature. The acquisition of articles has proved especially difficult for L2 learners who have no article system in their L1.

Research questions

- Will Chinese learners exhibit more non-native features in their use of articles than Spanish learners?
- Will difficulties be both grammatical and pragmatic for Chinese learners and exclusively pragmatic for Spanish learners?

Method

- Integrated contrastive model: comparison of article use in three L1 corpora (English, Chinese, and Spanish) and two L2 corpora (Chinese and Spanish learners). Obligatory context analysis based on annotated data.
- Corpora: compiled by the authors (the L2 Chinese corpus is part of ICLE).
- Software tool: WordSmith Tools.

Statistical tools

Chi-square and z-test.

Results

The results generally bear out the initial hypothesis that Chinese learners experience more difficulty than Spanish learners. The study provides a clear picture of the similarities and differences between the two L2 groups, among others the different hierarchies of accuracy of the definite (*the*), indefinite (*a*), and zero (0) articles.

studies that compare learners of different proficiency levels are in fact based on an underlying L1 norm. The same can be said of SLA studies reporting the results of grammaticality judgment tests. In LCR, the norm, rather than being implicit and intuition-based, is explicit and corpus-based (Mukherjee, 2005). Finally, L1–L2 comparisons are extremely powerful heuristic techniques which help bring to light hitherto undetected lexical, grammatical, and discourse features of learner language. These features can both inform theory-oriented studies and serve as a rich source of data for pedagogical implementation (see 'Pedagogical Implementation' below).

Relying on methods borrowed from corpus linguistics, learner corpus researchers have tended to analyze aggregated data, that is, data pooled together from a wide range of learners. The risk inherent in this approach has recently been pointed out by Durrant and Schmitt (2009, 168): "previous analyses of native vs. non-native writing have compared native and non-native corpora as wholes. This runs the risk of disguising differences between individual texts, and may therefore potentially produce misleading results." The solution is to apply statistical tests like the Student's t-test that take each text as an individual case, and more generally, as suggested by Reinhardt (2010, p. 95), to use "a mixed corpus and qualitative approach to the analysis of learner language."

Data Interpretation

LCR has so far been stronger on description than interpretation. This is perhaps understandable to a degree as the majority of the studies have focused on varieties of interlanguage that were badly in need of description, namely the upper intermediate and advanced stages of proficiency. It is time, however, to give more space to interpretation. The abundance of data provided by learner corpora, coupled with the plethora of corpora that can complement them – in particular, monolingual native/expert corpora and multilingual corpora – provide a very solid base from which to interpret L2 data. As suggested by Granger's (1996) integrated contrastive model, which combines multilingual and learner corpus data, and Jarvis's (2000) rigorous methodological framework, transfer studies in particular stand to gain from a multicorpus approach. Empirical evidence of transfer from L1 to L2 has often relied solely on the existence in the learner's L1 of a linguistic feature similar to that found in his or her L2. So, for example, Zhang (2000, p. 83) attributes the overuse of initial positioning of conjunctions in Chinese EFL learners to transfer on the basis that in Chinese "conjunction devices with similar meaning are mostly used at the beginning of a sentence." Similarly, overuse of the phrase *more and more* is presented as "most probably due to language transfer since a similar expression in the Chinese language *yue lai yue* was popularly used." In the absence of other corpus data, this interpretation can only be considered as highly tentative. Bilingual corpora, made up of data in both the L2 and the learner's L1, in this case English and Chinese, are needed to confirm or refute the similarity between the phenomena. In addition, multi-L1 learner corpora are necessary to tease out transfer effects from other effects. A look at the two phenomena mentioned by Zhang in the ICLE shows that they are in fact found in a wide range of learner populations and are therefore more likely to be developmental than transfer-related. As demonstrated by Osborne's (2008) study of adverb placement, the two effects often co-exist and the extent of the over- or underuse effect relates to the frequency of the linguistic phenomenon in the learner's L1 (for further discussion of transfer effects, see Paquot, 2010). See study box 2.4.

Study Box 2.4

Paquot, M. (2008). Exemplification in learner writing: A cross-linguistic perspective. In F. Meunier & S. Granger (Eds.), *Phraseology in foreign language learning and teaching* (pp. 101–119). Amsterdam and Philadelphia: John Benjamins.

Background

Comparisons of native and learner corpora of academic writing have highlighted a number of features of "unconventionality" in the phraseology of EFL learners. Although transfer has often been presented as a likely source, very few studies have tackled the issue systematically.

Research questions

- Does L1 have an influence on learners' production of multiword units that are typically used to fulfill an important rhetorical function (namely exemplification) in academic writing?
- Are semantically and syntactically compositional multiword units also transferable?

Method

- The use of five exemplifying items (*for example, for instance, example, illustrate,* and *exemplify*) is examined in light of Jarvis's (2000) unified framework for transfer studies and Granger's (1996) integrated contrastive model.
- Corpora used: five subcorpora of the ICLE (Dutch, French, German, Polish, and Spanish learners) and an extended version of the Louvain Corpus of Native English Essays (LOCNESS).
- Software tool: WordSmith Tools,

Statistical tools

Log-likelihood.

Results

The study shows that L1-related effects contribute significantly to learners' use of multiword units together with other factors like transfer of training and level of proficiency. Transfer of form often goes together with transfer of function as well as transfer of frequency and register.

Pedagogical Implementation

Although it is possible to carry out LCR in a strictly theoretical perspective, many learner corpus studies are carried out with a view to improving pedagogical tools and methods. The fields that have benefited most from learner corpus insights are lexicography, courseware, and language assessment. Rundell and Granger (2007) describe how learner and native corpus data was used to devise materials for inclusion in the *Macmillan English Dictionary for Advanced Learners*. The materials consisted of error notes intended to draw learners' attention to common pitfalls and an extended "improve your writing skills" section intended to help students write academic texts (see also Gilquin, Granger, & Paquot, 2007). Regarding courseware, Chuang and Nesi (2006) have error-tagged and analyzed academic texts written by Chinese students studying in the medium of English and designed a remedial online self-study package called GrammarTalk, which targets high-frequency errors such as article errors. A third field which stands to gain from LCR is language assessment. Carefully analyzed, learner corpora can help practitioners select and rank testing material at a particular proficiency level. Combined with natural language processing techniques, they can also be used to draw up automatic profiles of learner proficiency. The Direkt Profil analyzer, for example, provides a grammatical profile for L2 French and can be used to assess learners' grammatical level (Granfeldt et al., 2005).

Project Ideas and Resources

Space does not allow a detailed description of the multiplicity of resources that can help researchers embarking on a learner corpus project. In this section I list a few useful resources and refer the reader to two websites for further information:

- David Lee's meta-site 'Bookmarks for Corpus-Based Linguists': http://www.uow. edu.au/~dlee/CBLLinks.htm.
- Website of the Centre for English Corpus Linguistics (University of Louvain), which features an extended learner corpus bibliography: http://www.uclouvain. be/en-cecl-lcBiblio.html.

Learner Corpora

- Comprehensive list of learner corpora: http://www.uclouvain.be/en-cecl-lcworld. html.
- The ICLE, a 3.6-million-word corpus of argumentative writing by upper-intermediate to advanced learners of English from 16 mother-tongue backgrounds (Granger et al., 2009): http://www.uclouvain.be/en-277586.html.
- French Learner Language Oral Corpora, a web-based database of French learner oral corpora containing a range of corpora of learners of French as L2 at different developmental levels (Myles, 2005): http://www.flloc.soton.ac.uk.

Native Corpora

- Mark Davies's user-friendly interface to the 100-million-word British National Corpus and the 400+- million-word Corpus of Contemporary American English: http://corpus.byu.edu/bnc/ http://www.americancorpus.org/.

POS Taggers

- CLAWS7, POS tagger for English with an accuracy rate of c. 98%. Can be tested at http://ucrel.lancs.ac.uk/claws/trial.html.
- TreeTagger, a freeware program that can be used to tag several languages including English, French, Spanish, and German: http://www.ims.uni-stuttgart. de/projekte/corplex/TreeTagger/.

Concordancers

- WordSmith Tools, the most widely used commercial concordancer among (learner) corpus researchers: http://www.lexically.net/wordsmith/index.html.
- AntConc, a very good freeware concordance program: http://www.antlab.sci. waseda.ac.jp/antconc_index.html.

Corpus Annotation and Search Tool

Two freely available environments for corpus annotation:

- UAM CorpusTool: http://www.wagsoft.com/CorpusTool/.
- Dexter: http://www.dextercoder.org/slideshow/index.html.

Study Questions

1. What corpus format (raw vs. POS tagged) is it preferable to use to carry out a learner-corpus-based study of the following linguistic items?

    - The article *the*.
    - The preposition *to*.
    - The pronoun *you*.
    - Modal verbs.
    - The discourse marker *you know*.

2. You want to analyze the frequency and use of the connector *so* (e.g., *So the problem is pretty complicated*) in two learner corpora: a corpus of Spanish learner writing and a corpus of Chinese learner writing. Describe all the

methodological steps you need to go through before you have two valid sets of data to start your analysis.

3. You want to investigate subject–verb concord errors in a learner corpus. How will you go about it?

4. The table below gives the frequency of the connectors *therefore, thus,* and *however* in a subcorpus of the ICLE, which contains argumentative essays, and two native corpora: LOCNESS, a corpus of argumentative essays written by native American students, and Lancaster-Oslo-Bergen (LOB), a corpus of British English texts (mainly journalese and fiction). What conclusions can you draw from the figures?

Connector	ICLE	LOCNESS	LOB
therefore	36.4	136.7	47.0
thus	40.0	62.2	35.0
however	52.2	253.4	72.0

5. Figures 2.3 and 2.4 show a few right-sorted concordance lines of the word *as* extracted from the full concordance of *as* in the French and Chinese subcorpora of ICLE.

   (a) Examine each figure separately and try to identify the similarities and differences between the patterns used by French vs. Chinese learners.
   (b) Would it also be useful to draw up a left-sorted concordance of *as*?

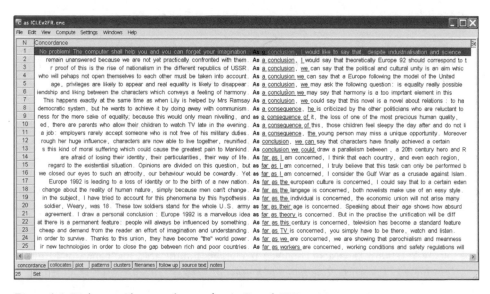

Figure 2.3 Right-sorted concordance of *as* in French EFL writing.

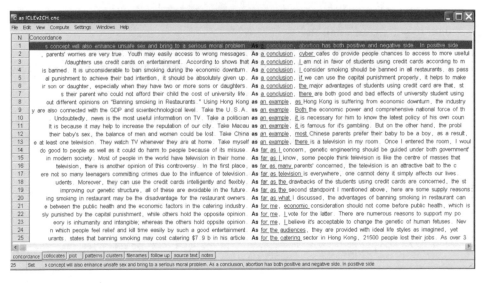

Figure 2.4 Right-sorted concordance of *as* in Chinese EFL writing.

Notes

1 See the Centre for English Corpus Linguistics website for a synthetic presentation of learner corpora around the world: http://www.uclouvain.be/en-cecl-lcworld.html. See also Schiftner (2008) for a recent survey of English and German L2 corpora.

2 It is important to point out, however, that research is never exclusively corpus-driven. Even in studies that are initially hypothesis-finding, theory underlies all subsequent stages of the analysis, from selection of the corpus to data interpretation.

References

Ädel, A. (2008). Involvement features in writing: Do time and interaction trump register awareness? In G. Gilquin, S. Papp, & B. Díez-Bedmar (Eds.), *Linking up contrastive and learner corpus research* (pp. 35–53). Amsterdam, Netherlands: Rodopi.

Altenberg, B., & Granger, S. (2001). The grammatical and lexical patterning of *make* in native and non-native student writing. *Applied Linguistics, 22*(2), 173–194.

Bley-Vroman, R. (1983). The comparative fallacy in interlanguage studies: The case of systematicity, *Language Learning, 33*, 1–17.

Botley, S., & Dillah, D. (2007). Investigating spelling errors in a Malaysian learner corpus. *Malaysian Journal of ELT Research, 3*, 74–93.

Callies, M. (2008). Easy to understand but difficult to use? Raising constructions and information packaging in the advanced learner variety. In G. Gilquin, S. Papp, & B. Díez-Bedmar (Eds.), *Linking up contrastive and learner corpus research* (pp. 201–226). Amsterdam, Netherlands: Rodopi.

Chen, C. W-Y. (2006). The use of conjunctive adverbials in the academic papers of advanced Taiwanese EFL learners. *International Journal of Corpus Linguistics, 11*(1), 113–130.

Chuang, F-Y., & Nesi, H. (2006). An analysis of formal errors in a corpus of Chinese student writing. *Corpora, 1*, 251–271.

Cobb, T. (2003). Analyzing late interlanguage with learner corpora: Québec replications of three European studies. *Canadian Modern Language Review/ Revue canadienne des langues vivantes, 59*(3), 393–423.

Connor, U., Pretch, K., & Upton, T. (2002). Business English: Learner data from Belgium, Finland and the U.S. In S. Granger, J. Hung, & S. Petch-Tyson (Eds.), *Computer learner corpora, second language acquisition and foreign language teaching* (pp. 175–194). Amsterdam, Netherlands: John Benjamins.

Dagneaux, E., Denness, S., & Granger, S. (1998). Computer-aided error analysis. *System, 26,* 163–174.

De Cock, S. (2002). Pragmatic prefabs in learners' dictionaries. In A. Braasch & C. Povlsen (Eds.), *Proceedings of the Tenth EURALEX International Congress. Vol. II* (pp. 471–781). Copenhagen, Denmark: Center for Sprogteknologi.

De Cock, S. (2004). Preferred sequences of words in NS and NNS speech. *Belgian Journal of English Language and Literatures (BELL), n.s. 2,* 225–246. Retrieved May 30, 2011 from http://hdl.handle.net/2078.1/75157.

Díaz-Negrillo, A., & Fernández-Domínguez, J. (2006). Error tagging systems for learner corpora. *RESLA, 19,* 83–102.

Díez-Bedmar, M. B., & Papp, S. (2008). The use of the English article system by Chinese and Spanish learners. In G. Gilquin, S. Papp, & B. Díez-Bedmar (Eds.), *Linking up contrastive and learner corpus research* (pp. 147–175). Amsterdam, Netherlands: Rodopi.

Durrant, P., & Schmitt, N. (2009). To what extent do native and non-native writers make use of collocations? *IRAL, 47,* 157–177.

Ellis, R. (1994). *The study of second language acquisition.* Oxford: Oxford University Press.

Gass, S. M., & Selinker, L. (2008). *Second language acquisition: An introductory course.* New York, NY: Routledge.

Gilquin, G. (2000/1). The integrated contrastive model: Spicing up your data. *Languages in Contrast, 3*(1), 95–123.

Gilquin, G. (2007). To err is not all: What corpus and elicitation can reveal about the use of collocations by learners. *Zeitschrift für Anglistik und Amerikanistik, 55*(3), 273–91.

Gilquin, G., Granger, S., & Paquot, M. (2007) Learner corpora: The missing link in EAP pedagogy. *Journal of English for Academic Purposes, 6*(4), 319–335.

Granfeldt, J., Nugues, P., Persson, E., Persson, L., Kostadinov, F., Agren, M., & Schlyter, S. (2005). Direkt Profil: A system for evaluating texts of second language learners of French based on developmental sequences. *Proceedings of the Second Workshop on Building Educational Applications Using Natural Language Processing,* 53–60. Retrieved May 29, 2011 from http://lup.lub.lu.se/luur/download?func=downloadFile&recordOId=530081&fileOId=624781.

Granger, S. (1996). From CA to CIA and back: An integrated approach to computerized bilingual and learner corpora. In K. Aijmer, B. Altenberg, & M. Johansson (Eds.), *Languages in contrast: Text-based cross-linguistic studies* (pp. 37–51). Lund Studies in English 88. Lund, Sweden: Lund University Press. Retrieved June 7, 2011from http://www.uclouvain.be/9002.html?publication=472006&entite=&zone_libre1=&matricule=00031717&annee=&portee=0&format=none&lang=en&urlAuteur=none&url=9002.html&sansEtat=1&tri=type,annee&Envoi=1.

Granger, S. (1997). Automated retrieval of passives from native and learner corpora: Precision and recall. *Journal of English Linguistics, 25*(4), 365–374.

Granger, S. (2008). Learner corpora. In A. Lüdeling & M. Kytö (Eds.), *Corpus linguistics: An international handbook. Vol. 1* (pp. 259–275). Berlin, Germany: De Gruyter.

Granger, S. (2009). The contribution of learner corpora to second language acquisition and foreign language teaching: A critical evaluation. In K. Aijmer (Ed.), *Corpora and language teaching* (pp. 13–32). Amsterdam, Netherlands: John Benjamins.

Granger, S., Dagneaux, E., Meunier, F., & Paquot, M. (2009). *The International Corpus of Learner English: Handbook and CD-ROM. Version 2.* Louvain-la-Neuve, Belgium: Presses Universitaires de Louvain.

Granger, S., & Tyson, S. (1996). Connector usage in the English essay writing of native and non-native EFL speakers of English. *World Englishes, 15*, 19–29.

Groom, N. (2009). Effects of second language immersion on second language collocational development. In A. Barfield & H. Gyllstad (Eds.), *Researching collocations in another language: Multiple interpretations* (pp. 21–33). Houndmills, England: Palgrave Macmillan.

Housen, A. (2002). A corpus-based study of the L2-acquisition of the English verb system. In S. Granger, J. Hung, & S. Petch-Tyson (Eds.), *Computer learner corpora, second language acquisition, and foreign language teaching* (pp. 77–116). Amsterdam, Netherlands: John Benjamins.

Jarvis, S. (2000). Methodological rigor in the study of transfer: Identifying L1 influence in the interlanguage lexicon. *Language Learning, 50*(2), 245–309.

Larsen-Freeman, D., & Long, M. H. (1991). *An introduction to second language acquisition research.* London, England: Longman.

Lee, S. H., Jang, S. B., & Seo, S. K. (2009). Annotation of Korean learner corpora for particle error detection. *CALICO Journal, 26*, 529–544.

Luzón, J. M. (2009). The use of *we* in a learner corpus of reports written by EFL engineering students. *Journal of English for Academic Purposes, 8*(3), 192–206.

Millar, N., & Lehtinen, B. (2008). DIY local learner corpora: Bridging gaps between theory and practice. *JALT CALL Journal, 4*(2), 61–72.

Mukherjee, J. (2005). The native speaker is alive and kicking: Linguistic and language-pedagogical perspectives. *Anglistik, 16*(2), 7–23.

Myles, F. (2005). Interlanguage corpora and second language acquisition research. *Second Language Research, 21*(4), 373–391.

Myles, F., & Mitchell, R. (2005). Using information technology to support empirical SLA research. *Journal of Applied Linguistics, 1*(2), 169–196.

Nesselhauf, N. (2004). Learner corpora and their potential in language teaching. In J. Sinclair (Ed.), *How to use corpora in language teaching* (pp. 125–152). Amsterdam, Netherlands: John Benjamins.

Odlin, T. (1989). *Language transfer: Cross-linguistic influence in language learning.* Cambridge, England: Cambridge University Press.

Osborne, J. (2008). Adverb placement in post-intermediate learner English: A contrastive study of learner corpora. In G. Gilquin, S. Papp, & B. Díez-Bedmar (Eds.), *Linking up contrastive and learner corpus research* (pp. 127–146). Amsterdam, Netherlands: Rodopi.

Paquot, M. (2008). Exemplification in learner writing: A cross-linguistic perspective. In F. Meunier & S. Granger (Eds.), *Phraseology in foreign language learning and teaching* (pp. 101–119). Amsterdam, Netherlands: John Benjamins.

Paquot, M. (2010). *Academic vocabulary in learner writing: From extraction to analysis.* London, England: Continuum.

Pendar, N., & Chapelle, C. (2008). Investigating the promise of learner corpora: Methodological issues. *CALICO Journal, 25*(2), 189–206.

Rankin, T. (2009). Verb second in advanced L2 English: A learner corpus study. In M. Bowles, T. Ionin, S. Montrul, & A. Tremblay (Eds.), *Proceedings of the 10th Generative Approaches to Second Language Acquisition Conference (GASLA 2009)* (pp. 46–59). Somerville, MA: Cascadilla Proceedings Project.

Reinhardt, J. (2010). Directives in office hour consultations: A corpus-informed investigation of learner and expert usage. *English for Specific Purposes, 29*, 94–107.

Rundell, M., & Granger, S. (2007). From corpora to confidence. *English Teaching Professional, 50*, 15–18.

Schiftner, B. (2008). Learner corpora of English and German: What is their status quo and where are they headed? *Vienna English Working Papers, 17*(2), 47–78. Retrieved May 29, 2011 from http://www.univie.ac.at/Anglistik/views_0802.pdf.

Sinclair, J. (1996). *EAGLES: Preliminary recommendations on corpus typology.* Retrieved May 20, 2011 from www.ilc.cnr.it/EAGLES/pub/eagles/corpora/corpustyp.ps.gz.

Tenfjord, K., Hagen, J. E., & Johansen, H. (2006). The hows and whys of coding categories in a learner corpus (or "How and why an error tagged learner corpus is not ipso facto one big comparative fallacy"). *Rivista di Psicolinguistica Applicata (RiPLA), 6*(3), 93–108.

Van Rooy, B. & Schäfer, L. (2003). Automatic POS tagging of a learner corpus: The influence of learner error on tagger accuracy. In D. Archer, P. Rayson., A. Wilson, & T. McEnery (Eds.), *Proceedings of the Corpus Linguistics 2003 Conference* (pp. 835–844). Technical Papers 16. Lancaster, England: Lancaster University Centre for Computer Corpus Research on Language.

Wulff, S., & Römer, U. (2009). Becoming a proficient academic writer: Shifting lexical preferences in the use of the progressive. *Corpora, 4*(2), 115–133.

Zhang, M. (2000). Cohesive features in the expository writing of undergraduates in two Chinese universities. *RELC Journal, 31*, 61–95.

3 Formal Theory-Based Methodologies

Tania Ionin

Background

This chapter examines data collection methods used in formal, generative second language acquisition (SLA) research. The ultimate goal of this field is to describe and explain the nature of second language (L2) learners' interlanguage (IL) grammar, and in particular to examine the extent to which IL grammar is constrained by Universal Grammar (UG; for overviews of the generative SLA approach, see Hawkins, 2001; White, 2003). Quantitative, empirical data on learners' production and comprehension of the target language are used to draw conclusions about the underlying grammar. Formal, generative SLA studies start with a research question (RQ) or hypothesis which stems from theoretical considerations and/or prior findings; the predictions generated by the research hypothesis are tested using production and/or comprehension methods. Although many SLA studies on morphosyntax examine L2 learners' naturalistic production (e.g., Lardiere, 1998; Prévost & White, 2000), typically, formal SLA studies use experimental methodologies, such as elicited production, grammaticality judgment tasks, and interpretation tasks. The focus of the present chapter is restricted to judgment and interpretation tasks; for more discussion of production tasks in SLA, see Mackey and Gass (2005).

The use of acceptability judgment tasks (AJTs) in generative SLA research is a consequence of the importance of judgments of grammatical acceptability in generative syntax (Chomsky, 1965, 1981). In generative syntactic theory, native speakers' judgments of (un)grammaticality are taken as primary evidence for the nature of speakers' linguistic competence: A sentence which is judged as grammatical by a native speaker is part of that speaker's mental grammar, while a sentence which is judged as ungrammatical is in violation of a linguistic rule of the speaker's mental grammar. Extending this reasoning to SLA, many researchers argue that L2 learners'

Research Methods in Second Language Acquisition: A Practical Guide, First Edition.
Edited by Alison Mackey and Susan M. Gass.
© 2012 Blackwell Publishing Ltd. Published 2012 by Blackwell Publishing Ltd.

grammaticality judgments can similarly inform us about the learners' linguistic competence in their target language (see White, 2003, for an overview). Generative syntactic theory has traditionally relied on introspective grammaticality judgments rather than controlled experiments, on the assumption that the judgments of an individual native speaker are representative of those of other native speakers (however, this assumption has been challenged, and use of controlled AJTs with native speakers is now increasingly common – see Cowart, 1997). Introspective judgments cannot be relied upon in SLA studies, and generative SLA research has from the start used experimental methods in order to control for variability among L2 learners. By keeping constant such factors as native language, proficiency level, type of L2 exposure, and age of acquisition, among others, an experimental SLA study can reduce variability among learners, and determine how learning proceeds within a given population (e.g., intermediate-level, adult classroom L1 Japanese L2 English learners). Alternatively, an experimental study can manipulate one or more of these factors (e.g., by comparing groups of different proficiency levels, and/or different native languages), in order to locate possible sources of learner variability.

The AJT in its traditional form asks participants to judge the grammatical (un)acceptability of isolated sentences, which are presented either in written form or auditorily (see study boxes 3.1 and 3.2).[1] The test contains both ungrammatical sentences which violate particular grammatical rules (e.g., a morpheme is missing or incorrect in an obligatory context, or the placement of negation is incorrect, or a *wh*-question is formed in a manner that violates syntactic principles), and their grammatical counterparts. Participants are given a binary response scale, such as "grammatical/ ungrammatical" or "YES/NO." Variations on this type of instrument provide participants with a Likert scale (e.g., from 1 to 7, or from –2 to +2), and ask them to rate the relative (un)acceptability of each sentence on this scale (see study box 3.3); yet another variant, magnitude estimation, asks participants to judge the (un)acceptability of each sentence relative to a baseline stimulus (see Sorace, 2010, for more discussion).

More recently, the use of AJTs in generative SLA research has been supplemented by the use of various interpretation tasks, which present sentences in context, rather than in isolation. One common interpretation task format is the truth-value judgment task (TVJT), which has its origins in first language (L1) acquisition research with young children (see Gordon, 1996; Crain & Thornton, 1998). In this task, participants are asked to judge the truth of the target sentence in the context of a preceding story, picture, or video. TVJTs used with young children are invariably oral in format, and typically involve a story either acted out with toys or told via a series of pictures. In the case of adult, literate L2 learners, the story can be provided in written form, possibly (but not necessarily) accompanied by a picture (see study box 3.4). Unlike AJTs, which explicitly focus on grammar, TVJTs focus on the meaning of the sentence, and are hence most appropriate for investigating phenomena at the syntax/semantics interface (e.g., interpretation of pronouns and reflexives, tense and aspect, definite and indefinite noun phrases, overt and null subject pronouns). In a correctly designed TVJT, the interpretation of a sentence as true or false in a given context depends on the syntactic structure assigned to the sentence. For example, consider the sentence in (1) (from Slabakova, 2003). The English present tense has a habitual interpretation,

Study Box 3.1

Johnson, J. S., & Newport, E. L. (1989). Critical period effects in second language learning: The influence of maturational state on the acquisition of English as a second language. *Cognitive Psychology, 21,* 60–99.

Background

This now classic study examines whether L2 acquisition is subject to critical period effects. According to the critical period hypothesis, adult L2 learners with late age of acquisition (AoA) should exhibit less target-like knowledge of the L2 than learners with an early AoA, as a result of cognitive maturation.

Research questions

- Is there an AoA effect on the L2 acquisition of grammar?
- What is the relationship between AoA and ultimate performance?
- What aspects of grammar are particularly problematic for different AoA groups?
- Can attitudinal variables (motivation, self-consciousness, and identification) explain all or some of the AoA effects?

Test instrument: GJT

- 276 sentences, 140 ungrammatical, 136 grammatical.
- 12 different rule types tested, including morphological rules (e.g., plural marking) and syntactic rules (e.g., question formation).
- Sample items:
    ungrammatical: The farmer bought two pig at the market.
    grammatical: The farmer bought two pigs at the market.
- Presentation of the stimuli: auditory.
- Rating scale: binary (YES/NO).

Participants

- 46 L1 Chinese and L1 Korean L2 English learners, all with five or more years of exposure to English; 23 early arrivals (AoA between 3 and 15) and 23 late arrivals (AoA between 17 and 39).
- 23 native English controls.

Statistical tools

- Correlational analyses between the different variables: AoA, test performance (overall, as well as on specific rule types), and scores obtained for attitudinal variables.

Results

For the early arrivals, there was an inverse correlation between AoA and test performance: as AoA increased, performance decreased. The late arrivals overall performed worse than the early arrivals, but there was no correlation between age and performance. These findings support the view that AoA effects are a result of brain maturation through puberty.

At the same time, AoA effects were not equally pronounced across all rule types: for example, AoA effects were more pronounced for determiners and plural marking than for progressive -*ing* marking and yes/no questions.

There were correlations between performance and some of the attitudinal variables, but AoA influenced test performance independently of attitudinal variables.

Study Box 3.2

White, L., & Genesee, F. (1996). How native is near-native? The issue of ultimate attainment in adult second language acquisition. *Second Language Research*, 12, 233–265.

Background

This study tests the hypothesis that the principles of UG are no longer accessible to L2 learners who are past the critical period. The study tests near-native and non-native L2 learners with different ages of acquisition (AoAs), in order to tease apart effects of proficiency from effects of AoA. The phenomena under investigation correspond to two principles of UG, Subjacency and the Empty Category Principle, which place restrictions on syntactic movement.

Research question

• Can any adult L2 learners achieve native-like competence?

Test instrument: GJT

• 60 *wh*-questions, half grammatical and half ungrammatical.
• 5 grammatical sentence types (5 different types of *wh*-questions).
• 5 ungrammatical sentence types (5 different violations of UG principles).
• 6 tokens per sentence type.
• Sample items:
    ungrammatical: What did you hear the announcement that Ann had received?
    grammatical: Who did John announce would be the new teacher?

- Presentation of stimuli: visual, on a computer; response times as well as accuracy recorded.
- Rating scale: binary (YES/NO).

Participants

- 89 L2 English learners (45 near-native, 43 non-native).
- 19 native English controls.

Statistical tools

- ANOVAs on both accuracy and reaction time data; comparisons across groups and across test categories.

Results

The near-native learners were found to be no different from native speakers on nearly every measure. Regardless of their AoA, near-natives correctly accepted grammatical sentences and correctly rejected ungrammatical sentences, which violated UG principles, providing evidence that native-like attainment is possible for late L2 learners.

Study Box 3.3

Montrul, S. (2005). On knowledge and development of unaccusativity in Spanish L2-acquisition. *Linguistics*, *43*, 1153–1190.

Background

According to prior literature (Oshita, 2001), L2 learners of English are initially insensitive to the differences between the two types of intransitive verbs: unaccusative verbs such as *arrive* and unergative verbs such as *laugh*. The present work extends the study of unaccusatives vs. unergatives to L2 Spanish, and furthermore tests whether more advanced learners are sensitive to lexical semantic differences among subclasses of unaccusatives.

Research questions

- Do L2 Spanish learners know the syntactic differences between unaccusative and unergative verbs, and how is this affected by proficiency level?
- Does the unaccusativity hierarchy proposed by Sorace (2000) play a role in the L2 acquisition of Spanish unaccusatives?

Test instrument: GJT

- 110 sentences, half grammatical and half ungrammatical.
- 9 unaccusative verbs (3 subtypes), 9 unergative verbs (3 subtypes), and 10 transitive verbs (distracters), each verb used in several different syntactic configurations.
- Sample items:

  unaccusative verb, preverbal subject: Juan llegó (Juan arrived) → *dispreferred.*

  unaccusative verb, postverbal subject: Llegó Juan (arrived Juan) → *preferred.*

  unergative verb, preverbal subject: Juan habló (Juan spoke) → *preferred.*

  unergative verb, postverbal subject: Habló Juan (spoke Juan) → *dispreferred.*

- Presentation of stimuli: visual.
- Rating scale: 5 points, from 1 (unacceptable) to 5 (acceptable).

Participants

- 71 L1 English L2 Spanish learners.
- 28 native Spanish controls.

Statistical tools

- Repeated-measures ANOVAs, followed up by pairwise comparisons.

Results

The low-proficiency learners did not distinguish between unergatives and unaccusatives, giving average ratings to all of them; however, the results were not fully consistent with Oshita's (2001) unaccusative trap hypothesis. Intermediate and advanced proficiency learners distinguished between the two verb classes, and furthermore showed sensitivity to different classes of unaccusatives, consistent with Sorace's (2000) unaccusativity hierarchy.

Study Box 3.4

Slabakova, R. (2003). Semantic evidence for functional categories in interlanguage grammars. *Second Language Research, 19,* 76–109.

Background

The functional category of aspect in English has a number of properties: The English simple present tense cannot be used to denote ongoing events;

progressive morphology must be used for ongoing interpretation; and English bare verb forms denote closed, completed events. None of these properties holds for Bulgarian, and only two of the three properties of English aspect are explicitly taught to Bulgarian students of English.

Research question

- Can L1 Bulgarian L2 English learners acquire the properties of English aspect that are not explicitly taught to them?

Test instrument: TVJT

- 60 items, each consisting of a story-sentence pair.
- 16 items with eventive verbs, crossing the interpretation provided by the story (habitual vs. ongoing) with the verb type (simple present vs. present progressive; e.g., *I fix my own car* vs. *I am fixing my own car*); 4 items for each context–verb-type combination.
- 16 items with stative verbs, crossing the interpretation provided by the story (habitual vs. ongoing) with the verb type (simple present vs. present progressive; e.g., *Cathy is lazy* vs. *Cathy is being lazy*).
- 16 items with perceptual reports, crossing the interpretation provided by the story (complete vs. incomplete event) with the form of the infinitival verb (bare vs. progressive; e.g., *I observed Matt eat a cake* vs. *I observed Matt eating a cake*).
- 12 distracter items.

Participants

- 112 L1 Bulgarian L2 English learners.
- 24 native English controls.

Statistical tools

- Mixed ANOVA crossing group, condition, target truth-value, and aspectual form of the verb.

Results

Higher-proficiency learners were quite target-like on all properties of English aspect, including the untaught property of perceptual reports. Across all learners, about half of the individual learners acquired the untaught property. It is argued that acquisition of the functional category of aspect leads to acquisition of all properties associated with it, including untaught properties.

so that a native English speaker should interpret (1) to mean that Jenna reads a French newspaper on a regular basis (e.g., she has a subscription to it). An L2-English learner might, erroneously, interpret *reads* as denoting the ongoing action of reading (since the simple present tense in many other languages allows for an ongoing interpretation); the learner would then interpret (1) as indicating that Jenna is reading a French newspaper right now. If (1) is presented in a context where the habitual interpretation is false (Jenna does not normally read a French newspaper) but the ongoing interpretation is true (she happens to be reading one right now), a response of "true" will indicate that the learner has assigned the wrong structure to the sentence, that of progressive aspect rather than perfective aspect (see example (8) below for a sample context for (1)).

(1)   Jenna reads a French newspaper.

A close relative of the TVJT is the picture matching task (PMT), which also has its origins in L1 acquisition research (see Gerken & Shady, 1996; Schmitt & Miller, 2010). Whereas the TVJT asks the learner to evaluate the truth of a sentence in the context of a single story or picture, the PMT presents a single sentence in the context of two or more pictures. The learner's job is to match the sentence to the correct picture. In a correctly designed PMT, the successful matching of the sentence to the correct picture depends on the syntactic structure assigned to the sentence. The exact opposite of the PMT is the sentence selection task, in which a single picture is presented with two sentences, and learners are asked to choose which sentence is a better match for the picture. While the PMT examines the interpretation assigned to a particular syntactic form, the sentence selection task examines which syntactic form best expresses a given interpretation (see study box 3.5).

Other tasks falling under the broad heading of interpretation tasks combine properties of both AJTs and TVJTs/PMTs: grammatical (un)acceptability is examined in the context of preceding stories or pictures. For example, participants might be asked to read pairs of sentences, and to judge the relative (un)acceptability of the second sentence as a continuation of the first. Alternatively, participants might be asked to read a story, and then be presented with a target sentence and asked to judge it as (un)acceptable in the context of the story. Unlike the TVJT, which asks participants to evaluate the truth of the sentence, such interpretation tasks ask participants to judge the appropriateness of a sentence in context.

An important issue to consider with all judgment and interpretation tasks is that of explicit vs. implicit knowledge. Generative SLA studies aim to test learners' underlying, implicit grammatical knowledge, in order to infer the learners' linguistic competence in their L2. However, the AJT is a rather explicit task, since it explicitly asks learners to think about grammar; if learners recognize which structure is being tested in the AJT, they may draw upon conscious, explicit knowledge, as learned in the classroom, and the results may not inform us about the learners' underlying grammatical intuitions. There are several ways of mitigating this problem. One is to hide the target items among many filler items, which look similar on the surface but test different structures; in this way, the learners may not be aware, at an explicit level, of what is being tested. Another way of reducing the possibility that learners

Study Box 3.5

Joo, H.-R. (2003). Second language learnability and the acquisition of the argument structure of English locative verbs by Korean speakers. *Second Language Research, 19*, 305–328.

Background

Some locative verbs in English enter into the locative alternation (e.g., *John loaded hay onto the wagon* vs. *John loaded the wagon with hay*), while others do not (e.g., *John poured water into the glass* but not *John poured the glass with water*). Constraints on the locative alternation include broad-range and narrow-range constraints; while English and Korean are similar in terms of the broad-range constraints on the locative alternation, they differ with regard to the narrow-range constraints: For example, some locative verbs which enter the locative alternation in Korean do not do so in English.

Research questions

- Do L1 Korean L2 English learners develop native-like knowledge of the English locative alternation, including the narrow-range constraints on which English and Korean differ?
- Does L1 transfer influence the acquisition of the English locative alternation?

Test instruments: picture selection task and sentence selection task

- 24 items in each task, with 12 different verbs each presented twice.
- The 12 verbs fell into six different subclasses of locative verbs, two per subclass.
- Format of the picture selection task and sample item: a single sentence (*John sprayed the door with paint* or *John sprayed paint onto the door*) presented with two pictures: (a) John sprays some paint on the door and then leaves; (b) John sprays the door completely and then leaves → participant chooses which picture is a better match for the sentence.
- Format of the sentence selection task and sample item: the two alternating variants (*John sprayed the door with paint* and *John sprayed paint onto the door*) presented with one of two pictures: (a) John sprays some paint on the door and then leaves; or (b) John sprays the door completely and then leaves → participant chooses which sentence is a better match for the picture.

Participants

- 59 L1 Korean L2 English learners.
- 17 native English controls.

Statistical tools

- Repeated-measures ANOVAs for each group and for each task with the type of picture or type of sentence, and the type of verb class, as the within-subjects variables.

Results

The learners had difficulty with the narrow-range constraints on the English locative alternation, while showing sensitivity to the broad-range constraints manifested in English as well as Korean. However, the learners' particular pattern of difficulty was not entirely due to L1 transfer.

are accessing explicit knowledge is to make the test timed (and/or present the stimuli auditorily), so that learners respond with their first intuitive judgment, and do not have time to access their explicit knowledge. Switching from a task that focuses on form (the AJT) to one that focuses on meaning (e.g., the TVJT, or the PMT) also makes it less likely that learners will draw upon explicit knowledge of form. See Ellis (2005) for more discussion of this issue.

How to Design Judgment and Interpretation Tasks

How to Design an Acceptability Judgment Task

An AJT in which sentences are presented in isolation is most appropriate when the RQ concerns a morphological or syntactic phenomenon: when the sentence is either grammatical or ungrammatical, independently of context. The following steps should be taken in designing an AJT.

Step 1

Formulate an RQ, and determine whether AJT format is appropriate. For example, an AJT can be used to examine an RQ on inflectional morphology, such as (2), or an RQ on syntactic movement, such as (3).

(2) "Do L2 English learners recognize that the -*s* suffix is required for verbs in the third person present tense singular, but not for other tense/person/number combinations?"

(3) "Do L2 English learners recognize that the auxiliary must be moved to the front of a question, preceding the subject?".

Step 2

Decide on exactly which *sentence types* will be examined. For the RQ in (2), one can choose to focus on sentences where third person present tense singular -*s* is used correctly vs. where it is omitted; it is also possible to include sentences where the third person -*s* is used incorrectly (e.g., with a first person subject). It is also necessary to decide whether only present-tense sentences with singular subjects will be examined, or whether sentences with plural subjects and/or in the past tense will be included as well. Similarly, for the RQ in (3), it is necessary to decide which auxiliaries will be tested (only the *be* auxiliary, or also the *do* auxiliary, the *have* auxiliary, and/or modal auxiliaries), and whether the focus will be on yes/no questions, *wh*-questions, or both.

Importantly, for every ungrammatical sentence type tested, the corresponding grammatical sentence type should be tested as well, whenever possible. For instance, if sentences with omitted third person -*s* are included, sentences where -*s* is used correctly should also be included; if the test includes ungrammatical *wh*-questions which lack subject–auxiliary inversion, corresponding grammatical *wh*-questions with inversion should be included as well. This is an important control, designed to ensure that the ungrammatical sentences are being rejected for the right reason: If a learner rejects both *wh*-questions with inversion and those without, then the lack of inversion cannot be the reason for the rejection. An additional way of ensuring that learners are rejecting ungrammatical sentences for the right reason is asking learners to provide a correction for each sentence rated as ungrammatical. A possible problem with this method, however, is that learners may rate sentences as grammatical in order to avoid the effort of making a correction. One way around this problem is to have the learners first rate sentences as grammatical vs. ungrammatical, without asking for corrections, and afterwards present the learners with all the sentences they rated as ungrammatical, and ask for corrections (see Gass & Alvarez-Torres, 2005, for an example).

It is possible – and indeed recommended – to include more than one type of grammatical phenomenon in the test: For example, a single AJT can be used to address the RQs in both (2) and (3), with different sentence types addressing each RQ. The different sentence types then serve as fillers for one another (see also Step 4 below).

In order to address the RQs in both (2) and (3) in a single task, it is necessary to include at least four test categories in the AJT, as illustrated in (4). More categories can be added, as long as each ungrammatical category has a corresponding grammatical category (e.g., if the category of "-*s* suffix used with a plural third person subject – ungrammatical" is added, the category of "no -*s* suffix used with a plural third person subject – grammatical" should also be added).

(4) Category 1: grammatical declarative sentence; the -*s* suffix present with a third person singular subject
     Category 2: ungrammatical declarative sentence; the -*s* suffix omitted with a third person singular subject
     Category 3: grammatical *wh*-question, with subject–auxiliary inversion
     Category 4: ungrammatical *wh*-question, with an uninverted auxiliary

Step 3

Create *tokens* for each category; in the case of the AJT, each token corresponds to a single sentence. There should be the same number of tokens in each category. The recommended number of tokens per category is four or more (some studies have as many as six or even ten). The number of tokens per category is determined in part by the number of categories (if the test already has ten categories, including six items per category makes for a fairly long test, especially once fillers are included as well – see Step 4 below). Sample tokens for the four categories in (4) are given in (5).

(5) Category 1: Julia eats breakfast every morning at 9 a.m.
Category 2: Tom eat dinner every evening at 6 p.m.
Category 3: What is Clyde cooking in the kitchen?
Category 4: What Roberta is watching on television?

Tokens across categories, and especially tokens in categories that are being compared directly (e.g., category 1 vs. 2, or 3 vs. 4 above) should be similar on factors such as length, plausibility, lexical complexity, and syntactic complexity. For more on how to design tokens in an AJT, see Cowart (1997).

Step 4

Decide whether *filler* items should be included in the test. Fillers (or distracters) are designed to distract participants' attention from the target items: They should look similar on the surface, but test different phenomena. Examples of possible filler categories and items for the categories in (4) are given in (6).

(6) Filler category 1: correct plural marking: Josh bought two books at the bookstore.
Filler category 2: missing plural marking: Margaret read two book last night.
Filler category 3: correct *wh*-word in a question: When did Joanna travel to Mexico?
Filler category 4: incorrect *wh*-word in a question: What did Bill travel to Germany?

Fillers should be included whenever the researcher wants to distract the learners' focus from the target structure(s), and make the test less explicit; the ratio of target items to fillers varies from one study to another, and depends on the extent to which the items from different target categories can serve as fillers for one another. Altogether, across both target items and fillers, there should be an equal number of grammatical and ungrammatical test items.

Step 5

Decide on the test modality and presentation. AJTs used in SLA research with adults are typically presented visually (on paper, or on a computer screen). However, some studies (e.g., Johnson & Newport, 1989) use the auditory modality, presenting stimuli to participants over headphones. The auditory modality is a must in research with low-literacy learners and with young children.

Traditionally, written AJTs have been presented in a paper-and-pencil format, but now it is becoming more common to present the task in electronic form. Various web-based survey tools now allow researchers to place AJTs (both written and auditory) on the internet, which facilitates the distribution of the task to participants in different physical locations. Such web-based tools record participant responses automatically, thus removing the step of manual data entry, which is often tedious as well as subject to human error.

Step 6

Decide on the rating scale. Some choices include a binary YES/NO scale, a Likert scale (typically, with anywhere between four and seven points on the scale), or the magnitude estimation method (see Sorace, 2010). A binary scale is appropriate for very clear and strong grammaticality contrasts, as in the above examples; a scale with more than two points, or the magnitude estimation method, is more appropriate for more subtle contrasts. Many studies include a "don't know" option which learners can choose if they are unsure of the response. It is important not to include a zero option: in a scale like "–2, –1, 0, +1, +2," the zero is supposed to stand for "neither very ungrammatical nor very grammatical," but learners may instead treat it as meaning "unsure" or "don't know." It is better to have a "don't know" option on the side. However, a possible danger in this case is that learners will over-rely on the "don't know" option, in order to avoid making a judgment; for this reason, many studies do not include a "don't know" option at all, and use only a numerical scale (with no zero midpoint). An alternative solution is to include a "don't know" option in the test, and to exclude from analysis all learners who over-rely on it (a numerical and/or statistical criterion should be set for determining over-reliance).

Step 7

Create the test instrument. All of the items (target items and fillers) should be randomized for order of presentation inside the test instrument. A blocking procedure can be used, by which the test instrument is divided into several blocks, where each block contains one token from each test category, and the corresponding number of fillers. For example, a 60-item AJT with 24 test items (four categories of six items each) and 36 filler items should have six blocks of 10 items each: each block would have one item from each of the four test categories, plus six filler items. The items within each block are randomized for order of presentation. Blocking ensures that items of the same type are not all clustered at the beginning or the end of the test instrument. It is recommended to furthermore create two different test orders, each administered to one half of the participants; the simplest way of doing so is to break the test into two halves (e.g., blocks 1 through 3 vs. blocks 4 through 6 in the above example), and reverse the order between the two halves. See Cowart

(1997) for more details on blocking, randomization, and test order, as well as on the benefits of creating multiple scripts of a single test instrument.

Step 8

Determine the participant groups. In addition to creating the test instrument, it is necessary to decide which groups to include in the study, as well as to decide on the inclusion and exclusion criteria for each group. Formal SLA studies with adult learners typically control for the learners' native language and proficiency level: For instance, if only one group is included in the study, all the learners in it would have the same native language and be of similar proficiency; alternatively, multiple groups can be compared, which differ from one another on native language and/or on proficiency. Some other factors that are often controlled for include length of exposure to the target language, the age of first target language exposure, the type of learning environment, and the level of education. In studies which test child L2 learners, children's chronological age as well as age of first target language exposure must be taken into account.

Formal SLA studies nearly always include a control group of adult native speakers of the target language. The control group is expected to perform at ceiling on all test categories. Pilot testing the test instrument with a small group of native speakers is a must: if native speakers are not performing at or near ceiling (i.e., are not saying "yes" to grammatical sentences and "no" to ungrammatical sentences), this may indicate problems with the test instrument, which should be corrected before further testing takes place. Beyond the native adult control group, other control groups and/or comparison groups may be necessary depending on the RQ and the experimental population. For example, studies with child L2 learners typically include control groups of monolingual children matched to the L2 children on chronological age and/or on proficiency in the target language.

Comparisons among L2 learners with different L1s are often done to examine the effects of L1 transfer, which can be manifested in any judgment or interpretation tasks. In an AJT, L1 transfer may cause learners to erroneously rate ungrammatical sentences as grammatical, because their counterparts in the learners' L1 are grammatical. In a TVJT or PMT, learners may say "true" instead of "false," or choose the non-target picture, because they assign to the sentence an interpretation that it would have in their L1, rather than in their L2. Thus, in designing judgment and interpretation tasks, researchers need to take into account not only what is grammatical/appropriate in the target language, but also what the interpretation of the corresponding sentences in the learners' L1s would be. At the same time, it is also possible that learners' errors are not due to L1 transfer, but rather reflect a general developmental pattern. In order to tease apart the effects of L1 transfer from transfer-independent developmental patterns, formal SLA studies often compare two different groups: for example, a group of L2 learners whose L1 behaves like the L2 in the relevant respect, and a different group whose L1 differs from the L2 in the relevant respect. These groups need to be balanced on factors such as proficiency, length of L2 exposure, and the learning environment.

How to Design an Interpretation Task

When the study's focus is on the link between form and meaning, rather than on form alone, it is more appropriate to present sentences in context, rather than in isolation. The basic logic of the AJT – deciding on the test categories, designing tokens, including fillers, and blocking and randomizing items for order of presentation – applies to interpretation tasks as well. However, the item format is different: Whereas an item in an AJT is a single sentence, an item in an interpretation task may be a pair of sentences, or a story followed by a sentence, or a picture or series of pictures followed by a sentence.

This can be illustrated with the topic of grammatical aspect, which is often investigated in formal SLA studies using interpretation tasks. Sentences with both simple verb forms (e.g., *The girl swims, The girl swam*) and progressive verb forms (e.g., *The girl is swimming*) are grammatical, but have different interpretations. An interpretation task can provide the context which will make the sentence with a simple verb form true/acceptable, and the one with the progressive verb form false/ unacceptable, and vice versa. The examples in (7) and (8) below illustrate how aspectual interpretation has been examined in SLA studies using two different types of interpretation tasks.

In (7a–b), the second sentence in the pair indicates that the event of singing two songs is not complete. The simple past in English entails completion, so in (7a), the second sentence is expected to be rated as unacceptable as a continua-tion of the first sentence (there is a conflict between the statements that the niece sang – that is, finished singing – two songs, and that she left after the first song). In contrast, the past progressive does not entail completion, so in (7b), the sec-ond sentence is expected to be rated an acceptable continuation of the first. Learners who have not acquired all the properties of the simple past or of the past progressive are then expected to be non-target-like on (7a) or (7b), respectively.

(7) **Example of interpretation task with sentence pairs (Gabriele, Martohardjono, & McClure, 2002):**
  a. *Category 1: sentence 1 contains simple past verb:*
      My niece **sang** two Christmas songs at church. She left after the first song.
  b. *Category 2: sentence 1 contains past progressive verb:*
      My niece **was singing** two Christmas songs at church. She left after the first song.

In the TVJT in (8), the context makes it clear that Jenna does not normally read a French newspaper, but is reading one today, because her neighbor left it for her by mistake. The simple present tense in English denotes habitual events, so (8a) is expected to be judged as "false" in the context in (8). In contrast, the present progressive denotes ongoing events, so (8b) is expected to be judged as "true" in this context. A different test category in the same task reverses this pattern, presenting a story which makes (8a) true and (8b) false.

(8) **Example of TVJT with story-sentence pairings (Slabakova, 2003):**
Story context: Jenna woke up late this morning. Her neighbor, a Frenchman, had picked up her newspaper instead of his French one, and left for his office. But reading in French is not too difficult … Tonight she will be able to tell him about her adventure with the French newspaper.
   a.   *Category 1: target sentence contains simple present verb:*
        Jenna reads a French newspaper.
   b.   *Category 2: target sentence contains present progressive verb:*
        Jenna is reading a French newspaper.

In a TVJT, it is important to have the same number of items (across targets and fillers together) that are designed to be true and that are designed to be false. Similarly, in other interpretation tasks, there should be the same number of items designed to be appropriate and inappropriate (and/or reflect different degrees of (in)appropriateness). Other decisions to be made with an interpretation task include: how much context to provide; whether to present the context and/or the target sentence visually or auditorily; and whether to include a picture, or multiple pictures, illustrating the story. For low-proficiency learners, an interpretation task consisting of a picture and a target sentence is more appropriate than a task containing a lengthy story which the learners may not fully comprehend. However, not every semantic contrast can be expressed using pictures. Other ways of ensuring that learners understand the context include (a) providing the context in the learners' native language (with only the target sentence presented in the target language); (b) using simple vocabulary, for example, vocabulary typically introduced during the first semester of instruction; (c) training the learners on the vocabulary used in the task; and (d) including an additional task checking learners' familiarity with the vocabulary. Options (b) through (d) should also be considered for AJTs, if there is any concern that the learners may not be familiar with the vocabulary.

In a PMT, the item format is different from that of other interpretation tasks: a single PMT item consists of a single sentence presented in the context of two or more pictures. One picture (the *match*) should match the target interpretation of the sentence, while another picture (the *mismatch*) should match a non-target interpretation that learners are expected to assign to the sentence given the research hypothesis. As an illustration, consider the sentences in (9), which are concerned with anaphor interpretation. Each sentence in (9) can be presented in the context of two pictures: picture A, which represents Snow White looking at Cinderella painting Cinderella; and picture B, which represents Snow White looking at Cinderella painting Snow White. Picture A is the match for (9a), because reflexives like *herself* must take a local antecedent (in this case, *Cinderella*), and picture B is the match for (9b), because pronouns like *her* may not take a local antecedent but may take a long-distance antecedent (in this case, Snow White), per Binding Theory principles (Chomsky, 1981). If learners chose the mismatch picture (picture B for (9a), or picture A for (9b)), this would indicate that they are misinterpreting reflexives or pronouns, respectively. Some studies also include a third distracter picture for each item: In this case, distracter picture

C might contain Cinderella looking at Snow White painting Cinderella. If learners choose the distracter picture, that would indicate that they are either not paying attention, or not fully comprehending the sentence. In any PMT, is important to ensure that the learners are familiar with the characters in the pictures (e.g., can tell apart Snow White and Cinderella).

(9) a. Snow White sees that Cinderella is painting herself.
     b. Snow White sees that Cinderella is painting her.

   Note that the sentences in (9) can be tested with a TVJT as well as with a PMT: in a TVJT, one item would present (9a) in the context of picture A, while another would present it in the context of picture B, and the same would happen with (9b); the learner's task then is to say whether the sentence matches the picture – that is, whether it is true in the context of the picture. In fact, precisely such a picture-based TVJT format has been used in studies on anaphor interpretation in both child language acquisition (Chien & Wexler, 1990) and SLA (Lee & Schachter, 1998; White, 1998). The advantage of the TVJT is that it allows the researcher to find out how a learner judges each picture–sentence mapping; in contrast, the PMT allows researchers only to find out which picture–sentence mapping is preferred, but does not inform them what the learner thinks about the dispreferred mapping. For example, if a learner correctly chooses picture A for sentence (9a) in a PMT, the researcher does not know whether the learner considers picture B an impossible match for (9a), or whether it is possible, but only dispreferred. For this reason, the TVJT format is often preferred to the PMT format. An advantage of the PMT is that it is half as long as the TVJT, and hence takes less time to administer: the PMT requires only two items (two sentences, each presented with two pictures) where the TVJT requires four items (each sentence repeated twice, with different pictures). The time-saving nature of the PMT is an important consideration, especially in work with child learners, who have shorter attention spans. Furthermore, there are cases where the researchers are in fact interested in preferences rather than absolute judgments, which also makes the PMT format appropriate.

Summary

In summary, there are many interpretation and judgment tasks for researchers to choose from. The choice of a particular method is determined by (a) the RQ; (b) the linguistic phenomena under investigation; (c) the population(s) being tested; and (d) the time and resources available to the researchers. Regardless of the task format, certain methodological guidelines should always be followed. These include (but are not limited to): having the same number of tokens per category; balancing the number of grammatical/ungrammatical, appropriate/inappropriate, or true/false items in the test instrument; using filler/distracter items; ensuring that the learners are familiar with the vocabulary used in the task, and/or with the characters in the pictures; and having a control group of native speakers.

Project Ideas and Resources

Analytical Tools

The results of AJTs, TVJTs, and other judgment or interpretation tasks can be analyzed with t-tests and ANOVAs. Since a judgment or interpretation task always compares at least two categories (e.g., grammatical vs. ungrammatical categories in an AJT; categories with the target TRUE vs. the target FALSE response in a TVJT), a statistical test which analyzes the effects of within-subjects variables is appropriate. A paired-samples t-test is appropriate for analyzing the response of a single group (e.g., a group of L2 learners) to two measures (e.g., grammatical vs. ungrammatical sentences in an AJT). If multiple groups (e.g., L2 learners and native speakers) are being compared, and/or if there are more than two measures, then an ANOVA should be used (an independent ANOVA if there are multiple groups, but only one measure, and a repeated-measures ANOVA if there are multiple measures taken from the same participants). For more discussion of statistical tools that can be used for an AJT, see Cowart (1997).

Further Reading

- AJTs: Schütze (1996); Cowart (1997).
- Interpretation tasks: Gerken and Shady (1996); Gordon (1996); Crain and Thornton (1998); Schmitt and Miller (2010).
- The magnitude estimation method of ratings: Sorace (2010).
- The use of judgment and interpretation tasks in SLA: Gass, Sorace, and Selinker (1999); Mackey and Gass (2005).
- The involvement of explicit vs. implicit knowledge in different tasks: Ellis (2005).
- Statistical analyses using SPSS software: Field (2006).

Study Questions

1. Consider each of the following data collection methods described in this chapter: (a) AJTs; (b) sentence-pair interpretation tasks, in which sentences are presented in pairs and judged for their contextual (in)appropriateness; (c) TVJTs; and (d) PMTs. For each task type, note its advantages and disadvantages; take into account whether the task taps into explicit and/or implicit knowledge, as well as how difficult the task is to construct and/or to administer.

2. The tasks discussed in this chapter can use either visual or auditory modality. What are the advantages and disadvantages of using each modality, and what is

the degree to which each modality can be used with different learner populations (e.g., L2 learners vs. foreign language learners, children vs. adults)? For tasks that present sentences in context (such as the TVJT), what are the relative advantages and disadvantages of using text vs. pictures?

3. Consider the RQ below. Propose how this RQ can be tested using an AJT in which sentences are presented in isolation, and judged for their grammatical (un) acceptability.

Do L2 English learners know the properties of English negation? Specifically, do they know that negation must follow auxiliaries (*She is not sleeping*), and precede lexical verbs, and that *do*-support is necessary in the absence of an auxiliary (as in *He does not like milk*)?

Following the steps outlined in this chapter, design a possible research study addressing this RQ. Decide on the relevant test categories (remember to include categories with both grammatical and ungrammatical sentences). Provide one sample item for each category, and decide on the total number of items that your test will need. Decide on possible filler items, and provide samples.

4. Consider the RQ below:

Do L2 English learners understand the meaning of sentences containing subject vs. object relative clauses in English? Specifically, do they know that in a sentence like *Bill met the girl that knows John*, the NP 'the girl' is the subject of the relative clause 'that knows John', but in a sentence like *Bill met the girl that John knows*, the NP 'the girl' is the object of the relative clause 'that John knows'?

This RQ can be tested using a TVJT. The two sentence variants (subject relatives and object relatives) both need to be presented in two different scenarios: a scenario that makes the sentence true on the subject relative reading and false on the object relative reading, and another scenario that does exactly the opposite, as represented in the table below, which shows the responses expected from native English speakers. Answer the questions that follow about this design.

Sentence \ Context	Story 1	Story 2
Subject relative (*Bill met the girl that knows John*)	TRUE	FALSE
Object relative (*Bill met the girl that John knows*)	FALSE	TRUE

(a) Create two stories that can fill in the "story 1" and "story 2" slots. Remember that the goal is to create stories that make one sentence true and the other false.

(b) Suppose that you administer this TVJT to a group of non-native English speakers (NNSs) with low-level English proficiency and a control group of native English speakers (NSs) and obtain the results in the table below. Explain what these results mean: In what way are the NNSs different from the NSs? How are they misinterpreting the sentences?

Sentence \ Context	Story 1	Story 2
Subject relative (*Bill met the girl that knows John*)	NS: 100% TRUE NNS: 100% TRUE	NS: 100% FALSE NNS: 10% TRUE, 90% FALSE
Object relative (*Bill met the girl that John knows*)	NS: 100% FALSE NNS: 80% TRUE, 20% FALSE	NS: 100% TRUE NNS: 100% TRUE

(c) Now, suppose that you would like to modify this TVJT by using pictures instead of stories. The target sentences in the two tables above are not easily translatable into pictures. Create a different pair of sentences (one with a subject relative and the other with an object relative), which describe more concrete actions, and then describe what the relevant pictures would look like. Remember that your pictures, like the stories in (a), should each make one sentence true and the other false.

5. Consider the RQ below:

   Do L2 English learners know that in English the definite article *the* is required for second-mention, with both singular and plural nouns?

This RQ is tested with an interpretation task, in which each item consists of a pair of sentences; the study participants judge whether the second sentence is an appropriate continuation of the first sentence, on a scale from 1 to 5. The task contains the four test categories below, which test article use with second-mention NPs (the task also contains other categories testing article use with first-mention NPs, as well as filler items). Each category contains six items; one sample item is given below to illustrate each category.

Category 1: correct use of 'the' with second-mention singular NP:

   Maryanne bought a book and a magazine. She read the book first.

Category 2: incorrect use of 'a' with second-mention singular NP:

   Joshua bought a newspaper and a magazine. He read a newspaper first.

Category 3: correct use of 'the' with second-mention plural NP:

Robert bought two sandwiches and three cookies. He ate the sandwiches first.

Category 4: incorrect use of no article with second-mention plural NP:

Lorraine bought two tomatoes and three cucumbers. She ate tomatoes first.

Consider the following dataset from 10 study participants: five native English speakers (NS) and five non-native English speakers (NNS).

	Mean rating on a scale from 1 to 5			
Subject	*Category 1*	*Category 2*	*Category 3*	*Category 4*
NS1	4.6	2.1	4.9	1.6
NS2	5.0	1.3	4.5	2.4
NS3	4.7	2.5	4.8	2.2
NS4	5.0	1.0	5.0	1.2
NS5	4.0	2.8	4.2	2.9
NNS1	4.5	2.9	4.4	2.7
NNS2	4.3	2.6	4.2	2.9
NNS3	4.5	4.2	4.6	4.8
NNS4	5.0	2.0	4.0	2.3
NNS5	4.9	2.3	4.5	2.5

Answer the following questions about this dataset:

(a) For each participant, compute that participant's average score on the two grammatical categories, and that participant's average score on the two ungrammatical categories. Also compute the group averages for each category, for the NS and NNS groups.

(b) How would you characterize the performance of the native speakers overall? Does it look as though the native speakers are making a contrast between acceptable and unacceptable sentences?

(c) How would you characterize the performance of the non-native speakers overall? Is it similar to, or different from, that of the native speakers? To the extent that there are differences between the NS and the NNS data, in what direction do these differences lie – are NNSs more likely than NSs to reject appropriate sentences, and/or to accept inappropriate sentences?

(d) An unanticipated finding is that the correct sentences (categories 1 and 3) are not being given the top ratings by some of the participants, NSs as well as NNSs. Discuss possible reasons for this. Suggest how the task might be modified to provide researchers with information about why grammatical sentences are not being given the top ratings.

Note

1 Many studies use the term "grammaticality judgment task" (GJT) rather than AJT. The term AJT is used here, following Cowart (1997); as discussed by Cowart, *grammaticality* refers to the abstract concept of grammatical well-formedness, whereas *acceptability* refers to whether sentences are considered acceptable by speakers. Experimental tasks can tap into speakers' judgments of acceptability, and the results can be used to make inferences about grammaticality.

References

Chien, Y-C., & Wexler, K. (1990). Children's knowledge of locality constraints in binding as evidence for the modularity of syntax and pragmatics. *Language Acquisition, 1,* 225–295.

Chomsky, N. (1965). *Aspects of the theory of syntax.* Cambridge, MA: MIT Press.

Chomsky, N. (1981). *Lectures on government and binding: The Pisa lectures.* Dordrecht, Netherlands: Foris.

Cowart, W. (1997). *Experimental syntax.* Thousand Oaks, CA: Sage.

Crain, S., & Thornton, R. (1998). *Investigations in universal grammar: A guide to experiments on the acquisition of syntax and semantics.* Cambridge, MA: MIT Press.

Ellis, R. (2005). Measuring implicit and explicit knowledge of a second language: A psychometric study. *Studies in Second Language Acquisition, 27,* 141–172.

Field, A. (2006). *Discovering statistics using SPSS.* Thousand Oaks, CA: Sage.

Gabriele, A., Martohardjono, G., & McClure, W. (2002). Why *swimming* is just as difficult as *dying* for Japanese learners of English. *ZAS Papers in Linguistics, 29,* 85–103.

Gass, S., & Alvarez-Torres, M. (2005). Attention when? An investigation of the ordering effect of input and interaction. *Studies in Second Language Acquisition, 27,* 1–31.

Gass, S., Sorace, A., & Selinker, L. (1999). *Second language learning: Data analysis.* Mahwah, NJ: Lawrence Erlbaum.

Gerken, L., & Shady, M. (1996). The picture selection task. In D. McDaniel, C. McKee, & H. Smith Cairns (Eds.), *Methods for assessing children's syntax* (pp. 125–145). Cambridge, MA: MIT Press.

Gordon, P. (1996). The truth-value judgment task. In D. McDaniel, C. McKee, & H. Smith Cairns (Eds.), *Methods for assessing children's syntax* (pp. 211–231). Cambridge, MA: MIT Press.

Hawkins, R. (2001). *Second language syntax: A generative introduction.* Oxford, England: Blackwell.

Johnson, J. S., & Newport, E. L. (1989). Critical period effects in second language learning: The influence of maturational state on the acquisition of English as a second language. *Cognitive Psychology, 21,* 60–99.

Joo, H-R. (2003). Second language learnability and the acquisition of the argument structure of English locative verbs by Korean speakers. *Second Language Research, 19,* 305–328.

Lardiere, D. (1998). Dissociating syntax from morphology in a divergent end-state grammar. *Second Language Research, 14,* 359–375.

Lee, D., & Schachter, J. (1998). Sensitive period effects in Binding Theory. *Language Acquisition, 6*, 333–362.

Mackey, A., & Gass, S. (2005). *Second language research: Methodology and design*. Mahwah, NJ: Lawrence Erlbaum.

Montrul, S. (2005). On knowledge and development of unaccusativity in Spanish L2-acquisition. *Linguistics, 43*, 1153–1190.

Oshita, H. (2001). The unaccusative trap hypothesis in second language acquisition. *Studies in Second Language Acquisition, 23*, 279–304.

Prévost, P., & White, L. (2000). Missing surface inflection or impairment in second language acquisition? Evidence from tense and agreement. *Second Language Research, 16*, 103–133.

Schmitt, C., & Miller, K. (2010). Using comprehension methods in language acquisition research. In S. Unsworth & E. Blom (Eds.), *Experimental methods in language acquisition research* (pp. 35–56). Amsterdam, Netherlands: John Benjamins.

Schütze, C. (1996). *The empirical base of linguistics: Grammaticality judgments and linguistic methodology*. Chicago, IL: University of Chicago Press.

Slabakova, R. (2003). Semantic evidence for functional categories in interlanguage grammars. *Second Language Research, 19*, 76–109.

Sorace, A. (2000). Gradients in auxiliary selection with intransitive verbs. *Language, 76*, 859–890.

Sorace, A. (2010). Using magnitude estimation in language acquisition research. In S. Unsworth & E. Blom (Eds.), *Experimental methods in language acquisition research* (pp. 57–72). Amsterdam, Netherlands: John Benjamins.

White, L. (1998). Second language acquisition and Binding Principle B: Child/adult differences. *Second Language Research, 14*, 425–439.

White, L. (2003). *Second language acquisition and Universal Grammar*. Cambridge, England: Cambridge University Press.

White, L., & Genesee, F. (1996). How native is near-native? The issue of ultimate attainment in adult second language acquisition. *Second Language Research, 12*, 233–265.

4 Instructed Second Language Acquisition

Shawn Loewen and Jenefer Philp

Background

This chapter focuses on research methods for investigating the nature and effectiveness of instruction on second language (L2) learning. Instructed second language acquisition (ISLA) has been defined as "any systematic attempt to enable or facilitate language learning by manipulating the mechanisms of learning and/or the conditions under which these occur" (Housen & Pierrard, 2005, p. 2). We begin by giving a brief overview of the ways in which research on ISLA has been carried out. We next focus on particular types of research, and the practicalities of carrying out each one. We then provide ideas and resources for conducting further research projects. It should be noted that this chapter will focus on general L2 classroom instruction, and will not specifically address reading and writing research as these topics are covered in chapters 9 and 8 respectively. Investigations of effects of individual differences, beliefs, and attitudes in instructed language learning are often captured through surveys (chapter 5), case studies (chapter 6), and use of statistical procedures (chapter 13). Additionally, we would like to point out that ISLA research is not a method in and of itself. Instead, ISLA research draws on many different methodologies to help provide answers about specific questions related to the effects of L2 instruction. As we shall see, particular research methods are often associated with particular theoretical perspectives, and were developed in order to provide answers to research questions within those perspectives.

Research Methods in Second Language Acquisition: A Practical Guide, First Edition.
Edited by Alison Mackey and Susan M. Gass.
© 2012 Blackwell Publishing Ltd. Published 2012 by Blackwell Publishing Ltd.

Brief Overview

Early ISLA research was represented by so-called "comparative method studies," in use as early as 1916 (see Chaudron, 2001), but associated with methodological and technological advancements in the teaching of languages in the 1960s and 1970s, such as the audiolingual method and use of language laboratories (Mitchell, 2009). These studies sought to compare the effectiveness of different kinds of teaching interventions through the use of matched pretests and posttests. This early research tended to compare intact classes, randomly assigned to experimental or control groups; teachers were asked to perform a certain intervention, or to refrain from using a certain method over a fixed period of time. Gain scores for students from the treatment and control groups were compared, and differences were attributed to the respective teaching methods. However, in these studies, there was often no attempt to verify, for example through observation or recording of classes, the teaching and learning processes that actually occurred. In a critique of these "black box" studies, Long (1980, p. 2) points out, "there is no guarantee ... that teachers have in fact implemented method A, B, or C as prescribed, or that methods do not overlap in some respects ... there is no way of knowing to what to attribute the differential performance." This lack of information about the teaching and learning processes that actually occurred has been the main limitation of this type of research. Although changes might occur following intervention, there is no way to demonstrate clearly that these changes were the result of the intervention itself, or what the precise nature of that intervention was.

Because of this limitation, subsequent research has generally reflected a greater emphasis on process rather than product alone, and on the inclusion of systematic and careful documentation of classroom interaction through observation, recording and classification. For instance, most research comparing classroom interventions seek to include data regarding the treatment itself in order to confirm that the intervention occurred as intended. Current studies of corrective feedback (e.g., Loewen, 2005) often attempt to report the number of feedback episodes provided in the treatment. However, information regarding the treatment data is not always accessible (e.g., Ammar & Spada, 2006). Researchers may encounter difficulties in gaining permission for the use of audio or video recording, or for observations, within the classroom. In this case it is important to ensure successful administration of the treatment in other ways, such as through the training and debriefing of classroom teachers.

Another concern with "black box" studies, and one critical to the usefulness of the research, is the choice of measures used to evaluate the effectiveness of an intervention. The importance of these assessment choices is illustrated in study box 4.1.

In summary, although initial ISLA research consisted of mainly "black box" studies, there is little to recommend such an approach to investigating the effectiveness of different types of instruction or intervention. A major limitation is the lack of data on the nature of the intervention in practice. For this reason, most researchers aim to provide description and verification of the instructional procedures.

Study Box 4.1

Morrison, F., & Pawley, C. (1986). *Evaluation of the second language learning (French) programs in the schools of the Ottawa and Carleton Boards of Education. Vol. I: French proficiency of immersion students at the grade 12 level*. Toronto, Canada: Ontario Dept. of Education.

Background

Morrison and Pawley compared two groups of grade 12 French students: one group of "early start" students who had experienced immersion French classes since at least grade 4, and a group who had started immersion classes in grade 6 or 7.

Research questions

- How does the ultimate attainment of the two groups compare?
- What are the effects of the program in terms of overall success?

Method

This study used a battery of tests, including multiple choice listening and reading tasks, cloze tests, dictations, and picture description tasks, to provide a nuanced picture of attainment.

Results

Both groups scored highly on general proficiency, particularly on written tests, while early starters scored significantly higher on measures of oral fluency and communicative competence. Differences between groups were detected "less often on multiple-choice tests of usage, reading and listening comprehension and more often on tests of oral communication and perhaps breadth of vocabulary" (p. 30). The findings suggest the importance of including a range of instruments to assess ISLA in such evaluations.

Observational Studies

When investigating the effects of L2 instruction, researchers have often begun by describing what occurs naturally in the classroom. Such descriptive types of studies have taken a variety of forms. For example, within the communicative language teaching approach, there has been an interest in determining which procedures and activities could be identified as communicative in the classroom. While it is possible for researchers to describe the nature of activities that occur in a classroom in their own terms, it is also possible for researchers to rely on existing coding frameworks. An obvious advantage of using such a framework is that it allows for relatively uniform comparison across studies. To that end, descriptive coding systems such as the Communicative Orientation of Language Teaching (COLT) have been developed (Spada & Fröhlich, 1995). The COLT consists of categories that are considered to be important components of communicative language teaching, such as the use of the target language and discourse initiation. The coding system is set up as a grid with columns for specific options in each category. In this way, researchers can easily keep a log of ongoing classroom activities. In using this system, a researcher can observe a class and then record the activities that occurred. Each different activity is recorded on a different row, along with the starting and ending time. Then the researcher ticks the appropriate columns regarding the characteristics of the activities that occurred. In this way, the researcher has a record of all the activities that occurred within a given class, as well as a description of some of the key elements related to communicative language teaching. Studies that have used the COLT include that by Lyster and Mori (2006), who compared the types of interaction occurring in a Japanese immersion class in the United States and a French immersion class in Canada.

One of the advantages of using instruments such as the COLT is that it is a standardized coding system that enables easy comparison of different studies. Thus, classrooms that have been observed in various contexts, such as US English as a second language (ESL) or Canadian immersion, can be compared for the level of communicativeness or other characteristics that are included on the COLT. In addition, the COLT is relatively easy to use in the classroom and provides researchers with a simple way of coding the data. Given the comparative ease of ticking boxes as the classroom activities unfold, this is a relatively low-tech way of conducting classroom observations. Although it might be more desirable to audio or video record the classroom, it is not absolutely necessary. Because the objects of interest in the classroom are clearly specified and can be identified fairly quickly, researchers using more traditional methods of data collection, such as the COLT, can come to similar conclusions to those of researchers using more advanced technology. As data collection may take place in situations where audio or video equipment might be difficult to obtain, or might be unnecessarily disruptive in the classroom context, research that does not depend on technology can be highly useful and even beneficial in certain contexts. In addition, it could be argued that these types of standardized coding schemes are of particular interest for pedagogical issues because they classify the classroom activities. One of the main criticisms of such coding schemes, however, is that they impose an outsider/researcher perspective on the classroom that may not be shared by the teacher and students in the classroom. There is more discussion of such insider perspectives below.

Another type of descriptive study that has been conducted in ISLA research occurs within an interactionist framework. These studies have also relied on classroom observation; however, they have taken a more discourse analysis approach to analyzing the classroom interaction. One of the classic studies in this tradition is Lyster and Ranta (1997), which incidentally used the COLT in their overall coding of the classroom activities (see study box 4.2).

Study Box 4.2

Lyster, R., & Ranta, L. (1997). Corrective feedback and learner uptake: Negotiation of form in communicative classrooms. *Studies in Second Language Acquisition, 19*(1), 37–66.

Background

This study was set in high school French immersion classrooms in Canada. These classes consisted of science, mathematics, social studies, etc.

Research question

• What types of corrective feedback and uptake occur in these classes?

Method

Lyster and Ranta observed and audio recorded 18.3 hours of instruction from 14 subject-matter lessons and 13 French language arts lessons. After the observations, the audiotapes were listened to and transcribed. After transcription, the data were analyzed using a coding system. First, all of the student errors in the transcripts were identified. After each error, the researchers identified whether there was corrective feedback or not. If there was, they coded the specific type of corrective feedback, as well as the type of uptake that occurred in response to the feedback. After these categories were coded, the overall occurrence of the categories in the dataset were tabulated. In this way the frequency of different types of corrective feedback and uptake could be described and compared. Only descriptive statistics were used.

Results

Lyster and Ranta found that about 60% of errors were followed by corrective feedback, with the most common type of feedback being recasts. However, repaired uptake occurred more frequently after other types of feedback that did not provide the correct form for the learners.

These types of descriptive studies were common in the 1990s and 2000s, particularly within interactionist approaches. Studies such as Ellis, Basturkmen, and Loewen (2001), Lyster and Panova (2001), Loewen (2004), and Sheen (2004) all relied upon similar methodologies to investigate the occurrence of corrective feedback in the classroom. Again, the strength of these types of studies is that they provide a picture of what is occurring in the classroom. And because these studies use similar methodologies and coding systems, the results of disparate studies in different contexts can be compared relatively easily. But like the previous studies that used coding systems such as the COLT, these types of descriptive studies also use externally derived coding systems. Although the coding categories were proposed as being of interest for theoretical reasons, the categories may or may not relate to the classroom participants' own perceptions of the classroom activities.

While the previous approaches have relied primarily on external viewpoints to interpret the classroom interaction, there are other approaches that take on a more insider perspective, employing approaches to classroom data such as ethnography and language socialization. Friedman (this volume, chapter 10) goes into more detail about these types of qualitative research.

Overall, the research methods and studies examined in this section have attempted to gain insight into what occurs in the classroom. As such they might not be as directly concerned with actual learning outcomes; however, they have provided insight into classroom activities so that other studies can build upon them. If the criticism of the black box studies was that researchers do not actually know what is happening in the classroom, then these descriptive studies have made progress in addressing that concern. However, ISLA research is not merely concerned with describing what happens in the classroom; it is also concerned with the learning that takes place there. Therefore, the following sections will examine studies that have more specifically addressed the issue of L2 learning.

Non-Interventionist Quasi-Experimental Studies

The next types of studies that we will consider are those that attempt to measure learning within the classroom. There is some agreement that comparative method types of studies cannot provide much insight into L2 learning processes in the classroom because such studies are too broad in scope to make valid comparisons. Instead, researchers now tend to identify specific types of instructional activities and investigate those more closely. One of the distinctions that can be made in these types of quasi-experimental studies is how much the researcher attempts to change and manipulate what is happening in the classroom. Some studies have not made any attempt to manipulate the variables that are of interest to the researcher, thus maintaining a non-interventionist approach. Such studies have typically been similar to the descriptive studies mentioned above; however, they have also involved the measurement of learning outcomes in some way. See study box 4.3 for an example.

An advantage of non-interventionist, quasi-experimental types of studies is that they have high ecological validity because they do not interfere with or manipulate the classroom context in any way. However, one of their disadvantages is that they cannot control extraneous or moderator variables. For example, Loewen (2005) was not able to provide a pretest since the linguistic items were not targeted ahead of time. Such limitations weaken the claims that can be made about L2 learning. In addition, for these types of studies, it is often difficult to have a control group that does not receive the same treatment. For example, it can be both ethically and logistically problematic in an intact class to exclude some students from potentially beneficial treatment sessions. Furthermore, using other classes as a control group introduces additional uncontrollable variation because of the individual and distinctive nature of each class, even where the teacher is the same.

Study Box 4.3

Loewen, S. (2005) Incidental focus on form and second language learning. *Studies in Second Language Acquisition, 27* (3), 361–386.

Background

This study examined corrective feedback and student-initiated focus on form in 12 ESL classrooms in New Zealand.

Research questions

- Does incidental focus on form occur in these classes, and if so, how?
- How effective is this incidental focus on form?

Method

The researcher observed and audio recorded 32 hours of communicative classroom interaction. The researcher identified any instances of corrective feedback or student questions about form. In addition to quantifying these instances in order to answer the first research question, he also designed individualized tests in order to see how well each student remembered the linguistic information provided during these classroom episodes. The tests were administered only to the student who directly received the feedback, and the test items consisted only of those items that were focused on in class.

Results

The results showed that students had a 50% accuracy rate one day after the classroom episodes and a 40% accuracy rate two weeks later. In addition, Loewen found that successful uptake was the main predictor of accurate test scores.

Another issue to consider in relation to non-interventionist, quasi-experimental research is the difference between longitudinal studies, which follow a small number of learners over a considerable period of time, and cross-sectional studies, which compare groups of learners at different proficiency levels. Although one of the primary goals of ISLA research is to determine learners' interlanguage development, there are several ways to measure this. Perhaps the ideal way is to follow learners for a period of time as they progress from being beginning learners of the L2 to more proficient learners. Indeed, some studies employed this longitudinal method, and examples are provided in study boxes 4.4 and 4.5. However, there is no consensus as to what constitutes the necessary length of time for a longitudinal study. Some studies are as short as a few months, while others span a year or more. (See Friedman in this volume, chapter 10, for more information on longitudinal research.) Finally, it

Study Box 4.4

Iwasaki, J. (2008). A longitudinal study of a young child from a processability theory (PT) perspective. In J. Philp, R. Oliver, & A. Mackey (Eds.), *Second language acquisition and the younger learner* (pp. 231–253). Amsterdam, Netherlands: John Benjamins.

Background

This was a study of a 7-year-old Australian child learning Japanese over one year in an immersion classroom.

Research question

• How do verbal morphosyntactic structures emerge in the interlanguage production?

Method

The researcher collected 24 90-minute samples of conversation between the child and other speakers of Japanese at two-week intervals. To facilitate conversation she employed eight different types of tasks, some of which were designed to elicit specific target forms. These forms had been identified in previous studies of adult Japanese interlanguage. The analysis was based on Pienemann's (1998) processability theory.

Results

The researcher was able to sample how the child communicated similar ideas at different points of time. There was no attempt to link development with classroom instruction, however.

Study Box 4.5

Cekaite, A. (2008). Developing conversational skills in a second language. In J. Philp, R. Oliver, & A. Mackey (Eds.), *Second language acquisition and the younger learner* (pp. 106–129). Amsterdam, Netherlands: John Benjamins.

Background

This longitudinal study traces development of conversational skills among young refugee and immigrant children in a primary school immersion classroom in Sweden over one year.

Research question

- How do beginner learners' interactional and linguistic skills develop over time within a situated context?

Method

The data consist of 90 hours of video recordings of children's classroom interactions taken at three times, from early to late in the year. Using a discourse analysis approach, the researcher identified any interactional moves in the data that were "designed to initiate (or re-initiate) an exchange with the teacher" (p. 109), in the context of the children carrying out communicative projects.

Results

Cekaite reports on how two of the children, both 7 years old, changed in their ability to gain the teacher's attention and recruit his or her conversational involvement. They did so through a range of strategies, gradually moving from the use of simple attention getters to more elaborate moves, eventually mastering "lexically more complex and informative initiating moves" (p. 126).

should be noted that many longitudinal studies are non-interventionist in nature, simply following learners as they progress through their normal course of study. In contrast, cross-sectional research is often interventionist, and is addressed in more detail in the subsequent section.

Interventionist Quasi-Experimental Studies

Because of the lack of control in non-interventionist studies that deal with naturalistic classroom data, researchers have also conducted interventionist studies which exert more control over some of the variables. Study box 4.6 describes one such study.

These types of interventionist studies have several strengths when compared to non-interventionist methodology. First, the researcher has much more control over the study's design and implementation. For instance, in interventionist studies the researcher is the one who decides ahead of time which linguistic features are going to be targeted, what types of testing instruments will be used, and what type of intervention will occur. In addition, the researcher can try to control confounding or interfering variables that they do not want to influence the study. Even though these studies have a high level of control, they can still be conducted in the classroom, and because they are often representative of natural instructional contexts, the studies may not differ appreciably from what students might do in their normal classes.

Disadvantages of interventionist research include the fact that the research conditions may impose some level of artificiality on the classroom. In addition,

Study Box 4.6

Ellis, R., Loewen, S., & Erlam, R. (2006). Implicit and explicit corrective feedback and the acquisition of L2 grammar. *Studies in Second Language Acquisition, 28*, 339–368.

Background

This study was conducted in several intact ESL classes in New Zealand. It examined the effectiveness of corrective feedback on English past tense and comparatives, as measured by several different testing instruments.

Research question

• Is there a difference in the effectiveness of implicit and explicit corrective feedback?

Method

This study identified three classes at similar levels of proficiency. The students underwent a pretest session, which consisted of an elicited imitation test and a grammaticality judgment test. Several days after the pretests, each class was visited by a researcher who led one hour of communicative activities that targeted the use of past tense and comparative *-er*. As these tasks were being conducted, the researcher provided feedback according to the designation of each class. One class received explicit, metalinguistic feedback about the nature of the error; one class received recasts on any errors; and one class did not receive any feedback on their errors. There were two treatment sessions, on different days. Then there was an immediate posttest, one day after the last treatment, followed by a delayed posttest two weeks later. In order to analyze the data, the test scores were subjected to mixed-design ANOVAs with the testing time (pretest, immediate posttest, and delayed posttest) and treatment group (explicit, implicit, no feedback) as independent variables.

Results

The results showed that the metalinguistic feedback group had improved accuracy on the delayed posttest, but that the groups did not differ on the immediate posttests.

classrooms are messy places and it may be difficult for researchers to control all of the potentially interfering variables.

In the previous section, we discussed some typical characteristics of longitudinal studies. Although longitudinal studies are designed to examine language development over time, the development of interlanguage proficiency does not necessarily occur rapidly, and it may take months or years for learners to progress to the target level that is under investigation by the researcher. In order to examine interlanguage development in a timelier manner, researchers may conduct cross-sectional research, an interventionist method in which different learners at different levels of proficiency are investigated. Any group differences are then generally attributed to interlanguage development. However, there is some concern that such claims might not be fully supported because other factors, such as differences in instructional quality or other interfering variables, may be influencing the performance of the groups. The cross-sectional nature of the learners might be determined in several ways. Some studies have used students' class level as a measure of proficiency (see Thomas, 2006). While this classification is relatively easy to make, the validity of the placement is dependent on the placement tests that are conducted by the institution, and such tests may not always be the most reliable in nature. Additionally, such placement tests may not target the specific linguistic features that the researcher has in mind. Other studies (e.g., Mackey & Philp, 1998; Mackey, 1999; Philp, 2003) have used developmental stages to classify learners. Thus, if learners are producing language at a low developmental stage, they are placed in one group, but if they are producing language at higher developmental stages, then they are placed in a different group. Although more time-consuming, such a careful means of assessing proficiency level has high construct validity because it provides researchers with up-to-date, specific measures of learners' linguistic abilities that are theoretically motivated and empirically tested.

Action Research

One other type of ISLA research that should be mentioned is action research (also known as practitioner research). Action research is conducted by teachers who are interested in finding out more about an issue that is specifically related to their own classrooms. Thus, such research is practically motivated and seeks to solve identified problems within the classroom context. These types of studies are generally very focused and very specific. Action research has a number of unique characteristics that differentiate it from the other research methods discussed above. For example, the researcher is a participant in the process under investigation: what is being investigated itself evolves over time as a function of the research. The research is thus context-specific, process-oriented, and often described as cyclical. Kemmis and McTaggart (1988), for example, propose a four-step loop: The first step, which may be preceded by a period of exploration and fact finding (Burns, 2005), is an initial planning stage in which the research topic is identified and developed, informed by the researcher's experience and knowledge of the context. This plan then leads to action; practical intervention in the teaching/learning process that moves toward improvement. The third stage involves observation, and is responsive as the researcher engages in documenting the action and its effects. This commonly involves classroom observation, audio and or video recording, and introspective techniques such as journals, or interviews with the participants (including the researchers themselves). The fourth stage, reflection, involves the participants' reflection and description of what occurred: the problems that arose, the constraints on implementation, and any unexpected repercussions. New perspectives, understandings, and ideas may arise at this point, providing input for further planning and implementation of new action.

One strength of action research is its practical outcomes. As this type of research is by nature situation-specific, it can help teachers solve problems they have identified in the classroom. In addition, action research can foster professional development through encouraging reflective teaching. A limitation of action research is that the outcomes are specific to a particular classroom at a specific point in time, and therefore the research findings are limited regarding generalizability, contributions to theory of ISLA, or understandings of language pedagogy (Mitchell, 2009). In other words, the primary contribution of action research is often to the teacher's own practice. See study box 4.7 for an example.

Study Box 4.7

Shart, M. (2008). What matters in TBLT: Task, teacher or team? An action research perspective from a beginning German language classroom. In J. Eckerth & S. Siekman (Eds.), *Task based language learning and teaching* (pp. 47–66). Berlin, Germany: Peter Lang.

Background

The author was both teacher and researcher as he sought to investigate, over one year, the implementation of a task-based language teaching approach in his intensive German language class for law students at a university in Japan.

Method

Shart was supported by an "outsider researcher," a doctoral student who was carrying out other research on the class. The outsider researcher observed classes, read the teacher's weekly reflections, and conducted email exchanges and individual and group interviews with the 13 student participants throughout the year. This data was first anonymized by the outsider researcher, and, with the permission of the students, then shared with the teacher-researcher where relevant to his study.

Research question

• How was a task-based language teaching approach implemented in this class?

Method

The study is briefly outlined here to illustrate Kemmis and McTaggart's (1988) four stages of action research.

1. Shart, the teacher of the class, initially identified a problem: how would he teach this class? In the context of a predominantly linear syllabus that

focused on linguistic structure, his weekly class sought to provide students with the opportunity to use the target language "creatively, imaginatively and meaningfully." At the planning stage, he drew on his previous experience in teaching the class to identify the most suitable approach. In choosing to do so, he needed to ensure that task content was "relevant to students' interests" and could "satisfy academic demands." He thus responded to the demands of the context: the requirements of the faculty and of the course itself, and the perceived linguistic, academic, and social needs of the students.

2.   In the process of implementing a task-based approach in his weekly classes, continual refinement in choice and presentation of tasks occurred. This ongoing process was in response to the teacher's observations and perceptions of what was happening, as well as feedback from the outsider researcher, which was gathered from the students on a weekly basis. Thus, during the action stage, the teacher reflected on the "data," comprised of his own observations, his diary, the outsider researcher's perspective (based on student interviews and classroom observation), and the students' perspectives (from anonymized emails). An example of this dynamic process of action, observation, reflection, and refinement is seen in the changes that occurred over several months. Shart reported that initially his diary records "abound with positive and enthusiastic perceptions ... active participation from all students;" he perceived the students as "open minded, accessible and vibrant with energy" (p. 61). After some weeks, however, he observed that the students split into three distinct groups, each reacting quite differently: two groups appeared less engaged and increasingly distant. This insight prompted a number of changes to teacher behavior, task selection, and organization (illustrating the dynamic nature of action research) as he sought to regain cohesion, engagement, and willingness to communicate among all students.

3.   The teacher's own observations and perceptions, which were based on his diary, were compared with student interview data and outsider researcher observations, leading to reflection on classroom management and instructional practice.

4.   Although this data confirmed the teacher's observations, it also suggested that the teacher's own behavior played a minimal role; "it is the whole constellation arising out of the way the tasks are organized and presented. The atmosphere during lessons seems to be dominated by the tension between the different groups and their perceptions and expectations" (p. 62). Thus triangulation of data allowed the teacher to better understand reasons for the problems that arose in the class, and the nexus between tasks, community of learning, and expectations.

Results

The researchers concluded that although the task-based language teaching design did allow students to become "small communities where creative and autonomous learning processes could happen," another important part of the equation was "a more topically balanced version of TBLT [task-based language teaching] ... that better integrates the expectations of different students" (p. 62).

ɔ Research

ɔ Do Observation Research

Select a classroom

While this may seem like an obvious step, it is a crucial one. Sometimes there are theoretical reasons for choosing a specific type of classroom. For example, a researcher who is interested in corrective feedback during communicative activities will need to find a classroom context that contains these characteristics. In some cases, finding specific types of classrooms is relatively easy. For example, a teacher might say that they teach communicatively and that you are welcome to come and observe their class. However, upon your arrival, you might find that (a) their definition of communicative teaching and yours are not the same and/or (b) the specific act of corrective feedback that you were hoping to investigate does not actually occur (or occur frequently enough for analysis). In these cases you may need to modify your research interests.

Although classes can be chosen on theoretical grounds, there is another, more mundane yet practical, rationale for choosing a classroom: access. In some studies, it is the case that the researcher investigates a specific classroom context because the teacher is friendly toward research in general and is welcoming of the researcher into the classroom. In these cases, the researcher may need to be more flexible in the focus of their research.

In selecting a classroom, it is important to gain permission from several sources. For instance, permission needs to be gained from the administration person that is responsible for the class. This may be the principal of a language school, the administrator of a school district, or a language program coordinator. Second, permission must be gained from the teacher, and finally the students must also consent to the research study.

2. Select a topic for research

Descriptive studies of classrooms may be approached from one of two perspectives. As discussed above, researchers may have specific research questions in mind before they go into the classroom. For example, Lyster and Ranta (1997) were interested in corrective feedback and uptake when they investigated their classes. However, some researchers may have a less focused research question, and may instead use their observations to help direct the topic under investigation.

3. Conduct the observations

There are several things to consider at this stage. One of them is what shape the actual observations will take. One important question to consider is who will do the observations. While it is generally the researcher who sits in the classes, sometimes a research assistant (RA) will conduct the observations. If this is the case, it will need to be explicitly clear what the RA ought to be paying attention to. Teachers can also serve as the observer or researcher. Although we will not consider studies in which the teacher is the researcher in this section, please see "Action Research" above for information about that scenario. Another question regards the role of the observer. Generally, the observer is a non-participant observer, meaning that they sit as quietly and unobtrusively as possible in the back of the classroom. However, it is also possible to be a participant observer, in which case the researcher interacts with the students (and teacher) in some way (e.g., Philp & Duchesne, 2008), though such a scenario is not common.

In addition to considering the observation arrangements, it is necessary to check and double check all of the recording equipment and observation methods that are going to be used. Thus, if pen-and-paper documents, such as the COLT, are going to be used, then the researcher needs to familiarize themselves with using the document in real-time situations. If recording equipment is going to be used, then researchers need to familiarize themselves with its functions and operation. Additionally, the researchers should consider how that recording equipment will determine the data that they get. For instance, audio recording obviously means that no visual record of the class will be obtained. Thus, the data will necessarily exclude any non-verbal communication, and, any visual aids, such those presented on overheard projectors, blackboards, or PowerPoint, will not be captured.

The position of the microphone is another consideration. If its location is stationary, then it will only record those classroom participants who are close to it. Some studies attach the microphone to the teacher, with the result that all of the teacher discourse is captured as well as any student interaction with that teacher (whether whole-class or in groups). However, any student group work in which the teacher is not present will not be recorded. A further possibility is to attach microphones to the students, in which case the students' interactions within the class will be captured. While one recording arrangement may not necessarily be better or worse than another, the researcher should be aware of how it constrains the research. For example, attaching a microphone to a teacher in a class in which students work mostly in groups with occasional teacher involvement will not yield as rich a dataset as would attaching a microphone to a student.

Similar considerations are necessary when video recording. Like that of the microphone, the placement of the camera affects what data is recorded. Not all classroom participants may be visible on the screen at the same time. Should the camera remain stationary or should it follow a specific person (often the teacher) as they move throughout the classroom? Another consideration is that the microphone on a video camera remains with the camera, and may not record conversations at the other side of the room. It should also be noted that recording in communicative classrooms with multiple groups talking at the same time can make it difficult to single out specific students, potentially leading to later transcription problems. In order to capture more data, several recording methods might be used.

4.   *Transcribe the data*

Generally, the next step in classroom research is to make a transcription of the audio/video recordings. This may be done after all the data has been collected or it may happen alongside the observation process. While some researchers may view transcribing as a tedious, but unavoidable, component of classroom research, it may also be viewed as a means by which the researcher becomes more intimately involved with and aware of their data. The type of transcription that should be employed depends on the goals of the research. For studies which use a conversation analysis approach to their data (e.g., Cekaite, 2008), a very fine-grained, detailed transcription is necessary in which aspects such as intonation, speed of delivery, precise length of pauses, hesitations and false starts, etc., are recorded. Studies which are interested in non-verbal aspects of the classroom, such as eye contact or facial expressions, must devise a way to incorporate these gestures into the written record. Sometimes a more broad transcription, which approximates regular orthography, is sufficient.

Additionally, the researcher must consider whether it is necessary to transcribe the entirety of the observations or whether segments of the class will suffice. For example, if a researcher is only looking at corrective feedback, then it may not be necessary to transcribe all of the interaction, but only that which contains corrective feedback. However, if the research is also trying to record all of the students' errors in the interaction, then it may be necessary to transcribe the interaction in its entirety. Furthermore, if the primary interest is in the teacher's discourse, then it may not be necessary to transcribe the student discourse. Regardless of which decisions are made regarding transcription, it should be realized that transcription is already a part of the process of interpreting the data.

5.   *Code the data*

There are several ways to go about coding the data. In studies where there is an a priori established research question, the coding system is usually based on existing taxonomies. Thus, it is necessary for the researcher to decide whether the existing taxonomy fits the data as-is, or whether it needs to be modified. In many cases, the researcher will code the data initially by themselves, and then submit some or all of the data to another individual in order to determine how reliably the coding system can be applied to the data. Careful training improves coding reliability. Sometimes the researcher will code only a portion of the data before giving it to another individual in order to identify and modify any inconsistencies in the coding before the entire dataset is coded. There is no hard-and-fast rule for how much of the data should be double-coded; however, 15–20% is a commonly accepted amount, particularly if the agreement in coding is high. Statistical methods for calculating inter-rater reliability include simple percentage agreement and Cohen's kappa, which is a more conservative measure because it adjusts for chance agreement.

If one is taking a more qualitative approach to the study, then there may not be an established coding scheme to draw upon. In such cases, coding the data usually follows an iterative process of identifying themes in the data. See Friedman (this volume, chapter 10) for more detail.

How to Do Non-Interventionist Quasi-Experimental Studies

The purpose of non-interventionist quasi-experimental studies is to investigate the effectiveness of existing classroom practices. In some senses, then, this type of research is similar to action research; however, it is not necessarily the teacher who conducts the study, and the study is not conducted with only the local context in mind. Finally, action research is often conducted to address primarily pedagogical questions, while quasi-experimental studies generally address more theoretical questions.

Since this type of study does not manipulate the classroom environment, the researcher needs to be as unobtrusive as possible. Researchers would generally follow many of the same steps as for classroom observation studies; however, the classroom participants are usually asked to do something beyond (and generally outside of) their normal classroom activities. For example, learners may be asked to take pretests and posttests to determine the effects of a particular instructional activity, or students and/ or teachers may be asked to provide introspective data. Such data might be elicited through diaries, journals, and interviews, or gathered by employing a stimulus which the participants comment upon. Using an open elicitation instrument has the advantage of allowing the participants to comment on things that are important or relevant to them. However, a more controlled elicitation, including measures such as multiple choice or open-ended questions, has the advantage of allowing the researcher to gain insight into an aspect of the classroom that is of particular interest and that might not be commented on otherwise by the participant. Although non-interventionist-type research has high ecological validity because it investigates real classrooms and real classroom activities, a drawback is that the researcher has very little control over what happens in the classroom, and thus, the teacher and students may not engage in the types of activities that the researcher is hoping to investigate.

How to Do Interventionist Quasi-Experimental Studies

Interventionist quasi-experimental studies require a considerable amount of planning because the researcher is trying to manipulate certain variables and to control other variables.

1. Select a research question

The first thing to do is decide on the topic that is to be investigated. For the purposes of this chapter, research questions address issues related to L2 instruction; however, as opposed to descriptive and non-observational studies, which may not isolate specific features, this type of research attempts to distill one or two qualities to investigate.

2.   *Identify participants*

This type of research can be done either in the classroom or in a laboratory. Thus, it is important to decide whether the researcher will be able to use the necessary class time in order to conduct the study, or whether it is better to conduct the study outside of class time. While some lab-based studies attempt to recreate classroom conditions (for example, by having multiple students involved in the activities), other studies may investigate one or two students at a time.

3.   *Design the data collection instruments*

Because this type of research addresses specific research questions, it is necessary to design precise instruments to collect the necessary data. For example, if the research question addresses the effectiveness of an instructional technique, then a pretest and posttest are necessary. These tests must be designed so that they can effectively measure the treatment. For example, an oral production test is probably not the best way to measure the effects of written corrective feedback.

4.   *Pilot the instruments*

Before using the instruments for actual data collection, it is necessary to make sure that they function in the way that they are intended. Piloting may involve several different populations. A researcher may want to pilot their instrument on a set of knowledgeable experts in the field to make sure that the instrument reflects their perceptions. For example, teachers' opinions of the difficulty of an instrument or its relevance to the classroom may be sought. Another potential pilot group is native speakers of the target language. Often it is important to assess how a baseline group of participants perform a task in order to then contrast and compare how L2 learners perform on the task. If native speakers do not perform well on a grammaticality judgment test, for example, there may be design problems that need to be addressed. Finally, it is advisable to pilot the instruments on participants from the target population. In this way, the researcher can gain information regarding the reliability of the assessment and how the potential sample population will perform on the instruments.

The designing and piloting stages of research are generally cyclical, meaning that the information gleaned from piloting is then incorporated back into the research design and then piloted again. While this is a time-consuming process, it is a critical stage in order for the research to have a high level of validity.

5.   *Conduct the experiment*

Following the selection of participants and the design and piloting of measurement materials, the day comes when the experiment is ready to be conducted and all the systems are put into place. Generally this stage "simply" involves implementing what one has already decided to do. However, it is inevitable that difficulties, such as technology malfunction or participant attrition, will occur and will need to be addressed.

6. *Analyze the data*

In general, the types of data that are generated from interventionist type studies are quantitative in nature, and the reader is referred to chapter 13 (this volume) for more information about statistical analysis.

Project Ideas and Resources

For further examples of research projects, and further discussion of how to carry out research in the classroom, see the following:

Allwright, D. (1997). Quality and sustainability in teacher-research. *TESOL Quarterly, 37,* 368–70.

Burns, A. (1999). *Collaborative action research for English teachers.* Cambridge, England: Cambridge University Press.

Crookes, G., & Chandler, P. (2001). Introducing action research into the education of postsecondary foreign language teachers. *Foreign Language Annals, 34,* 131–40.

Ellis, R., & Barkhuizen. (2005). *Analysing learner language.* Oxford, England: Oxford University Press.

Freeman, D. (1988). *Doing teacher research.* Toronto, Canada: Heinle & Heinle.

Study Questions

1. What are the advantages and disadvantages of using outsider and insider viewpoints in ISLA?
2. What might Lyster and Ranta's (1997) study (study box 4.1) have looked like if they had taken an ethnographic approach?
3. Are some classroom contexts more suited to specific types of research?
4. Like the study by Loewen (2005; see study box 4.3), Cekaite's study (2008; see study box 4.5) deals with naturalistic classroom data, but it differs in a number of ways. Discuss the differences.
5. Iwasaki (2008) and Cekaite (2008; see study boxes 4.4 and 4.5) both employ longitudinal studies of child learners. Discuss the similarities and differences in their approach in terms of research focus, data collection, and data analysis. How do these reflect the methodological approaches of each?
6. In what ways does action research, as illustrated in study box 4.7, differ from interventionist quasi-experimental research?

7. What are the benefits of carrying out action research?
8. What are some of the limitations of action research?

References

Ammar, A., & Spada, N. (2006). One size fits all? Recasts, prompts and L2 learning. *Studies in Second Language Acquisition, 28*(4), 543–574.

Burns, A. (2005). Action research: An evolving paradigm? *Language Teaching, 38,* 57–74.

Cekaite, A. (2008). Developing conversational skills in a second language. In J. Philp, R. Oliver, & A. Mackey (Eds.), *Second language acquisition and the younger learner* (pp. 106–129). Amsterdam, Netherlands: John Benjamins.

Chaudron, C. (2001). Progress in language classroom research: Evidence from the *Modern Language Journal,* 1916–2000. *Modern Language Journal, 85,* 57–76.

Ellis, R., Basturkmen, H., & Loewen, S. (2001). Learner uptake in communicative ESL lessons. *Language Learning, 51*(2), 281–318.

Ellis, R., Loewen, S., & Erlam, R. (2006). Implicit and explicit corrective feedback and the acquisition of L2 grammar. *Studies in Second Language Acquisition, 28,* 339–368.

Housen, A., & Pierrard, M. (2005). *Investigations in instructed second language acquisition.* New York, NY: De Gruyter.

Iwasaki, J. (2008). A longitudinal study of a young child from a processability theory (PT) perspective. In J. Philp, R. Oliver, & A. Mackey (Eds.), *Second language acquisition and the younger learner* (pp. 231–253). Amsterdam, Netherlands: John Benjamins.

Kemmis, S., & McTaggart, R. (1988). *The action research planner.* Melbourne, Australia: Deakin University.

Loewen, S. (2004). Uptake in incidental focus on form in meaning-focused ESL lessons. *Language Learning, 54*(1), 153–187.

Loewen, S. (2005). Incidental focus on form and second language learning. *Studies in Second Language Acquisition, 27*(3), 361–386.

Long, M. H. (1980). Inside the "black box": Methodological issues in classroom research on language learning. *Language Learning, 30*(1), 1–42.

Lyster, R., & Mori, H. (2006). Interactional feedback and instructional counterbalance. *Studies in Second Language Acquisition, 28,* 269–300.

Lyster, R., & Panova, I. (2002). Patterns of corrective feedback and uptake in the adult ESL classroom. *TESOL Quarterly, 36*(4), 573–595.

Lyster, R., & Ranta, L. (1997). Corrective feedback and learner uptake: Negotiation of form in communicative classrooms. *Studies in Second Language Acquisition, 19*(1), 37–66.

Mackey, A. (1999). Input, interaction and second language development: An empirical study of question formation in ESL. *Studies in Second Language Acquisition, 21,* 557–587.

Mackey, A., & Philp, J. (1998). Conversational interaction and second language development: Recasts, responses and red herrings? *Modern Language Journal, 82*(3), 338–356.

Mitchell, R. (2009). Current trends in classroom research. In M. Long & C. Doughty (Eds., *The handbook of language teaching.* (pp. 675–705) Oxford, England: Wiley-Blackwell.

Morrison, F., & Pawley, C. (1986). *Evaluation of the second language learning (French) programs in the schools of the Ottawa and Carleton Boards of Education. Vol. I: French proficiency of immersion students at the grade 12 level.* Toronto, Canada: Ontario Dept. of Education.

Philp, J. (2003). Constraints on "noticing the gap": Nonnative speakers' noticing of recasts in NS–NNS interaction. *Studies in Second Language Acquisition, 25*(1), 99–126.

Philp, J., & Duchesne, S. (2008). When the gate opens: The interaction between social and linguistic goals in child second language development. In J. Philp, R. Oliver, & A. Mackey (EWds.), *Second language acquisition and the younger learner: Child's play?* (pp. 83–104). Amsterdam, Netherlands: John Benjamins.

Pienemann, M. (1998). *Language processing and second language development: Processability theory*. Amsterdam, Netherlands: John Benjamins.

Shart, M. (2008). What matters in TBLT: Task, teacher or team? An action research perspective from a beginning German language classroom. In J. Eckerth & S. Siekman (Eds.), *Task based language learning and teaching* (pp. 47–66). Berlin, Germany: Peter Lang.

Sheen, Y. (2004). Corrective feedback and learner uptake in communicative classrooms across instructional settings. *Language Teaching Research, 8*(3), 263–300.

Spada, N., & Fröhlich, M. (1995). *The Communicative Orientation of Language Teaching Observation Scheme: Coding conventions and applications*. Sydney, Australia: National Centre for English Language Teaching and Research, Macquarie University.

Thomas, M. (2006). Research synthesis and historiography: The case of assessment of second language proficiency. In J. M. Norris & L. Ortega (Eds.), *Synthesizing research on language learning and teaching* (pp. 279–298). Amsterdam, Netherlands: John Benjamins.

5 How to Design and Analyze Surveys in Second Language Acquisition Research

Zoltán Dörnyei and Kata Csizér

The aim of this chapter is to describe how survey studies are carried out in the context of SLA research. After a general introduction, we explain the required steps to design a survey that can provide valid and reliable data. Then we look at the main aspects of quantitative data analysis to be applied to questionnaire data, followed by a discussion of reporting survey results. Finally, we present an illustration of how the various principles of questionnaire design have been put into actual practice, with information on further resources that might be helpful in planning to conduct a questionnaire survey.

Background to the Questionnaire Surveys

Survey research is a quantitative research method which aims to collect self-report data from individuals, and the typical instrument used for this purpose is the written questionnaire (although market researchers, for example, often use structured interviews as well). Both survey methodology and questionnaire design have their origins in the social sciences. The basic idea behind survey research is the recognition that the characteristics, opinions, attitudes, and intended behaviors of a large population (e.g., second language (L2) learners in a country) can be described and analyzed on the basis of questioning only a fraction of the particular population. The development of survey methodology for research purposes has gone hand in hand with political public opinion research, as survey results about people's political preferences have an obvious link to actual election results (Babbie, 2007). However, surveys of large populations have also been employed in many other fields of study (e.g., sociology, psychology, education, and market research), and questionnaire

Research Methods in Second Language Acquisition: A Practical Guide, First Edition.
Edited by Alison Mackey and Susan M. Gass.
© 2012 Blackwell Publishing Ltd. Published 2012 by Blackwell Publishing Ltd.

surveys have made a substantial contribution to second language acquisition (SLA) research as well (for detailed summaries, see Brown, 2001; Dörnyei, 2010). Survey studies can inform us about:

- language learners' intended language behavior, that is, how students plan to respond to certain language learning situations (e.g., how much effort they are willing to invest in L2 learning);
- people's opinions and attitudes concerning specific L2s and the language learning process in general (e.g., how much they like certain aspects of learning a foreign language);
- participants' feelings (e.g., anxiety about language use) and beliefs about certain L2-related issues (e.g., the optimal age or method of learning an L2);
- learners' knowledge of certain issues in SLA. (e.g., their awareness of different varieties of English);
- various background information and biodata from the students (e.g., facts about their language learning history).

In sum, surveys can target a wide variety of language-related issues and allow researchers to make inferences about larger L2 learning populations; this obviously facilitates decision making and policy formation in an informed and principled manner.

How to Design a Questionnaire

The backbone of any survey study is the instrument used for collecting data. The most common way of obtaining large amounts of data in a relatively short period of time in a cost-effective way is by means of standardized questionnaires. Questionnaire design requires a rigorous process if we want to produce an instrument that yields reliable and valid data and, accordingly, whole volumes have been written on how to construct instruments of good quality (for a review, see Dörnyei, 2010). In the following we discuss what we see as the six key design issues.

Issue 1: The Sampling of Questionnaire Content and the Use of "Multi-Item Scales"

The first step in preparing questionnaire items is to specify their content in explicit terms. Although this may sound obvious, it does not always happen, and vague content specifications can pose a serious threat to the validity and reliability of the instrument, particularly in two areas: (a) the *sampling of content* and (b) the preparation of "*multi-item scales.*"

- *Appropriate sampling of content*: Ad hoc questionnaire design involves jotting down a few seemingly relevant questions without any rigorous procedure to ensure that the coverage is comprehensive. The problem with this method, as Davidson (1996, p. 10) highlights, is that "You cannot analyze what you do not measure." That is, not even the most sophisticated data analysis techniques will be able to compensate for leaving out some important questions from the data collection by accident. Certain omissions are bound to occur even in otherwise very thorough studies (as attested by the anecdotes one hears at professional conferences), but when the sampling of the content is not theory-driven, the chances of something irrecoverable happening are obviously much greater. Here are three suggestions to help to ensure appropriate content sampling. (a) Carefully clarify the research problem and identify the critical concepts that are likely to play a defining role in shaping the issue in question – these variables will need to be addressed by the questionnaire. (b) Eliminate all the questions that are only of peripheral interest but not directly related to the variables and hypotheses that the questionnaire has been designed to investigate. (c) Avoid making the questionnaire too long by covering every possible angle; focus on the key issues.

- *Using "multi-item scales"*: The notion of multi-item scales is the central component in scientific questionnaire design, yet this concept is surprisingly little known in the L2 profession. The core of the issue is that when it comes to assessing abstract, mental variables not readily observable by direct means (e.g., attitudes, beliefs, etc.), the actual wording of the questions assumes an unexpected amount of importance: minor differences in how a question is formulated and framed can produce radically different levels of agreement or disagreement, or a completely different selection of answers (Gillham, 2008). Because of the fallibility of single items, there is a general consensus among survey specialists that more than one item is needed to address each identified content area, all aimed at the same target but drawing upon slightly different aspects of it. How many is "more than one"? Professional scales often contain as many as 10–20 items focusing on a target issue, but even if we want to shorten the scales to be able to target more issues in the questionnaire it is risky to go below four items per subdomain, because if the post hoc item analysis (see below for details) reveals that certain items did not work in the particular sample, their exclusion will result in too short (or single-item) scales.

Issue 2: Main Types of Questionnaire Items

The typical questionnaire is a highly structured data collection instrument, with most items either asking about very specific pieces of information or giving various response options for the respondent to choose from, for example by ticking a box or circling the most appropriate option. Most professional questionnaires are primarily made up of "closed-ended" items, which do not require the respondents to produce any free writing. The most famous type of closed-ended item is undoubtedly the *Likert scale*, which consists of a characteristic statement accompanied by five or six response options for respondents to indicate the extent to which they "agree" or "disagree" with it by marking (e.g., circling) one of the responses ranging from "strongly agree" to "strongly disagree." For example:

Applied linguists are genuinely nice people.
| Strongly disagree | Disagree | Neither agree nor disagree | Agree | Strongly agree |

Another frequently applied way of eliciting a graduated response is the *semantic differential scale*, in which respondents are asked to indicate their answers by marking a continuum (with a tick or an "X") between two bipolar adjectives at the extremes. For example:

Listening comprehension tasks are:
difficult ___:___:___:___:___: X :___ easy
useless ___: X :___:___:___:___:___useful

Finally, *numerical rating scales* involve giving "so many marks out of so many" (e.g., five points to applied linguists on a scale from one to five for being nice people; see the sample questionnaire near the end of the chapter for an illustration).

Issue 3: Writing Items that Work

Over the past 50 years, survey researchers have accumulated a considerable body of knowledge and experience about what makes a questionnaire item good and what the potential pitfalls are. However, most specialists also emphasize that item construction is not a 100% scientific activity, because in order to write good questions one also needs a certain amount of creativity and lots of common sense. Indeed, it is generally recommended that when we get down to writing the actual items we should let our imagination go free and should try and create as many potential items as we can think of – the resulting collection of items is referred to as the *item pool* (DeVellis, 2003). During the generation of the item pool, item designers can draw on two sources in addition to their own verbal creativity:

- *Qualitative, exploratory data* gathered from respondents, such as *notes* taken during talks and brainstorming in focus or discussion groups; recorded unstructured/semi-structured *interviews*; and *student essays* written around the subject of the inquiry (see e.g., Tseng, Dörnyei, & Schmitt, 2006).
- *Borrowed questions* from established questionnaires. Questions that have been used frequently before must have been through extensive piloting and therefore have a certain "track record." Of course, we will need to acknowledge the sources precisely, and it is important to note that even if we adopt most items from existing instruments, our questionnaire will still need to be piloted for the specific population that we intend to use it for.

What are the main rules about writing good items? Here are five key strategies for producing items that work:

- *Aim for short and simple items*. Whenever possible, questionnaire items should be short, rarely exceeding 20 words.
- *Use simple and natural language*. As a rule, in questionnaire items we should always choose the simplest way to say something.
- *Avoid ambiguous or loaded words and sentences*. Any element that might make the language of the items unclear, ambiguous, or emotionally loaded needs to be avoided.
- *Avoid negative constructions*. Items that contain a negative construction (i.e., including "not," "doesn't," or "don't") are deceptive because, although they read OK, responding to them – especially giving a negative response – can be problematic.
- *Avoid double-barreled questions*. Double-barreled questions are those that ask two (or more) questions in one, while expecting a single answer (e.g., *Is the relationship with your parents good?*).

Issue 4: The Format of the Questionnaire

The format and layout of the questionnaire are frequently overlooked as an important aspect of the development of the instrument. This is a mistake because producing an attractive and professional design is half the battle in motivating respondents to produce reliable and valid data. Here are some points to consider:

- *Length*: The optimal length of a questionnaire depends on how important the topic is for the respondent (if we feel very strongly about something, we are usually willing to spend longer answering questions). However, most researchers agree that anything that is more than 4–6 pages long and requires over half an hour to complete is likely to be considered too much of an imposition. So a good rule of thumb is to stay within a four-page limit, which tends not to exceed the 30-minute completion limit.
- *Space economy*: We want to make the pages full because respondents are much more willing to fill in a two-page rather than a four-page questionnaire even if the two instruments have exactly the same number of items. However, we must not make the pages look crowded by economizing on the spaces separating different sections of the questionnaire. Effective ways of achieving this trade-off involve reducing the margins, using a space-economical font, and utilizing the whole width of the page, for example by printing the response options next to each question rather than below it.
- *Mixing up the scales and items*: The items from different scales need to be mixed up as much as possible to create a sense of variety and to prevent respondents from simply repeating previous answers.
- *Factual (or "personal") questions at the end*: Starting the questionnaire with a rather forbidding set of personal background questions (as in passport application forms) is offputting and may also ring "privacy alarm bells" in the students – such questions are best left to the end of the questionnaire.

Issue 5: Translating the Questionnaire

The issue of how to translate questionnaires from one language to another typically been marginalized and treated as an addendum in questionnaire design, whereas translating questionnaires as a practice is surprisingly common, due to the frequency of multinational research teams (including supervisor–research-student teams) and the widespread – and we believe correct – belief that the quality of the obtained data improves if the questionnaire is presented in the respondents' own mother tongue (for an overview, see Harkness, 2008).

The main challenge in translating a questionnaire is to reconcile two somewhat contradictory criteria: (a) the need to produce a close translation of the original text so that we can claim that the two versions are equivalent, and (b) the need to produce natural-sounding texts in the target language. For most parts of the questionnaire we are likely to find easy solutions to this challenge, but there will be a few places where a close or literal translation will not express the real meaning and the pragmatic function of the text well. This is a point where team-based brainstorming and negotiation are particularly useful, and even in small-scale projects we should make an effort to recruit some competent help to deal with these problem issues.

After the initial translation is completed, it is necessary to ensure the equivalence of the two versions. We have two basic options: to consult bilingual external reviewers or to recruit an independent translator to back-translate the target language version into the source language (Brislin, 1970).

Issue 6: Piloting the Questionnaire

Piloting the questionnaire involves administering the instrument to a sample of participants who are similar to the target group of people for whom it has been designed. The results of the pilot study are invaluable in helping the researchers to (a) fine-tune the final version of the questionnaire in order to eliminate ambiguous, too difficult/easy, or irrelevant items; (b) improve the clarity of the item wordings and the instructions; (c) finalize the layout; (d) rehearse the administration procedures; (e) dry run the analysis in order to see whether the expected findings will potentially emerge from the data; (f) time the completion of the questionnaire; and (g) generally double-check that there are no mistakes left in the instrument.

The first stage of piloting usually involves assessing the item pool by carrying out a think-aloud protocol with three or four people (usually friends, colleagues, or family) who answer the items and provide detailed feedback. Based on their responses, we can normally put together a near-final version of the questionnaire, which is then tried out with 50–100 participants who are in every way similar to the target population the instrument is designed for. The obtained data is then submitted to item analysis, which usually involves checking three aspects of the response pattern:

- *Missing responses* and possible signs that the instructions were not understood correctly. If some items are left out by several respondents, that should serve as an indication that something is not right.
- The *range of the responses* elicited by each item. We should avoid including items that are endorsed by almost everyone or by almost no one, because they are difficult if not impossible to process statistically.
- The *internal consistency* of the multi-item scales. Multi-item scales are only effective if the items within them work in concert, that is, if they measure the same target area. To check the coherence of each scale and to identify items that do not fit in with the others, researchers usually conduct reliability analyses (see below).

Sampling and Data Collection

The most frequent question asked by novice researchers who are planning to use questionnaires in their investigation is "How many people do I need to survey?" In measurement terms this question can be formulated as "How large should my sample be?" And a second question to follow is "What sort of people shall I select?" Or, in other words, "Whom shall my sample consist of?" Let us start answering these key questions by first looking at the second issue, the principles of quantitative sampling.

Issue 1: Sampling Procedures

The *sample* is the group of people whom the researcher actually examines and the *population* is the larger group of people whom the survey is about. That is, the target population of a study consists of all the people to whom the survey's findings are to be applied or generalized. For example, the population in a study might be English as a foreign language (EFL) learners in Taiwanese secondary schools and the actual sample might involve three Taiwanese secondary classes.

The main point of sampling is to save resources. We could, in principle, survey the whole population – as the census does – but by adopting appropriate *sampling procedures* to select a smaller number of people to be questioned we can still come up with accurate results at a much lower cost (as demonstrated by opinion polls). To achieve this, we need to choose a sample that is similar to the target population in its most important general characteristics (e.g., age, gender, ethnicity, educational background, academic capability, social class, socioeconomic status, etc.) as well as in all the more specific features that are known to be significantly related to the items included on the questionnaire (e.g., L2 learning background or the amount and type of L2 instruction received). That is, the sample needs to be *representative* of the whole population, and various sampling procedures have been developed to ensure this representativeness.

Broadly speaking, sampling strategies can be divided into two groups: (a) scientifically sound "probability sampling," which involves complex and expensive procedures that provide a truly representative sample; and (b) "non-probability sampling," which involves a number of strategies that try to achieve a trade-off, that is, a reasonably representative sample while using resources that are within the means of the ordinary researcher. Because probability sampling is typically beyond the means of most applied linguists, we will introduce "random sampling", the crucial element of this approach, only briefly before we describe several non-probability sampling procedures.

- *Random sampling* involves the selection of members of the population to be included in the sample on a completely random basis, a little bit like drawing numbers from a hat. In this way the selection is based entirely on chance rather than on any extraneous or subjective factors. As a result, a sufficiently large sample is generally believed to contain subjects whose characteristics are similar to the population as a whole. Combining random sampling with some form of rational/purposeful grouping is a particularly effective method for research with a specific focus: in "stratified random sampling" the population is divided into groups, or "strata," and a random sample of a proportionate size is selected from each group.
- *Convenience or opportunity sampling* is the most common non-probability sampling type in L2 research, where an important criterion of sample selection is the convenience to and resources of the researcher. Members of the target population are selected only if they meet certain practical criteria, such as geographical proximity, availability at a certain time, or easy accessibility. Captive audiences such as students in the researcher's own institution are prime examples of convenience samples. To be fair, convenience samples are rarely completely convenience-based but are usually partially purposeful, which means that besides the relative ease of accessibility, participants also have to possess certain key characteristics that are related to the purpose of the investigation.
- *Snowball sampling* involves a "chain reaction," whereby the researcher identifies a few people who meet the criteria of a particular study and then asks these participants to identify appropriate further members of the population. This technique is useful when studying groups whose membership is not readily identifiable (e.g., teenage gang members or particularly test-anxious learners).
- In *quota sampling* the researcher defines certain distinct subgroups (e.g., boys/girls or age cohorts) and determines the proportion of the population that belongs to each of these subgroups (e.g., when targeting language teachers, determining that the female–male ratio among them is 70:30 in a particular setting). The actual sample, then, is selected in a way as to reflect these proportions (i.e., 70% of the teacher sample will be women). Thus, quota sampling is similar to stratified random sampling without the "random" element.

We must not forget, however, that no matter how principled a non-probability sample strives to be, the extent of generalizability in this type of sample is often negligible. Therefore, we need to describe in sufficient detail the limitations of such samples when we report the results, while also highlighting the characteristics that the particular sample shares with the defined target population.

Issue 2: How Large Should the Sample Be?

When researchers ask the question, "How large should the sample be?" what they usually mean is, "How small a sample can I get away with?" Therefore, the often-quoted principle "the larger, the better" is usually rather unhelpful for them. Unfortunately, there are no hard-and-fast rules in setting the optimal sample size; the final answer to the "how large/small?" question should be the outcome of the researcher considering several broad guidelines:

1. In the survey research literature a range of between 1% and 10% of the population is usually mentioned as the "magic" sampling fraction, depending on how careful the selection has been (i.e., the more scientific the sampling procedures applied, the smaller the sample size can be, which is why opinion polls can produce accurate predictions from samples as small as 0.1% of the population).

2. From a purely statistical point of view, a basic requirement is that the results obtained from the sample should have a *normal distribution*, and a rule of thumb to achieve this, offered by Hatch and Lazaraton (1991), is that the sample should include 30 or more people. However, this is not an absolute rule, because smaller sample sizes can be compensated for by using certain special *non-parametric statistical procedures* (see Dörnyei, 2007).

3. From the perspective of *statistical significance*, the principal concern is to sample enough learners for the expected results to be able to reach significance. Because in L2 studies meaningful correlations reported in journal articles have often been as low as 0.30 and 0.40, a good rule of thumb is that we need around 50 participants to make sure that these coefficients are significant and thus we do not lose potentially important results. However, certain multivariate statistical procedures require more than 50 participants; for factor analysis or structural equation modeling, for example, we need a minimum of 100 (but preferably more) subjects.

4. A further important consideration is whether there are any distinct subgroups within the sample which may be expected to behave differently from the others. If we can identify such subgroups in advance (e.g., in most L2 studies of schoolchildren, girls have been found to perform differently from boys), we should set the sample size so that the minimum size applies to the *smallest subgroup* to allow for effective statistical procedures.

5. When setting the final sample size, it is advisable to leave a decent *margin* to provide for unforeseen or unplanned circumstances. For example, some participants are likely to drop out of at least some phases of the project; some questionnaires will always have to be disqualified for one reason or another; and – in relation to point 4 above – we may also detect unexpected subgroups that need to be treated separately.

Issue 3: Administering the Questionnaire

There is ample evidence that questionnaire administration procedures play a significant role in affecting the quality of the elicited responses. The key question is this: why would the respondents take the survey seriously when they have usually nothing to gain from participating in the research? The answer is that people in general do not mind expressing their opinions and answering questions as long as they think that the particular survey they are invited to participate in is a serious study, related to a worthy cause, and that their opinion matters. Thus, if we take sufficient care planning and executing the administration process, we can successfully build on this human characteristic and can secure the cooperation of our informants (for a range of administration strategies suitable for different questionnaire formats, see Dörnyei, 2010).

How to Analyze Survey Results

After we have designed the questionnaire and administered it to an appropriate sample, we need to process the obtained data. The main stages of this stepwise process are as follows:

Step 1: Preparing the Raw Data to Processing

The first step in processing questionnaire data involves a series of procedures to transform the respondents' markings on the actual questionnaires into a neat data file that contains figures recorded in a way that is appropriate for statistical analysis:

- *Coding questionnaire data*: The respondents' answers are converted to numbers by means of *coding procedures* in order to be able to use the vast arsenal of statistical techniques available for numerical data. With numerical variables such as test scores, the coding is simple, and with closed-ended questionnaire items, such as Likert scales, the process is similarly straightforward (with each response option assigned a consecutive number). For simple open-ended questionnaire items (e.g., some background information), the coding frame is more complex because it can have as many values as the number of the different answers in all the questionnaires, and other open-ended questions require an elaborate and principled interpretive scheme.
- *Inputting the data*: First we should create a new data file within a computer program into which the data will be recorded. Next, the data needs to be keyed in – SPSS, which is the most frequently used statistical package in the social sciences, has its own Data Editor screen, which provides a convenient, spreadsheet-like method for creating and editing data files.
- *Data cleaning*: The initial data file will always contain mistakes. Some of these are the result of human error occurring during the data entry phase (e.g., typing

the wrong number) and some are mistakes made by the respondents when filling in the questionnaire. Data cleaning involves correcting as many of these errors and inaccuracies as possible before the actual analyses are undertaken. This is an indispensable phase of preparing the data because some mistakes can completely distort our results.

- *Data manipulation*: This involves making changes in the dataset prior to the analyses in order to make it more appropriate for certain statistical procedures. One particularly important issue here is to decide how to handle missing data, and another is to recode any negatively worded items.

Step 2: *Reducing the Number of Variables in the Questionnaire*

The actual analysis of questionnaire data always starts with *reducing the number of variables* measured by the questionnaire to manageable proportions so that the mass of details does not prevent us from seeing the forest for the trees. Thus, data reduction involves creating fewer but broader variables by merging items. Most researchers apply one of two approaches (or a combination of these) to determine which items belong together:

- The statistical technique of *factor analysis* is particularly suited to reducing the number of variables to a few values that still contain most of the information found in the original variables, because it explores the interrelationships of the items and tries to find patterns of correspondence – that is, common underlying themes – among them. The outcome is a small set of underlying dimensions, referred to as *factors* or *components*.
- Based on the theoretical considerations guiding the construction of the questionnaire, we form clusters of items that are hypothesized to hang together (i.e., the original multi-item scales) and then conduct an internal consistency check to determine whether our assumptions are borne out in practice. The *Reliability Analysis* procedure in SPSS not only computes "Cronbach Alpha" reliability coefficients describing the homogeneity of the items in a cluster (or, as it is usually referred to, a "scale"), but also advises us whether the exclusion of one or more items would increase the scale's internal reliability. The *Cronbach Alpha coefficient* is a figure usually ranging between 0 and +1, and during item analysis we should aim at coefficients in excess of .70; if the Cronbach Alpha of a scale does not reach .60, this should sound warning bells.

Step 3: *Analyzing the Data through Statistical Procedures*

The standard method of analyzing quantitative questionnaire data involves submitting it to various statistical procedures. These include a wide range of different techniques, from calculating item means on a pocket calculator to running complex statistical analyses. It is beyond the scope of this chapter to provide a detailed analysis of the available procedures (for non-technical discussions of statistics, see Dörnyei,

2007; Pallant, 2007; Salkind, 2008). Instead, we would like to emphasize one crucial aspect of statistical data analysis that is often misunderstood or ignored by novice researchers, namely the distinction between *descriptive statistics* and *inferential statistics*:

- *Descriptive statistics*, such as mean, range, and standard deviation, are used to summarize sets of numerical data in order to conserve time and space. However, these statistics are only specific to the given sample and do *not* allow the drawing of any general conclusions that would go beyond the sample.
- *Inferential statistics* are the same as descriptive statistics except that the computer also tests whether the results observed in our sample (e.g., mean differences or correlations) are powerful enough to generalize to the whole population. If they are, we can say that our results are statistically "significant," and we can then draw some more general lessons from the study.

Thus, *statistical significance* denotes whether a particular result is powerful enough to indicate a more generalizable phenomenon. If a result is non-significant, this means that we cannot be certain whether it occurred in the particular sample only because of chance (e.g., because of the unique composition of the respondents examined). Accordingly, statistically non-significant results *must be ignored* in research studies. That is, we must not say things like "Although the mean difference between boys' and girls' scores did not reach significance, girls tended to do better than boys."

Reporting Survey Results

Survey data can be used for a great variety of purposes and each of these might require somewhat different types of summaries and reports of the findings. It is obvious, for instance, that a PhD dissertation will have to meet criteria that are very different from the presentation requirements of a summary of student achievement at a school staff meeting. There are, however, certain common issues shared by many different types of research reports of survey results. Here we highlight three such issues: the question of how much to generalize, the technical information that we need to include in a survey report, and presenting results in tables.

Issue 1: How Much to Generalize

Researchers need to exercise great caution when pitching the level of generalization in their research reports; this is particularly so in light of Lazaraton's (2005) warning that using high-powered parametric procedures may easily tempt scholars to overgeneralize their results and to make grand claims regarding their findings. The other side of the coin is, however, that research in most cases is all about the need to produce generalizable findings, and along with the Task Force on Statistical Inference of the American Psychological Association (TSFI; see Wilkinson & TFSI, 1999, p. 602), we would encourage researchers not to be afraid "to extend your interpretations to a general class or population if you have reasons to assume that your results apply." The question, then, is when generalization becomes *over*generalization. Unfortunately, there are no hard-and-fast rules about where the threshold is, so we need to strive for a delicate balance between the following two considerations: on the one hand, we may wish to be able to say something of a broader relevance, since without this our audience would be very limited; on the other hand, big claims can usually be made only on the basis of big studies. Having said that, Dörnyei (2010) also points out that some seminal papers in the research literature have made some very big claims based on rather small studies.

Issue 2: Technical Information to Accompany Survey Results

In order for the readers to be able to interpret (and believe) the claims made in a research report, they will have to be convinced that the methodology used to produce the particular findings was appropriate. This does not mean that we can only report results if our study did not have any methodological limitations but it does mean that we must provide a concise and yet detailed summary of the main aspects of the survey, including any known limiting factors. There is no perfect study and it is up to the readers (and the journal editors) to decide on the value of the findings. Table 5.1 presents a summary of the points to be covered by the description.

Issue 3: Presenting the Results in Tables

Questionnaire studies typically produce a wealth of data, and therefore developing effective and digestible – that is, reader-friendly – ways of presenting the data is an essential skill for the survey researcher. A rule of thumb is that we should present as much of the information as possible in *tables* rather than in the running text. Having said that, we should realize that for the sake of space economy, some international journals encourage the reporting of some statistical results within the main body of text, so we must not overdo using tables. The big advantage of tables is that they can summarize large amounts of data about the respondents and their responses, and they are also ideal for presenting the results of statistical analyses. Their drawback is that these numerical results are less digestible without any textual context, particularly for the uninitiated.

There are two technical points that we would like to highlight about tables. First, if we present statistics in tables, we should *not* repeat the figures in the text as well, except when we want to underscore some particularly noteworthy results. Second, we should note that statistics tables have certain canonical forms, both in content (i.e., what information to include) and format (e.g., usually we do not use vertical lines in them). These need to be observed closely, which means that simply importing a table from SPSS into a manuscript is most likely to be inappropriate.

Table 5.1 Checklist for the main points to be covered by the technical description part of a survey report.

Participants
- *Description of the sample*, including the participants' total number, age, gender, ethnicity, first language, level of L2 proficiency, L2 learning history, L2 teaching institution (if applicable), type of tuition received, and any relevant grouping variable (e.g., number of courses or classes they come from).
- The *sampling method* used for the selection of the participants.
- Any necessary *additional details* depending on the particular study, such as general aptitude (or academic ability), socioeconomic background, occupation, amount of time spent in an L2 host environment, etc.

Questionnaire
- *Description* of and *rationale* for the main content areas covered by the items.
- *Factual description* of the instrument (e.g., number of items, response options, language).
- Details about the *piloting* of the instrument.
- Any available data concerning the *reliability* and *validity* of the instrument.

Questionnaire administration
- *Procedures* used to administer the questionnaire.
- *Length of time* that was needed to complete the questionnaire.
- Questionnaire *return rate*.

Variables (if the study contains several complex variables)
- *Complete list* of the variables derived from the raw questionnaire data, including details of how they were operationalized.
- With *multi-item scales*: the number of constituent items and the Cronbach Alpha internal consistency reliability coefficient for each scale.

Project Ideas and Resources

Analyzing a Questionnaire

We would like to present a questionnaire adapted from a published study (Kormos & Csizér, 2008; original version in Hungarian; for a description of the study, see study box 5.1) to illustrate how the various principles of questionnaire design have been put into actual practice. Following the questionnaire and further reading suggestions, we list some study questions that help to analyze the instrument. While no instrument is perfect and some readers might find that they would have done some aspects differently, this particular questionnaire has delivered the "proof of the pudding" – it worked.

Study Box 5.1

Kormos, J., & Csizér, K. (2008). Age-related differences in the motivation of learning English as a foreign language: Attitudes, selves and motivated learning behavior. *Language Learning, 58*, 327–355.

Background

The aim of the investigation was two-fold. First, the authors wanted to investigate any possible differences among three distinct learner groups who studied English in the same context in Budapest, the capital city of Hungary. The second objective was to test empirically the two main constructs of Dörnyei's L2 motivational self-system, namely the Ideal L2 Self and the Ought-to L2 Self, and explore the relationship of these variables with more traditional motivational and attitudinal constructs such as integrativeness and instrumentality.

Research questions

- What are the main dimensions describing students' foreign language learning motivation?
- What age-related differences can be found across the three samples?
- What dimensions influence motivated learning behavior in a significant way?

Method

A cross-sectional questionnaire survey with three independent samples of learners: secondary school students (N = 202; average age = 16.5 years), university students (N = 230; average age = 21.5 years), and adult language learners (N = 191; average age = 33.7 years). After extensive piloting, the final version of the questionnaire was mailed or personally delivered to the participating secondary schools, universities, colleges, and language schools, where a person who agreed to take charge of the administration of the questionnaires distributed them among the teachers and later collected the completed questionnaires.

Statistical tools

A range of descriptive and inferential statistical procedures including ANOVA, correlation, and regression analysis.

Results

The main factors affecting students' L2 motivation were language learning attitudes and the Ideal L2 self, which provides empirical support for the main construct of the theory of the L2 motivational self-system. Models of motivated behavior varied across the three investigated learner groups; for the secondary school pupils, it was their interest in English-language cultural products that affected their motivated behavior most, whereas international posture emerged as an important predictive variable in the two older age groups.

College and university student questionnaire (extract; original language: Hungarian)

We would like to ask you to help us by answering the following questions concerning foreign language learning. This is not a test so there are no "right" or "wrong" answers and you don't even have to write your name on it. We are interested in your personal opinion. Please give your answers sincerely as only this will guarantee the success of the investigation. Thank you very much for your help!

I. In the following section please answer the questions by simply giving marks from 1 to 5.

5 = very much   4 = quite a lot   3 = so-so   2 = not really   1 = not at all

For example, if you like "apples" very much, "bean soup" not very much, and "spinach" not at all, encircle the following numbers:

How much do you like apples?	⑤	4	3	2	1
How much do you like bean soup?	5	4	3	②	1
How much do you like spinach?	5	4	3	2	①

Please encircle one (and only one) number for each item, and please don't leave out any of them. Thanks.

5 = very much   4 = quite a lot   3 = so-so   2 = not really   1 = not at all

1. How much do you like the TV programs made in the United States?	5	4	3	2	1
2. How much do you think knowing English would help your future career?	5	4	3	2	1
3. How much do you like English?	5	4	3	2	1
4. How much do you like the films made in the United States?	5	4	3	2	1
5. How much do you like the pop music of the USA?	5	4	3	2	1
6. How much would you like to become similar to the people who speak English?	5	4	3	2	1

| 7. How much do you like the magazines made in the United States? | 5 | 4 | 3 | 2 | 1 |
| 8. How much do you like meeting foreigners from English-speaking countries? | 5 | 4 | 3 | 2 | 10 |

II. Now there are going to be statements some people agree with and some people don't. We would like to know to what extent they describe your own feelings or situation. After each statement you'll find five boxes. Please put an 'X' in the box which best expresses how true the statement is about your feelings or situation. For example, if you like skiing very much, put an 'X' in the first box:

	Absolutely true	Mostly true	Partly true partly untrue	Not really true	Not true at all
I like skiing very much.	X				

There are no right or wrong answers – we are interested in *your* personal opinion.

	Absolutely true	Mostly true	Partly true partly untrue	Not really true	Not true at all
9. People around me tend to think that it is a good thing to know foreign languages.					
10. My parents really encourage me to study English.					
11. Learning English is really great.					
12. The things I want to do in the future require me to speak English.					
13. I am willing to work hard at learning English.					
14. My parents encourage me to practice my English as much as possible.					
15. I really enjoy learning English.					
16. Whenever I think of my future career, I imagine myself being able to use English.					
17. Nobody really cares whether I learn English or not.					

	Absolutely true	Mostly true	Partly true partly untrue	Not really true	Not true at all
18. It is very important for me to learn English.					
19. My parents consider foreign languages important school subjects.					
20. My parents have stressed the importance English will have for me in my future.					
21. I find learning English really interesting.					
22. I like to think of myself as someone who will be able to speak English.					
23. My parents feel that I should really try to learn English.					
24. I can honestly say that I am really doing my best to learn English.					
25. When I think about my future, it is important that I use English.					
26. I am determined to push myself to learn English.					
27. Learning English is one of the most important aspects in my life.					

III. **Finally, would you please answer a few personal questions – we need this information to be able to interpret your answers properly.**

28. If you had a choice, which foreign languages would you choose to learn next year at school (or work)? Please mark three languages in order of importance.

> 1)...................
> 2)...................
> 3)...................

29. Your gender? (Please underline):   male   female
30. How old are you (in years)? ....
31. What foreign language(s) are you currently learning besides English?
   ....
32. What college/university do you attend? ....
   ....
33. What do you study? ....
   ....
34. How old were you when you started learning English? ....

THANK YOU VERY MUCH – WE REALLY APPRECIATE YOUR HELP!

Further Reading

- The most comprehensive text on questionnaires in L2 research is Dörnyei (2010). Brown (2001) also offers a valuable discussion of survey research, including information on interview surveys.
- For further information on various aspects of research methodology in SLA, please refer to Dörnyei (2007) and Mackey and Gass (2005).
- With regard to statistics, a good starting point is Salkind's (2008) book entitled *Statistics for People Who (Think They) Hate Statistics* – the title says it all.
- With regard to the use of SPSS, one of the most informative and user-friendly texts we are aware of is Pallant (2007) – and it also contains statistical advice.
- Finally, the largest-ever attitude/motivation survey in SLA has been Dörnyei, Csizér, and Németh (2006), which also contains extensive appendices that include all the instruments and other materials used in the study.

Study Questions

1. Look again at the questionnaire above, adapted from Kormos and Csizér (2008):

   (a) Identify the main parts of the questionnaire.
   (b) Provide numerical codes for the different types of questions in the questionnaire.
   (c) The main aim of Kormos and Csizér's (2008) study was to investigate what factors influenced students' motivated learning behavior in a significant way. Motivated learning behavior was defined as the amount of effort students were willing to invest into foreign language learning. The final multi-item scale contained *five* items, which are scattered around in the adapted version of the questionnaire presented in this chapter. Try to identify the questions that successfully measured motivated learning behavior.

2. The following set of items was used by Clément, Dörnyei, and Noels (1994) to measure the extent of group cohesiveness in learner groups. If the first item is excluded from the scale, the overall internal consistency reliability coefficient of the scale (i.e., Cronbach Alpha) goes up from .77 to .80. Discuss what could be wrong with this item.

   (a) Sometimes there are tensions among the members of my group and these make learning more difficult.
   (b) Compared to other groups like mine, I feel that my group is better than most.
   (c) There are some cliques in this group.
   (d) If I were to participate in another group like this one, I would want it to include people who are very similar to the ones in this group.

(e)   This group is composed of people who fit together.

(f)   There are some people in this group who do not really like each other.

(g)   I am dissatisfied with my group.

3.   There are two mistakes in the following sentence. Can you spot them?

As can be seen in table below, the correlation between motivation and learning achievement is highly significant (r = .64, p < .001).

References

Babbie, E. R. (2007). *The basics of social research* (12th ed.). Belmont, CA: Thomson & Wadsworth.

Brislin, R. W. (1970). Back-translation for cross-cultural research. *Journal of Cross-Cultural Psychology, 1,* 185–216.

Brown, J. D. (2001). *Using surveys in language programs*. Cambridge, England: Cambridge University Press.

Clément, R., Dörnyei, Z., & Noels, K. (1994). Motivation, self-confidence and group cohesion in the foreign language classroom. *Language Learning, 44,* 417–448.

Davidson, F. (1996). *Principles of statistical data handling*. Thousand Oaks, CA: Sage.

DeVellis, R. F. (2003). *Scale development: Theory and applications* (2nd ed.). Thousand Oaks, CA: Sage.

Dörnyei, Z. (2007). *Research methods in applied linguistics: Quantitative, qualitative and mixed methodologies*. Oxford, England: Oxford University Press.

Dörnyei, Z. (2010). *Questionnaires in second language research: Construction, administration, and processing*. New York, NY: Routledge.

Dörnyei, Z., Csizér, K., & Németh, N. (2006). *Motivation, language attitudes and globalisation: A Hungarian perspective*. Clevedon, England: Multilingual Matters.

Gillham, B. (2008). *Developing a questionnaire* (2nd ed.). London, England: Continuum.

Harkness, J. A. (2008). Comparative survey research: Goals and challenges. In E. D. De Leeuw, J. J. Hox, & D. A. Dillman (Eds.), *International handbook of survey methodology* (pp. 56–77). New York, NY: Lawrence Erlbaum.

Hatch, E., & Lazaraton, A. (1991). *The research manual: Design and statistics for applied linguistics*. New York, NY: Newbury House.

Kormos, J., & Csizér, K. (2008). Age-related differences in the motivation of learning English as a foreign language: Attitudes, selves and motivated learning behavior. *Language Learning, 58,* 327–355.

Lazaraton. A. (2005). Quantitative research methods. In E. Hinkel (Ed.), *Handbook of research in second language teaching and learning* (pp. 209–224). Mahwah, NJ: Lawrence Erlbaum.

Mackey, A., & Gass, S. M. (2005). *Second language research: Methodology and design*. Mahwah, NJ: Lawrence Erlbaum.

Pallant, J. (2007). SPSS survival manual: A step by step guide to data analysis using SPSS for Windows (Version 15) (3rd ed.). Maidenhead, England: Open University Press and McGraw-Hill Education.

Salkind, N. J. (2008). *Statistics for people who (think they) hate statistics*. Los Angeles, CA: Sage.

Tseng, W.-T., Dörnyei, Z., & Schmitt, N. (2006). A new approach too assessing the strategic learning: The case of self-regulation in vocabulary acquisition. *Applied Linguistics, 27*, 78–102.

Wilkinson, L., & TFSI. (1999). Statistical methods in psychology journals: Guidelines and explanations. *American Psychologist, 54*, 594–604.

6 How to Carry Out Case Study Research

Patricia A. Duff

Background

Case study research is a potentially powerful yet quite practical form of inquiry and theory building that has led to important insights since the inception of the field of second language acquisition (SLA) (e.g., Hatch, 1978). Its focus is a small number of research participants – language learners or teachers typically – and sometimes just one individual (a focal participant or case) is involved. The individual's behaviors, performance, knowledge, and/or perspectives are then studied very closely and intensively, often over an extended period of time, to address timely questions regarding language acquisition, attrition, interaction, motivation, identity, or other current topics in applied linguistics. In this chapter I describe SLA case study research, one of the most common forms of qualitative inquiry. I then provide procedures for conducting case studies and some recent examples. (See Duff, 2008, for a more detailed history, description, and exemplification of this approach.)

Case Study Methodology

Case study research involves not only a type of *data* but also a type of *research design* and *written report* that highlights cases. Research design refers to the conceptualization of research: "the logic and coherence of your research study – the components of your research and the ways in which these relate to one another" (Maxwell, 2005: xii). The design in case studies and other types of qualitative research is not fixed, however; it often changes as the study unfolds. If a longitudinal study is underway and the learner moves to another city or country, the data collection might need to proceed

Research Methods in Second Language Acquisition: A Practical Guide, First Edition.
Edited by Alison Mackey and Susan M. Gass.
© 2012 Blackwell Publishing Ltd. Published 2012 by Blackwell Publishing Ltd.

differently – at different intervals, via Skype or email rather than face-to-face, by self-recorded digital audio files, or by the selection of a new local participant. If an aspect of language learning or use not originally expected to be relevant becomes salient in the study, then new procedures for examining that particular aspect might need to be designed and others eliminated. Maxwell (2005) recommends that qualitative research design, including case study, should take an interactive, emergent approach. One of the advantages of working with cases is that there is quite a bit of flexibility in design that would simply be impracticable or unnecessary in larger-scale qualitative studies or quantitative studies.

The "case" (person) in a case study is not normally the phenomenon itself being studied (Dyson & Genishi, 2005); it is a case *of something* – of a phenomenon of interest. The phenomenon may be patterns of SLA in instructional or naturalistic settings, fossilization, negotiation of meaning, code-switching, multilingual literacies, first language (L1) or second language (L2) attrition, language transfer, or acculturation. Case studies can be exploratory, descriptive, or explanatory (Yin, 2003a, 2003b). They can be confirmatory or disconfirmatory; that is, they can corroborate previous findings or disconfirm them, a very important role in theory development. The greatest strength of case study is its ability to exemplify larger processes or situations in a very accessible, concrete, immediate, and personal manner. In the most illuminating studies, new directions for the field may result from insights generated by the case. Case study research seeks depth rather than breadth in its scope and analysis. Its goal is not to universalize but to particularize and then yield insights of potentially wider relevance and theoretical significance.

Case study research in SLA traditionally paralleled work in psychology and linguistics, particularly in L1 acquisition. Brown's (1973) multiple-case study of three children's acquisition of English (L1) set an early, quite rigorous, and informative precedent. However, case study has enjoyed a much longer history of use – and scrutiny – across the social sciences, life sciences, and humanities, as well as in other academic and professional fields. A large proportion of case studies in SLA and L2 education today reflect developments in sociology and in the humanities, with an emphasis on families or communities as cases with unique linguistic ecologies and social dynamics. Examining the linguistic or cognitive performance or dispositions of a single individual in relative isolation is now less common (e.g., see study box 6.1 below).

Because of its diverse disciplinary origins and the research traditions found across them (e.g., psychology vs. anthropology), case studies may involve different units of analysis (e.g., a country, a city, a child, the testing of an innovation). They may be highly analytical, technical, and experimental, providing relatively little information about the broader context (e.g., in linguistics, psychology, and SLA traditionally) or even the participants' lives, past or present; or they may be highly holistic and naturalistic (e.g., in much educational case study research), with a "thick description" (Geertz, 1973) of the case and context and less analysis of one particular area or attribute of the case (e.g., the grammar system) but a more global description and analysis of settlement, integration, and identity issues. In some work, the researcher's interpretations are privileged; in other work, the research participant may also play a central role in ascribing meanings to his or her own SLA experiences and to interpreting learning processes and abilities, sometimes in discussion with the researcher and other times more independently.

Study Box 6.1

Caldas, S. J. (2007). Changing bilingual self-perceptions from early adolescence to early adulthood: Empirical evidence from a mixed-methods case study. *Applied Linguistics, 29,* 290–311.

Background

The study examined the "changing bilingual self-perceptions of three children, identical twin girls and their older brother, from early adolescence through early adulthood" (p. 290). Data were collected over a 13-year period. Framing the study in part in terms of group socialization (psychology), language socialization (linguistic anthropology), and identity construction, Caldas examined how, and why, the children's attitudes toward being bilingual (or multilingual) vacillated over time. It is part of a larger study of the children's incipient bilingualism/multilingualism.

Research question

Although it is not explicitly stated, the following question is addressed: How do the French/English bilingual identities of three Canadian-American children evolve from early adolescence through early adulthood, and what factors might account for changes?

Method

Two questionnaires were given to the children – a self-report of their L2 proficiency and of their bilingualism/biculturalism – at three times, spanning 13 years. Then, "paired-sampled t-tests and correlations were generated between and among the children at Time1, Time2, and Time3. The author's ethnographic field notes, interviews with the children, and a quantitative measure of French preference are used to help interpret the results" (p. 290).

Statistical tools

t-tests of proficiency ratings and correlations.

Qualitative data analysis

The life histories and linguistic ecologies of the children's and family's life and education in both the USA and Canada were described. Ethnographic descriptions of home language practices and how they evolved were included based on participant observation, recordings, and interviews.

Results

As the children reached young adulthood, they were happier about being bilingual or multilingual. Earlier, socialization into peer-group norms of monolingualism challenged the bilingual values, opportunities, and Francophone culture and identities into which the parents tried to socialize their children.

Generalizability

"Of course, it is difficult to generalize from a case study of only three subjects to a broader population. However, the children's initial responses on the surveys are consistent with the literature that stresses that adolescence is the time of life that an individual seeks his or her own identity apart from parents and other authorities, and within the context of their peer groups" (p. 308).

The general philosophy underlying case study research is that much can be learned by looking both holistically and in close detail at the behaviors, performance, knowledge, or perspectives of just a few rather than many research subjects at one time. The cases can reveal important developmental patterns or perspectives that might be lost or obscured in a larger-scale study of populations or in larger sample sizes. These patterns or insights then contribute to theorizing about the phenomenon under investigation. By studying small numbers of research subjects, complex and dynamic interactions between the individual and the local social, cultural, and linguistic environment can be observed, although in SLA that is not always the focus of studies. Examining interactions within or among linguistic subsystems (e.g., across phonology, morphology, and syntax; or among various types of morphology, or across different task environments in which within-case variation is observed) may suffice in some studies.

Case Studies in Second language Acquisition: Historical Perspective

Most case studies in SLA and in other domains of applied linguistics are qualitative, though they may represent different epistemological and ontological approaches (see Friedman, this volume, chapter 10; Duff, 2008, 2010). That is, they may be positivist, testing hypotheses or looking for cause–effect relationships and seeking an objective reality or "truth" about the nature of SLA under scrutiny; they may be interpretive, trying to understand the experiences, abilities, and performance of learners, or their perceptions of those experiences and reconstructions of them through narratives or interviews, for example; or they may be critical, examining learners in terms of larger social issues related to power, oppression, and discrimination.

SLA case studies, at least traditionally, have examined factors influencing people's L2 development and have sought linguistic or other evidence for claims. Quantifying or statistically testing the significance of observed patterns, test results, or other manifestations of L2 development and use is not normally desired, required, or even possible. Furthermore, testing cause–effect relationships between a small number of variables is usually not the goal either. However, some SLA case studies are quantitative, looking for such causal relationships or otherwise quantifying relationships or patterns. They test the significance of findings statistically and may employ an experimental design to test whether, and to what degree of certainty, development or change has occurred and, if so, how it might be characterized and accounted for. Single-case time series experiments are one such approach, where the case generates its own baseline data (typical patterns of linguistic behavior) prior to an intervention of some kind (e.g., instruction regarding a particular grammatical point), after which the effects of the intervention are noted and compared with the developmental trend established by that same person prior to the intervention (e.g., Mellow, Reeder, & Forster, 1996). Marked change in performance following the intervention suggests that the intervention or experimental treatment was largely responsible for that change.

Since this single-case experimental approach to case study research is relatively uncommon in applied linguistics, in this chapter qualitative and mixed-method case studies are discussed. Stand-alone case studies in SLA and L2 education are now more interpretive than positivist in orientation. In mixed-method studies, such as surveys combined with case studies, there may be quantification of the survey (questionnaire) data and then a more in-depth, personalized, qualitative description of the topic by choosing a few cases to provide a more concrete illustration of the phenomenon.

The first wave of published SLA studies that appeared in the mid-to-late 1970s and 1980s examined linguistic aspects of development in bilingual learners, such as children in bilingual homes, or L2 learners across a variety of contexts (e.g., studies in Hatch, 1978). The focus was how these learners acquired or used particular L2 forms to express particular meanings (grammatically or ungrammatically), kept their two languages separate, transferred aspects of their L1 to their L2, or built up their utterance structure or discourse grammar. The populations examined were varied. Studies in Europe often involved predominantly male migrant-worker populations (e.g., Klein & Perdue, 1992) who had moved from, say, Morocco to Germany or Portugal to Denmark and were learning their new L2 naturalistically. Other studies focused on adolescent and adult male and female immigrants, or international university students, examining strategies used in various skill areas, for example (see Duff, 2008). Alternatively, studies examined sociolinguistic development by focusing on how learners acquired the appropriate pragmatic means to express politeness involving speech acts such as complaints, apologies, or requests. Studies also explored the cognitive, psychological, and neurobiological attributes of highly talented or successful language learners, sometimes in contrast with much less successful learners, some of whom seemed to have plateaued or "fossilized" (ceased developing) in their L2 generally or in particular grammatical or phonological domains.

The next wave of SLA case studies, in the 1990s, began to examine social and affective factors to a greater extent, drawing less on linguistics, social psychology, and psychology and more on sociology. A larger number of research participants included immigrant women coping with SLA in the context of domestic duties, difficulties entering the labor market, or gaining access to effective language instruction or social interaction in the L2, sometimes because of issues of power and discrimination (e.g., Norton, 2000). Issues of not just L2 or third language (L3) learning but also L1 loss were addressed as well, as people shifted from their mother tongue to the language of the dominant culture in post-immigration contexts typically (e.g., Kouritzen, 1999; Pavlenko & Lantolf, 2000). The descriptions of language loss in such studies were not first and foremost linguistic, but were personal ruminations, life histories, describing the deep sense of loss experienced by people who had successfully learned another language because of the impact of the transition on their linguistic and cultural roots.

The most recent wave of SLA case studies, within the past decade, have expanded the populations and contexts to study-abroad learners (e.g., Kinginger, 2008); heritage-language learners (He, 2008; Guardado, 2009); learners immersed in language learning and use mediated by the internet or other technologies (e.g., Lam, 2004); and Generation 1.5 learners, those who immigrated in their school years but have quite unique linguistic and literacy profiles and experiences many years later, especially when they enter college or university (e.g., Kim, 2008). Transnational learners are also of greater interest than before: that is, language learners or users who move back and forth across national or linguistic borders with some regularity and must negotiate their (L1, L2, and/or L3) proficiency, identities, and community affiliations. This latter trend is connected with globalization and cosmopolitanism among workers and families.

In addition to the changing populations of language learners, users, and losers now included in SLA research, epistemologies, methods, and levels of contextualization are also expanding. As mentioned earlier, positivist and (linguistic) structural research examining incremental, categorical changes in linguistic abilities or intuitions, for example, is no longer the dominant approach in case studies. Interpretive and critical research incorporating sociological and sociocultural theory (e.g., notions of identity and agency) is increasing. In addition, the data collection methods in case studies in SLA are no longer primarily oral proficiency interviews, tests, or other highly structured interviews or test items designed to elicit L2 samples, grammaticality judgments, or measures of attitudes and motivation toward L2 learning. Narrative research, involving life history interviews, memoirs, diary studies, and even multi-modal and multilingual representations of SLA are becoming more pervasive as well (Pavlenko, 2007, 2008).

The reason for these changes in epistemology and methods is perhaps because sociolinguists, educators, and applied linguists not principally concerned with linguistic theories or theories of cognitive development have become more engaged in case study research, building on earlier generations of SLA but following the so-called social or narrative turn (e.g., Block, 2003). These researchers are less interested in charting technical aspects of learners' morphological, phonological, or syntactic development in either oral or written language or in testing linguistic or (social/cognitive) psychological theory. Rather, they are more concerned with understanding how the learners' developmental pathways affect them as individuals within particular communities (and vice versa): as members of society, as parents, children, immigrants, sojourners, or workers. Cognitive and purely linguistic aspects of learning have therefore been backgrounded to some extent and social aspects and their relationship to learners' linguistic and social identities foregrounded, examining race, gender, and socioeconomic and migration status.

Finally, qualitative (multiple-)case study research combined with other research methods, such as pretesting and posttesting of proficiency or attitudes and motivation, is now less rare than before and offers possibilities for capturing both linguistic and socio-experiential aspects of SLA. Two mixed-method case studies of French language learning follow in study boxes 6.1 and 6.2, by Caldas (2007) and Kinginger (2008), respectively. Both combine traditional foci in SLA on language proficiency and social-psychological orientations, and current trends examining socialization and identity, set within the larger sociopolitical or cultural context. Caldas's represents an unusually long study of French–English familial bilingualism, whereas Kinginger's deals with American university students' French L2 study-abroad experiences during a semester in France. (See related study questions near the end of the chapter.)

Study Box 6.2

Kinginger, C. (2008). Language learning in study abroad: Case studies of Americans in France. *Modern Language Journal*, 92(1), 1–124.

Background

Framed by sociocultural theory and the impact of globalization and current political events on SLA, this study investigates the L2 experiences of 24 undergraduate study-abroad students from a US university during their one-semester sojourn in France.

Research questions

Chapter 1 provides the theoretical and educational rationale for the study but research questions are not explicitly stated. The author wanted to "see why [students] choose to study abroad and, in this context, what language learning means to them" (p. 12). The study also "seeks to understand the relationship among the participants' histories as American foreign language learners, the nature of their investment in language learning, the qualities of their experience, and documented outcomes" (p. 13).

Method

24 participants planning to study abroad were recruited; 6 were selected as focal case participants (3 more advanced, 3 elementary-intermediate). A questionnaire

obtained information about students' prior and anticipated French study. Quantitative data included a standardized French proficiency test, speech samples from role plays, a language awareness interview (sociolinguistic/pragmatic aspects; awareness of colloquial words). Qualitative data were collected from the six via in-country logs (hours per day of French vs. English use), journals, oral interviews before and after their sojourn, and on-site observations.

Statistical tools

Descriptive statistics on pre-test vs. post-test scores; non-parametric statistics on use of informal vs. formal address pronouns pre- and post-; t-tests on some pre-post measures of L2 skills (e.g., reading, listening; speech acts), etc.

Qualitative data analysis

Thematic (narrative) analysis, exemplification, discussion related to such themes as how Americans were perceived abroad (during beginning of Iraq War; national vs. personal identities); frustration and isolation (and role of gender); complexity of experiences; uniqueness of each case. Extended description of each participant's profile and experiences, in turn.

Results

"Study abroad is a productive – if imperfect – environment for the development of communicative competence in foreign languages" (p. 107). Students in the cohort showed overall "marked" improvement in their L2 proficiency, with considerable individual variation. The focal students' "dispositions toward language learning" (p. 107) proved very powerful and also variable in their experiences abroad, including in their access to meaningful opportunities to practice the L2 outside of class (e.g., with host families) and their expectations regarding, and satisfaction with, their study-abroad sojourn and their identities as L2 learners and users. Two out of three reported "success stories" were male.

Generalizability

"The findings of this study are similar to those of previous research investigating language learning in study-abroad contexts ... [However,] considerable variation was documented for individual students" (p. 107). Kinginger notes that a strength of the study is looking not only at the individuality of each case and context (e.g., type of home-stay environment, gendered experience) but also the complex local conditions of study abroad based on life histories, current affairs, ideologies of nationalism, settings, and students' own investments in their SLA experiences and identities as L2 users. "The primary limitation of this project – the fact that it is a case study of a cohort and of individual students – is also its greatest strength" (p. 113).

Doing Case Studies

Conducting case studies can be very practical because only a small number of individuals or sites are normally involved, and thus participants may be easier to recruit and obtain permissions from than in a study with a different design for which hundreds of permissions (from institutions, parents, children, or others) might be required.

However, to characterize case study research as "practical" does not mean that it is necessarily any easier to conduct or publish than other approaches. L2 learners often represent a mobile population–migrants, in a region for just a short period of time to work or study; children who may move to another school district or city as their parents' employment requires; or adults learning an additional language to pursue job opportunities or travel in another region. Therefore, longitudinal studies may prove difficult to sustain. Also, committee members or readers might question the representativeness, generalizability, and significance of the findings. For that reason, case study researchers must design studies carefully, and select research participants, sites, and data collection and analysis methods in anticipation of such critiques.

Getting Started

Becoming familiar with the existing literature and issues in SLA

Case study research must be guided by a *conceptual framework* which includes "theories, beliefs, and prior research findings" directly relevant to the goals of the study being undertaken (Maxwell, 2005, p. 4). For that reason, case study researchers need to be familiar with the field; the current issues, debates, and methods in SLA, recent related research (case study and other types); and relevant theoretical frameworks. Surveying recent SLA textbooks can provide an overview of the field to begin with (e.g., Ellis, 2008; Gass & Selinker, 2008; Ortega, 2009). Recent issues of journals that publish SLA research should also be examined (e.g., *Language Learning, Studies in Second Language Acquisition, Applied Linguistics, Modern Language Journal, TESOL Quarterly, Journal of Language, Identity, and Education*) to see what other case studies have been published or to find topics of particular interest that may have been studied using other research designs but not case studies. In addition, consulting recent textbooks on case study research methodology in education and the social sciences generally, as well as in SLA, will provide familiarity with different theoretical, epistemological/ontological, and methodological orientations to current qualitative SLA research. This also provides concrete examples of studies (e.g., Stake, 1995, 2005; Merriam, 1998; Merriam & Associates, 2002; Yin, 2003a, 2003b; Duff, 2008). Another strategy involves examining recent case studies (theses, dissertations, research articles) from across a number of areas of SLA then deciding which topics are most interesting, and why, and considering which approach to reporting the research seems most engaging or convincing. Duff (2008: ch. 3) provides an overview or sampling of case studies across the SLA spectrum, and I usually ask new SLA students which studies or topics they found most interesting.

Apart from library research, researchers might already have identified an important and intriguing issue or research problem/question to address or might have located interesting possible case study participants. Nevertheless, being able to situate your research in the wider existing literature is important because this knowledge provides justification that your research is original, timely, and likely to contribute new knowledge to the field.

Finding a general research "problem" or domain

The second important step, informed by your library research and your own experiences as a language teacher, learner, tester, and/or academic, is to decide what it is you would like to learn more about through your research and how case study methods might facilitate that. Whether you are interested in linguistic development, such as the development of tense/aspect systems in an L2, or in sociocultural issues, such as how learners exert their agency in SLA, you need to identify the issues and theoretical constructs being investigated. However, other studies may already have been undertaken, and normally researchers need to find an original new angle to pursue. For example, although there have been studies done of the acquisition of the aspectual marker *le* (for completed events) in Chinese as a second language (CSL)–a notoriously difficult form to master–there may not have been any longitudinal case studies done on it. Alternatively, as someone with expertise in Arabic, you might be particularly interested in the experiences of heritage-language learners of Arabic (L2) in the United States, not from a linguistic perspective but in terms of identity; the communities they belong to or wish to belong to; the kinds of social, cultural, and political issues that arise; or perhaps their preferences for particular varieties of Arabic, and reasons for those choices. Or you might examine the effects of L2 learning on L3 language and literacy development; for instance, for English L1 learners who have previously learned Japanese and are now learning Mandarin; or English L1 learners who have previously learned German and are now learning Mandarin.

Focusing the research question and constructs

Once an area of research, a topic, and a population have been identified, very clear research questions must be articulated. You should also define the theoretical terms (constructs and learner types) you plan to use, such as *heritage language, Generation 1.5, Chinese as a second language learner, or English language learner*; or linguistic terms such as *aspect* or *very proficient*.

Designing the research

Will the case study serve as a pilot study for a larger study later? Will it be part of a mixed-method study – and, if so, will the quantitative portion precede, follow, or be concurrent with the case study? Will you study individuals at one primary point in time, over a relatively short time period, or is the design longitudinal, allowing you to track changes in proficiency, linguistic structures, attitudes, or experiences over six months to a year (or longer)? What kinds of methods for collecting and analyzing data suit the purposes, scope, and timeline of the study (a term paper vs. a dissertation), and also your expertise and training as a researcher? Do you plan to triangulate, or bring together, data of different types or from different sources, such as interviews, written data, test scores, and observational data, or do you plan to focus on just one type of data? If the latter, you must anticipate the trade-offs in doing so.

Selecting the case (participants)

This next step is really a matter of design. In case study it is especially important to consider the kinds and number of participants you wish to study closely, and the criteria for their recruitment and selection, since they are the very core of case study research. Your criteria and rationale for selecting participants will affect the kinds of descriptions and inferences you can make based on your data. My own recommendation for a small-scale pilot study would be to choose one participant meeting your general target criteria (e.g., by proficiency level, years of L2 or L3 study, gender, or other categories that are relevant to your study); but for a larger study, such as a thesis, dissertation, or key research article, to recruit several participants. Three or four can be very rich, especially for a thesis or dissertation. With more than one participant, you have the assurance that if one drops out of the study, for whatever reason, or is less suitable than expected, at least one other will remain. On the other hand, a single case might be sufficiently representative (or, rather, unique), fascinating, complicated, triangulated, longitudinal, and so on, for your purposes. Perhaps others fitting the criteria and constructs cannot be found and only this one case is needed to refute previous findings or to reveal new possibilities and insights in SLA (see Yin, 2003a). In some kinds of SLA research, it may also be possible to use existing data from case studies conducted by others (e.g., the CHILDES corpus) for new analyses, if permissions have been obtained to do so and if enough contextual information germane to your study and interpretation is included in the dataset.

   In sum, having several participants gives you more options for sampling, for reporting on your findings, and for noting similarities and differences across cases. It may also yield a richer set of experiences or observations to draw upon than just one or two cases would. Your sampling may target participants who are similar in demographic or linguistic terms; alternatively, you can sample for contrasting cases or for variation, according to gender, proficiency level, attitudes toward the L2, or previous language learning experience, among other possible variables. But you must consider carefully the theoretical significance of sampling for diversity. If you choose two females and two males instead of four females (with either similar or different profiles), is there some reason to think that gender will have some bearing on the students' SLA experiences? Or, why choose three learners at different proficiency levels rather than three who are at about the same level (regardless of gender)? If you choose all three at the same general level and from the same L1, you might see some variation in development or performance, regardless. Such choices must be thought through in advance to the extent possible. A third option would be to sample for typicality or representativeness: that is, because these subjects are most typical of the wider population from which they are drawn and might assist with questions of (external) validity or generalizability or even relevance (Duff, 2006). A fourth option (among many others) would be to sample for extreme cases: one or two cases who are extremely successful, motivated, proficient, invested in their L2, or whatever you are interested in; and one or two at the opposite extreme.

Recruiting research participants (cases)

Once you have decided on your ideal participants, from both practical and theoretical standpoints, consider how you will recruit them. Do you already know people in the target demographic whom you could approach? If so, you might be able to locate other possible participants by snowball sampling (word of mouth or referral) once you get your first participant. What is your relationship to the participant or the target population (or even the phenomenon being analyzed) and how might this influence your recruitment, analysis, and findings or interpretations? Your reflexivity about such matters is also important to disclose in case study and other qualitative research, without breaching confidentiality agreements. Among other things, it helps establish your connections to the target languages and communities, your status as an insider or outsider, as someone who understands the experiences or language backgrounds of the participants based on your own prior SLA, for example, and your possible investment in this topic and population/sample.

Undertaking an ethical review of the study

Before recruitment of human subjects can take place, most universities require that you go through the procedures for a review of your research protocol – which normally includes specifying your research questions and methods, your recruitment procedures, whether participants can provide consent on their own behalf and in what language(s), what the possible risks and benefits are to participating, how you will maintain the anonymity of your participants, what kinds of time or other resources will be required of them, and how you might compensate or reward them. Because ethical reviews usually require appended sample interview and observation protocols and questions, these should be worked out and perhaps piloted with volunteer non-participants before you start. Beyond institutional requirements, case studies do raise various ethical questions because of the intensity of participants' involvement and the possibility that they will be identified in later reports (see study question 4 below).

Conducting the study: methods and procedures

This component is the crux of data collection and analysis for any type of study. What methods will be effective, valid, and suitable for addressing your research questions? What kinds of evidence (data) do you need? How do you plan to observe participants, and for how long? How will the data be recorded, transcribed, and analyzed? If you plan to interview participants, it is important to practice questions or prompts that will enable you to elicit the structures or perspectives you seek access to. Consider also how your role as interviewer will affect the data and findings. In what language will interviews or instructions be given – participants' L1 or L2? And what language will they use to respond, and why, and with what possible consequences? If the study is going to be longitudinal, how will you manage to communicate with your participants in an ongoing manner about future data collection sessions and how will you track changes over time?

Analyzing data

Once methods for collecting data have been determined, consider how best to manage, organize, and analyze the data. Digital equipment confers many advantages for the retrieval, organization, and sharing of data, and for transcribing, sorting, coding, and presenting the data and analyses as well. Ambitious case studies – those with multiple participants, multiple sources and modalities of data (oral, written, visual from video, etc.), and multiple data collection occasions as in longitudinal work – may require learning how to use sophisticated qualitative data analysis software to assist with data management. Such software also permits you to link various forms of data to the same individual or event and to see relationships among observations (e.g., occurrences of particular linguistic structures, themes, patterns). Learning to use the software effectively (e.g., NVivo, ATLAS-ti) takes some time initially but will be well worth the investment of time and money for a bigger study (see Baralt, this volume, chapter 12). However, for a less ambitious case study, say a pilot study with just one or two participants being interviewed at one point in time, more traditional data transcription and manual or electronic coding via simple word processors may be more efficient. For coding data and quantifying occurrences of particular structures in bigger datasets, computers can be more efficient and accurate than humans, though.

Often case study researchers do not seek the assistance of other coders or analysts to demonstrate the consistency, accuracy, or validity of their transcription, coding, counting, or interpretations. However, it is certainly valuable to consider having someone else examine at least a subset of your data to check for consistency (inter-coder reliability) and for the transparency, logic, or clarity of themes in relation to the larger study.

In multiple-case studies, often an analysis is presented of individual cases first, and then a cross-case analysis is done of issues or themes that arose across the set, with a discussion of how they relate to the literature reviewed earlier. In theses or dissertations, one chapter may be devoted to each focal case, followed by a chapter containing a cross-case analysis with a discussion of the similarities or differences across the cases (see Miles & Huberman, 1994; Stake, 2006). In addition, some case studies have focal participants (e.g., 4–6) and then describe them in detail, and provide a cross-case analysis of those participants plus the larger set from which they may have originally been drawn in a two-stage or even three-stage data collection and analysis process (e.g., Kouritzen, 1999). There is no set limit on how many cases can be part of a multi-case study. However, if there are too many cases (e.g., 12–20), less intensive scrutiny and presentation of each one are possible and some of the main advantages of case study research (internal and ecological validity, vividness of the case) are thereby lost. For that reason, eight or fewer focal cases per study are generally preferable. In Kinginger's study of 24 American study-abroad students in France (see study box 6.2), she settled on six focal participants for her in-depth case study analysis.

Many case studies involve an analysis of either linguistic structures or themes related to participants' perspectives on their SLA; some involve both, of course. For linguistic studies, the unit of analysis will normally be a particular linguistic form (e.g., a formulaic expression, or sentence particle), a function associated with that form (e.g., a speech act or meaning), a recast of an incorrect form, a question type, and so on. Ellis and Barkhuizen (2005) provide options and examples of how to analyze SLA data of various types. Although linguistic analysis sounds quite straightforward, inference may be involved, especially with L2 data where it may not always be clear what the speaker's (or writer's) intended meaning was and therefore what the appropriate category of form or function should be for coding purposes. In such cases, triangulating data, seeking input from the participant about his or her intended meaning, and examining data of different types or from different tasks may all help to reveal the learner's current level of development or performance.

A thematic analysis might focus on issues or expressions of identity, agency, motivation, community membership, frustration, or (other) affective stances toward the learning or use of the L2. It is very important to be able to account for how and why you chose the themes identified and for choosing the examples included in the written report. Are these highly representative, or just the most interesting or amusing? If the former, how do you know? If the latter, what were some counter-examples that might be less interesting but equally valid or salient or perhaps even more representative of the larger data set? Also, if doing a thematic or content analysis, consider in advance the theoretical status of those themes. What have other researchers said about them? How have they been theorized or operationalized (defined)? Try not to broach too many themes in any one study, or at least in any one report of it, especially if they are quite unrelated, because it may reduce the depth, logic, and coherence of your discussion.

Writing and defending the case study report

I discuss the various options, in terms of organization, stylistics, and substance, for preparing a case study-based thesis, dissertation, or journal article in Duff (2008). In brief, the more complex the research design, the more decisions one has to make (and more options) about how to organize the findings. If it is a single-case study involving only one primary source of data, the written report should be quite straightforward. But if multiple participants, methods, and timescales are involved, and multiple themes or linguistic areas are analyzed, more decisions must be made about how to do so in a way that is informative and not too disjointed. You must decide whether to describe the data and findings case by case or, rather, theme by theme (and exemplified with data from different cases as is relevant for a given theme).

Both are valid. You might need to do a mock-up of two different organizational structures before settling on one of them. When publishing articles from a dissertation or thesis with multiple-case studies (e.g., 4–6), it is not uncommon to choose a subset of the cases (e.g., 2) or themes in a given article because of space constraints (see e.g., Norton Peirce, 1995; Morita, 2004).

Case study research is often very engaging because the researcher is closely involved with just one or a few participants with whom a direct and personal research relationship may be maintained for a considerable period of time, or at least an intensive period of time in a shorter study (Harklau, 2008). Readers, too, often find case studies very interesting, engaging, and informative for the same reason that well-written biographies or fictional accounts of individuals or families are popular with many. However, case studies can also be problematic and challenging when, for instance, the cases are very atypical or unsatisfactory in terms of the kinds of development or reflections that were sought or anticipated. Researchers must be able to justify to professors, colleagues, examiners, reviewers, and other readers the meaningfulness or validity of the study and the findings based on the small number of participants. Readers also typically want to understand the case's "story" – circumstances, contexts, behaviors, and so on – but also want to understand that the study has been undertaken rigorously and with integrity, and that the findings or interpretations have merit. Readers want to know that in reading the account, they can learn something about the participant(s) in question but also about the broader (or technical) SLA issues being addressed. To achieve that, you must be able to create a coherent account of the participant within the local and theoretical context and demonstrate that a key aspect of the study is original and helpful to others as well as being interesting and well written (see Edge & Richards, 1998; Duff, 2008, regarding criteria for assessing case studies).

Project Ideas and Resources

As study boxes 6.1 and 6.2 show, case study can involve a variety of data collection and analysis tools, from standardized oral or written language proficiency tests or tests of social-psychological orientation toward the target language and community to much more narrative approaches, based on semi-structured or open-ended interview and journal formats that allow learners to describe their own experiences with SLA. How these data are analyzed depends a great deal on the purposes of the research, the preferences of the researcher, the theoretical and methodological orientation of the work, and the audience.

Oral Interviews

Because oral interviews of various types (from highly structured or test-like to highly unstructured) are used in many case studies, it is important to understand your options and also the consequences of various interview format choices for your analysis and interpretations. Practice interviewing techniques and questions with friends or colleagues to determine their effectiveness and whether any equipment being used is satisfactory, consistent, and effective. As Talmy and Richards (2011) argue, interviews are co-constructed speech events based on social relationships and interaction; they do not necessarily generate complete or accurate versions of interviewees' perspectives or proficiency. They yield a partial representation of reality (or truth), a (re)construction of past events in the case of retrospective interviews. The interviews create a special discourse context in which the interviewee is being tested, is performing in a particular role, or is being prompted or constrained by the interviewer (whom the interviewee might want to please or, perhaps, whose judgment might be feared) in untold ways (see also Gubrium & Holstein, 2002, 2003 ; Seidman, 2006; Fontana & Prokos, 2007; Kvale & Brinkman, 2009; Roulston, 2010; Talmy, 2010). Interview data should be interpreted accordingly.

Narrative Research

One of the most common data collection strategies in case study research is oral interviews that contain narratives of language learning or written narratives (e.g., in diaries, journals, or other projects). Narrative research is a very broad and interdisciplinary field, however. There are many structural and interpretive approaches to studying narratives or stories and for representing findings. Pavlenko (2007, 2008) reviews narrative research in SLA and bilingualism including case studies, memoirs, and autobiographies, and Benson and Nunan (2004) present case studies of SLA embracing narrative methods. Other resources on narrative inquiry in other fields include Chase (2008) and Gubrium and Holstein (2008).

Generalizability

Questions about generalizability, a type of validity, are almost inevitable with case study research. Some research attempts to generalize from findings to the wider population from which the sample was drawn. This is known as statistical generalization (see Yin, 2003a). In a study of Korean international students in a particular type of English language learning situation abroad, the intended generalization might be to Korean international students and perhaps other international students with similar characteristics in similar learning contexts. However, another goal might be (instead) to induce general principles based on the findings of Korean international students' experiences and apply them to models of acculturation or socialization. This is sometimes called analytic or theoretical generalization. Both approaches must be taken with considerable caution, but a constrained version of the latter is a more typical goal in SLA case study research. Generalizability is closely related to case selection and sampling and the larger population of cases from which the sample is ostensibly drawn. See Duff (2006, 2008), Chalhoub-Deville, Chapelle, and Duff (2006), Lincoln and Guba (2000), and Donmoyer (1990) for a fuller discussion of this issue.

Examine the study summarized in study box 6.3, for example, and issues of generalizability and sampling/selection that it raises.

Study Box 6.3

DaSilva Iddings, A. C., & Jang, E-Y. (2008). The mediational role of classroom practices during the silent period: A new-immigrant student learning the English language in a mainstream classroom. *TESOL Quarterly,* 42(4), 567–590.

Background

The study examines the "silent period" among children, especially, in immigrant contexts, learning their L2, English. The study is framed in terms of contemporary "ecological" and sociocultural approaches to activity (and to silence) as well as intentionality and emergentism in SLA. The larger one-year study had four Spanish-speaking English language learners newly arrived from Mexico in a mainstream kindergarten class in the USA. This article focuses on just one of the students who remained relatively silent throughout the year.

Research question

The study examines "how a kindergarten student [Juan] undergoing the silent period began to create and express meaning in the new linguistic and cultural environment of school, while also attending to the tasks of becoming a legitimate member of the classroom, learning a new language, and gaining knowledge of the content of instruction" (p. 571).

Method

Researchers were participant observers for an academic year at the school, observing students' in-class and out-of-class (e.g., cafeteria) behaviors regularly. Interviews were conducted with teachers and students. Three types of classroom activities were examined.

Statistical tools

Not applicable.

Qualitative data analysis

Each of the three activity types is discussed, drawing on observational data, in conjunction with Juan's (mostly non-verbal) participation in the activity and how his participation changed over time.

Results

The authors conclude that for Juan "language learning was not merely a result of repetition or mimicking, but instead, it was an intentional, transformative, and complex process of meaning-making involving an understanding and creation of shared semiotic systems through joint participation in sign-mediated activities" (p. 586); and that "for students undergoing the silent period, the joint-attentional frames that are formed through students' participation in classroom tasks can serve as an important tool to mediate between language and the learners, and without this type of engagement in such tasks, meaning-making [or language learning] may be difficult to achieve" (p. 567).

Generalizability

This is not mentioned. The authors claim that students in the silent period are in fact actively constructing meanings and are participating psychologically in lessons in various ways, many of them non-verbal but foundational to their later oral and literate development in English. This is a kind of analytic generalization. There is no explanation about how typical Juan's case was of the four participants in the larger study, and no explanation about why only he was included in this article.

Other Resources on Case Study and Qualitative Research

Handbooks of qualitative research (or inquiry) in education and the social sciences, including chapters on case study research methods, abound (e.g., Hatch, 2002; Denzin & Lincoln, 2003, 2005; Gall, Gall, & Borg, 2003, 2005; Silverman, 2004; Berg, 2007). Heigham and Croker (2009) is a practical survey of qualitative methods in applied linguistics (including case study), and Dyson and Genishi (2005) is an introduction to case study research in (L1) language and literacy education. Richards's (2003) *Qualitative Inquiry in TESOL* provides a useful overview as well.

Study Questions

1. What aspects or examples of SLA case studies that you are already familiar with, including the findings, have appealed to you most, and why? If you are new to SLA research, think of an individual you know with a particularly intriguing SLA profile (it could be you) or someone who has perhaps experienced many challenges as a language learner. If you were to do a study of that person's SLA, what would you focus on and why?

2. What are the advantages and disadvantages of serving as your own research subject, that is, by doing an autobiographical study (through diaries, memoirs, or other procedures) of your own experiences of SLA versus studying someone else's? If you were starting to learn a language typologically unrelated to English, such as Mandarin, in a study-abroad context for a half year or full year, but you also got to

know others in the same situation, consider the trade-offs and also your preferred focus in studying yourself versus studying one or more others in your program.

3. Alternatively, discuss the advantages and disadvantages in SLA case study research of having participants themselves become more involved in the analysis, interpretation, and representation of their L2 data together with you, the researcher. If participants cannot help you with aspects of analysis and interpretation, how can you ensure that your interpretations are valid, reasonable, or even plausible – that you are not misrepresenting subjects' abilities, experiences, perceptions, perspectives, or performance?

4. Caldas (2007; see study box 6.1 above) conducted a longitudinal study of his children's English–French bilingualism through their childhood and into adolescence, as they lived in the USA (Louisiana) and summered in French-speaking Canada with Caldas (English L1) and his Francophone wife. Both parents "desperately wanted the children to speak French" (p. 307). First, what are the pros and cons of conducting a study as long in duration as this one? Second, what issues arise in conducting a study with your own relatives rather than with others' families (e.g., involving enforced home language practices, interviews, tests with them on a regular basis, "six years of tape recordings made weekly during family meals in both Québec and Louisiana" (p. 294), and the children's educators regularly filling survey instruments out about the children's French ability)? Caldas concedes, "our eagerness to rear our children to be bilingual–biliterates almost certainly tainted all aspects of this project" (p. 298). How might participating in such a research project change the family dynamics (including language use patterns) and children's attitudes toward bilingualism, especially given the tensions between the parental expectations regarding French use and the children's peers' expectations regarding English use?

5. Refer to Kinginger's (2008) study above (study box 6.2). Consider the advantages of combining quantitative measures of language proficiency (pre- and post-sojourn) with a multiple-case narrative-based study of American study-abroad students' experiences of learning French during a sojourn in France. Are there any disadvantages of using mixed methods? What would be lost if only the quantitative (proficiency-related) data were included, without the in-depth analysis of six students' experiences in France in a narrative fashion, and vice versa? If you were to do a case study of study-abroad L2 students, what would you focus on?

References

Benson, P. & Nunan, D. (Eds.). (2004). *Learners' stories: Difference and diversity in language learning*. Cambridge, England: Cambridge University Press.

Berg, B. L. (2007). *Qualitative research methods for the social sciences* (6th ed.). Boston, MA: Pearson.

Block, D. (2003). *The social turn in second language acquisition*. Edinburgh, Scotland: Edinburgh University Press.

Brown, R. (1973). *A first language*. Cambridge, MA: Harvard University Press.

Caldas, S. J. (2007). Changing bilingual self-perceptions from early adolescence to early adulthood: Empirical evidence from a mixed-methods case study. *Applied Linguistics, 29,* 290–311.

Chalhoub-Deville, M., Chapelle, C., & Duff, P. (Eds.). (2006). *Inference and generalizability in applied linguistics: Multiple research perspectives.* Amsterdam, Netherlands: John Benjamins.

Chase, S. (2008). Narrative inquiry: Multiple lenses, approaches, voices. In N. K. Denzin & Y. S. Lincoln (Eds.), *Collecting and interpreting qualitative materials* (3rd ed., pp. 57–94). Thousand Oaks, CA: Sage.

DaSilva Iddings, A. C., & Jang, E-Y. (2008). The mediational role of classroom practices during the silent period: A new-immigrant student learning the English language in a mainstream classroom. *TESOL Quarterly, 42*(4), 567–590.

Denzin, N. K., & Lincoln, Y. S. (Eds.). (2003). *Collecting and interpreting qualitative materials.* Thousand Oaks, CA: Sage.

Denzin, N. K., & Lincoln, Y. S. (Eds.). (2005). *The handbook of qualitative research* (3rd ed.). Thousand Oaks, CA: Sage.

Donmoyer, R. (1990). Generalizability and the single-case study. In E. Eisner & A. Peshkin (Eds.), *Qualitative inquiry in education: The continuing debate* (pp. 175–200). New York, NY: Teachers College Press.

Duff, P. (2006). Beyond generalizability: Context, credibility and complexity in applied linguistics research. In M. Chalhoub-Deville, C. Chapelle, & P. Duff (Eds.), *Inference and generalizability in applied linguistics: Multiple research perspectives* (pp. 65–95). Amsterdam, Netherlands: John Benjamins.

Duff, P. (2008). *Case study research in applied linguistics.* New York, NY: Lawrence Erlbaum.

Duff, P. (2010). Research methods in applied linguistics. In R. Kaplan (Ed.), *Handbook of applied linguistics* (2nd ed., pp. 45–59). Oxford, England: Oxford University Press.

Dyson, A. H., & Genishi, C. (2005). *On the case: Approaches to language and literacy research.* New York, NY: Teachers College Press.

Edge, J., & Richards, K. (1998). May I see your warrant, please? Justifying outcomes in qualitative research. *Applied Linguistics, 19,* 334–356.

Ellis, R. (2008). *The study of second language acquisition* (2nd ed.). Oxford, England: Oxford University Press.

Ellis, R., & Barkhuizen, G. (2005). *Analysing learner language.* Oxford, England: Oxford University Press.

Fontana, A., & Prokos, A. H. (2007). *The interview: From formal to postmodern.* Walnut Creek, CA: Left Coast Press.

Gall, J., Gall, M. D., & Borg, W. T. (2005). *Applying educational research* (5th ed.). Boston, MA: Pearson.

Gall, M. D., Gall, J. P., & Borg, W. T. (2003). *Educational research* (7th ed.). White Plains, NY: Pearson.

Gass, S., & Selinker, L. (2008). *Second language acquisition* (3rd ed.). Mahwah, NJ: Lawrence Erlbaum.

Geertz, C. (1973). Thick description: Toward an interpretive theory of culture. In C. Geertz (Ed.), *The interpretation of cultures* (pp. 3–30). New York, NY: Basic Books.

Guardado, M. (2009). Learning Spanish like a boy scout: Language socialization, resistance, and reproduction in a heritage language scout troop. *Canadian Modern Language Review, 66,* 101–29.

Gubrium, J. F., & Holstein, J. A. (Eds.). (2002). *Handbook of interviewing: Context and method.* Thousand Oaks, CA: Sage.

Gubrium, J. F., & Holstein, J. A. (Eds.). (2003). *Postmodern interviewing.* Thousand Oaks, CA: Sage.

Gubrium, J. F., & Holstein, J. A. (2008). *Analyzing narrative reality.* Thousand Oaks, CA: Sage.

Harklau, L. (2008). Developing qualitative longitudinal case studies of advanced language learners. In L. Ortega & H. Byrnes (Eds.), *The longitudinal study of advanced language capacities* (pp. 23–35). New York, NY: Routledge.

Hatch, E. (Ed.). (1978). *Second language acquisition.* Rowley, MA: Newbury House.

Hatch, J. A. (2002). *Doing qualitative research in education settings.* Albany: State University of New York Press.

He, A. W. (2008). An identity-based model for the development of Chinese as a heritage language. In A. He & Y. Xiao (Eds.), *Chinese as a heritage language* (pp. 109–124). Honolulu: National Foreign Language Resource Center, University of Hawai'i.

Heigham, J., & Croker, R. A. (Eds.). (2009), *Qualitative research in applied linguistics: A practical introduction.* Basingstoke, England: Palgrave Macmillan.

Kim, J. (2008). *Negotiating multiple investments in languages and identities: The language socialization of Generation 1.5 Korean-Canadian university students.* Unpublished PhD dissertation, University of British Columbia, Canada.

Kinginger, C. (2008). Language learning in study abroad: Case studies of Americans in France. *Modern Language Journal, 92*(1), 1–124.

Klein, W., & Perdue, C. (1992). *Utterance structure: Developing grammars again.* Philadelphia, PA: John Benjamins.

Kouritzen, S. (1999). *Face[t]s of first language loss.* Mahwah, NJ: Lawrence Erlbaum.

Kvale, S., & Brinkman, S. (2009). *InterViews: Learning the craft of qualitative research interviewing* (2nd ed.). Thousand Oaks, CA: Sage.

Lam, W. S. E. (2004). Second language socialization in a bilingual chat room: Global and local considerations. *Language Learning and Technology, 8*(3), 44–65.

Lincoln, Y,. & Guba, E. (2000). The only generalization is: There is no generalization. In R. Gomm, M. Hammersley, & P. Foster (Eds.), *Case study method* (pp. 27–44). London, England: Sage.

Maxwell, J. A. (2005). *Qualitative research design: An interactive approach* (2nd ed.). Thousand Oaks, CA: Sage.

Mellow, J. D., Reeder, K., & Forster, E. (1996). Using time-series research designs to investigate the effects of instruction on SLA. *Studies in Second Language Acquisition, 18,* 325–350.

Merriam, S. (1998). *Qualitative research and case study applications in education.* (2nd ed.). San Francisco, CA: Jossey-Bass.

Merriam, S., & Associates. (Eds.). (2002). *Qualitative research in practice.* San Francisco, CA: Jossey-Bass.

Miles, M., & Huberman, A. M. (1994). *Qualitative data analysis* (2nd ed.). Thousand Oaks, CA: Sage.

Morita, N. (2004). Negotiating participation and identity in second language academic communities. *TESOL Quarterly, 38,* 573–603.

Norton, B. (2000). *Identity and language learning: Gender, ethnicity and educational change.* London, England: Longman/Pearson.

Norton Peirce, B. (1995). Social identity, investment, and language learning. *TESOL Quarterly, 29,* 9–31.

Ortega, L. (2009). *Understanding second language acquisition.* London, England: Hodder.

Pavlenko, A. (2007). Autobiographic narratives as data in applied linguistics. *Applied Linguistics, 28,* 163–188.

Pavlenko, A. (2008). Narrative analysis in the study of bi- and multilingualism. In M. Moyer & W. Li (Eds.), *The Blackwell guide to research methods in bilingualism* (pp. 311–325). Oxford, England: Wiley-Blackwell.

Pavlenko, A., & Lantolf, J. P. (2000). Second language learning as participation and the (re) construction of selves. In J. P. Lantolf (Ed.), *Sociocultural theory and second language learning* (pp. 155–177). New York, NY: Oxford University Press.

Richards, K. (2003). *Qualitative inquiry in TESOL*. New York, NY: Palgrave Macmillan.

Roulston, K. (2010). *The reflective researcher: Learning to interview in the social sciences*. Thousand Oaks, CA: Sage.

Seidman, I. (2006). *Interviewing as qualitative research: A guide for researchers in education and the social sciences* (3rd ed.). New York, NY: Teachers College Press.

Silverman, D. (2004). *Qualitative research: Theory method and practice* (2nd ed.). Thousand Oaks, CA: Sage.

Stake, R. (1995). *The art of case study research*. Thousand Oaks, CA: Sage.

Stake, R. (2005). Qualitative case studies. In N. Denzin & Y. Lincoln (Eds.), *Handbook of qualitative research* (3rd ed., pp. 443–466). Thousand Oaks, CA: Sage.

Stake, R. (2006). *Multiple case study analysis*. New York, NY: Guilford Press.

Talmy, S. (2010). Qualitative interviews in applied linguistics. *Annual Review of Applied Linguistics, 30*, 128–148.

Talmy, S., & Richards, K. (Eds.). (2011). Qualitative interviews in applied linguistics: Discursive perspectives [Special issue]. *Applied Linguistics, 32*(1).

Yin, R. K. (2003a). *Case study research: Design and methods* (3rd ed.). Thousand Oaks, CA: Sage.

Yin, R. K. (2003b). *Applications of case study research* (2nd ed.). Thousand Oaks, CA: Sage.

7 How to Use Psycholinguistic Methodologies for Comprehension and Production

Kim McDonough and Pavel Trofimovich

Background

Psycholinguistics is the study of the psychological processes involved in language, and its main goals are to understand how people comprehend and produce language. For a skilled language user, understanding and producing language seem deceptively simple. For a psycholinguist, however, language comprehension and production involve a complex interaction of various processing components, which include accessing the lexicon, building a syntactic structure, and encoding and decoding the sound patterns of a language, as well as interpreting and expressing intended pragmatic messages. By studying these various components, psycholinguists attempt to figure out what processes, mechanisms, or procedures underlie language use and learning.

Psycholinguists typically study language comprehension and production as separate sets of processes. One reason for this is that comprehension and production both pose distinct challenges to language users. For example, language comprehension involves extracting meaning from a speech signal or printed text whereas language production involves converting a preverbal message into speech or text using appropriate lexicon, grammar, and phonology or orthography. Another reason is that compared to comprehension, production appears to be much harder to study experimentally. This is because researchers often find it difficult to control input and elicit relevant output when studying language production. Indeed, it is much easier to manipulate words and sentences to be read or heard than to control the ideas and means of expression used for speaking and writing. It is not surprising, then, that even after decades of psycholinguistic research, comprehension tends to be studied more extensively than production (see Bock, 1996, for additional reasons).

Research Methods in Second Language Acquisition: A Practical Guide, First Edition.
Edited by Alison Mackey and Susan M. Gass.
© 2012 Blackwell Publishing Ltd. Published 2012 by Blackwell Publishing Ltd.

Psycholinguists have developed a number of ingenious methods for studying how people comprehend and produce language. The goal of this chapter is to describe four of these methods, with a particular focus on their use in second language (L2) research. The methods we highlight have been used extensively in research with first language (L1) speakers. They allow for the study of language comprehension and production at different levels of analysis (words, sentences, longer discourse), and they are adaptable to L2 research contexts. In discussing each method, we first describe it, then contextualize it within its relevant theoretical framework, and finally raise some methodological considerations. Because space limitations do not allow for a complete inventory of psycholinguistic methods, we refer interested readers to other sources listed under 'Further Reading' near the end of the chapter.

Language Comprehension

Self-Paced Reading Task

Description of the task

In a self-paced reading task, participants are seated at computers with programs such as E-prime, PsyScope, or DMDX and read text from a computer screen. The text is segmented into words or short phrases, and participants press a keyboard key or a response button to display each consecutive segment until they reach the end. For example, the sentence *The bad boys | watched almost every day | were playing | in the park* could be presented to participants in four consecutive segments marked by vertical bars. This sentence, taken from Juff's (1998) study, illustrates that readers can encounter temporary ambiguity in interpreting some structures. The second segment above could be interpreted as both a reduced relative clause (with the relative pronoun and auxiliary verb omitted) or as a main clause with a past tense verb. The third segment is critical because it signals that *were playing* is the main verb and that *watched almost every day* is a reduced relative clause. The logic of self-paced reading is that the time needed to read each segment reflects the cognitive workload experienced in processing that segment. Thus, the measure of interest in self-paced reading is the amount of time between two successive button presses, especially for the ambiguous segments.

Several versions of the task have been developed. These versions are illustrated in figure 7.1. In the "stationary-window" version of the task (row A), each subsequent segment replaces the preceding segment, usually in the center of the screen. In the "moving-window" version (rows B and C), the text is masked by a pattern of dashes and spaces, and each consecutive segment appears on the screen sequentially, replacing the dashes. The "moving-window" version can be used with a cumulative or a non-cumulative presentation. The cumulative presentation (row B) reveals increasingly more segments with the previous segments remaining on screen. The non-cumulative presentation (row C) presents a subsequent segment but removes or covers up the previous segments. The cumulative moving-window presentation is less preferred because participants tend to reveal multiple segments in order to read them all at once.

Figure 7.1 A schematic illustration of the first three display screens for the sentence *The bad boys watched almost every day were playing in the park* in stationary-window (A), cumulative moving-window (B), and non-cumulative moving-window (C) versions of the task.

Theoretical frameworks

L1 comprehension   Self-paced reading is typically used in L1 research that investigates syntactic parsing (or simply parsing), which is the process by which people analyze the syntactic structure of a string of words to arrive at a correct interpretation. Skilled language users usually process syntactic information in print and speech rapidly, encountering little comprehension difficulty. Therefore, researchers use sentences that create difficulties for comprehension, such as "garden-path" sentences that are initially misinterpreted and must be reanalyzed. Structures typically manipulated in garden-path sentences include reduced relative clause–main verb ambiguity, relative clause attachment (Dussias, 2003), subject–object ambiguity (Hopp, 2006), and *wh*-extraction (Jackson & Bobb, 2009).

Because the comprehension process involves several levels of processing (e.g., grapheme/phoneme, word, sentence, text) and includes several subprocesses (van Gompel & Pickering, 2007), two key theoretical questions have been raised. Do people entertain only one interpretation of something they read or listen to, or do they consider several plausible interpretations simultaneously? How do people use the many sources of information available to them (e.g., syntax, semantics, discourse, prosody, etc.)? Self-paced reading has been used extensively to address these two questions, with a focus on the theoretical debate between interactive and modular theories of sentence comprehension. Interactive theories (constraint-based or one-stage theories) assume that people entertain several sources of information simultaneously (e.g., semantics, discourse constraints, frequency of use) in order to interpret a syntactic structure (e.g., Trueswell & Tanenhaus, 1994). In contrast, modular theories (two-stage theories) posit that people use only syntactic information to create an initial interpretation of a sentence and that other sources of information (e.g., semantics, context) are used later in the comprehension process (e.g., Frazier, 1990). This theoretical debate continues due to strong evidence in support of both views (see van Gompel & Pickering, 2007).

Bilingual/L2 comprehension   Current bilingual and L2 research investigates the parsing strategies employed by L2 users. The central issue is whether L2 users develop syntactic parsing strategies that are specific to the L2 or whether they use L1-based parsing strategies, or perhaps strategies that are found in neither language (see Dussias & Piñar, 2009, for a recent summary). Briefly, the syntactic parsing of

L2 users is influenced by many factors. Some of these factors are linguistic in nature (i.e., specific to the lexical, semantic, or syntactic information available in sentences). Other factors are related to L2 users' experiences with a language (i.e., proficiency or type of exposure) and to individual differences (e.g., working memory). It appears that many of these factors interact in determining precisely how L2 users' parsing strategies in the L2 are similar to or different from those used in the L1. A sample self-paced reading study that investigates syntactic parsing in L2 users is summarized in study box 7.1.

Study Box 7.1

Rah, A., & Adone, D. (2010). Processing of the reduced relative clause versus main verb ambiguity in L2 learners at different proficiency levels. *Studies in Second Language Acquisition*, 32, 79–109.

Purpose

Examine how L2 learners of different proficiency levels process the main verb versus reduced relative clause ambiguity (*The bad boys watched almost every day were playing in the park*).

Participants

22 intermediate- and 22 advanced-level German learners of English, all students at a German university; 22 native English speakers.

Task design

The 30 target sentences included (1) unambiguous sentences, (2) ambiguous sentences with a good cue that ruled out a transitive reading of the sentence, and (3) ambiguous sentences with a poor cue, which left the transitive interpretation plausible until the disambiguating region (italicized).

(1) The brown sparrow | seen | by the hungry cat | *pecked* | at an insect.
(2) The brown sparrow | noticed | on an upper branch | *pecked* | at an insect.
(3) The brown sparrow | noticed | almost every day | *pecked* | at an insect.

Procedure

A stationary (non-cumulative) centered self-paced presentation was used; 10 sentences were followed by a comprehension question.

Analysis

Data analyzed using $2 \times 3 \times 3$ (group × sentence type × region) ANOVA followed by univariate ANOVAs and pairwise comparisons.

Results

Reading patterns for the learners and the native speakers were similar. The learners of different proficiency levels differed in overall speed of reading, but not in pattern of processing.

Methodological considerations

There are several methodological considerations to keep in mind when designing self-paced reading experiments. Because self-paced reading is used to test claims about comprehension processes, the task must encourage participants to comprehend the sentences. To accomplish this, researchers typically ask participants to answer a comprehension question (Rah & Adone, 2010), judge grammaticality (Juffs, 1998), decide whether another sentence conveys the same meaning (Hopp, 2006), or make a plausibility judgment (Williams, Möbius, & Kim, 2001). Usually researchers only analyze the reading times for the sentences which are responded to correctly. Before analyzing the data, researchers also often try to confirm that all participant groups are matched for comprehension rates on these tasks. This helps ensure that potential differences in reading times can be attributed to the kinds of materials being manipulated rather than to participants' processing strategies (e.g., reading for comprehension vs. skimming the text).

Another consideration involves the need to create target and baseline materials which are maximally comparable so that participants' performance can be interpreted appropriately. For example, it is important to match the target and baseline materials for word length and for lexical content, especially before the disambiguating segment, or the region where researchers expect to find reading time differences. This ensures that potential differences in reading times are not due to different lexical content across sentences. It is also important to match the length of disambiguating segments across all materials in terms of total character length and frequency. This helps ensure that these segments are equally "salient," given the fact that shorter and more frequent words are often read quickly or even skipped over in reading (see Ferreira & Clifton, 1986, for a statistical procedure to adjust reading times for segment length). Finally, the disambiguating segments should not be placed at the ends of sentences. This helps minimize sentence wrap-up effects, or the tendency for reading times to be slower and more variable at sentence and clause boundaries.

Researchers wishing to use self-paced reading to study language comprehension need to be aware of certain limitations. One concern is that self-paced reading is prone to spillover effects. This refers to the tendency for processing effects to "carry over" from one segment to the next. For example, when researchers present readers with the sentence *The bad boys | watched almost every day | were playing | in the park*, they expect to find longer reading times for the third segment (compared to the same segment in a baseline condition) because this segment will signal to readers that they have been led on a "garden path" and will need to reinterpret the sentence.

However, due to spillover effects, longer reading times associated with this segment could manifest themselves much later, for example, when readers process one of the following segments. To minimize spillover effects, researchers should avoid using word-by-word presentations (e.g., *The | bad | boys |* etc.) and should carefully match materials for number of words, especially for segments preceding the disambiguating segment (Mitchell, 1984). Another concern about self-paced reading is that processing might be affected by a particular text segmentation strategy. In other words, it is possible that researchers could find different results depending on how they segment their materials (*The bad boys | watched almost every day | were playing | in the park* vs. *The bad boys | watched | almost every day | were | playing | in the park*). Although "there is no solid evidence that researchers have ever been misled by segmentation biases in the self-paced reading task" (Mitchell, 2004, p. 26), researchers may wish to replicate their findings using a number of different segmentation strategies.

Self-Paced Listening Task

Description of the task

Self-paced listening (or the auditory moving-window technique) is the auditory equivalent of self-paced reading. Compared with self-paced reading, this task is relatively new. It was first described by Ferreira, Henderson, Anes, Weeks, and McFarlane (1996) in a study of lexical and syntactic processing with L1 speakers. In a self-paced listening task, listeners hear sentence segments presented one at a time, pressing a button to play the next segment. For example, ambiguous sentences like *When | Roger | leaves | the house | is | dark* and *When | Roger | leaves | the house | it's | dark* could be played to participants in several separate segments, demarcated here by vertical bars (Titone et al., 2006). The end of a sentence is usually marked by a tone, which is often followed by a comprehension question (or a related task) which ensures that participants process each sentence. The logic behind this task is identical to that of self-paced reading: the time participants take to listen to each segment reflects the processing load (and therefore, the processing difficulty) they experience in comprehending that segment. At least two temporal variables can be measured in this task: (a) inter-response time, or the time between each consecutive press of the button (Ferreira et al., 1996) and (b) pause duration, or the time between the offset of one segment and participants' press of the button to initiate the next one (Titone et al., 2006).

Theoretical frameworks

L1 comprehension   In L1 research, self-paced listening has been used to address the same topics examined with self-paced reading tasks, such as how listeners interpret the structure of spoken utterances and what information they use to do so. For example, Ferreira et al. (1996) showed that listeners, just like readers, take longer to process syntactically ambiguous than unambiguous sentences. In addition, these researchers also showed that sentence prosody (metrical and intonational structure of utterances) influences syntactic processing, such that pitch contours and pausing that are congruent with the syntactic structure make ambiguous sentences easier to process. This finding suggests that listeners use prosody (along with other lexical and contextual information) to comprehend spoken sentences.

Self-paced listening has been used in L1 research to compare child and adult processing of syntactically complex and simple utterances (Booth, MacWhinney, & Harasaki, 2000), compare younger and older adults' processing of spoken passages (Titone, Prentice, & Wingfield, 2000), test the relationship between speech processing and working memory (Waters & Caplan, 2004), and investigate the processing of spoken sentences by individuals with brain damage (Caplan & Waters, 2003) and children with language impairments (Marshall, Marinis, & van der Lely, 2007). In contrast, relatively little bilingual and L2 research to date has used self-paced listening, which we believe is a reflection of L2 researchers' relatively low familiarity with this task. We are aware of only one published study (de Jong, 2005) and a few conference presentations (e.g., Heredia, Stewart, & Cregut, 1997) that have used self-paced listening. Clearly, the advantages and limitations of this method need to be explored in future L2 research. In study box 7.2, a sample L1 self-paced listening study is summarized.

Study Box 7.2

Titone, D. A., Koh, C. K., Kjelgaard, M. M., Bruce, S., Speer, S. A., & Wingfield, A. (2006). Age-related impairments in the revision of syntactic effects of prosody. *Language and Speech*, 49, 75–99 (Experiment 1).

Purpose

Investigate the role of prosody in younger and older adults' processing of syntactically ambiguous sentences.

Participants

24 younger (aged 18–28) and 24 older (aged 65–83) adults, all native speakers of English.

Task design

18 syntactically ambiguous sentence pairs patterning according to "early" and "late closure" (see example below), recorded in three prosodic conditions: when sentence contained no prosodic information (baseline prosody), when prosodic and syntactic boundaries coincided (cooperating prosody), and when prosodic and syntactic boundaries conflicted (conflicting prosody). | = segmentation locations, * = prosodic boundary, *italics* = ambiguous region.

Baseline prosody
Late closure   When | Roger | *leaves* | *the house* | it's | dark
Early closure   When | Roger | *leaves* | *the house* | is | dark

Cooperating prosody
Late closure   When | Roger | *leaves* | *the house** | it's | dark
Early closure   When | Roger | *leaves** | *the house* | is | dark

Conflicting prosody
Late closure   When | Roger | *leaves** | *the house* | it's | dark
Early closure   When | Roger | *leaves* | *the house** | is | dark

Procedure

Participants listened to a sentence in a self-paced listening task, then repeated or paraphrased that sentence (to ensure that they processed it for comprehension and resolved syntactic ambiguity). Pause duration was recorded in the disambiguating segment *it's/is*.

Analysis

Data analyzed using a 2 × 2 × 3 (age × syntax × prosody) ANOVA, followed by planned pairwise comparisons.

Results

Younger and older adults were similar in their interpretation of sentences and in their use of prosody for sentence comprehension. However, younger adults appeared faster than older adults at using congruent prosodic patterns for sentence comprehension.

Methodological considerations

Because self-paced listening is modeled after self-paced reading, the methodological issues described in the previous section are important. However, additional issues stemming from the auditory nature of the task should also be addressed. One issue relates to preparation of task materials. Unlike printed text, speech does not have clear-cut boundaries between adjacent words, with sounds produced in an overlapping fashion. This makes it hard for researchers to divide a continuous speech stream into segments. To address this problem, some researchers record each individual word (or segment) separately and present their materials as sequences of individually recorded segments (Booth et al., 2000). Other researchers segment a continuous stream of speech, trying to ensure that the transitions between adjacent segments are smooth and that words at segment boundaries are intelligible (Ferreira et al., 1996).

Yet other researchers, especially those interested in processing of longer texts, segment their recordings where naturally occurring pauses are present, for example, at clause or sentence boundaries (Titone et al., 2000).

A related issue concerns the role of prosody in comprehension of speech. In spoken language, variations in pitch, pausing, and duration all signal important information about the structural configuration of an utterance. Put differently, prosodic and syntactic patterns of spoken utterances are normally closely aligned, and listeners rely on both syntax and prosody in comprehension of speech. This relationship between prosody and syntax could introduce an unwanted confound in a self-paced listening study if prosodic factors are not the focus of investigation. There are several ways of minimizing the unwanted effects of prosody. One solution is to record each word (or segment) of an utterance in isolation and out of sequence, for example, by reading them from a list. Sentences recorded in this fashion lack coarticulatory and prosodic cues (Booth et al., 2000). Another solution is to use a digital splicing technique whereby researchers take a single prosodic pattern (e.g., from a neutral, baseline utterance) and splice it into their target materials using speech editing software (Felser, Marinis, & Clahsen, 2003). This allows researchers to create materials that are comparable in their prosodic content across conditions (see Ferreira, Anes, & Horine, 1996, on prosody in self-paced listening).

Another consideration to take into account is the choice of the dependent measure. As noted earlier, researchers typically collect two principal measurements in self-paced listening. Using inter-reponse times as the primary measure in self-paced listening could be problematic if the segments of interest are not matched for duration across conditions. Because longer segments are processed more slowly than shorter segments, longer inter-response time may simply reflect processing time rather than comprehension difficulty. Pause duration (which is equivalent to the "difference time" measure proposed by Ferreira et al., 1996) at least in part avoids this problem because this measure excludes the duration of the segment.

Language Production

Picture–Word Interference Task

Description of the task

The picture–word interference task is often described as a Stroop-like task because it similarly directs speakers to articulate words while ignoring distracting information (see Dell'Acqua, Job, Peressotti, & Pascali, 2007, and van Maanen, van Rijn, & Borst, 2009, for similarities and differences between these tasks). In the Stroop task, speakers articulate the font color while ignoring the name of the color written in orthography (e.g., *green* written in purple font). In the picture–word interference task, speakers name objects depicted through pictures while ignoring aural or visual distracters (e.g., naming the picture of a dog while seeing the word *cat*). The picture–word interference

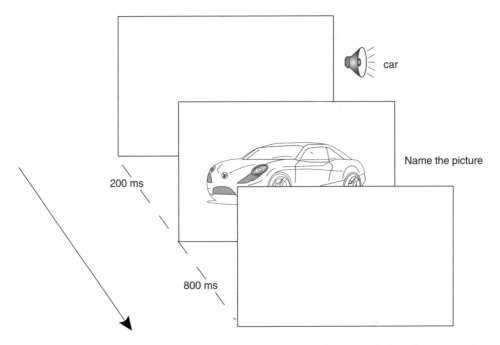

200 ms

800 ms

car

Name the picture

Figure 7.2 A schematic illustration of the picture–word interference task (based on Hantsch, Jescheniak, & Schriefers, 2009). This illustration depicts the following sequence of events for each trial: (1) a semantically related auditory distracter *car* (the picture's basic-level name) is presented 200 ms before the picture, (2) the target picture (Porsche) is presented for 800 ms, and (3) the participant names the picture (i.e., says *Porsche*) as quickly as possible.

task elicits reaction times in the form of naming latencies, which are believed to provide insight into the nature of lexical retrieval. The logic behind the task is that the distracters activate their corresponding lexical representations and this interferes with picture naming, making it slower and more difficult. Two variables are measured in this task: (a) naming latency, which is the amount of time required for speakers to name the picture, and (b) accuracy, which is whether the object names accurately represent the illustrations. Slower naming latencies (compared to a baseline condition) indicate that the distracters interfere with lexical selection of the target words, while faster naming latencies indicate that the distracters facilitate selection.

To carry out the picture–word interference task, individual speakers are seated at computers with programs such as E-prime, PsyScope, or DMDX and high-quality voice-activated recorders. The typical presentation of stimuli involves a fixation point which remains on screen briefly (e.g., 500 ms), after which a blank screen appears (e.g., 500 ms). Then the picture appears on screen with the distracter word written on or near the picture. Alternatively, distracters may be presented aurally instead of visually. Depending on the focus of the experiment, the distracter may be presented with the onset of the picture, shortly before, or shortly after the picture. The target picture remains on screen for about 2 seconds and the trial terminates immediately after the naming response is provided or after the 2 seconds elapse. There is usually a 1-second interval between items. A sample procedure for a picture–word interference task is illustrated in figure 7.2.

Theoretical frameworks

L1 production The picture–word interference task has been used in L1 speech production research to test claims about lexical selection. Contemporary speech production models are in agreement that the basic architecture of the production system consists of three stages (for an overview, see Griffin & Ferreira, 2006). These include conceptualization (preverbal message), formulation (lexical selection, grammatical processing, and phonological assembly), and articulation (physical articulation of overt speech). However, current models diverge in terms of specific claims about (a) the process of lexical selection (competition during activation or selection), (b) the association of grammatical properties with lexical selection (automatic or subsequent), and (c) the impact of phonological encoding on lexical selection (feed-forward or cascading).

Picture–word interference tasks have been used to investigate the timing of the lexical and phonological assembly phases within the formulation stage. These studies have shown that compared to unrelated distracters, semantically related distracters lead to slower naming latencies, which is the semantic interference effect (e.g., Hantsch et al., 2009). For example, hearing or seeing the word *cat* at the same time as or 400 ms before a picture of a dog is presented slows picture naming when compared to unrelated distracters, such as *table*. In contrast, phonologically similar but semantically unrelated distracters facilitate naming latencies when they are presented after the object to be named, which is the phonological facilitation effect (e.g., Bi, Xu, & Caramazza, 2009; Zhang, Chen, Weekes, & Yang, 2009). For example, hearing or reading the word *doll* milliseconds after a picture of a dog facilitates naming latencies compared to a phonologically unrelated distracter, such as *book*.

Bilingual/L2 production One main question for bilingual speech production is the extent to which the language not in use, referred to as the non-response language, affects production in the response language. For example, if a Spanish–English bilingual is asked to name a picture of a dog in English, do the corresponding lexical items in each language, dog and perro, become activated? Contemporary models of bilingual speech production assume that the conceptual system is shared by the two languages and that activation from the conceptual system is not specific to the response language. This implies that the relevant lexical items in both languages get activated (for review, see Costa, 2004). To explain how bilinguals manage to produce the appropriate lexical item in the appropriate language, one account posits an inhibitory process that suppresses activation of the words in the non-response language, while alternative accounts assume the existence of a selection mechanism that ignores activation of words in the non-response language.

Picture–word interference tasks have been used to determine whether activation of the non-response language interferes with lexical selection in the response language. Costa and his colleagues have shown that distracters that are translation equivalents of the target words facilitate naming latencies compared to unrelated distracters (Costa & Caramazza, 1999; Costa, Miozzo, & Caramazza, 1999). For example, a Spanish–English bilingual would name a picture of a dog in Spanish (would say *perro*) faster if the distracter were the English word *dog* as opposed to a non-translation equivalent, such as *table*. These results have been used to support the lexical selection mechanism, as opposed to inhibitory processes. Costa and his colleagues have also shown that non-target-language distracters that are phonologically related to the targets can impact naming latencies (Costa et al., 1999), which suggests that both lexical and phonological activation of the non-target language occurs. A sample study using a modification of the picture–word interference task, in which the distracters are pictures rather than words, is summarized in study box 7.3.

Study Box 7.3

Colomé, A., & Miozzo, M. (2010). Which words are activated during bilingual word production? *Journal of Experimental Psychology: Learning, Memory, and Cognition, 36*, 96–109 (Experiment 2).

Purpose

Determine whether distracters that are phonologically related to the non-response language affect naming latencies in the response language. It was predicted that phonologically related distracters would facilitate naming latencies.

Participants

24 Catalan–Spanish bilinguals with high proficiency in both languages who acquired their second language before age six.

Task design

Target pictures were 21 objects to be named in Catalan. They were paired with a distracter picture that was a cross-language similar name or a phonologically and semantically unrelated name. The target pictures were green, while the distracter pictures were red. Composite images were created so that the target picture and distracter picture were partially overlapping. For example, a picture of a vest to be named in Catalan (*armilla*) was paired with a picture of a squirrel, which is *ardilla* in Spanish, or a picture of a beak, which is *pico* in Spanish. None of the target and distracter picture pairs was semantically related to any other. The 21 target pictures were also paired with another set of semantically and phonological unrelated distracters that served as fillers and were not analyzed. The target pictures were presented in three blocks, with each block consisting of six pictures from each distracter type (phonologically related, unrelated, or fillers).

Procedure

Individual testing in soundproof booths at a computer with voice key recording. Preliminary activities included a familiarization phase for the pictures and object names with feedback, practice picture naming, instructions to name the green picture while ignoring the red picture, and practice items. Each trial began with a fixation point (500 ms), followed by a blank screen (500 ms) and the composite picture (400 ms). Recording of response latencies began when the picture appeared, and continued for up to 2 seconds with a 1-second blank interval separating the trials.

Analysis

No responses were discarded for recording failures or fast responses. Responses in which participants produced unintended names or had verbal dysfluencies (stuttering, repairs, non-verbal sounds) were coded as errors (3.2%) and entered into error analyses, which revealed no significant results.

Results

A t-test indicated that naming latencies were significantly faster for pictures that had related versus non-related distracters.

Methodological considerations

Because the picture–word interference task uses naming latencies and accuracy rates as evidence of interference or facilitation, the experimental materials manipulate the semantic and phonological relationships between the distracters and the objects to be named. The distracters should have varying relationships with the objects to be named, such as semantically related, phonologically related, or unrelated controls, and should be matched for length and frequency. When cognate distracters are used in bilingual experiments, they should share a significantly larger number of phonemes in identical word position than non-cognates. Most studies typically have small object sets and use a single object with multiple distracters, which can artificially decrease picture naming latency due to repetition practice. This potential problem can be avoided by using a unique picture for each trial (Knupsky & Amrhein, 2007), which increases the breadth of the stimuli and improves the ecological validity of the task.

In terms of the location of the distracter word, it is usually presented in the center of the image. However, its position has been manipulated in order to disambiguate recognition of the distracter, as reflected in eye movements to it, from interference of the distracter, as reflected by naming latencies (Kaushanskaya & Marian, 2007). Another modification is to present two images in the visual array and then present the distracters aurally. This allows for greater testing of relationships as some distracters can relate to the target picture, while others can be associated with the picture to be ignored (Oppermann, Jescheniak, & Schriefers, 2008). And in the picture–picture interference task, one picture is the distracter while the other picture is the object to be named. In this version of the task, color is typically used to indicate which picture should be named (Navarrete & Costa, 2005; Colomé & Miozzo, 2010).

All participants must be familiar with the pictures and the objects to be named prior to carrying out the experimental tasks. During the familiarization phase, feedback is generally provided to ensure that the participants recognize the objects in the pictures and use the appropriate words to name them. For example, the familiarization phase would help ensure that participants name the object previously shown in figure 7.2 using the word *Porsche* instead of *car*. Practice trials help ensure that the participants understand the instructions, which is particularly important in the picture–picture interference task where color indicates which picture should be named (e.g., "Name the object in the green picture but ignore the red picture"). In terms of analyzing responses, not only unintended object names but also no responses, self-corrections, or dysfluencies are typically coded as errors, but responses that were not detected due to technical problems are generally excluded. Outliers are responses that deviate more than two standard deviations from a mean (the participant or item mean), and those scores are either excluded or replaced with the cell mean.

Sentence Preamble Task

Description of the task

The sentence preamble task is most often used to elicit errors in subject–verb number agreement, although pronoun agreement has also been tested with this task. Speakers are given a phrase that serves as the subject of a sentence and are asked to generate a complete sentence. The subject phrases, or sentence preambles, contain two noun phrases. The first noun phrase is the grammatical subject of the sentence, and the second noun phrase is embedded in a prepositional phrase or a relative clause. The grammatical number of the first noun (the head noun) and the second noun (the local noun) are manipulated in order to increase or reduce number conflict. For example, the preamble *the key to the cabinets* has number conflict between *key* and *cabinets*, while the preamble *the key to the cabinet* does not. Speakers are asked to generate full sentences using the preambles as the subjects (e.g., *The key to the cabinets is in my desk drawer*), and their predicates are analyzed for subject–verb agreement errors. The logic of the task is that agreement errors should be greater when the head and local noun phrases mismatch in number as opposed to when they match.

The sentence preamble task (illustrated schematically in figure 7.3) is presented through experimental software such as PsyScope or DMDX with high-quality voice-activated recorders. The typical presentation of stimuli begins with a fixation point, such as a dot, an X, or a cross, which remains on screen for approximately 800 ms. Next, the preamble is presented either aurally or visually, with on-screen presentation time for visual preambles adjusted by their length. When the preamble ends, a visual cue appears, such as an exclamation point, at which point speakers repeat and complete the preamble. If the experimental design involves manipulation of semantic relationships or plausibility, then the task is adjusted by specifying a word to be

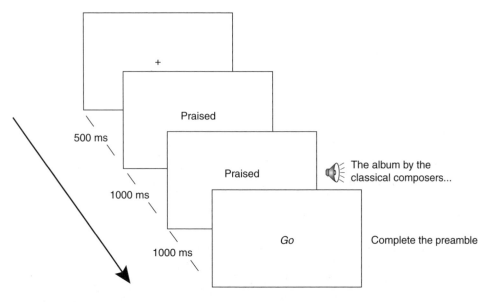

Figure 7.3 A schematic illustration of the sentence preamble task (based on Thornton &
MacDonald, 2003). This illustration depicts the following sequence of events for each trial:
(1) a fixation point (+) is presented; (2) the verb to be used in preamble completion is shown
after 500 ms; (3) a preamble is played after 1000 ms, and the verb stays on screen for the
duration of the preamble; (4) after a 1000-ms delay, *Go* appears on screen as the cue for
participants to repeat the preamble and complete the sentence in the passive voice.

included in the predicate, such as a verb or an adjective. In this modification, this
additional word is typically presented after the initial fixation point and remains on
screen for about 600 ms. The sentence-preamble task is usually self-paced with the
participant pressing the space bar to move to the next preamble.

Theoretical frameworks

L1 production Within the three-stage speech production model described previously,
grammatical encoding occurs in two phases within the formulation stage. First,
functional processing assigns grammatical functions (i.e., subject or object) and
morphological information to lexical representations, which creates hierarchical
relationships. Next, the output of the functional processing stage is subject to
positional processing, which imposes serial word order on the elements within
phrases and between phrases within the utterance, which is referred to as linearization
(see Ferreira & Engelhardt, 2006, for an overview of syntax in production).
Researchers have used sentence preamble tasks initially to test claims that non-
syntactic information has no impact on grammatical encoding. However, subsequent
studies have shown that non-syntactic information, such as the notional number of
the head noun (i.e., its semantic properties as opposed to grammatical number), also
impacts grammatical agreement (Eberhard, 1999; Barker, Nicol, & Garret, 2001;
Thornton & MacDonald, 2003; Humphreys & Bock, 2005). For example, the head

noun in the preamble *the label on the wine bottles* is grammatically singular but notionally plural as it can be interpreted as referring to multiple labels. A sample study is summarized in study box 7.4.

Study Box 7.4

Humphreys, K., & Bock, K. (2005). Notional number agreement in English. *Psychonomic Bulletin and Review, 12,* 689–695.

Purpose

Determine whether notional number influences subject–verb agreement in both the visual and auditory modalities. It was predicted that, if notional number plays a role in agreement, plural verbs will be more frequent after spatially distributed phrases (*the gang near the motorcycles*) than spatially collective phrases (*the gang on the motorcycles*). It was predicted that, if modality influences subject–verb agreement, plural verbs will be more frequent when preambles are read rather than heard.

Participants

144 college-age native English speakers.

Task design

18 sentence preambles were created with a head noun and prepositional phrase modifier. Six versions of each preamble were created by manipulating the head noun (collective or plural), the local noun in the prepositional phrase (singular or plural), and the prepositions (distributed or collective construal). Six lists were created consisting of three versions of each preamble and 50 fillers.

Procedure

Participants carried out the task individually using Macintosh computers with PsyScope experimental software. Half of the participants heard the preambles over external speakers, while the other half read the preambles on screen. When cued by the program, they repeated and completed the preamble.

Analysis

Responses were transcribed and verb number was classified into four categories: (1) singular, (2) plural, (3) uninflected (such as past tense verbs), and (4) miscellaneous (incorrect, unintelligible, or dysfluent preambles; no verb produced, preambles not used as the subject).

Results

ANOVAs were carried out with the percentage of plural verbs as the dependent variable and head noun, local number/construal, and modality as the factors, followed by planned pairwise comparisons. The main findings were (a) more plural verbs occurred after plural local nouns than singular local nouns, (b) more plural verbs occurred after distributed construals than collective construals, and (c) modality had little impact on agreement performance.

Bilingual/L2 production In terms of grammatical processing, bilingual speech production researchers have questioned the relationship between the grammatical properties of the two languages and how it impacts production of the response language. Previous studies have shown that speakers of Spanish, Italian, French, and Dutch are more sensitive to notional number than are English speakers. In other words, unlike English speakers, they make more agreement errors when the head noun, while grammatically singular, can be interpreted as conceptually plural. Bilingual studies have used the sentence preamble task to explore whether bilingual speakers' agreement errors are similar to L1 or L2 patterns. For example, while low-proficiency Spanish L2 speakers appear to carry over their English agreement errors when speaking Spanish, Spanish-dominant bilinguals with native proficiency in English show Spanish error patterns when speaking English (Nicol, Teller, & Greth, 2001).

Methodological considerations

In terms of task design, the most important consideration is the design of the sentence preambles. A set of basic sentence preambles is created first, and then manipulated so that there is one version of each preamble for every condition being tested. The post-modifying constituent with the local noun is typically a prepositional phrase, as studies which included relative clauses found that they elicit fewer subject–verb agreement errors (Bock & Cutting, 1992). The constituents that modify the head noun need to be matched in length. The filler preambles should avoid the relationships being targeted in the experimental conditions, but should have similar length and complexity. Some studies provide a verb to be used when completing the preamble in order to have greater control over the plausibility relations among the head noun, local noun, and the verb (Thornton & MacDonald, 2003). When the sentence preambles manipulate semantic factors, pilot testing is needed to control ratings of plausibility or distributed versus collective interpretations across the experimental conditions (Thornton & MacDonald, 2003; Humphreys & Bock, 2005).

For the analysis, the preamble completions are transcribed and then classified based on subject–verb agreement. Typically four categories are used to capture the logical possibilities. Correct completions are generally defined as correct repetition of the preamble and completion using a verb with correctly marked agreement. Agreement errors are defined as correct repetition of the preamble with incorrectly marked agreement, such as using a plural verb after a grammatically singular head noun due to the presence of a plural local noun. Uninflected responses are defined as a correct repetition of the preamble along with a completion with a verb that lacks number inflection or occurs in past tense. The final category is often termed "other" or "miscellaneous" and includes situations in which the preamble was not repeated or was incorrectly repeated, or there was no response, or the preamble was not used as the subject in the completion.

Concluding Remarks

As this brief overview has made apparent, psycholinguistic methodologies typically involve individual speakers who are asked to comprehend or produce words or sentences in isolation. Garnham, Garrod, and Sanford (2006) acknowledged that this focus on individual speakers persists despite the fact that dialogue is the most natural and basic form of language use, and expressed hope that future studies would investigate language processing during dialogue. We too are hopeful that L2 researchers interested in psycholinguistics will expand their research methodologies to explore language processing during situated language use. Of course, not all of the tasks described here could be adapted for conversation, but it is possible to design communicative tasks that have semantically and phonologically related distracters or present pictures with potentially facilitating or inhibiting images.

We also share Sears's (1986) concern that the inferences made from research carried out with a narrow database, specifically college students tested in a laboratory with academic-like tasks, may skew a field's understanding of basic processes. Like Sears's field of social psychology, L2 research also over-represents late adolescents in academic settings and under-represents other age groups in more varied contexts. And certainly Grosjean's (2008) advice concerning the need for caution when using experimental tasks designed for monolinguals with bilingual speakers warrants reiteration. Issues such as language proficiency and dominance, language mode, and the comparability of stimuli across languages can influence the extent to which research findings represent bilingual and L2 processing generally as opposed to task-specific processing. Finally, we would like to encourage L2 researchers to also consider using these comprehension and production methodologies as a tool for exploring the processes involved in language acquisition.

Project Ideas and Resources

Further Reading

Clahsen, H. (2008). Behavioral methods for investigating morphological and syntactic processing in children. In I. A. Sekerina, E. M. Fernández, & H. Clahsen (Eds.), *Developmental psycholinguistics: On-line methods in children's language processing* (pp. 1–27). Amsterdam, Netherlands: John Benjamins.

Ferreira, F., & Anes, M. (1994). Why study spoken language? In M. A. Gernsbacher (Ed.), *Handbook of psycholinguistics* (pp.33–56). New York, NY: Academic Press.

Heredia, R., & Stewart, M. T. (2002). On-line methods in bilingual spoken language research. In R. R. Heredia & J. Altarriba (Eds.), *Bilingual sentence processing* (pp. 7–28). Amsterdam, Netherlands: Elsevier.

McDonough, K., & Trofimovich, P. (2008). *Using priming methods in second language research*. New York, NY: Routledge.

Study Questions

1. In applied linguistics research, are comprehension and production typically studied separately or together? What are some areas of research within applied linguistics that either integrate or separate the study of comprehension and production?
2. In the self-paced reading task, researchers typically ask participants to do a secondary task, such as answer a comprehension question or make a plausibility judgment, in order to increase the likelihood that the sentences are comprehended. In what situations might the secondary task influence the participants' performance?
3. Why might a researcher decide to use inter-response time instead of pause duration as the dependent measure for the self-paced listening task?
4. Considering their similarities, in what situations might it be more appropriate to use the picture–word interference task instead of the Stroop task?
5. All of the tasks described in this chapter are administered to individuals seated at computers that have been programmed with experimental software. How could these tasks be adapted for use in low-tech environments or for group administration, such as in L2 classrooms?

References

Barker, J., Nicol, J., & Garrett, M. (2001). Semantic factors in the production of number agreement. *Journal of Psycholinguistic Research, 30*, 91–114.

Bi, Y., Xu, Y., & Caramazza, A. (2009). Orthographic and phonological effects in the picture–word interference paradigm: Evidence from a logographic language. *Applied Psycholinguistics, 30*, 637–658.

Bock, J. K. (1996). Language production: Methods and methodologies. *Psychonomic Bulletin and Review, 3*, 395–421.

Bock, K., & Cutting, J. (1992). Regulating mental energy: Performance units in language production. *Journal of Memory and Language, 31*, 99–127.

Booth, J. R., MacWhinney, B., & Harasaki, Y. (2000). Developmental differences in visual and auditory processing of complex sentences. *Child Development, 71*, 981–1003.

Caplan, D., & Waters, G. (2003). On-line syntactic processing in aphasia: Studies with auditory moving window presentation. *Brain and Language, 84*, 222–249.

Colomé, A., & Miozzo, M. (2010). Which words are activated during bilingual word production? *Journal of Experimental Psychology: Learning, Memory, and Cognition, 36*, 96–109.

Costa, A. (2004). Speech production in bilinguals. In T. Bhatia & W. Ritchie (Eds.), *The handbook of bilingualism* (pp. 201–223). Malden, MA: Blackwell.

Costa, A., & Caramazza, A. (1999). Is lexical selection language specific? Further evidence from Spanish–English bilinguals. *Bilingualism: Language and Cognition, 2*, 231–244.

Costa, A., Miozzo, M., & Caramazza, A. (1999). Lexical selection in bilinguals: Do words in the bilingual's two lexicons compete for selection? *Journal of Memory and Language, 41*, 365–397.

De Jong, N. (2005). Can second language grammar be learned through listening? An experimental study. *Studies in Second Language Acquisition, 27*, 205–234.

Dell'Acqua, R., Job, R., Peressotti, F., & Pascali, A. (2007). The picture–word interference effect is not a Stroop effect. *Psychonomic Bulletin and Review, 14*, 717–722.

Dussias, P. E. (2003). Syntactic ambiguity resolution in L2 learners: Some effects of bilinguality on L1 and L2 processing strategies. *Studies in Second Language Acquisition, 25*, 529–557.

Dussias, P. E., & Piñar, P. (2009). Sentence parsing in L2 learners: Linguistic and experience-based factors. In W. C. Ritchie & T. K. Bhatia (Eds.), *The new handbook of second language acquisition* (pp. 295–317). Bingley, England: Emerald.

Eberhard, K. (1999). The accessibility of conceptual number to the processes of subject–verb agreement in English. *Journal of Memory and Language, 41*, 560–578.

Felser, C., Marinis, T., & Clahsen, H. (2003). Children's processing of ambiguous sentences: A study of relative clause attachment. *Language Acquisition, 11*, 127–163.

Ferreira, F., Anes, M. D., & Horine, M. D. (1996). Exploring the use of prosody during language comprehension using the auditory moving window technique. *Journal of Psycholinguistic Research, 25*, 273–290.

Ferreira, F., & Clifton, C. (1986). The independence of syntactic processing. *Journal of Memory and Language, 25*, 348–368.

Ferreira, F., & Engelhardt, P. (2006). Syntax and production. In M. Traxler & M. Gernsbacher (Eds.), *Handbook of psycholinguistics* (2nd ed., pp. 61–91). Amsterdam, Netherlands: Elsevier.

Ferreira, F., Henderson, J. M., Anes, M., Weeks, P. A., & McFarlane, D. K. (1996). Effects of lexical frequency and syntactic complexity in spoken-language comprehension: Evidence from the auditory-moving window technique. *Journal of Experimental Psychology: Learning, Memory, and Cognition, 22*, 324–335.

Frazier, L. (1990). Exploring the architecture of the language-processing system. In G. T. M. Altmann (Ed.), *Cognitive models of speech processing: Psycholinguistic and computational perspectives* (pp. 383–408). Cambridge, MA: MIT Press.

Garnham, A., Garrod, S., & Sanford, A. (2006). Observations on the past and future of psycholinguistics. In M. Traxler & M. Gernsbacher (Eds.), *Handbook of psycholinguistics* (2nd ed., pp. 1–18). Amsterdam, Netherlands: Elsevier.

Griffin, Z., & Ferreira, V. (2006). Properties of spoken language production. In M. Traxler & M. Gernsbacher (Eds.), *Handbook of psycholinguistics* (2nd ed., pp. 21–60). Amsterdam, Netherlands: Elsevier.

Grosjean, F. (2008). *Studying bilinguals*. Oxford, England: Oxford University Press.

Hantsch, A., Jescheniak, J., & Schriefers, H. (2009). Distractor modality can turn semantic interference into semantic facilitation in the picture–word interference task: Implications for theories of lexical access in speech production. *Journal of Experimental Psychology: Learning, Memory, and Cognition, 35*, 1443–1453.

Heredia, R. R., Stewart, M. T., & Cregut, I. (1997, November). Bilingual online sentence processing: Frequency and context effects in code switching. Poster presented at the 38th annual meeting of the Psychonomic Society, Philadelphia, PA.

Hopp, H. (2006). Syntactic features and reanalysis in near-native processing. *Second Language Research, 22,* 369–397.

Humphreys, K., & Bock, K. (2005). Notional number agreement in English. *Psychonomic Bulletin and Review, 12,* 689–695.

Jackson, C. N., & Bobb, S. C. (2009). The processing and comprehension of *wh*-questions among second language speakers of German. *Applied Psycholinguistics, 30,* 603–636.

Juffs, A. (1998). Main verb versus reduced relative clause ambiguity resolution in L2 sentence processing. *Language Learning, 48,* 107–147.

Kaushanskaya, M., & Marian, V. (2007). Bilingual language processing and interference in bilinguals: Evidence from eye tracking and picture naming. *Language Learning, 57,* 119–163.

Knupsky, A., & Amrhein, P. (2007). Phonological facilitation through translation in a bilingual picture naming task. *Bilingualism: Language and Cognition, 10,* 211–223.

Marshall, C., Marinis, T., & van der Lely, H. (2007). Passive verb morphology: The effect of phonotactics on passive comprehension in typically developing and Grammatical-SLI children. *Lingua, 117,* 1434–1447.

Mitchell, D. C. (1984). An evaluation of subject-paced reading tasks and other methods for investigating immediate processes in reading. In D. Kieras & M. A. Just (Eds.), *New methods in reading comprehension research* (pp. 69–89). Hillsdale, NJ: Lawrence Erlbaum.

Mitchell, D. C. (2004). On-line methods in language processing: Introduction and historical review. In M. Carreiras & C. Clifton, Jr. (Eds.), *The on-line study of sentence comprehension: Eyetracking, ERPs and beyond* (pp. 15–32). New York, NY: Psychology Press.

Navarrete, E., & Costa, A. (2005). Phonological activation of ignored pictures: Further evidence for a cascade model of lexical access. *Journal of Memory and Language, 53,* 359–377.

Nicol, J., Teller, M., & Greth, D. (2001). The production of verb agreement in monolingual, bilingual, and second language speakers. In J. Nicol (Ed.), *One mind, two languages: Bilingual language processing* (pp. 117–133). Oxford, England: Blackwell.

Oppermann, F., Jescheniak, J., & Schriefers, H. (2008). Conceptual coherence affect phonological activation of context objects during object naming. *Journal of Experimental Psychology: Learning, Memory, and Cognition, 34,* 587–601.

Rah, A., & Adone, D. (2010). Processing of the reduced relative clause versus main verb ambiguity in L2 learners at different proficiency levels. *Studies in Second Language Acquisition, 32,* 79–109.

Sears, D. (1986). College sophomores in the laboratory: Influences of a narrow data base on psychology's view of human nature. *Journal of Personality and Social Psychology, 51,* 513–530.

Thornton, R., & MacDonald, M. (2003). Plausibility and grammatical agreement. *Journal of Memory and Language, 48,* 740–759.

Titone, D. A., Koh, C. K., Kjelgaard, M. M., Bruce, S., Speer, S. A., & Wingfield, A. (2006). Age-related impairments in the revision of syntactic effects of prosody. *Language and Speech, 49,* 75–99.

Titone, D., Prentice, K. J., & Winfield, A. (2000). Resource allocation during spoken discourse processing: Effects of age and passage difficulty as revealed by self-paced listening. *Memory and Cognition, 28,* 1029–1040.

Trueswell, J. C., & Tanenhaus, M. K. (1994). Toward a lexicalist framework of constraint-based syntactic ambiguity resolution. In C. Clifton & L. Frazier (Eds.), *Perspectives on sentence processing* (pp. 155–179). Mahwah, NJ: Lawrence Erlbaum.

van Gompel, R. P. G., & Pickering, M. J. (2007). Syntactic parsing. In M. G. Gaskell (Ed.), *The Oxford handbook of psycholinguistics* (pp. 289–308). Oxford, England: Oxford University Press.

van Maanen, L, van Rijn, H., & Borst, J. (2009). Stroop and picture–word interference are two sides of the same coin. *Psychonomic Bulletin and Review, 16*, 987–999.

Waters, G. S., & Caplan, D. (2004). Verbal working memory and on-line syntactic processing: Evidence from self-paced listening. *Quarterly Journal of Experimental Psychology, 57A*, 129–163.

Williams, J. N., Möbius, P., & Kim, C. (2001). Native and non-native processing of English *wh*-questions: Parsing strategies and plausibility constraints. *Applied Psycholinguistics, 22*, 509–540.

Zhang, Q., Chen, H., Weekes, B., & Yang, Y. (2009). Independent effects of orthographic and phonological facilitation in spoken word production in Mandarin. *Language and Speech, 52*, 113–126.

8 How to Research Second Language Writing

Charlene Polio

Background: Overview of Second Language Writing Research

Empirical studies of second language (L2) writing can be classified in different ways. One is by the focus of the study (Cumming, 1998; Polio, 2003; Silva & Brice, 2004, Leki, Cumming, & Silva, 2008), and the other is by the research method. With regard to the focus of the study, the researcher might target, for example, the texts that L2 writers produce; the writers themselves, including their writing processes and attitudes or motivation; or the context in which they write, including their needs in content classes or at work. Another way to classify studies is by research method, which is what I will do in this chapter. I have classified empirical studies of L2 writing into eight categories. Because several of these methods are covered elsewhere in this volume, I will focus on the two that are more specific to L2 writing (i.e., text analysis and process analysis), and I give examples of all eight below. Overall, this chapter has a quantitative and cognitive focus. Although producing written language is a cognitive activity and sometimes used to support general language learning, we also need to consider why L2 writers learn to write and what particular genre they need to master. Indeed, qualitative, social research is more common, but the basics of qualitative research are covered elsewhere in this volume (see Duff, chapter 6, Friedman, chapter 10, and Baralt, chapter 12) and are not specific to L2 writing.

The eight types of methods or techniques are surveys, interviews, meta-analysis, classroom observation, ethnography, content analysis, text analysis, and process research, with the last two including several different subtechniques. Certainly, there is some overlap in these categories, and some studies may (and should) use more than one method. I have not included case studies in this list even though they are

Research Methods in Second Language Acquisition: A Practical Guide, First Edition.
Edited by Alison Mackey and Susan M. Gass.
© 2012 Blackwell Publishing Ltd. Published 2012 by Blackwell Publishing Ltd.

very common in L2 writing research. Such studies may focus on specific students, classes, or programs. Case studies can include most of the other techniques including observations, interviews, surveys, content analysis, and process and text analysis. Study box 8.1 provides an example of a case study on students' perceptions of teacher feedback (Lee, 2008). It is exemplary because it uses a variety of methods including observations, content analysis, interviews, and questionnaires collected over an extended period of time. The variety of methods allowed the researcher to triangulate the data, and the prolonged data collection allowed for a more representative sample of data as opposed a brief view of what was happening in the instructional context. For a detailed discussion of how to do case study research see Duff (2008, this volume).

Study Box 8.1

Lee, I. (2008). Student reaction to teacher feedback in two Hong Kong secondary classrooms. *Journal of Second Language Writing, 17,* 144–164.

Background

Although many studies have shown that students want and value a variety of types of teacher feedback, much of this research on students' preferences has been conducted using questionnaires instead of examining what students do with actual feedback in the context of a real classroom. This study sees feedback as a social act and attempts to get a full picture of how students perceive and deal with feedback in one specific setting.

Research questions

• What are the characteristics of teacher feedback and the instructional context in which feedback is given?
• How do students react to the feedback provided by their teacher in their specific context?
• What factors might have influenced student reactions to teacher feedback? (p. 146)

Method

36 high-proficiency and 22 low-proficiency students aged 12–13 and their two teachers, all Cantonese speakers, in two Hong Kong secondary schools were studied. Data were collected in a variety of ways over the course of one school year. All students completed questionnaires, and a randomly selected subset completed a checklist and interview after receiving teacher feedback. Teachers were observed and interviewed and had their feedback examined.

Results

In both classes, the majority of teacher feedback was directed toward grammatical errors, although more so in the lower-level class. All students wanted teacher comments on their essays in addition to grammar feedback, but the less proficient students did not value the error feedback as much as the more proficient students and sometimes did not understand it. In neither class were students required to revise their essays based on teacher feedback.

Table 8.1 provides examples of each type of study, the first six of which I briefly discuss here. Surveys (see Dörnyei & Csizér, this volume, chapter 5) and interviews are quite common in L2 writing research and often used to uncover student attitudes or experiences as well as teacher beliefs and practices. Interviews can be revealing but are more helpful when triangulated with other types of data (see Friedman, this volume, chapter 10). The same is true of classroom observations. When used in L2 writing research, they tend to be components of case studies providing a way for the researcher to corroborate students' and teachers' perceptions of what is happening in the classroom. Ethnographies, like case studies, may include the above techniques. True ethnographies that are holistic and longitudinal are quite rare in L2 writing research. Instead, ethnographies that address L2 writing tend to discuss the skill as part a wider portrayal of the language learning context (e.g., McKay & Wong, 1996, but see Ramanathan & Atkinson, 1999, for a discussion of ethnography as applied to L2 writing research). Meta-analyses (see Plonsky & Oswald, this volume, chapter 14), too, are quite rare, perhaps because in order for a meta-analysis to be completed, a substantial volume of quantitative research on a particular topic needs to have accumulated. The effectiveness of written error correction has prompted a large number of empirical studies; thus one of the few meta-analyses on L2 writing has been completed on that topic (Truscott, 2007).

Before moving on to studies that focus on writers' texts or writing processes, I note the various types of content analysis that can be included in L2 writing research. Content analysis is a broad category that involves the researcher examining some type of texts or documents. In L2 writing research, a researcher may analyze a set of writing textbooks or syllabi to determine how writing is taught in a specific context. In Lee's (2008) case study, she coded and quantified teacher feedback on the students' texts. Generally, in content analysis, the researcher has to develop a reliable coding system to describe the data quantitatively. (In this volume see Friedman, chapter 10, Baralt, chapter 12, and Révész, chapter 11, for a discussion of coding qualitative and quantitative data.)

A more common goal of content analysis, however, is to describe written texts that L2 writers may have to produce. For example, John Swales has spent much of his career characterizing how research articles are organized in English (Swales, 1990, 2000, 2004). The goal is that these detailed descriptions will make explicit certain conventions for L2 writers. His work is considered to be one type of what is called genre analysis. Another approach to analyzing target texts is through corpus

Table 8.1 Examples of studies that use different research methods.

Type of method	Citation	Research question(s)	Comments
Survey	Montgomery & Baker (2007)	What is the quantity and type of current teacher feedback? What is the relationship between teacher self-assessments and students' perceptions of teacher-written feedback? What is the relationship between teacher self-assessments of written feedback and their actual performance? Throughout the process, do teachers focus their comments on the aspects of writing the way they should? (p. 86)	In addition to using student and teacher questionnaires, teachers' feedback on student papers was examined.
Interviews	Harwood, Austin, & Macaulay (2009)	What experience do those who proofread students' papers have? What are the proofreaders' beliefs and practices regarding the proofreading of students' papers? What type of experiences have proofreaders had proofreading students' texts?	
Classroom observations	Reichelt & Waltner (2001)	What do teachers and students perceive the purpose of writing in a foreign language class to be? How does writing fit into the curriculum?	In addition, interviews of the teachers and some students were conducted, questionnaires were administered, and teaching materials were examined. This study can also be considered a case study.

Method	Author (year)	Research question	
Ethnography	Atkinson & Ramanathan (1995)	What are the differences in attitudes and practices between L1 and L2 university writing programs?	
Meta-analysis	Truscott (2007)	Does written error correction help learners write more accurately?	
Content analysis (not including writers' texts)	Gillaerts & Van de Velde (2010)	How are interactional discourse markers (e.g., hedges, boosters, attitude markers) used in research article abstracts?	
Text analysis (descriptive)	Chan (2010)	What types of lexicogrammatical errors do Cantonese English as a second language (ESL) learners make?	
Text analysis (causal-comparative/correlational)	Ceyala & Navés (2009)	What are the differences in the writing of learners who start a foreign language early (at age 8) and those who start later (at age 11)?	
Text analysis (experimental)	Hartshorn et al. (2010)	Does a program of dynamic written corrective feedback lead to changes in students' writing with regard to accuracy, rhetorical competence, fluency, and complexity?	
Process analysis (descriptive)	Murphy & Roca de Larios (2010)	Do English as a foreign language (EFL) learners struggle to solve lexical problems when composing at advanced levels of proficiency? Do these advanced learners use their mother tongue in their attempts to solve these lexical problems? (p. 64)	This study also asks research questions related to task differences, and thus also has elements of an experimental study.
Process analysis (causal comparative/correlational)	Wang & Wen (2002)	Does the amount of L1 used in the L2 composing process vary with the writers' L2 development? (p. 228)	This study also examined task differences.
Process analysis (experimental)	Sengupta (2000)	In what ways do learning revision strategies influence student writers' perceptions of writing and revision? (p. 99)	This study also examined the effect of revision instruction on writers' texts.

linguistics (see Granger, this volume, chapter 2). By focusing on a specific structure or set of lexical items in a certain genre (e.g., research article, business letter), the analysis can provide teachers and students with a description of the language that needs to be mastered for writing in a specific context. The *Journal of English for Academic Purposes* publishes many studies of this type.

Analysis of Writers' Texts

There are various reasons that researchers may choose to analyze students' texts. These reasons may be classified by purpose in that they may (a) describe a group of L2 writers' text to help teachers and curriculum developers focus on problematic areas, (b) compare the texts of two different groups of writers, or (c) study the effects of some type of intervention or task on students' writing. I have called these descriptive, causal comparative/correlational, and experimental, respectively. The studies may also be classified with regard to what they analyze including accuracy, complexity, fluency, cohesion, and organization. (See Leki et al., 2008, for a more detailed taxonomy of ways to analyze writers' texts.)

Studies that simply describe writers' text often do so in hopes of providing teachers, curriculum developers, or textbook writers with areas in which a specific group of writers may need additional instruction. For example, Chan (2010) recently analyzed the essays of 387 Cantonese speakers, creating a taxonomy of morphological, syntactic, and lexical errors. Certainly, teachers may informally examine the texts of their own students' writing to determine areas that need improvement, but such published studies are not very common.

Instead, published studies tend to compare different groups of writers' texts, most commonly native versus non-native speakers or students at different proficiency levels. These studies can be called causal-comparative in that they compare groups on the basis of some group difference that is inherent in them and not manipulated by the researcher. Correlational research is similar but instead of comparing two groups, it correlates some text feature with some other variable, most commonly a measure of proficiency or overall text quality. When comparing two groups of writers' texts, the researcher may choose to study students at different levels of proficiency in hopes of learning more about the developmental stages of writing (e.g., Sasaki, 2000). Another possible variable for comparison is the writers' native language (e.g., Reynolds, 1995). Similarly, a study may correlate scores of essay quality or students' overall proficiency scores with some text variable. Liu and Braine (2005), for example, examined students' essays for cohesive features using Halliday and Hasan's (1976) three categories of cohesion (i.e., reference, lexical, conjunction) and found that essay quality correlated with the overall number of cohesive ties as well as the number of lexical ties. Note that in a correlation study such as Liu and Braine's, a method for quantifying overall text quality as well as the text feature under investigation needs to be chosen.

Many studies examine writers' texts to determine the effects of some type of intervention or the effects of different types of writing tasks. A common vein of research is to examine the effects of various types of written feedback on students' writing. (For reviews of error correction research see Ferris, 2002; Guénette, 2007; Truscott, 2007.) An example of research examining the effect of different task types can be found in study box 8.2.

Study Box 8.2

Kuiken, F., & Vedder, I. (2008). Cognitive task complexity and written output in Italian and French as a foreign language. *Journal of Second Language Writing, 17,* 48–60.

Background

This study examines students' writing on a more and less complex tasks. It aims to test whether a more complex task will cause various text features to suffer, as predicted by Skehan's limited attentional capacity model (Skehan, 1998; Skehan & Foster, 2001), or whether the text features will stay the same or improve, as predicted by Robinson's cognition hypothesis (2001, 2005).

Research questions

- What is the effect of manipulating cognitive task complexity on syntactic complexity, lexical variation, and accuracy of learner output?
- Is the output of low- and high-proficient learners affected by the manipulation of task complexity? (p. 51)

Method

91 Dutch learners of Italian and 76 Dutch learners of French at different proficiency levels were given two writing tasks that involved making a choice of a place to stay on an upcoming trip. Several variables needed to be operationalized including the independent variable (task complexity and learner proficiency) and the dependent variables (syntactic complexity, lexical variation, and accuracy). Cognitive task complexity was determined by the number of factors to be discussed in making a choice in a writing task, and proficiency was measured using a cloze test. Syntactic complexity was measured by clauses per T-unit and the degree of embedding per clause. Lexical variation was calculated through by a type/token ratio. Accuracy was measured by error-free T-units classified into three levels of severity.

Results

t-tests showed that students wrote more accurate essays on the complex writing task, but syntactic complexity and lexical variation were not significantly different on the two writing tasks. An ANOVA revealed no interaction effect for task and proficiency level.

A wide variety of measures can be used to analyze students' texts. Take, for example, a study that divides students into groups where one group gets no feedback, one group gets feedback on language, and one group gets feedback on content and organization. Constructs that one might want to measure include accuracy, complexity, fluency, organizational quality, content, and cohesion. While space limitation prevent a detailed description of each of these constructs, Polio (2001) provides a more extensive discussion of each, and additional references are listed under "Resources" below. I will use the examples of accuracy and complexity to illustrate the issues involved in applying these measures.

Accuracy can be measured in several ways (Polio, 1997; Wolf-Quintero, Inagaki, & Kim, 1998). For example, one may count the number of errors in an essay and divide the tally by the total number of words (error per words) or count the number of error-free T-units (consisting of an independent clause and its dependent clauses) to determine the number of error-free T-units per total T-units. With these examples, two problems are evident. First, determining what an error is can be problematic. Two native speakers will often not agree on whether something is an error; sometimes a phrase or sentence may sound awkward, but one is hesitant to label it an error. Second, some studies include spelling and punctuation errors in accuracy measures and some do not; and getting two native speakers to agree on where writers need commas is nearly impossible. In any case, researchers need to develop detailed guidelines on how the coding of errors was determined and preferably provide them in the appendices of the study.

Calculating accuracy by number of errors or error-free T-units provides only a rough calculation of accuracy. Not all errors would be seen as equal by a teacher or grader of an essay or by a reader outside of an educational setting. A missing article, for example, would probably be considered less severe than a word order problem that rendered a sentence incomprehensible. Thus, some studies attempt to code errors by type, but this can also be difficult; one ungrammatical sentence can be corrected in a variety of ways and the researcher may not know what the writer intended. The Kuiken and Vedder (2008) study in study box 8.2 classifies errors into three error types depending on severity.

Complexity may comprise both syntactic and lexical complexity. The most common way to measure syntactic complexity is to calculate the number of dependent clauses per T-unit. Thus, a sentence like *My flight was cancelled because there was a storm* (two clauses) would be less complex than *The flight that I was scheduled to take was cancelled because there was a storm* (three clauses). Although this measure is common, it can be problematic. First, clauses can be defined in different ways (Wolfe-Quintero et. al., 1998). For example, are infinitive clauses to be considered? Second, certain written features common to academic writing, arguably more complex, would be ignored, such as nominalization (e.g., Hyland & Tse, 2007), passive constructions, or modification through prepositional phrases. Housen and Kuiken (2009, p. 464) state that complexity in learner language includes "*size, elaborateness, richness*, and *diversity* of the learner's linguistics L2 system" (italics in original). A writer who used the same type of dependent clause repeatedly might receive a high numerical score on a measure of clauses per T-unit but would not seem to have a wide range of grammatical structures at his or her disposal. Norris and Ortega (2009) describe a variety of methods for measuring complexity in both speaking and writing and provide a useful discussion of the differences. Ultimately, they argue that complexity is complex and needs to be characterized through a variety of measures.

Lexical complexity needs to be considered as well and there are a variety of ways to measure that construct (Wolfe-Quintero et al., 1998). A simple type/token ratio is quite common. Using this measure, the number of different words is divided by the total number of words. Thus, a writer whose vocabulary was not diverse would receive a lower lexical complexity score. (See Malvern & Richards, 2002, for a discussion of this measure.) Because these calculations are generally done using a computer program, lexical errors are often not considered. Other methods (e.g., Laufer & Nation, 1995) may also consider the frequency of a lexical item; a writer using less common words would receive a higher lexical complexity score.

Whatever construct is being measured, the reliability and validity need to be considered. Reliability, the consistency of the measure, is relatively straightforward. The researcher needs to ensure that anyone coding the data will get similar results each time. To check inter-rater (or inter-coder) reliability, at least two coders code all or a subset of the data. Depending on the type of measure, a variety of statistics can be calculated to determine how well the two coders agree. The lower the reliability is, the more error is introduced into the measure. A study using a measure with low reliability might fail to find significant differences that would be found using a more reliable method. Validity has to do with whether the measure indeed measures what it is intended to. Returning to the example of complexity, the measure of clauses per T-unit probably does not capture a full view of what we might perceive complexity in writing to be.

In studies comparing groups, the researcher has to be careful that the intended comparison variable accounts for group differences. For example, a researcher may want to compare the organization styles of a group of Japanese speakers and a group of German speakers. It might be the case, however, that one group is simply more proficient in English and thus proficiency and not native language is the causal variable. Similarly, in a correlational study, one has to be careful not to imply a cause–effect relationship where there is none.

In studies comparing the effects of an intervention or task, measuring only one construct can be misleading. The classic problem among error correction studies is that they measure only the effects of the treatment on accuracy. Clearly, attention to accuracy could help their accuracy but harm the fluency or the complexity of their writing. It is important to get a holistic picture of the effects of any intervention. Study box 8.2 above details a study comparing two different writing tasks. Kuiken and Vedder (2008) investigated the effects of having students complete a more and a less complex writing task. The researchers analyzed the students' texts with regard to syntactic complexity, lexical variation, and accuracy.

Note that some studies of texts do not measure anything. This is particularly true of studies in the realm of contrastive rhetoric that examine how the writers from different first language (L1) backgrounds organize their writing. (For a review, see Connor, 2002.) Other studies might use their own unique coding system to study, for example, how students paraphrase (Keck, 2006) or incorporate outside sources into their writing (Shi, 2010).

Finally, much of the literature on writing assessment, which is beyond the scope of this chapter, is useful to anyone studying L2 writers' texts. L2 writing assessors have studied the reliability and validity of a variety of both holistic and analytic grading scales that can be used in L2 writing research. Analytic scales may cover constructs that a researcher wants to measure such as organization and content. In addition, numerous studies correlate holistic measures with more objective measures that might be used in research studies. Cumming et al. (2005) examined the correlation between holistic Test of English as a Foreign Language (TOEFL) scores and a variety of textual measures not discussed here, including quality of argument structure and orientations to source.

Analysis of the Writing Process

Researchers analyze the writing process for the same reasons that they analyze students' texts: to diagnose problems, to compare groups of writers, and to study the effect of an intervention or task. Learners' writing processes are generally studied through introspective methods (i.e., think-aloud protocols) and retrospective methods (i.e., stimulated recall, interviews, questionnaires). In addition, less common methods not discussed here include observations (Sasaki, 2004), computer keystroke logging (Miller, Lindgren, & Sullivan, 2008), and eye tracking (Wengelin et al., 2009).

Some of the research on the writing process describes how L2 writers write. For example, Roca de Larios, Murphy, and Manchón (1999) described how Spanish EFL learners use restructuring strategies as they wrote. More commonly, however, researchers compare groups of L2 writers, usually at higher and lower levels of general language proficiency or writing expertise. Rosa Manchón, Liz Murphy, and Julio Roca de Larios have conducted several cross-sectional studies on the writing processes of Spanish learners of English composing in both English and Spanish. For example, Roca de Larios, Manchón, and Murphy (2006) studied the amount of time that writers devoted to formulation and found, not surprisingly, that more time was spent formulating when writing in the L2 than in the L1. More interesting is that that time allocation did not change with proficiency, but what did change was the type of problem addressed. Less common is research that attempts to influence students' writing processes. When there is an intervention, it is usually an attempt to get students to revise differently, sometimes to do global revisions instead of simply sentence-level editing. These interventions tend to look only at students' texts for changes (e.g., Berg, 1998), or use questionnaires or interviews (Sengupta, 2000) and do not actually observe the revision process directly.

Despite concerns sometimes expressed over the use of think-aloud protocols, these tend to be the most common method used for studying the writing process, with stimulated recall and interviews and questionnaires being somewhat less common. During a think-aloud protocol (also called concurrent verbal protocol) writers speak aloud about what they are doing as they write. The goal is to get participants to verbalize what is currently going through their minds. For example, a participant may say, "I need to start the essay with a strong introduction. Maybe I should use an example here. Or maybe I should start with a general statement." With a stimulated recall (also called retrospective verbal protocols), the participants are usually shown a video of themselves writing. They are then asked to talk about what they were thinking at the time that they were writing. For example, a participant might say, "I paused there because I thought that sentence sounded funny. I was trying to decide if I should choose another word."

Much has been written about concurrent and retrospective verbal protocols, and three comprehensive books are listed in "Resources" under "Verbal protocols" for anyone planning to use these methods. Briefly, the issue with think-aloud protocols is that there is some concern that thinking aloud while writing can change the participants' writing process or the texts that they produce. This is called the reactivity problem. For example, talking aloud might cause a writer to plan more before writing or notice more errors while editing. Many researchers have studied how thinking aloud does or does not change what one normally does, but more so with other tasks such as problem solving or reading. (For a review, see Bowles, 2010.) Furthermore, a researcher has to make a variety of decisions such as how much to train the participants and what language the participants should speak while writing (the L2 or both the L1 and the L2). For both think-alouds and stimulated recall, there is a concern that what the participants say is an accurate and complete account of what they were thinking. This is called the veridicality problem. For think-alouds, most would agree that a participant cannot verbalize every thought, and thus the researcher is limited in the type of information that they have access to. With stimulated recall, there is the danger that the participants verbalize what they are thinking during the recall and not while they were writing. For example, a participant might say, "Oh, what a terrible sentence. I shouldn't have made that error." A true stimulated recall accesses only what the participant was doing in the task, although comments that participants make while reflecting on the completed task can still provide useful information.

Study box 8.3 details a longitudinal study of the writing process by Sasaki (2004). In that study, she followed 11 students over 3.5 years and analyzed their essays and their writing processes. She chose to conduct a stimulated recall. She videotaped the participants writing and then met with them to watch the video. After transcribing the stimulated recall, she coded the transcripts for different types of writing strategies (e.g., global planning, rhetorical refining) to determine how students' writing process changed over time. In addition, she observed the students writing. What one can tell from observing is limited, but she was able to determine how long it took students to start writing and for how long they wrote. As with studies of writers' texts, researchers need to determine reliable ways to code both think-aloud and stimulated recall data. Sasaki modified a coding scheme from a previous study and had a second researcher code a subset of the data to check for inter-coder reliability.

Finally, an increasing number of studies on collaborative writing are being conducted (for a review, see Storch, in press). In these studies, the interaction between students completing a writing task can serve as a way to observe the writing process. By observing students interacting about writing, the researcher can get some insight as to what students are focusing on.

Study Box 8.3

Sasaki, M. (2004). A multiple-data analysis of the 3.5-year development of EFL student writers. *Language Learning, 54*, 525–582.

Background

Sasaki and Hirose (Hirose & Sasaki, 1994; Sasaki & Hirose, 1996; Sasaki, 2000, 2002) conducted studies to determine how Japanese writers of English progressed in their writing. Because the studies were cross-sectional, Sasaki completed this longitudinal study targeting variables proposed in Grabe and Kaplan's (1996) model of writing: language performance output (overall composition scores and fluency), language competence (overall L2 proficiency), and verbal processing (writing strategies).

Research questions

- What changes could be identified in the students' general L2 proficiency?
- What changes could be identified in their L2 composition quality?
- What changes could be identified in their L2 writing fluency?
- What changes could be identified in their L2 writing strategy use?
- What changes could be identified in their L2 writing style?
- What characteristics of L2 writing experts did they acquire? (p. 534)

Method

11 students in their first year at a Japanese university were studied for 3.5 years with data collected at four times during the study period. Six of these students studied abroad during this time. Quantitative data including proficiency and composition scores were collected. Sasaki also studied the students' writing strategies through the use of a stimulated recall and by calculating the time students spent writing and planning before they wrote. The stimulated recall transcripts were coded for five strategies: global planning, local planning, thematic planning, translating from L1 to L2, and rhetorical refining. Students were also interviewed about their attitudes toward writing.

Results

Students showed improvement in the measures of writing quality and language proficiency, but the students who studied abroad showed more changes and developed a wider variety of writing strategies. All students felt that writing in English had become easier for them. Not surprisingly, however, students had not reached the level of L2 writing experts from Sasaki's other studies.

How to Complete an Experimental Writing Study

To illustrate the steps in conducting a research project, I have chosen a sample research question. Let us assume that the researcher is working in an EFL context where students have had little instruction on how to plan and revise their essays. The teachers and curriculum developers in that context want to try to use a method that instructs students in prewriting and revision, and they want to know whether such instruction results in any improvement. Thus a starting research question might be:

> Are students who are taught to modify their writing process successful and do they produce better-quality texts?

The independent variable (i.e., the intervention or treatment) is the instruction. The researcher first has to determine the nature of the instruction. Possibilities include having the students fill out questionnaires about their own writing processes, having the teacher model a process that involved planning and revision, and giving students questions to answer about their own writing before revising. This instruction is given to the experimental group whereas the control group receives the instruction that is the status quo. As with any experimental study, random assignment is preferred. In addition, it is best to keep other variables such as teacher, setting, and class time constant. Of course, both groups cannot meet at the same time with the same teacher. Another possible study design is to divide students into two groups within each class and have students in the experimental group participate in the treatment individually online. In this case, students in the control group would need to be given a filler activity to keep the overall amount of instruction time or the overall amount of writing completed equal.

Once the treatment is chosen, the researcher needs to determine how to measure the two dependent variables: the writing process and text quality. To study the writing process, the researcher needs to choose a method such as stimulated recall or think-aloud protocols. If stimulated recall is chosen, the researcher has to meet individually with every participant to play back the video immediately after the student writes. In this case, think-aloud protocols may be easier to administer if the researcher has access to a language lab. Still, the researcher has to decide how to train the participants without biasing them. In other words, if the researcher models the think-aloud by talking about his or her own writing process, the students may follow the same process. Thus, many researchers choose to model the think-aloud using an alternative task such as a math problem. Furthermore, the researcher needs to decide whether the students are allowed to use their native language during the think-aloud. Once the data are collected and transcribed, the researcher has to decide how to code them.

Next the researcher needs to determine the writing task on which to assess improvement. Most experimental studies students have students write in a controlled setting without access to outside sources. This is done to reduce the effects of uncontrolled variables and ensure the internal validity of the study. The result, however, is that the writing becomes unrealistic, and the study has no ecological validity. With regard to the prompt, some studies use a single question like those sometimes found on general proficiency tests, such as *Should parents control their children's access to the internet?* or have students describe a series of pictures. Some studies try to provide a simulated context in which students are asked to write a letter about a specific problem, in hopes of providing a more meaningful and realistic context. In addition, the researcher needs to determine whether a pretest is to be given. If a study has a very large sample size of fairly homogeneous students randomly divided into groups, a pretest is not required. Often, however, studies have small sample sizes or use intact classes without random assignment. In these cases, a pretest is needed to determine whether the groups are equivalent. The pretest should be somewhat similar to the type of writing task required for the posttest. If the researcher wants to draw any conclusions about how the students' writing changes over time, a pretest must be given and the writing tasks need to be counterbalanced, meaning that half the students in each group write on task A as the pretest and task B as the posttest, while the other half do the reverse.

The other dependent variable, text quality, can be operationalized in a number of ways. It is important to use a variety of measures to get an overall picture of how the students' writing has or has not changed. In this case, one might want to use a holistic scale such as those found on general proficiency tests that assign one score to the essay on the basis of a number of factors. But such a score will not shed light on the components of the essay that have or have not changed. Some composition grading scales are analytic assigning individual scores to areas such as vocabulary, content, grammar, and organization. The problem with such scales is that they are often not fine-grained enough to detect small changes in students' writing. Thus, many studies use measures such as those described earlier. But again, measuring only accuracy and complexity does not fully characterize the students' writing; the content or organization of the students' writing may have changed as well. Whatever measures are used, the researcher needs also to determine the reliability of these measures. Once the data are quantified, the researcher can use a variety of statistics to analyze group differences depending on the sample size and normality of the data.

Finally, in a study such as this, supplementing the quantitative data with qualitative data would be extremely useful. First, the researcher must do class observations to ensure that the instruction is being conducted as intended. If the students are assigned to the instruction individually, the researcher needs to ensure that they are completing the assignments. Second, interviews with the students and instructors would be useful, particularly if it was found that the treatment had no effect. It is possible that the students and instructors could highlight problems with the treatment that the researcher had not foreseen.

Project Ideas and Resources

Projects

1. Develop a somewhat realistic writing task such as writing an email request in a specific context. With a classmate, exchange tasks and observe that person think aloud. Reflect on the difficulty of trying to write and think at the same time. What were you thinking that you couldn't verbalize?

2. Ask an L2 learner to write while you video record the student. One way to do this is to use the screen recorder Camtasia (see"Resources" under "Programs for capturing the writing process" below), which records the computer screen so that it can be played back to the student. Ask the student to talk about what he or she was thinking while writing. Consider the following:

    *   What is the best way to give instructions to the student?
    *   Should you model the activity?
    *   Can the student fully express his or her thoughts in the L2?
    *   What do you think would happen if the student spoke in the L1 but wrote in the L2?

Transcribe the data and propose categories for coding the data. Then look at some other studies that have used stimulated recall in L2 writing research. Were your categories similar?

3. Imagine that you teach at a university that offers no ESL writing instruction for graduate students. You are asked to complete a case study of two engineering students, one who has the minimum required TOEFL score and one who is more proficient, to determine whether they have writing problems and how the university might best address them. After reading Duff, this volume, chapter 6, make a plan as to how you would go about conducting such a case study. How would you determine the students' writing needs? Would you examine their written texts and writing processes? If so, how?

4. Get examples of essays from low- and high-level L2 writers. Circle and code all the errors and label them according to type (e.g., article, verb tense). Compare your results to those of some classmates. Where and why did you disagree on what was an error or how to code it?

5. Read the abstract below from Min (2006, p. 118). Make a list of the independent and dependent variables. What are some ways that they could be operationalized? After you do this, read the whole article and see how the author operationalized the variables. Note that you will need to operationalize variables not discussed above, including student revisions. Min details how this can be done and refers to other studies that have coded revision.

    This preliminary classroom study aims to examine the impact of trained responders' feedback on EFL college students' revisions, both in terms of revision types and quality. After a 4-hour in-class demonstration and a 1-hour after-class reviewer-teacher conference with each student ($n = 18$), the instructor/researcher collected students' first drafts and revisions, as well as reviewers' written feedback, and compared them with those produced prior to training. Results show that students incorporated a significantly higher number of reviewers' comments into revisions post peer review training. The number of peer-triggered revisions comprised 90% of the total revisions, and the number of revisions with enhanced quality was significantly higher than that before peer review training. The researcher concludes that with extensive training inside and outside of class, trained peer review feedback can positively impact EFL students' revision types and quality of texts directly.

Resources

Research summaries

Hyland, K. (2002). *Teaching and researching writing.* Harlow, England: Pearson.

Leki, I., Cumming, A., & Silva, A. (2008). *A synthesis of research on second language writing.* New York, NY: Routledge/Taylor & Francis.

Polio, C. (2003). An overview of approaches to second language writing research. In B. Kroll (Ed.), *Exploring the dynamics of second language writing* (pp. 35–65). Cambridge, England: Cambridge University Press.

Text measures

Housen, A., & Kuiken, F. (Eds.). (2009). Complexity, accuracy, and fluency (CAF) in second language acquisition research [Special issue]. *Applied Linguistics, 30.*

Norris, J., & Ortega, L. (2009). Towards an organic approach to investigating CAF in instructed SLA: The case of complexity. *Applied Linguistics, 30,* 555–578.

Polio, C. (1997). Measures of linguistic accuracy in second language writing research. *Language Learning, 47,* 101–143.

Polio, C. (2001). Research methodology in second language writing research: The case of text-based studies. In T. Silva & P. Matsuda (Eds.), *On second language writing* (pp. 91–116). Mahwah, NJ: Lawrence Erlbaum.

Wolfe-Quintero, K., Inagaki, S., & Kim, H. Y. (1998). *Second language development in writing: Measures of fluency, accuracy, and complexity.* Technical Report #17. Honolulu: National Foreign Language Resource Center.

Verbal protocols

Bowles, M. (2010). *The think-aloud controversy in second language research.* New York, NY: Routledge/Taylor & Francis.

Gass, S., & Mackey, A. (2000). *Stimulated recall methodology in second language research.* Mahwah, NJ: Lawrence Erlbaum.

Smagorinsky, P. (Ed.). (1994). *Speaking about writing: Reflections on research methodology.* Thousand Oaks, CA: Sage.

Qualitative research

Duff, P. (2008). *Case study research in applied linguistics.* Mahwah, NJ: Lawrence Erlbaum.

Ramanathan, V., & Atkinson, D. (1999). Ethnographic approaches and methods in L2 writing research: A critical guide and review. *Applied Linguistics, 20,* 44–70.

Writing assessment

Weigle, S. (2002). *Assessing writing.* Cambridge, England: Cambridge University Press.

Programs for capturing the writing process

Screen recorder: www.techsmith.com/camtasia.asp.
Keystroke logger: www.inputlog.net.

References

Atkinson, D., & Ramanathan, V. (1995). Cultures of writing: An ethnographic comparison of L1 and L2 university writing/language programs. *TESOL Quarterly, 29*, 539–568.

Berg, E. C. (1999). The effects of trained peer response on ESL students' revision types and writing quality. *Journal of Second Language Writing, 8*, 215–241.

Bowles, M. (2010). *The think-aloud controversy in second language research.* New York, NY: Routledge/Taylor & Francis.

Ceyala, M. L., & Navés, T. (2009). Age-related differences and associated factors in foreign language writing: Implications for L2 writing theory and school curricula. In R. M. Manchón (Ed.), *Writing foreign language contexts: Learning, teaching, and research* (pp. 130–155). Bristol, England: Multilingual Matters.

Chan, A. (2010). Toward a taxonomy of written errors: Investigation into the written errors of Hong Kong Cantonese ESL learners. *TESOL Quarterly, 44*, 295–319.

Connor, U. (2002). New directions in contrastive rhetoric. *TESOL Quarterly, 36*, 493–510.

Cumming, A. (1998). Theoretical perspectives on writing. *Annual Review of Applied Linguistics, 18*, 61–78.

Cumming, A., Kantor, R., Baba, K., Erdosy, U., Eouanzoui, K., & James, M. (2005). Differences in written discourse in independent and integrated prototype tasks for next generation TOEFL. *Assessing Writing, 10*, 5–43.

Duff, P. (2008). *Case study research in applied linguistics.* Mahwah, NJ: Lawrence Erlbaum.

Ferris, D. (2002). *Treatment of error in second language student writing.* Ann Arbor: University of Michigan Press.

Gillaerts, P., & Van de Velde, F. (2010). Interactional metadiscourse in research article abstract. *Journal of English for Academic Purposes, 9*, 128–139.

Grabe, W., & Kaplan, R. B. (1996). *Theory and practice of writing.* London, England: Longman.

Guénette, D. (2007). Is feedback pedagogically correct? Research design issues in studies of feedback on writing. *Journal of Second Language Writing, 16*, 40–53.

Halliday, M. A. K., & Hasan, R. (1976). *Cohesion in English.* London, England: Longman.

Hartshorn, K., Evans, N., Merrill, P., Sudweeks, R., Strong-Krause, D., & Anderson, N. (2010). Effects of dynamic corrective feedback on ESL writing accuracy. *TESOL Quarterly, 44*, 84–109.

Harwood, N., Austin, L., & Macaulay, R. (2009). Proofreading in a UK university: Proofreaders' beliefs, practices, and experiences. *Journal of Second Language Writing, 18*, 166–190.

Hirose, K., & Sasaki, M. (1994). Explanatory variables for Japanese students' expository writing in English: An exploratory study. *Journal of Second Language Writing, 3*, 203–229.

Housen, A., & Kuiken, F. (2009). Complexity, accuracy, and fluency in second language acquisition. *Applied Linguistics, 30*, 461–473.

Hyland, K., & Tse, P. (2007). Is there an academic vocabulary? *TESOL Quarterly, 41*, 235–253.

Keck, C. (2006). The use of paraphrase in summary writing: A comparison of L1 and L2 writers. *Journal of Second Language Writing, 15*, 261–278.

Kuiken, F., & Vedder, I. (2008). Cognitive task complexity and written output in Italian and French as a foreign language. *Journal of Second Language Writing, 17*, 48–60.

Laufer, B., & Nation, P. (1995). Vocabulary size and use: Lexical richness in L2 written production. *Applied Linguistics, 16*, 307–322.

Lee, I. (2008). Student reaction to teacher feedback in two Hong Kong secondary classrooms. *Journal of Second Language Writing, 17*, 144–164.

Leki, I., Cumming, A., & Silva, A. (2008). *A synthesis of research on second language writing*. New York, NY: Routledge/Taylor & Francis.

Liu, M., & Braine, G. (2005). Cohesive features in argumentative writing produced by Chinese undergraduates. *System, 33*, 623–636.

Malvern, D., & Richards, B. (2002). Investigating accommodation in language proficiency interviews using a new measure of lexical diversity. *Language Testing, 19*, 85–104.

McKay, S. L., & Wong, S. C. (1996). Multiple discourses, multiple identities: Investment and agency in second-language learning among Chinese adolescent immigrant students. *Harvard Educational Review, 66*, 577–608.

Miller, K., Lindgren, E., & Sullivan, K. (2008). The psycholinguistic dimension in second language writing: Opportunities for research and pedagogy using computer key stroke logging. *TESOL Quarterly, 42*, 433–454.

Min, H. (2006). The effects of trained peer review on EFL students' revision types and writing quality. *Journal of Second Language Writing, 15*, 118–141.

Montgomery, J., & Baker, W. (2007). Teacher-written feedback: Student perceptions, teacher self-assessment, and actual teacher performance. *Journal of Second Language Writing, 16*, 82–99.

Murphy, L., & Roca de Larios, J. (2010). Searching for words: One strategic use of the mother tongue by advanced Spanish EFL writers. *Journal of Second Language Writing, 19*, 61–81.

Norris, J., & Ortega, L. (2009). Towards an organic approach to investigating CAF in instructed SLA: The case of complexity. *Applied Linguistics, 30*, 555–578.

Polio, C. (1997). Measures of linguistic accuracy in second language writing research. *Language Learning, 47*, 101–143.

Polio, C. (2001). Research methodology in second language writing research: The case of text-based studies. In T. Silva & P. Matsuda (Eds.), *On second language writing* (pp. 91–116). Mahwah, NJ: Lawrence Erlbaum.

Polio, C. (2003). An overview of approaches to second language writing research. In B. Kroll (Ed.), *Exploring the dynamics of second language writing* (pp. 35–65). Cambridge, England: Cambridge University Press.

Ramanathan, V., & Atkinson, D. (1999). Ethnographic approaches and methods in L2 writing research: A critical guide and review. *Applied Linguistics, 20*, 44–70.

Reichelt, M., & Waltner, K. (2001). Writing in a second-year German class. *Foreign Language Annals, 34*, 235–245.

Reynolds, D. (1995). Repetition in nonnative speaker writing: More than quantity. *Studies in Second Language Acquisition, 17*, 185–210.

Robinson, P. (2001). Task complexity, task difficulty, and task production: Exploring interactions in a computational framework. *Applied Linguistics, 22*, 27–57.

Robinson, P. (2005). Cognitive complexity and task sequencing: Studies in componential framework for second language task design. *International Review of Applied Linguistics, 43*, 1–32.

Roca de Larios, J., Manchón, R., & Murphy, L. (2006). Generating text in native and foreign language writing: A temporal analysis of problem solving formulation processes. *Modern Language Journal, 90,* 100–114.

Roca de Larios, J., Murphy, L, & Manchón, R. (1999). The use of restructuring strategies in EFL writing: A study of Spanish learners of English as a foreign language. *Journal of Second Language Writing, 8,* 13–44.

Sasaki, M. (2000). Toward an empirical model of EFL writing processes: An exploratory study. *Journal of Second Language Writing, 9,* 259–291.

Sasaki, M. (2002). Building an empirically-based model of EFL learners' writing processes. In S. Ransdell & M.-L. Barbier (Eds.), *New directions for research in L2 writing* (pp. 49–80). Amsterdam, Netherlands: Kluwer.

Sasaki, M. (2004). A multiple-data analysis of the 3.5-year development of EFL student writers. *Language Learning, 54,* 525–582.

Sasaki, M., & Hirose, K. (1996). Explanatory variables for EFL students' expository writing. *Language Learning, 46,* 137–174.

Sengupta, S. (2000). An investigation into the effects of revision strategy instruction on L2 secondary school learners. *System, 28,* 97–113.

Shi, L. (2010). Textual appropriation and citing behaviors of university undergraduates. *Applied Linguistics, 31,* 1–24.

Silva, T., & Brice, C. (2004). Research in teaching writing. *Annual Review of Applied Linguistics, 24,* 70–106.

Skehan, P. (1998) *A cognitive approach to language learning.* Oxford, England: Oxford University Press.

Skehan, P., & Foster, P. (2001). Cognition and tasks. In P. Robinson (Ed.), *Cognition and second language learning* (pp. 183–205). Cambridge, England: Cambridge University Press.

Storch, N. (in press). Collaborative writing in L2 contexts: Processes, outcomes, and future directions. *Annual Review of Applied Linguistics.*

Swales, J. (1990). *Genre analysis: English in academic and research settings.* Cambridge, England: Cambridge University Press.

Swales, J. (2000). *English in today's research world: A writing guide.* Ann Arbor: University of Michigan Press.

Swales, J. (2004). *Research genres: Explorations and applications.* Cambridge, England: Cambridge University Press.

Truscott, J. (2007). The effect of error correction on learners' ability to write accurately. *Journal of Second Language Writing, 16,* 255–272.

Wang, W., & Wen, Q. (2002). L1 use in the L2 composing process: An exploratory study of 16 Chinese EFL writers. *Journal of Second Language Writing, 11,* 225–246.

Wengelin, A., Torrance, M., Holmqvist, K., Simpson, S., Galbraith, D., Johansson, V., & Johansson, R. (2009). Combined eyetracking and keystroke-logging methods for studying cognitive processes in text production. *Behavior Research Methods, 41,* 337–351.

Wolfe-Quintero, K., Inagaki, S., & Kim, H. Y. (1998). *Second language development in writing: Measures of fluency, accuracy, and complexity.* Technical Report #17. Honolulu: National Foreign Language Resource Center.

9 How to Do Research on Second Language Reading

Keiko Koda

Background

Doing research on second language (L2) reading is a challenging enterprise. As a multidimensional construct, reading involves a wide range of subskills and their acquisition depends on various learner-internal (e.g., cognitive abilities and linguistic knowledge) and learner-external factors (e.g., print-related experience at home, reading instruction, community-wide literacy practices). Because of these multiple diversities, no single approach can adequately address all aspects of reading. As a result, reading has been tackled from diverse perspectives, using a variety of methodologies. Under cognitive views, for example, reading is regarded as a process of text-meaning construction, entailing linguistic information processing and conceptual manipulation. From sociocultural vantage points, reading is seen as a socially constructed pursuit, shaped by the everyday experiences of members in a particular social community. Thus, empirical probing of reading development encompasses the broad range of subskills required and the varied factors affecting their acquisition. In doing research on L2 reading, it is critical to clarify the theoretical and methodological orientations in relation to the problem that motivates the study.

In this chapter, reading is viewed as a psycholinguistic process involved in reconstructing the message intended by the author based on visually encoded information. As such, it consists of three major operations: (a) *decoding* (extracting linguistic information directly from print); (b) *text-base building* (assembling the extracted information into larger text units, such as phrases and sentences); and (c) *message construction* (integrating the assembled text information with prior knowledge). When reading is learned in an L2, the complexities increase exponentially because all subskills required for each operation entail two languages and their interactions. L2 reading research must explain how previously acquired

Research Methods in Second Language Acquisition: A Practical Guide, First Edition.
Edited by Alison Mackey and Susan M. Gass.
© 2012 Blackwell Publishing Ltd. Published 2012 by Blackwell Publishing Ltd.

first language (L1) reading subskills are integrated in L2 reading development; how integrated L1 subskills interact with L2 print input; and how the involvement of two languages alters the course of L2 reading development in linguistically diverse L2 learners.

The objectives of the chapter are three-fold: (a) explaining how L1 and L2 linguistic knowledge jointly constrain L2 reading development, (b) clarifying what constitutes evidence for such dual-language constraints, and (c) demonstrating how such evidence can be obtained in empirical studies. The chapter focuses on the conceptual and methodological foundations for empirical explorations of dual-language impacts on L2 development decoding.

Research Perspectives

Conceptual Foundations

Traditionally, L2 reading research has based its orientations on principles derived from L1 research. Because dual-language involvement is unique to L2 reading, the issues arising from cross-linguistic interactions cannot be tackled properly within the models of monolingual L1 reading. L2 reading research must go beyond research-based claims from L1 reading studies to illuminate the variables explaining the unique nature of L2 reading – dual-language involvement, in particular. To this end, cross-linguistic variations in learning to read must be clarified by analyzing (a) how reading acquisition is linguistically constrained; and (b) how reading subskills, as outcomes of such constraints, vary across languages.

These clarifications are not easy because languages differ in a number of significant ways – for example, their meaning-making conventions, devices for signaling those conventions, and methods of graphically encoding those devices. Although cross-linguistic variations can occur in all subskills involved in linguistic information processing, some variations are more critically related to reading development than others. In identifying those critical variations, the notion of reading universals is important, as it specifies the requisite operations for reading acquisition imposed on all learners in all languages, and in so doing, sets the limits on possible variations in learning to read across languages.

According to the universal grammar of reading (Perfetti, 2003; Perfetti & Liu, 2005; Perfetti & Dunlap, 2008), reading is the dynamic pursuit embedded in two interrelated systems: a language and its writing system. Because writing systems depend on language in decoding and encoding meaning, reading acquisition requires a linkage between the two systems. This means that in learning to read in all languages, children must first uncover which spoken language element (e.g., phoneme, syllable, morpheme) is directly encoded in the writing system (the *general mapping principle*) and then learn how it is encoded (the *mapping details*). Systematic comparisons of how the universally demanded operations are accomplished in diverse languages enable us to identify the language-specific demands imposed by the properties of the writing system in typologically diverse languages.

A small but growing body of evidence suggests that different languages require distinct symbol-to-sound mappings for phonological information extraction. In learning to read, children must become aware that spoken language elements systematically relate to print, and use the awareness in learning to map spoken sounds onto the graphic symbols that encode them (e.g., McBride-Chang, Wagner, Muse, Chow, & Shu, 2005; Ziegler & Goswami, 2005, 2006; Geva, 2008). The direct connection between the structural sensitivity and symbol-to-sound correspondences offers a clear methodological advantage. By analyzing the orthographic properties, the language-specific demands for learning to read can be uncovered within the reading universal framework.

To illustrate, in uncovering the *general mapping principle*, children learning to read English must recognize that each letter represents a distinct sound – either a consonant or a vowel (the alphabetic principle) – and then gradually work out the details of its symbol-to-sound relationships. Although the same (alphabetic) realization is required of children learning to read Korean, they must understand that individual symbols have to be packaged into syllable blocks, and then learn the specific way in which syllable blocks are formed. In contrast, children learning to read Chinese need to be aware that each symbol (character) corresponds to the meaning and the sound of a morpheme, and subsequently learn how single-unit characters are combined to form compound characters.

These variations have critical implications for L2 reading theories. Unlike monolingual L1 reading, L2 learning to read involves previously acquired skills integrated through cross-linguistic transfer. For transferred L1 skills to be functional in the new language, they must be adjusted to L2 orthographic properties. Hence, L2 decoding subskills are shaped jointly, but differently, by L1 and L2 orthographic properties. While L1 properties induce *deviations in L2 decoding behaviors* by virtue of transferred L1 skills, L2 properties explain *variances in L2 decoding efficiency* via evolving L2 orthographic knowledge. Empirical research must illuminate the subtle ways in which two languages coalesce in forming an additional set of decoding subskills in the new language. Presumably, research outcomes derived from studies incorporating such cross-linguistic analysis can explain systematic variations in L2 decoding development among learners with diverse L1 orthographic backgrounds.

Methodological Foundations: Construct Analysis

As a multifaceted, multilingual construct, empirical explorations of L2 reading development call for a specification of the skills to be investigated and the linguistic requirements for their utilization in each language involved. Because reading and linguistic knowledge are both complex abilities, the functional connection between the two cannot be fully understood unless their components are isolated and the functions of each are clarified. Such clarification requires a sequence of analyses, including (a) construct analysis (isolating the requisite skills for a particular operation in reading comprehension), (b) linguistic analysis (identifying the properties of the linguistic facet directly related to the subskills under consideration), and (c) cross-linguistic analysis (determining how the properties of the relevant linguistic facet vary between two languages). Incrementally, these analyses allow researchers to convert highly complex dual-language issues into empirically testable hypotheses.

In the initial phase of the analyses, the central construct of reading must be dissected into its constituent subskills. The *component skills approach*, proposed by Carr and Levy (1990), provides a methodological foundation for isolating the requisite skills for each operation involved in text-meaning construction. Several assumptions underlie this approach (Carr, Brown, Vavrus, & Evans, 1990): Reading is the product of a complex information-processing system; it involves a constellation of closely related mental operations; each operation is theoretically distinct and empirically separable, serving an identifiable function; each operation entails a unique set of processing skills; and the component skills interactively facilitate perception, comprehension, and memory of visually presented language.

The approach has been adopted in a large number of L1 reading studies (e.g., Leong, Shek, Loh, & Hau, 2008). The first step in this approach is to specify a reading component model to be tested based on accepted reading theories. The model can be used to select the subskills to be examined in a study and a battery of assessment tasks for measuring the selected skills. The scores from those tasks are first subjected to simple correlations. The resulting correlational matrix is then converted into a distance metric by squaring each correlation to obtain the proportion of simple variance shared by any two subskills. The reciprocal of the squared correlation is then calculated, producing a number between 1.0 and infinity, with the smaller numbers representing greater shared variances. The functional distance among the measured skills can thus be represented graphically in the form of a map. The utility of cognitive maps lies in their capacity for disentangling interconnected subskills involved in complex cognitive tasks, such as reading. A clearer understanding of the functional relationships among component skills enables researchers to pinpoint the sources of reading impediments. Study box 9.1 shows a sample L1 reading study using this approach.

The component skills approach is particularly suitable for examining multiple variations in L2 reading development, because it offers a reliable means of dissecting the very construct of reading into its component subskills, and in so doing, allows us to compare the functional interconnections among those subskills both within and across languages. In short, the approach permits two-layered analyses of reading development – one contrasting variations within individual learners when reading in L1 and L2, and the other comparing performance variances across linguistically diverse L2 learner groups.

Dual-Language Impacts on Second Language Reading Development

As noted, dual-language involvement is a defining characteristic of L2 reading. The basic premise is that L2 reading skills are shaped through cross-linguistic interaction between transferred L1 skills and L2 print input. On this premise, L2 decoding development can be seen as the process of reshaping transferred L1 skills to accommodate L2-specific orthographic properties. This means that we can make specific and testable predictions as to qualitative and quantitative variations in L2

Study Box 9.1

Leong, C. K., Shek, K. T., Loh, K. Y., & Hau, K. T. (2008). Text comprehension in Chinese children: Relative contribution of verbal working memory, pseudoword reading, rapid automatized naming, and onset–rime phonological segmentation. *Journal of Educational Psychology, 100*(1), 135–149.

Purpose

To examine the relative contribution of four subskills to text comprehension in Chinese.

Participants

518 grade 3–5 Chinese children in Hong Kong.

Method

Participants did the following tasks:

- *Text comprehension*: Read eight short passages and answered three questions per passage. Points from 0 to 3 were awarded for each answer.
- *Working memory*: Listened to 13 sets of two, three, and five sentences. Wrote down short answers to comprehension questions and the last word in each sentence of each set.
- *Pseudoword reading*: Read aloud 72 Chinese two-character compound pseudowords (pronounceable but meaningless character combinations).
- *Rapid automatized naming (RAN)*: Read aloud 15 letters and numbers as rapidly and as accurately as possible in two separate sessions.
- *Onset–rime phonological segmentation*: Listened to a spoken character or one-syllable word, deleted the end sound or the beginning sound of the character/word, and then said what was left (e.g., listen to /gold/, delete /g/, and say /old/).

Analysis

The relative impacts of the three subskills (working memory, RAN, phonological skill) on pseudoword reading (decoding) and text comprehension were compared using structural equation modeling and hierarchical regression analysis.

Results

Working memory contributed to both decoding and comprehension to a much greater extent than the other subskills.

decoding subskills by analyzing differences and similarities in the facets of L1 and L2 orthographic properties directly related to the decoding subskill under investigation. To date, L2 reading research has presented empirical evidence for (a) L1 involvement in L2 decoding, (b) L1-induced variations in L2 decoding behaviors, and (c) L1 and L2 joint impacts on the formation of L2 decoding subskills.

In this research, the most fundamental question is whether L1 skills are indeed involved in L2 print information processing. Over the past thirty years, the pursuit of the question has been guided, in the main, by the *developmental interdependence* hypothesis. Its main contention is that L1 cognitive abilities are the chief determinant of L2 literacy and academic achievement (Cummins, 1979, 1991). Early bilingual studies showed that L1 and L2 reading test scores were highly correlated (e.g., Skutnabb-Kangas & Toukomaa, 1976; Troike, 1978; Legarretta, 1979; Cummins, Swain, Nakajima, Handscombe, & Green, 1981), and thus provided partial support for the role of L1 skills in L2 reading development. In these studies, however, reading was uniformly treated as a single unitary construct. The studies provide little information regarding individual subskills and their functional interconnections either within or across languages.

Within the component skills approach, recent studies have demonstrated systematic relationships in decoding and other related subskills between two languages, including phonological awareness (Durgunoglu, Nagy, & Hancin, 1993; Wade-Woolley & Geva, 2000; Bialystok, McBride-Chang, & Luk, 2005; Wang, Perfetti, & Liu, 2005; Branum-Martin et al., 2006), decoding (Durgunoglu et al., 1993; Da Fontoura & Siegel, 1995; Abu-Rabia, 1997; Geva & Siegel, 1999; Gholamain & Geva, 1999; Wade-Woolley & Geva, 2000), and working memory (Abu-Rabia, 1995; Da Fontoura & Siegel, 1995; Geva & Siegel, 1999; Gholamain & Geva, 1999). These studies have yielded far more detailed information about reading subskills and their cross-linguistic relationships than had been available in the earlier literature. It is important to note, however, that these studies are primarily correlational, and their results, even from non-zero order correlations, constitute only indirect evidence of reading skills transfer. To substantiate the hypothesized dual-language impacts, more direct evidence is needed. The section that follows describes a methodological approach to the empirical testing of this and other related hypotheses. A sample study is summarized in study box 9.2.

Investigating Dual-Language Impacts on Second Language Reading

Although dual-language impacts are presumed to be observable in any subskills, this chapter, as noted earlier, focuses on linguistic information extraction simply because more research-based information is available on decoding than on any other operations in the current L2 reading literature. Using a well-established research base is advantageous in describing a methodological approach in an emerging area of inquiry. Defined as the process of extracting linguistic information from visually

Study Box 9.2

Bialystok, E., McBride-Chang, C., & Luk, G. (2005). Bilingualism, language proficiency, and learning to read in two writing systems. *Journal of Educational Psychology, 97,* 580–590.

Purpose

To examine cross-linguistic relationships in phonological awareness and decoding among three groups of children (monolingual, bilingual, and L2 learner).

Participants

204 children in three language groups across two grade levels (kindergarten or grade 1): 64 monolingual English speakers in Canada; 70 English–Cantonese bilingual speakers in Canada; and 70 L2 English learners in Hong Kong.

Method

Participants did the following tasks:

- *Peabody Picture Vocabulary Tasks (English and Cantonese)*: Shown four pictures on a plate in a booklet, heard one of them named, and pointed to the picture that corresponded to the word. Testing terminated when the child made eight errors in a set of 12 items.
- *Syllable deletion (English and Cantonese)*: Heard a three-syllable word and reproduced the word without one of the syllables as specified by the experimenter (16 items).
- *Phoneme onset deletion (English and Cantonese)*: Heard a monosyllabic word and reproduced the word without the beginning sound (8 real words and 8 non-words).
- *Phoneme counting (English only)*: Counted the total number of sounds they heard by using finders or a set of counter chips (8 for the Canadian groups and 15 for the Hong Kong group).
- *Word decoding (English and Cantonese)*: Read aloud a list of simple words (30 for English and 25 for Cantonese).

Analysis

The effect of bilingualism (three groups) on decoding was tested using 2 (grade: kindergarten vs. Grade 1) × 3 (language group: monolingual, bilingual vs. L2 learner) ANOVAs. The cross-linguistic relationships were examined using second-order correlations between English and Cantonese phonological tasks and decoding measures.

Results

Phonological awareness was more strongly related between English and Cantonese than decoding. No overall effect of bilingualism was found.

presented words, decoding entails two subskills: word segmentation (analyzing a word into its sublexical constituents) and mappings (mapping the segmented information onto the graphic symbols encoding the information).

In testing the hypothesized dual-language impacts, the language-specific demands for the requisite symbol-to-sound mappings in two languages must be accurately described for cross-linguistic comparisons, because the disparity in the demands between the languages can be used as the basis for making the predictions to be tested, as well as for devising the tasks for measuring the mapping skills in each language. For the purpose of illustration, the orthographic properties in three languages, each representing a distinct type of writing system, are described: English as a phonologically opaque alphabetic system, Korean as a phonologically transparent alphabetic system, and Chinese as a logographic system.

Language-Specific Demands for Learning to Read

Insofar as languages differ in the way they encode phonological information of spoken words in their respective writing systems, the skills optimal for symbol-to-sound mappings vary across languages. Within the reading universal framework, the critical variations in learning to read are presumed to lie in two dimensions: the general mapping principle and mapping details.

As an alphabetic system, English orthography is governed by phonemic constraints. Its strong tendency to preserve morphological information in the visual display makes it a phonologically opaque system. Because of this tendency, many spelling irregularities are more readily explained by morphological rather than phonemic constituents. Reflecting the dual-unit (morpheme and phoneme) representation, phonological information extraction in English necessitates the skill to manipulate intra-syllabic sound units, such as onset, rime, and phoneme, through assembling and dissembling constituent letters of a printed word, as well as the ability to use orthographic analogy for mapping particular sounds onto recurring letter clusters (e.g., Shankweiler & Liberman, 1972; Ehri, 1998). L1 reading research has shown that competent readers are uniformly adept at pronouncing both individual letters and pronounceable letter strings (e.g., Hogaboam & Perfetti, 1978; Siegel & Ryan, 1988; Wagner, Torgesen, & Rashotte, 1994); and that skilled readers have more solid knowledge of sound–symbol correspondences than poor readers (e.g., Seidenberg & McClelland, 1989; Adams, 1990; Ehri, 1994, 1998).

The Korean writing system, Hangul, is also alphabetic, but it employs a non-Roman script, in which each symbol represents a single consonant or vowel. In contrast to the linear horizontal alignment in English orthography, Hangul symbols are packaged into syllable blocks using simple formation rules (Park, 2008). For example, the word, 깊훈 (/ki-phɨn/ 'deep') consists of two syllable blocks, 깊 /kip/ and 훈/hun/, each containing three Hangul symbols (깊 → ㅋ /k/ + ㅣ /i/ + ㅍ /p/; 훈 → ㅎ /h/ ㅜ/u/ ㄴ/n/).

There are 24 basic Hangul symbols, including those for 14 consonants (representing 19 phonemes) and 10 vowels. Although grapheme-to-phoneme correspondences are highly consistent and reliable at the individual symbol level, syllable blocks do not always correspond to spoken syllable boundaries because some Hangul spelling conventions, or syllable-block formations, tend to conform to the word's morphological composition, rather than to the phonetic constituents (Sohn, 1999). The dual-level (phoneme and syllable) representation in the Hangul script demands that Korean children be sensitized to both syllables and phonemes. In fact, phonological manipulation skills at the two levels are both strong predictors of Korean word-reading ability (McBride-Chang et al., 2005).

In logographic Chinese, the basic unit of character formation is radical (e.g., Chen, Allport, & Marshall, 1996; Shu & Anderson, 1997). *Radical* refers to recurrent stroke patterns, each having a clearly identifiable function. Many radicals themselves are single-unit characters and used both as independent lexical morphemes and as components of compound characters. Of several character-formation procedures, semantic–phonetic compounding is by far the dominant method, used in the vast majority (roughly 80–90%) of compound characters (Zhang, 1994). This formation method involves a non-linear integration of two radicals, each providing either phonological or semantic information. For instance, the character 妈 (/ma/ tone1; 'mother') consists of two radicals placed side by side. The radical 女 ('woman') on the right provides partial semantic information of the character (the character refers to a type of woman) while the radical on the left, 马 (/ma/tone3), indicates the character's pronunciation.

To extract phonological information from compound characters, logographic readers must segment a character into its graphic components; determine which radical provides phonological information; and then retrieve its phonological information from lexical memory. In principle, the sound of a character can be accessed through its phonetic radical, but phonological information extraction is not as straightforward as it seems because less than half the compound characters have the same phonetic value as their radicals (Zhou, 1978; DeFrancis, 1989; Perfetti, Zhang, & Berent, 1992). Logographic readers must activate phonological information simultaneously at the character and radical levels.

In sum, the language-specific demands for phonological information extraction are closely aligned with the symbol–sound relationships in the language in which reading is learned. By describing and comparing those relationships in two languages, we can identify differences and similarities in the subskills optimal for the required mappings between the two languages. The analysis is also useful as it provides the basis for making accurate predictions of how transferred L1 skills and L2 input jointly shape L2 decoding subskills.

Hypothesis Formulation

Based on the descriptions above, it seems reasonable to assume that the critical contrast between alphabetic and logographic literacy lies in the grain sizes that are required for phonological information extraction. Because the requisite mappings occur at the phonemic level in alphabetic systems, decoding in alphabetic literacy requires phoneme identification and manipulation. In contrast, in logographic systems, phonology is encoded holistically at the morphemic level in a single character. Their phonological information extraction relies primarily on graphic analysis to segment a visually complex symbol into its graphic components, and then determine which component provides phonological information. Based on the disparity in the requisite mappings in alphabetic and logographic literacy, several hypotheses can be formulated for empirical testing.

One such hypothesis is that L2 learners of English (English as a second language, or ESL) with alphabetic and logographic L1 orthographic backgrounds engage in phonological and graphic analyses in different degrees during L2 decoding. Empirical testing of this hypothesis involves systematic comparisons of the relative magnitudes of interference caused by two types of experimental manipulation: one blocking phonological information and the other distorting graphic displays. English orthography offers an ideal condition for such comparisons because its dual-unit (morphophonemic) representation necessitates two distinct procedures for phonological information extraction – that is, grapheme-to-phoneme translation (phonological analysis) and orthographic analogy (graphic analysis). If L1 subskills are involved in L2 phonological information extraction, the magnitude of disruption, resulting from each type of manipulation, should vary between two groups of ESL learners each representing a distinct L1 orthographic background. While the blocking of phonological information will seriously hinder decoding performance among alphabetic ESL learners, graphic distortion will impede phonological information extraction more severely among logographic ESL learners. Differential degrees of performance decline, if they occur as predicted, can be taken as direct evidence of L1 subskills involvement. As for L2-based variances, the extent to which the two types of manipulation affect both groups can be used as the basis for gauging the impact stemming from the sensitivity to L2-specifc properties.

Empirical Testing

A series of experimental studies have tested the hypothesis presented above, using a variety of experimental manipulations, including case alteration (replacing *read* with *ReAd*; Akamatsu, 1999), heterographic homophones (replacing *ate* with *eight*; Koda, 1989), and spelling regularity (contrasting regularly and irregularly spelled pseudowords; Hamada & Koda, 2008). These studies have shown that L2 learners with alphabetic and logographic L1 backgrounds respond differently to varying manipulations (e.g., Brown & Haynes, 1985; Green & Meara, 1987; Koda, 1998, 1999; Akamatsu, 1999; Hamada & Koda, 2010, in press); and that the observed differences are consistent with the processing behaviors predicted on the basis of the participants' respective L1 writing systems (e.g., Koda, 1989, 1990, 1993; Ryan & Meara, 1991). These results have been interpreted as suggesting that L1 decoding skills are used in L2 phonological information extraction; and that L1 orthographic properties have a measurable impact on L2 decoding development. In study box 9.3, a sample study is summarized.

Study Box 9.3

Hamada, M., & Koda, K. (2010). The role of phonological decoding in second language word-meaning inference. *Applied Linguistics*, 31, 513–531.

Purpose

To examine how L1–L2 orthographic similarity facilitates L2 decoding efficiency, and how L1-induced difference in L2 decoding efficiency, if any, affects word-meaning inference during text comprehension.

Participants

Two groups of proficiency-matched college-level ESL learners with similar (alphabetic; N = 16) and dissimilar (logographic; N = 17) L1 orthographic backgrounds.

Method

Participants did the following tasks:

- *Naming*: Read aloud English words and pseudowords (20 items each) as accurately and as quickly as possible. The stimulus items were randomized and presented on the computer screen one at a time for a maximum of 2,500 ms.
- *Word-meaning inference task*: Read a passage containing eight pseudowords, answered comprehension questions, and wrote down inferred meanings of the pseudowords.

Analysis

The effect of L1 orthographic background on decoding was tested using 2 (language group: Chinese vs. Korean) × 2 (word type: real words vs. pseudowords) ANOVAs. The effect of L2 decoding efficiency on word-meaning inference was examined using two-tailed t-tests.

Results

The two ESL groups differed in L2 decoding efficiency, with the Korean group being more efficient. However, the decoding efficiency did not systematically relate to word-meaning inference.

Once L1 involvement is empirically demonstrated, the next step is to determine how transferred L1 skills interact with L2 orthographic properties. Of late, interest in such cross-linguistic interactions has risen, and a growing number of studies is currently underway. These initial studies have explored the relative influences of L1 and L2 factors on L2 decoding performance, using an assortment of tasks, such as semantic category judgment (Wang, Koda, & Perfetti, 2003), naming (Hamada & Koda, 2010), and word identification (Wang & Koda, 2005). Typically, in these studies, L2 stimulus words are manipulated both phonologically and graphically to distinguish the impacts stemming from each language involved. The magnitude of each manipulation is then compared both within and between two participant groups representing contrasting (alphabetic and logographic) L1 orthographic backgrounds. As noted earlier, the extent to which a particular manipulation affects both groups is used as the basis for gauging the L2 impact, and the extent to whicht the effect of each manipulation varies between the participant groups serves as an index of the L1 impact. Study box 9.4 presents a summary of a sample study.

The studies have demonstrated that L2 decoding efficiency significantly declined when any type of interference was present regardless of L1 background. The magnitude of interference, however, varied between the two types of manipulation (graphic vs. phonological), as well as between two participant groups (alphabetic vs. logographic L1 background). As predicted, graphic distortion affected ESL learners with a logographic L1 background more seriously than phonological distraction, whereas phonological interference disrupted processing efficiency among ESL learners with an alphabetic L1 background more severely than graphic alteration. Interestingly, the *manipulation* by *L1 background* interaction was not significant in any of the studies. The non-significant interaction effect has been taken to indicate that the impact stemming from L2 orthographic properties overrides the variance attributable to L1 properties. Viewed collectively, these findings suggest that L1 orthographic properties have lasting effects on L2 print information extraction, but L2 print input is the stronger force in shaping L2 decoding subskills. The emerging database, though still limited, lends support for the hypothesized dual-language impacts on L2 reading development.

Study Box 9.4

Wang, M., & Koda, K. (2005). Commonalities and differences in word identification skills among learners of English as a second language. *Language Learning, 55*, 71–98.

Purpose

To examine the joint impact of L1 and L2 orthographic properties on L2 word identification.

Participants

Proficiency-matched college-level ESL learners with Chinese (N = 18) and Korean (N = 16) L1 backgrounds.

Method 1: Naming

Participants did the following task:

- Read aloud a word shown on the computer screen for 500 ms. The 120 stimulus words included (a) high-frequency regular words (e.g., *best*), (b) high-frequency exception words (e.g., *both*), (c) low-frequency regular words (e.g., *slam*), (d) low-frequency exception words (e.g., *swamp*), and (e) non-words (e.g., *foth*).

Analysis

Accuracy and reaction times (RT) data were analyzed using 2 (frequency: high vs. low) × 2 (regularity: high vs. low) × 2 (language group: Chinese vs. Korean) repeated-measures ANOVAs. The percentages of regularization errors (i.e., naming exception words by analogy to regular words) were compared using 2 (frequency) × 2 (language groups) ANOVAs.

Results

The Korean group was more accurate and faster in naming English words than the Chinese group. Korean participants also made more regularization errors. The two L2 variables (word frequency and spelling regularity) had a stronger impact on naming efficiency than did L1 background.

Method 2: Oral Semantic Category Judgment

Participants did the following tasks:

- Read a category name presented on the computer screen for 500 ms, heard a sound of a word, and decided whether the word heard was an exemplar of the category on the screen. Five common categories of concrete nouns (furniture, reading materials, occupation, clothing, and vehicle) were used. There were six items in each category (60 items). An equal number of control items was selected and matched on frequencies with the experimental items (60 items).

Analysis

Accuracy and RT data were analyzed using t-tests.

Results

The Korean group performed faster and more accurately than did the Chinese group.

Data Construction and Interpretation

For the constructed data to be interpretable in an experimental study, the induced variances must be unequivocally linked to the experimental manipulations employed. This section explains how such unambiguous relationships can be established by illustrating the data collection and analysis procedures used in one of the studies cited above (Wang et al., 2003). Because this study directly addressed the above-mentioned hypothesis through the use of phonological and graphic manipulations, detailed descriptions of the logic and design of the study should illuminate what it takes to capture highly intricate phenomena, such as cross-linguistic interactions, by eliciting particular patterns of behaviors experimentally.

Experimental Procedures: An Illustration

In the Wang et al. study (2003), semantic category judgment was employed. In the task, the participants were first presented with a category description, such as *flower*, followed by a stimulus word. The participants were asked to decide whether the word was a member of the category. The stimulus words were manipulated either phonologically or graphically. In the "phonological" manipulation, the target word for a given category was replaced with its homophone. For instance, *rows* as a homophone of the category-member exemplar *rose* was shown immediately after the category description *flower*. If participants relied on phonological information in accessing stored word information, it should have taken them longer to reject *rows* as a member of the *flower* category than to deny its non-homophonic, non-member control. In contrast, in the "graphic" condition, each target word was replaced with a similarly spelled non-member word. For example, *fees* was used, in lieu of *feet*, as the target word for the *body part* category. If participants relied heavily on graphic analysis in retrieving lexical information, the manipulation should have disrupted their judgment performance.

Wang et al.'s data demonstrated that the two types of manipulation seriously affected category judgments of all ESL learners irrespective of their L1 orthographic background. At the same time, the magnitude of the interference stemming from each type of manipulation varied between the groups. As predicted, Korean ESL learners were considerably less efficient when judging homophonic items, whereas Chinese participants' performance declined more visibly when dealing with graphically manipulated items. As indicated above, the effect of *group* (Chinese vs. Korean) by *manipulation* (phonological vs. visual interference) interaction was not statistically significant, indicating that the within-group variances (L2 impact) are greater than the between-group variances (L1 impact). These results were taken as suggesting that both L1 and L2 orthographic properties explain variations in L2 decoding behaviors; and that, of the two, L2 influence is stronger in L2 decoding subskills development.

The Logic and the Design: An Explanation

What ensures the interpretability of the data gathered through particular experimental manipulations? In evaluating the validity and accuracy of data interpretation, two factors are particularly pertinent: (a) characteristics of the elicited behavior and (b) involvement of extraneous variables. The former concerns the correspondence between the processing behavior elicited and the construct under consideration. If the elicited behavior cannot be warranted as a behavioral manifestation of the focal construct, it is not possible to make valid inferences about the construct based on the data in hand. The latter has to do with the likelihood that extraneous variables explain greater portions of the observed variances in the elicited performance than the experimental manipulations. Using the Wang et al. study (2003) again as an example, this section explains how the logic and design of a study affect the interpretability of experimental data.

To determine whether semantic category judgment is an appropriate task for eliciting a processing behavior that is analogous to print information extraction, one must first analyze what is required for performing this task. In order to make judgments about each word's category membership, participants must extract the core semantic information from the word's visual display. Thus, the task simulates the operation that transpires during decoding, and in so doing, elicits the processing behavior as it occurs during decoding in non-experimental situations.

Inasmuch as lexical access necessitates both graphic and phonological analyses, the processing behavior elicited by the category judgment task is susceptible to any manipulation designed to block either graphic or phonological information. To establish an unambiguous link between the induced variances and the experimental manipulations, no other factors should be allowed to explain greater portions of the variances in the elicited performance. If, for example, the exemplars in the Wang et al. study, such as *rose* and *feet*, had been differentially familiar to the participants, word familiarity could have explained the variances in semantic category judgments to a greater extent than either type of manipulation. Similarly, if the two participant groups had not been matched on their English proficiency and other related factors (e.g., L1 literacy, educational level, and so on), the between-group variances in their judgment performances could have been accounted for by an unintended learner-related variable, rather than L1 orthographic backgrounds.

Drawing Out Pedagogical Implications

In any applied field, there is a general expectation that empirical studies yield information of utility in solving real-life issues and problems. Given that a growing number of students worldwide struggle to read in their second or later acquired languages, it is particularly important that research-based information on L2 reading development be properly incorporated into instruction. However, drawing out pedagogical implications is not simple because not all insights brought to light in empirical studies can be taught, or even have direct bearing on improving reading performance. Careful attention must be given to the unique characteristics of L2 reading when translating research into practice. As a case in point, it is critical to make sure that the subskill to be trained is *causally* related to reading comprehension. For the planned intervention to be effective, the targeted skill should be accessible in the conscious mind of learners, so they can monitor and regulate what they are trained to do during practice. In addition, the focal group of learners should be linguistically ready for the intended intervention. These issues are considered further in what follows.

First, correlational relationships do not indicate any causal direction between the variables measured. Caution must be exercised in implementing correlational findings. When a particular skill is related to comprehension performance, it may seem logical to provide explicit training on the skill. If, however, their relationship is correlational, such training is not likely to be effective. To illustrate, high- and low-ability readers markedly differ in many eye-movement indices, including fixation frequency, fixation duration, and backtracking (e.g., Balota, Pollasek, & Rayner, 1985; Just & Carpenter, 1987). Would it be legitimate to take those differences as suggesting that successful comprehension depends on specific eye-movement patterns? If so, could we improve comprehension performance by teaching weak readers how to move their eyes? The answer is "no" to both because eye movements are merely an indicator of reading ability, rather than a *cause* of reading problems.

Second, psycholinguistic experimentation provides a glimpse of real-time text-information processing. Because many processing subskills are automated, their execution occurs at no cost of attentional capacity. This means that automated subskills cannot be examined directly by asking readers to describe what they do, or by observing ongoing behaviors during comprehension. Instead, many psycholinguistic studies rely on indirect measures. Those methods exploit the fact that automated processing is non-volitional, transpiring under any (experimental) circumstances, irrespective of the reader's intent. Readers are purposely presented with anomalous items designed to disrupt automated processes (e.g., case-altered words, heterographic homophones). Based on their reactions, inferences can be drawn on how print information is extracted and integrated. Given the "tricky" nature of the data construction, any recommendation for classroom practice made solely on the basis of study outcomes without probing their instructional utility would be precarious. Specifically, interventions designed to modify L2 processing operations that involve automated L1 subskills, such as decoding, are not likely to be effective because learners can neither monitor nor control automated L1 subskills involved in L2 processing. Thus, research information of considerable value in understanding processing behaviors may not be of direct utility for classroom teaching.

Finally, L1-induced variations must be taken into account in evaluating the applicability of findings from L1 reading instruction studies. Measurable gains in comprehension performance have been reported as a result of explicit instruction on a variety of comprehension subskills, such as word–meaning inference (Sternberg, 1987), metacognitive comprehension strategies (Pressley, Almasi, Schuder, Bergman, & Kurita, 1994), and text-structure analysis (Baumann & Bergeron,

1993). These findings are potentially beneficial to L2 learners if they are implemented selectively on the basis of learners' functional readiness. For example, comprehension operations depend on well-developed decoding competence, and delays in achieving optimal decoding efficiency result in comprehension problems. Given that L1 and L2 orthographic distance directly relates to the rate at which L2 decoding efficiency develops (Muljani, Koda, & Moates, 1998), in all probability, linguistically heterogeneous learners are differentially ready for comprehension subskills instruction at a given point in time in L2 learning to read. Should this be the case, interventions aiming to improve comprehension subskills are not likely to be effective uniformly across diverse learner groups.

Future Research Directions

Cumulative evidence collected over the past three decades has begun to disentangle multilayered complexities arising from cross-linguistic interactions in L2 reading development. Future research agendas can be built to purposefully expand the current investigative scopes. Three areas seem particularly promising: (a) including a wider variety of languages, (b) incorporating a broader range of subskills, and (c) tracking the long-term impacts of dual-language involvement.

In the current database, scant information is available on reading development in languages other than English. Because empirical probing of dual-language impacts necessitates accurate descriptions of how reading development is linguistically constrained in two languages, the paucity severely restricts the scope of the cross-linguistic analysis integral to this research. Because the approach described in this chapter is grounded in the notion of the dual-level – that is, universal and language-specific – constraints on learning to read, it is vital that we be clear about what constitutes "prior literacy experience" in elucidating how the universally demanded requirements are achieved in the languages involved. In the absence of such clarification, it is virtually impossible to estimate the disparity between what has been previously learned and what has yet to be acquired by a particular group of L2 learners.

Although reading entails a wide range of subskills, the extant studies are almost exclusively focused on phonological decoding and related subskills. To more fully appreciate L2 reading development, it is essential that the current scope be expanded to other subskills, particularly those involved in information integration and conceptual manipulation. Because many of the comprehension subskills are developmentally interdependent, it is highly desirable to probe their functional relationships both within and across languages. Properly executed, empirical examinations of higher-order comprehension subskills will yield significant additional insights into cross-linguistic variations in L2 text-meaning construction.

Different subskills develop at disparate rates in accordance with their respective timetables. It is difficult to isolate the impacts stemming from two languages, if subskills are measured only once at a given point in time. To better understand the long-term effects of dual-language involvement, it is important to track changes in a particular subskill longitudinally in L2 reading development. It would be of considerable benefit, for example, to determine to what extent developmental acceleration of the focal subskill is attributable to similarities in the properties of the relevant facet in two languages, and then explore how differential degrees of acceleration alter higher-order operations whose functionality depends on the mastery of the subskill under investigation.

As noted earlier, L1 and L2 orthographic distance is known to be largely responsible for differences in L2 decoding efficiency. In the absence of longitudinal data, we know little about what happens to the initial disparity in decoding efficiency over the course of L2 reading development. Although it is possible that the gap may close over time, entailing little consequence for subsequent reading development, this could have a lasting impact on the acquisition of higher-order subskills. If the latter is the case, the initial decoding differences may induce procedural variations in L2 text-meaning construction. Despite their direct bearing on instruction, the long-term effects of L1 and L2 linguistic distance remain largely unexplored. Clearly, future studies should explore dual-language involvement through longitudinal observations of multiple skills development.

Closing Remarks

This chapter has described a methodological approach to empirical examinations of dual-language impacts on L2 reading development. Because L2 reading is a multifaceted, multilingual competence, its development cannot be adequately addressed solely on the basis of L1 reading theories. To tackle complex cross-linguistic issues, more refined models of reading have yet to emerge. To that end, future research should incorporate a series of analyses as its integral phase: (a) determining the subskill to be examined, (b) clarifying the linguistic demands for its utilization, and (c) identifying differences in such demands between two languages. It is only through such finely tuned analyses that we can come to grips with the multilayered diversities inherent in L2 learning to read.

Project Ideas and Resources

Further Reading

Bernhardt, E. B. (2010). *Understanding advanced second language reading*. New York, NY: Routledge.

Duke, N. K., & Mallette, M. H. (Eds.). (2004). *Literacy research methodologies*. New York, NY: Guilford Press.

Grabe, W. P. (2008). *Reading in a second language: Moving from theory to practice*. New York, NY: Cambridge University Press.

Hamada, M., & Koda, K. (2008). Influence of first language orthographic experience on second language decoding and word learning. *Language Learning, 58*, 1–31.

Koda, K., & Zehler, A. M., (Eds.). (2008). *Learning to read across languages*. New York, NY: Routledge.

McKenna, M. C., & Stahl, S. A. (2003). *Assessment for reading instruction*. New York, NY: Guilford Press.

Study Questions

1. Extracting linguistic information from printed words is a vital operation for successful text comprehension. The skills for print information extraction are shaped to accommodate the specific way in which language elements are graphically represented in the writing system. Select one language, other than English, and describe what linguistic information is encoded in each graphic symbol in the language (the general mapping principle) and how those symbols are combined to represent spoken words (the mapping details). Discuss how the grapheme–language relationships differ between English and the language of your choice.

2. Based on the analysis in question 1, consider how the identified structural differences between the two languages would be manifest in processing behaviors. In order to obtain empirical evidence of cross-linguistic variation in the required grapheme-to-language mappings in the two languages involved, what tasks would you use to capture subtle differences in the mapping behaviors that are not directly observable?

3. In recent studies, reading is seen as a constellation of abilities, rather than a single unitary skill. Reflecting such a view, many studies treat reading as a multifaceted construct, examining a subset of component skills identified through construct (reading) analysis and decomposition. Discuss the advantages and disadvantages of using the component view of reading as a methodological foundation in L2 reading research.

4. Although this chapter has focused on a psycholinguistic approach to L2 reading research, reading can be studied from diverse perspectives. What approaches are you familiar with? Discuss what types of issues are most commonly addressed in those approaches. Consider how research outcomes in each approach inform L2 reading theory and practice.

References

Abu-Rabia, S. (1995). Learning to read in Arabic: Reading, syntactic, orthographic and working memory skills in normally achieving and poor Arabic readers. *Reading Psychology, 16*, 351–394.

Abu-Rabia, S. (1997). Verbal and working memory skills of bilingual Hebrew–English speaking children. *International Journal of Psycholinguistics, 13*, 25–40.

Adams, M. J. (1990). *Beginning to read*. Cambridge, MA: MIT Press.

Akamatsu, N. (1999). The effects of first language orthographic features on word recognition processing. *Reading and Writing, 11*(4), 381–403.

Balota, D., Pollasek, A., & Rayner, K. (1985). The interaction of contextual constraints and parafoveal visual information in reading. *Cognitive Psychology, 17,* 364–390.

Baumann, J. F., & Bergeron, B. S. (1993). Story map instruction using children's literature: Effects on first graders' comprehension of central narrative elements. *Journal of Reading Behavior, 25,* 407–437.

Bialystok, E., McBride-Chang, C., & Luk, G. (2005). Bilingualism, language proficiency, and learning to read in two writing systems. *Journal of Educational Psychology, 97,* 580–590.

Branum-Martin, L., Fletcher, J. M., Carlson, C. D., Ortiz, A., Carlo, M., & Francis, D. J. (2006). Bilingual phonological awareness: Multilevel construct validation among Spanish-speaking kindergarteners in transitional bilingual education classrooms. *Journal of Educational Psychology, 98,* 170–181.

Brown, T., & Haynes, M. (1985). Literacy background and reading development in a second language. In T. H. Carr (Ed.), *The development of reading skills* (pp. 19–34). San Francisco, CA: Jossey-Bass.

Carr, T. H., Brown, T. L., Vavrus, L. G., & Evans, M. A. (1990). Cognitive skill maps and cognitive skill profiles: Componential analysis of individual differences in children's reading efficiency. In T. H. Carr & B. A. Levy (Eds.), *Reading and its development: Component skills approaches* (pp. 1–55). San Diego, CA: Academic Press.

Carr, T. H., & Levy, B. A. (Eds.). (1990). *Reading and its development: Component skills approaches.* San Diego, CA: Academic Press.

Chen, Y. P., Allport, D. A., & Marshall, J. C. (1996). What are the functional orthographic units in Chinese word recognition: The stroke or the stroke pattern? *Quarterly Journal of Experimental Psychology, 49*(A), 1024–1043.

Cummins, J. (1979). Linguistic interdependence and educational development of bilingual children. *Review of Educational Research, 49,* 222–251.

Cummins, J. (1991). Interdependence of first- and second-language proficiency in bilingual children. In E. Bialystok (Ed.), *Language processing in bilingual children* (pp. 70–89). New York, NY: Cambridge University Press.

Cummins, J., Swain, M., Nakajima, K., Handscombe, J., & Green, D. (1981). *Linguistic interdependence in Japanese and Vietnamese students.* Report prepared for the Inter-America Research Associates, June. Toronto: Ontario Institute for Studies in Education.

Da Fontoura, H. A., & Siegel, L. S. (1995). Reading syntactic and memory skills of Portuguese-English Canadian children. *Reading and Writing: An International Journal, 7,* 139–153.

DeFrancis, J. (1989). *Visible speech: The diverse oneness of writing systems.* Honolulu: University of Hawai'i Press.

Durgunoglu, A. Y., Nagy, W. E., & Hancin, B. J. (1993). Cross-language transfer of phonemic awareness. *Journal of Educational Psychology, 85,* 453–465.

Ehri, L. C. (1994). Development of the ability to read words: Update. In R. Ruddell, M. Ruddell, & H. Singer (Eds.), *Theoretical models and processes of reading* (4th ed., pp. 323–358). Hillsdale, NJ: Lawrence Erlbaum.

Ehri, L. C. (1998). Grapheme–phoneme knowledge is essential to learning to read words in English. In J. L. Metsala & L. C. Ehri (Eds.), *Word recognition in beginning literacy* (pp. 3–40). Mahwah, NJ: Lawrence Erlbaum.

Geva, E. (2008). Facets of metalinguistic awareness related to reading development in Hebrew: Evidence from monolingual and bilingual children. In K. Koda & A. M. Zehler (Eds.), *Learning to read across languages: Cross-linguistic relationships in first and second language literacy development* (pp. 154–187). New York, NY: Routledge.

Geva, E., & Siegel, L. S. (2000). Orthographic and cognitive factors in the concurrent development of basic reading skills in two languages. *Reading and Writing, 12*, 1–30.

Gholamain, M., & Geva, E. (1999). Orthographic and cognitive factors in the concurrent development of basic reading skills in English and Persian. *Language Learning, 49*, 183–217.

Green, D. W., & Meara, P. (1987). The effects of script on visual search. *Second Language Research, 3*, 102–117.

Hamada, M., & Koda, K. (2008). Influence of first language orthographic experience on second language decoding and word learning. *Language Learning, 58*, 1–31.

Hamada, M., & Koda, K. (2010). The role of phonological decoding in second-language word-meaning inference. *Applied Linguistics, 31*, 213–231.

Hamada, M., & Koda, K. (in press). The role of the phonological loop in English word learning: A comparison of Chinese ESL learners and native speakers. *Journal of Psycholinguistic Research*.

Hogaboam, T. W., & Perfetti, C. A. (1978). Reading skill and the role of verbal experience in decoding. *Journal of Educational Psychology, 70*, 717–729.

Just, M. A., & Carpenter, P. A. (1987). *The psychology of reading and language comprehension*. Boston, MA: Allyn & Bacon.

Koda, K. (1989). The effects of transferred vocabulary knowledge on the development of L2 reading proficiency. *Foreign Language Annals, 22*, 529–542.

Koda, K. (1990). The use of L1 reading strategies in L2 reading. *Studies in Second Language Acquisition, 12*, 393–410.

Koda, K. (1993). Transferred L1 strategies and L2 syntactic structure during L2 sentence comprehension. *Modern Language Journal, 77*, 490–500.

Koda, K. (1998). The role of phonemic awareness in L2 reading. *Second Language Research, 14*, 194–215.

Koda, K. (1999). Development of L2 intraword structural sensitivity and decoding skills. *Modern Language Journal, 83*, 51–64.

Legarretta, D. (1979). The effects of program models on language acquisition of Spanish speaking children. *TESOL Quarterly, 13*, 521–534.

Leong, C. K., Shek, K. T., Loh, K. Y., & Hau, K. T. (2008). Text comprehension in Chinese children: Relative contribution of verbal working memory, pseudoword reading, rapid automatized naming, and onset–rime phonological segmentation. *Journal of Educational Psychology, 100*(1), 135–149.

McBride-Chang, C., Wagner, R. K., Muse, A., Chow, B. W-Y., & Shu, H. (2005). The role of morphological awareness in children's vocabulary acquisition in English. *Applied Psycholinguistics, 26*, 415–435.

Muljani, M., Koda, K., & Moates, D. (1998). Development of L2 word recognition: A connectionist approach. *Applied Psycholinguistics, 19*, 99–114.

Park, E. C. (2008). Literacy experience in Korean: Implications for learning to read in a second language. In K. Koda & A. M. Zehler (Eds.), *Learning to read across languages: Cross-linguistic relationships in first and second language literacy development* (pp. 201–221). New York, NY: Routledge.

Perfetti, C. A. (2003). The universal grammar of reading. *Scientific Studies of Reading, 7*, 3–24.

Perfetti, C. A., & Dunlap, S. (2008). Learning to read: General principles and writing system variations. In K. Koda & A. M. Zehler (Eds.), *Learning to read across languages: Cross-linguistic relationships in first and second language literacy development* (pp. 13–38). New York, NY: Routledge.

Perfetti. C. A., & Liu, Y. (2005). Orthography to phonology and meaning: Comparisons across and within writing systems. *Reading and Writing, 18*, 193–210.

Perfetti, C. A., Zhang, S., & Berent, I. (1992). Reading in English and Chinese: Evidence for a "universal" phonological principle. In R. Frost & L. Katz (Eds.), *Orthography, phonology, morphology, and meaning* (pp. 227–248). Amsterdam, Netherlands: North-Holland.

Pressley, M., Almasi, J., Schuder, T., Bergman, J., & Kurita, J. A. (1994). Transactional instruction of comprehension strategies: The Montgomery County, Maryland, SAIL program. *Reading and Writing Quarterly: Overcoming Learning Difficulties, 10,* 5–19.

Ryan, A., & Meara, P. (1991). The case of invisible vowels: Arabic speakers reading English words. *Reading in a Foreign Language, 7,* 531–540.

Seidenberg, M. S., & McClelland, J. L. (1989). A distributed, developmental model of word recognition and naming. *Psychological Review, 96,* 523–568.

Shankweiler, D., & Liberman, I. Y. (1972). Misreading: A search for causes. In J. F. Kavanaugh & I. G. Mattingly (Eds.), *Language by eye and by ear* (pp. 293–317). Cambridge, MA: MIT Press.

Shu, H., & Anderson, R. C. (1997). Role of radical awareness in the character and word acquisition of Chinese children. *Reading Research Quarterly, 32,* 78–89.

Siegel, L. S., & Ryan, E. B. (1988). Development of grammatical sensitivity, phonological, and short-term memory in normally achieving and learning disabled children. *Developmental Psychology, 24,* 28–37.

Skutnabb-Kangas, T., & Toukomaa, P. (1976). *Teaching migrant children's mother tongue and learning the language of the host country in the context of the sociocultural situation of the migrant family.* Helsinki: Finnish National Commission for UNESCO.

Sohn, H. (1999). *The Korean language.* Cambridge, England: Cambridge University Press.

Sternberg, R. J. (1987). Most vocabulary is learned from context. In M. G. McKeown & M. E. Curtis (Eds.), *The nature of vocabulary acquisition* (pp. 89–103). Hillsdale, NJ: Lawrence Erlbaum.

Troike, R. C. (1978). Research evidence for the effectiveness of bilingual education. *NABE Journal, 3,* 13–24.

Wade-Woolley, L., & Geva, E. (2000) Processing novel phonemic contrasts in the acquisition of L2 word reading. *Scientific Studies of Reading, 4,* 295–311.

Wagner, R. K., Torgesen, J. K., & Rashotte, C. A. (1994). The development of reading-related phonological processing abilities: New evidence of bi-directional causality from a latent variable longitudinal study. *Developmental Psychology, 30,* 73–87.

Wang, M., & Koda, K. (2005). Commonalities and differences in word identification skills among learners of English as a second language. *Language Learning, 55,* 71–98.

Wang, M., Koda, K., & Perfetti, C. A. (2003). Alphabetic and non-alphabetic L1 effects in English semantic processing: A comparison of Korean and Chinese English L2 learners. *Cognition, 87,* 129–149.

Wang, M., Perfetti, C. A., & Liu, Y. (2005). Chinese–English biliteracy acquisition: Cross-language and writing system transfer. *Cognition, 97,* 67–88.

Zhang, H. C. (1994). Some studies on the recognition of Chinese characters. In Q. Jing, H. Zhang, & D. Peng (Eds.), *Information processing of Chinese language* (pp. 1–11). Beijing, China: Beijing Normal University.

Zhou, Y. G. (1978). To what degree are the "phonetics" of present-day Chinese characters still phonetic? *Zhougguo Yuwen, 146,* 172–177.

Ziegler, J. C., & Goswami, U. (2005). Reading acquisition, developmental dyslexia, and skilled reading across languages: A psycholinguistic grain size theory. *Psychological Bulletin, 131,* 3–29.

Ziegler, J. C., & Goswami, U. (2006). Becoming literate in different languages. Similar problems, different solutions. *Developmental Sciences, 9,* 425–436.

10   How to Collect and Analyze Qualitative Data

Debra A. Friedman

Background

The last 15 years or so have seen the emergence of "the social turn" (Block, 2003) in second language acquisition (SLA) research and the rise of theoretical and analytical frameworks such as sociocultural theory (e.g., Lantolf, 2000), community of practice (e.g., Haneda, 2006), second language (L2) socialization (e.g., Watson-Gegeo, 2004), and learner identity (e.g., Norton, 2000). While varying in terms of methods employed, these frameworks share a focus on language learning as a social process and an emphasis on the contexts of learning. This focus has been accompanied by increasing use of qualitative approaches as alternatives to quantitative and experimental research for the study of language teaching and learning. While a survey of articles appearing in major applied linguistics journals between 1991 and 1997 found that only 10% could be classified as qualitative (Lazaraton, 2000), in a later survey covering 1997 to 2006 the percentage had grown to 22% (Benson, Chik, Gao, Huang, & Wang, 2009). In addition, a number of journals, including *Applied Linguistics* (Zuengler & Mori, 2002; Talmy & Richards, 2011), the *Modern Language Journal* (Markee, 2004), and *Studies in Second Language Acquisition* (Gullberg & McCafferty, 2008), have published special issues featuring qualitative studies. It is therefore important to develop an understanding of what qualitative research is and what it can contribute to the field.

This chapter explores qualitative inquiry as an approach to research in SLA. It begins with an overview of the philosophical underpinnings, characteristics, and major traditions of qualitative research. It then proceeds step by step through the process of designing and conducting a qualitative research project, including theoretical and practical aspects of qualitative methods for data collection and analysis. The chapter concludes with projects and study questions for further discussion and application of the concepts and methods presented.

Research Methods in Second Language Acquisition: A Practical Guide, First Edition.
Edited by Alison Mackey and Susan M. Gass.
© 2012 Blackwell Publishing Ltd. Published 2012 by Blackwell Publishing Ltd.

What Is Qualitative Research?

Although we speak of qualitative *methods*, what distinguishes qualitative inquiry from quantitative or experimental research goes beyond procedures used to collect or analyze data. Qualitative research is a distinct approach to scholarly inquiry that may also entail a different set of beliefs regarding the nature of reality (*ontology*) and ways of knowing (*epistemology*). These sets of beliefs, or *paradigms*, can be classified and labeled in various ways; those summarized in table 10.1 are drawn from a typology proposed by Lincoln and Guba (2000, p. 168). The essential distinction is between *post-positivism* (historically the dominant paradigm in the sciences) and so-called *postmodern* paradigms such as *constructivism* and *critical theory*. The primary supposition underlying post-positivism is that a single reality exists and that the function of research is to uncover it (to the extent possible given the limitations of our methods). Constructivists and critical theorists, however, assume that there are multiple perspectives on reality and that the aim of research is to explore and document this diversity. While these distinctions may appear to be esoteric and abstract, the paradigm in which researchers are operating can have a profound effect on how they collect and interpret data.

Quantitative and qualitative approaches do not map neatly onto post-positivist (quantitative) and postmodern (qualitative) paradigms; qualitative research in SLA has been and continues to be conducted from a post-positivist perspective. Nevertheless, postmodern approaches have become increasingly common in the field, and both of these approaches will be incorporated into the discussions throughout this chapter.

Characteristics of Qualitative Research

The diversity of approaches, methods, techniques, and philosophical stances that constitute qualitative research eludes simple definition. The following list summarizes some major features; however, these features are not necessarily found in all types of qualitative research, and they are not necessarily absent from quantitative research (e.g., much classroom-based research, both quantitative and qualitative, may be said to be *naturalistic*).

- *Open inquiry*: Qualitative research is approached in the spirit of *open inquiry*. Rather than establishing a set of hypotheses to be tested and specific research questions to be investigated, researchers typically begin a project with an open mind about what they may find, allowing the focus of the research to emerge during data collection and analysis. There is also a tendency to avoid pre-set coding schemes to analyze data in favor of developing coding categories based on the data at hand.
- *Inductive*: Unlike *deductive* approaches, which are designed to test a theory or hypothesis, qualitative research is *inductive*; that is, it aims to build theory (i.e., explanations of a phenomenon) from the detailed study of particular instances.

Table 10.1   Ontology and epistemology in qualitative research (Lincoln & Guba, 2000).

	Post-positivism	*Constructivism*	*Critical theory*
Ontology	Reality exists, but we perceive it imperfectly and incompletely.	Reality is relative; it is co-constructed through social interaction.	Each person's reality is a product of social, political, and historical forces.
Epistemology	Objectivist; research findings are "probably" true.	Subjectivist; research findings are created through the interaction of researchers and their participants.	Subjectivist; research findings are mediated by social values.

- *Naturalistic*: Qualitative researchers do not attempt to control or manipulate variables by, for example, designing tasks for research participants to perform. Instead, the aim is to examine how participants think or behave in the course of their everyday activities. For example, a researcher may observe and record teachers and students as they participate in their routine activities in a classroom.
- *Descriptive and interpretive*: The aim of qualitative research is to generate *rich description* of the setting and phenomena being studied. Elements of rich description might include a detailed account of the setting, activities and behaviors of those acting in the setting, and research participants' perspectives on these activities and behaviors. The researcher then brings these elements together to *interpret* the significance of these phenomena within the larger issues that are the focus of the research (e.g., how the organization of classroom activities affects opportunities for learning).
- *Multiple perspectives*: As part of rich description, qualitative research incorporates both *emic* (insider) and *etic* (outsider) perspectives. Rather than privileging the researcher's interpretations, there is an effort to include multiple points of view and multiple voices through methods such as interviews with participants or close attention to how participants orient to an utterance or activity. Another technique is *member checking*, in which the researcher allows participants to read and comment upon the researcher's interpretations, with these comments subsequently being incorporated into the final analysis.
- *Cyclical*: We often envision research proceeding in a linear fashion: establish research questions, design a study, collect data, analyze them, and present findings. In qualitative research, however, analysis typically begins during data collection, and preliminary findings may shape subsequent data collection. For example, in the initial stages of a classroom observation a researcher may notice certain recurring patterns of interaction. The researcher may then devise interview questions to obtain participants' perspectives on these phenomena, and the results of these interviews may in turn redirect the focus of future observations.
- *Attention to context*: A basic tenet of qualitative research is that one cannot understand a phenomenon without attending to the context in which it occurs.

For most qualitative researchers, the term *context* refers not only to the general setting (e.g., English as a foreign language (EFL) context), but also to features of the research site. For example, a classroom-based study may incorporate micro-level features such as the physical layout of the classroom, materials and objects, lesson organization, activities, and teacher–student and student–student relationships, as well as macro-level features such as curriculum, institutional culture, or state education policy. The presence of the researcher may also be considered as part of the context and incorporated into the analysis.

- *Focus on the particular*: Qualitative research tends to operate on a small scale with the goal of providing a detailed and nuanced picture of individual settings, participants, or instances of interaction. It does not aim to generate statistically significant findings or report on research participants in the aggregate as representatives of a category (e.g., Japanese learners of English), but instead endeavors to bring out individual characteristics or differences and to explore these in depth.

Qualitative Research Traditions in Second Language Acquisition

Many qualitative researchers operate within a research *tradition*, that is, an established approach to research that utilizes a generally agreed upon methodology. Guidelines for qualitative research published in *TESOL Quarterly* (Chapelle & Duff, 2003) recognize three traditions: case study, (critical) ethnography, and conversation analysis, and Benson et al. (2009) confirm that these are among the most common qualitative research traditions represented in applied linguistics journals (although these researchers also found that many of the studies in their survey did not fit neatly into any established research tradition). The following presents a brief overview of two SLA research traditions: ethnography and conversation analysis (for case study, see Duff, this volume, chapter 6).

Ethnography

- *Background*: Ethnography studies the practices of human social and cultural groups. Developed in anthropology, it was taken up in the late 1960s by education researchers interested in examining the cultural organization of classrooms. A recent trend is *critical ethnography*, which seeks not only to describe but also to critique classroom practices by situating them within larger political contexts (e.g., state language policies).
- *Basic principles*: Ethnography can be distinguished from other types of observational research by its *longitudinal* research design. The aim of ethnography is to understand what a group's practices mean to its members, and developing this understanding requires immersion in the research setting for an extended period of time. At the same time, however, the researcher must maintain some degree of

detachment in order to observe, describe, and analyze community practices that members may take for granted. Ethnography also takes a *holistic* orientation that considers all aspects of the research context as potentially relevant to an analysis.

- *Data collection*: Primary methods of data collection include observation and field notes, interviews, collection of artifacts, and recordings of culturally salient interactions. In a classroom ethnography, a researcher would typically spend a semester or more at the research site (studies lasting one or more years are the norm), observe and record lessons on a regular basis, interview teachers, students, parents, and school staff, and collect materials such as textbooks, handouts, exams, and student records. *Participant observation*, in which the researcher participates directly in the community (e.g., as a teacher's aide), is often employed. Ethnographers might also conduct observations outside of the classroom (e.g., in students' homes or in the local community) in order to situate classroom practices within a larger context.
- *Data analysis*: Ethnographic analysis endeavors to build what anthropologist Clifford Geertz (1973) called *thick description*, that is, a description that is rich in detail and incorporates multiple perspectives. This is done through *triangulation*, in which multiple methods, theories, viewpoints, and sources of data are applied to the analysis. For example, a thick description of an instance of error correction might include a micro-analysis of the correction sequence itself, comparisons with other error-correction sequences, perspectives of teacher and students on corrective feedback, analysis of how the textbook presents rules of usage, and attitudes of the local community regarding correct language.

Conversation analysis

- *Background*: Conversation analysis (CA) originated in sociology and was developed in the late 1960s and early 1970s by Harvey Sacks, Emmanuel Schegloff, and Gail Jefferson to analyze talk in interaction as a primary locus of social organization (e.g., Sacks, Schegloff, & Jefferson, 1974). CA research can be divided into *pure CA*, which looks for instances of a phenomenon across different contexts in order to establish what interactional resources are available, and *applied CA*, which investigates how these resources are employed in specific instances of interaction (ten Have, 1999).
- *Basic principles*: CA researchers take a "radically emic" (Kasper, 2006, p. 84) approach to the analysis of talk; that is, they are interested in what the talk means to participants, not to the analyst. In practice, this means that the analyst does not apply pre-determined categories to the data, but instead examines how participants orient to the talk and to each other through the talk. For CA practitioners, *context* refers to the local interactional context, that is, the talk preceding and following a particular utterance. Features that are outside of the interaction itself (e.g., participants' gender or social relationships, the setting) are not taken into account unless the participants show through their talk that these features are relevant.

- *Data collection*: Data collection consists of audio or video recordings of naturally occurring (i.e., non-elicited) talk. Recordings are transcribed with a high level of detail on the assumption that even seemingly minor phenomena (e.g., an audible intake of breath) can be of import. Other forms of data collection, such as interviews or stimulated recalls, are not used in CA, as the analytical focus is not on participants' subsequent accounts of what they thought or intended at a given point in the interaction, but on how they visibly oriented to it at the time.
- *Data analysis*: The central unit of analysis is the *sequence*, a series of turns at talk that implement a course of action. A CA analysis focuses on how turns are constructed and how they build upon one another to construct sequences. Analyses based on video-recorded interactions also incorporate objects that participants orient to in the talk and paralinguistic features such as eye gaze and gestures.

Designing and Conducting a Qualitative Study

Purpose

Although qualitative inquiry embraces open inquiry, it has often been noted that beginning a study with an open mind does not mean beginning it with an empty mind. Like any research, qualitative inquiry has a purpose; before you can design a study, or even determine whether a qualitative approach is appropriate, you must first have some sense of why you are doing the research. A study that seeks to establish causal relationships between a given teaching practice and language acquisition or one that aims to generate results that can be generalized across a range of contexts is not a good candidate for a qualitative approach. However, an inquiry into how language is used in a particular setting or how individuals feel about their language learning experience might well be undertaken through a qualitative research design.

Qualitative research typically begins with a broadly worded research question or statement of purpose that is refined as the research progresses and findings begin to emerge. For example, an ethnography might propose to "investigate the integration of English language learners into mainstream classrooms," while a CA study might begin with an interest in "examining the sequential organization of talk in small group work." Such research questions provide a general framework, but make no a priori assumptions about what the researcher will find or what specific phenomena to focus on.

Sampling

Because of the volume of data generated and a preference for focusing on the particular, qualitative research generally involves small sample sizes (as few as one in a case study). In classroom-based qualitative research the sample may consist of one or more classrooms, or the researcher may select individual teachers or students as *focal participants*. Qualitative research may use either a *purposive sample*, in which the site and participants are selected in accordance with specified criteria, or a *sample of convenience*, in which they are selected because they are accessible to the researcher. For example, a researcher may choose to focus on Chinese learners of English because they are representative of the English as a second language (ESL) learner population in a particular setting (a purposive sample) or because the researcher speaks Chinese and is thus able to interview them in their first language (a sample of convenience). While either kind of sampling is acceptable, those who are concerned with the generalizability of their research should take care to select a representative sample (see Duff, 2006).

Data Collection

The most common methods of qualitative data collection in SLA research include observations, audio or video recordings, and various form of data elicitation, such as interviews, open-ended questionnaires, and journals. When selecting among these methods, the researcher must consider how much and what kind of data are needed to adequately address the research questions or purpose of the study and generate credible results. Qualitative research often draws upon multiple methods and sources of data in order to achieve triangulation and strengthen the validity of interpretations. For example, consider the inquiry into the integration of English language learners into mainstream classrooms that was proposed at the beginning of this section. If a researcher were to rely on interviews with teachers to investigate this question, the study might be open to challenges regarding the accuracy of the picture presented (i.e., do the teachers really do what they say they do?). To avoid this problem, the researcher could supplement teacher interviews with classroom observations and interviews with students that would bring together an etic (i.e., researcher) perspective with multiple emic perspectives, thus creating a more complete and multilayered description. In addition, researchers working within an established tradition should ensure that their methods are consistent with that tradition. For example, ethnography requires long-term engagement in the field, while CA does not employ interviews.

The discussion below addresses some major theoretical and practical issues related to these data collection methods. As only a brief description can be provided here, those intending to use any of these methods should first consult the list of resources provided near the end of this chapter under 'Further Reading'.

Observations

Observations can be broadly divided into two types. *Closed* or *structured observations* utilize pre-defined categories that may be spelled out in an *observation schedule*, a form that is filled out during the observation sessions (e.g., Spada & Lyster, 1997). In *open observations*, on the other hand, the researcher develops categories based on what emerges during the observation itself; rather than fill out a form, the observer takes detailed field notes. While open observation is more common in qualitative research, these approaches are not mutually exclusive; a researcher often begins with open observation and then moves to a more structured observation once a phenomenon has been identified as possible focus.

Learning to see as a researcher is a skill that takes time and practice to develop. Novice researchers often face two main obstacles when conducting open observations. The first is overcoming an initial impression that there is "nothing to see," a particularly pervasive problem in familiar settings (such as classrooms). The second problem is exactly the opposite; there is too much to see. The researcher tries to record everything, but finds this to be impossible and ends up feeling overwhelmed. A number of checklists have been devised to guide researchers through the initial stages of open observation (e.g., Spradley, 1980; Richards, 2003); these checklists include features such as the following:

1. *Setting*: What does the physical space look like? What objects are there? Are there designated areas for specific activities?
2. *People* (or *actors*): Who uses the space? How do they use it? How does the space facilitate or constrain their actions? How do they interact with each other?
3. *Behavior*: How do people behave in the space? Are there rules governing behavior (e.g., turn-taking in a classroom)? What routine activities take place?

Another issue is the so-called *observer's paradox*, a term coined by sociolinguist William Labov (1972), which proposes that the presence of an observer changes the behavior of those being observed. One's perspective on the observer's paradox depends on the paradigm in which one is working. For post-positivists, it reflects an assumption that reality exists when we are not there to observe it. While this problem can never be eliminated entirely, it might be mitigated over time as participants become used to the researcher's presence. For constructivists, on the other hand, the observer is one more feature of the context to be taken into account in an analysis.

Audio and video recordings

Advances in technology have made it easier to make recordings of naturally occurring interactions as part of data collection. While some advocate audio recording as less intrusive (and thus less likely to generate the observer's paradox), a strong case can be made for video recording, as it facilitates identification of speakers (an issue when recording in settings such as classrooms that involve multiple participants) and allows for incorporation of non-verbal features such as eye gaze and gestures into an analysis.

Elicited data

Unlike the data collection methods described above, data elicitation involves use of an instrument (e.g., interview questions, a questionnaire, a prompt) to generate data. Data elicitation methods play a major role in case studies, ethnographies, and other qualitative classroom-based research as well as in mixed-methods studies. Study box 10.1 gives an example of research using elicited data.

The most common data elicitation method is interviews, which may be *structured*, *semi-structured*, or *unstructured*. In structured interviews, the same set of questions is asked of all participants in order to permit cross-case comparisons. At the opposite end of the spectrum, unstructured interviews do not use pre-planned questions, but resemble a conversation in which the researcher proposes a topic that is explored with the interviewee in depth. Most qualitative interviews fall between these two extremes and follow a semi-structured format. In semi-structured interviews the researcher prepares a set of questions (or *interview guide*) as the basis for the interviews; however, he or she may deviate from the guide in order to pursue topics that arise during the course of the interview. As a result, different questions may be asked of each interviewee.

When preparing an interview guide the first consideration is determining the focus of the interview and the topics to be investigated. The interviewer then writes several questions for each topic, following these general guidelines:

1. Minimize use of *closed ended* (i.e., yes/no) questions in favor of *open-ended* questions. For example, rather than asking, "Do you like the textbook?" one might ask, "What do you think of the textbook?"
2. Avoid *leading questions*, that is, questions that lead the interviewee to a particular kind of response. For example, asking, "What is stressful about speaking English?" imposes a point of view (i.e., that speaking English is stressful) upon the interviewee and asks him or her to comment on it. A preferable approach would be to begin with a question such as, "How do you feel when speaking English?" If the interviewee brings up the topic of stress, the interviewer can follow up by asking why speaking English is stressful.
3. Avoid *complex questions* that ask about several things at once, for example, "What do you think of the textbook and if you don't like it how would you improve it?" Such questions are difficult to answer, as it is not clear what the interviewee should focus on.
4. Consider whether your questions will be *comprehensible* to interviewees. This is important not only when interviewing people in their L2; for example, an ESL teacher might not necessarily understand a question such as "How often do you use reactive focus on form?"

Piloting the interview guide (i.e., using it to conduct practice interviews) is also recommended, as it enables the researcher to identify potential problems and to revise the questions as needed before beginning data collection.

When conducting a semi-structured interview one should treat the interview guide as just that – a guide, not a checklist to be strictly followed. Depending on how the interview develops, the interviewer might change the order of questions, add further questions to clarify, follow up, or probe more deeply into a response, or drop some questions entirely. As the purpose of an interview is to explore a topic from the interviewee's perspective, the interviewer must take care not to dominate.

Study Box 10.1

Gan, Z., Humphreys, G., & Hamp-Lyons, L. (2004). Understanding successful and unsuccessful EFL students in Chinese universities. *Modern Language Journal, 88*, 229–244.

Background

This study followed up on a large-scale quantitative survey of Chinese university students that examined links between motivations, self-directed strategies for learning English, and learning outcomes. It aimed to delve more deeply into these issues among a smaller group of students and to investigate the variation found in the quantitative study.

Research questions

- Are there any typical attitudinal differences between successful and unsuccessful tertiary-level Chinese EFL students?
- What strategies do they report using in their English learning?
- How are they typically motivated into carrying out their English learning?

Method

Participants were 18 Chinese university English language learners (9 "successful" and 9 "unsuccessful"). Data were collected through interviews (two per student), diaries in which participants reflected on their language learning, and follow-up emails. Results from analyzing the first interview and diaries determined questions for the second interview. Grounded theory was used to analyze the data.

Results

Successful and unsuccessful language learners differed in terms of how they conceptualized language learning, attitudes toward instruction, use of out-of-class opportunities to practice English, perceptions of control over their learning, and motivation. The authors conclude that interaction among these factors accounts for different outcomes and propose that research on learner differences take a more holistic approach.

The interviewee should do most of the talking; the role of the interviewer is to pose questions to stimulate reflection on the topic and to encourage further talk by providing supportive feedback.

Interviews may also incorporate *stimulated recall*; for example, a researcher might play a recording involving the interviewee and ask him or her to stop the tape and comment at any point. Alternatively, the researcher may select specific segments of the recording and ask the interviewee some general questions (e.g., "What is happening here?" or "What were you thinking at this point?") to prompt a response. For most qualitative researchers the purpose of a stimulated recall is not to determine participants' thought processes, but to allow participants to provide interpretations of their own or others' actions. These interpretations are not taken as fact, but as one of many possible perspectives.

Open-ended questionnaires may be seen as variations on the interview theme. Like interviews, they consist of questions, but answers are provided in writing. The advantages of questionnaires are that they are easier to administer (especially when done online), allow participants more time to formulate responses, and do not need to be transcribed. On the other hand, the researcher cannot follow up, clarify, or probe answers, and participants' responses may be limited. The choice between interviews or questionnaires depends on the researcher's purpose; questionnaires work well to survey opinions, but for more in-depth explorations of a topic interviews are preferred.

Journals or diaries involve the least amount of researcher control; the usual procedure is to provide general instructions (e.g., "record situations in which you use English outside of class"), leaving the specific content up to the participant. Journals can be a useful means of documenting participants' activities when a researcher is not present to observe them and can also be used to prompt participants to reflect on their experiences or feelings. One must always remember, however, that such data are invariably selective and subjective; that is, they represent a participant's view of an event, not the event itself.

Transcription

Audio- or video-recorded data are transformed into written documents, or *transcripts*. There are a number of established transcription conventions in circulation, many of which are based on those developed in CA (e.g., Atkinson & Heritage, 1984; Markee & Kasper, 2004). These offer a range of symbols that can be used to represent features of talk such intonation, word stress, sound stretches, overlapping talk, relative pitch and loudness, etc.

Transcription involves numerous decisions regarding what will be included on the transcript and how these elements will be rendered on the page; for example:

1. How do you transcribe speech? Do you use standard orthography or do you attempt to reflect pronunciation by using a phonetic alphabet or non-standard spelling (e.g., *becuz* for *because*)?
2. Do you include features of imperfect speech, such as hesitation markers (*er, uh*), cut-offs and restarts (e.g., "I thi- I thought …"), pauses, or fillers (e.g., "I was *like, you know*, real upset about it")?
3. Do you include non-verbal features (e.g., eye gaze, gestures)? If so, how do you describe them?

Answers to these questions depend on research purpose, tradition, and philosophical or ideological stance (Green, Franquiz, & Dixon, 1997). For example, an interview will usually be transcribed at a lower level of detail than a segment of classroom interaction, as the researcher is likely to be more interested in what the interviewee said than how he or she said it. On the other hand, a CA analyst will endeavor to incorporate as many features of the talk as possible into the transcript on the assumption that "nothing that occurs in interaction can be ruled out, *a priori*, as random, insignificant, or irrelevant" (Atkinson & Heritage, 1984, p. 4). A transcript can therefore never be objective, but must be viewed as a product of multiple subjective decisions. As these decisions can subsequently shape the analysis, transcribers should be aware of what decisions they are making and why they are making them.

Qualitative analysis

Analysis in qualitative research is not a stage of research, but begins during data collection and continues throughout the research process. Richards (2003, p. 272) notes a number of "activities" that are involved in this process, including (a) collecting data, (b) thinking about how the data relate to the research purpose, (c) categorizing the data, (d) reflecting on the process of analysis, (e) organizing the data to look for patterns and themes, (f) connecting emergent themes to larger concepts and theories, and (g) collecting more data. Along the way, researchers write *analytical memos* or keep a *research diary* to record observations, reflections, preliminary interpretations, questions for further exploration, etc.

Content analysis

One approach to qualitative data analysis is *content analysis*, which involves coding data in a systematic way in order to discover patterns and develop well-grounded interpretations. One of the most widely used approaches to content analysis is *grounded theory*, which was developed by social scientists Glaser and Strauss (1967) to strengthen the validity and reliability of qualitative analysis (see also Strauss & Corbin, 1998). As its name implies, grounded theory eschews imposing existing theory upon data in favor of generating theory that is grounded in data. Coding proceeds in three stages:

1. *initial coding* (or *open coding*), in which the researcher goes through a subset of the data line by line and assigns labels or codes that designate actions, events, or topics;
2. *axial coding*, which involves finding patterns in the data by comparing coding categories within and across cases (e.g., different accounts of the same incident by different participants, different points in time for a single participant), relating larger categories to subcategories, and establishing connections between categories;
3. *selective coding* (or *focused coding*), in which selected codes from the initial coding (e.g., the most frequent) are applied to the rest of the dataset and are further developed or refined.

Throughout this process the researcher evaluates the coding categories based on (a) how well they fit the data, (b) whether they provide an explanation for the phenomenon being studied, (c) relevance to the real-world issues or problems that are the focus of the research, and (d) how easily the categories may be modified as further data are collected. Grounded theory also involves *theoretical sampling*, that is, collecting additional data to fill in gaps identified during analysis. When all new data fit into existing categories, the data are said to have achieved *saturation* and the process ends.

In recent years researchers have increasingly turned to various software packages designed to facilitate the coding process. Software allows researchers to enter codes into a database for easy sorting and retrieval, link data across cases, and create graphic displays. More on coding in qualitative analysis, including a detailed account of using qualitative data analysis software, can be found in Baralt (this volume, chapter 12).

Discourse analysis

An alternative approach to content analysis is *discourse analysis*, a loosely defined term that can refer to any procedure in which the analyst focuses on linguistic or structural features rather than content. Some researchers adopt an established approach to discourse analysis, such as *interactional sociolinguistics*, *ethnography of communication*, *critical discourse analysis*, *narrative analysis*, or CA, each of which comes with its own theoretical underpinnings, analytical apparatus, and ideological stance (see Schiffrin, 1994, for an overview). Others, however, simply state that they are doing discourse analysis, without specifying any particular approach.

Analyzing interaction begins with a few basic steps (adapted from Richards, 2003, pp. 184–188):

1. Review the recording. Transcripts are useful tools; however, we analyze data, not transcripts. Reviewing recordings before beginning analysis often reveals details that were missed or inaccurately rendered during transcription and re-engages the researcher with the original data.
2. Establish a general picture. Take note of major features such as (a) setting, (b) participants and their relationships, (c) activities in which participants are engaged, and (d) what each participant is doing.
3. Focus on structural features. Look at how the interaction is constructed. Does one person dominate? How do participants get a chance to take the floor? How do turns relate to each other? What do objects or non-verbal features contribute to the interaction?
4. Begin to develop an analysis by identifying patterns, recurrent features, or other notable aspects of the interaction.

How the analysis develops beyond this preliminary stage will depend on the purpose of the research and the phenomena that have been selected as the primary foci (see study box 10.2).

Study Box 10.2

Cekaite, A. (2007). A child's development of interactional competence in a Swedish L2 classroom. *Modern Language Journal, 91,* 45–62.

Background

This case study draws from a larger ethnographic study of immigrant children in a Swedish immersion classroom. Using a language socialization framework, it focuses on one child's development of interactional competence, with a focus on turn-taking.

Research question

- How does a child's participation in classroom activities change as she becomes increasingly competent in multiparty classroom talk?

Method

The focal child was a 7-year-old Kurdish girl in a "reception classroom" for immigrant children in Sweden. Primary data collection comprised recordings of children's interactions in class and on the playground at three points during the school year (total 90 hours). The micro-analysis of the data draws upon the conversation analytic literature on turn-taking.

Results

Development passed through three stages: the "silent child," with limited linguistic resources in Swedish; the "noisy child," with increasing linguistic skills but limited knowledge of appropriate participation; and the "skillful student," who demonstrated ability to gain a turn-at-talk in an appropriate manner. The results demonstrate the benefits of examining learner identities and participation over time.

Like much else in qualitative research, choosing between content analysis and discourse analysis depends on the researcher's purpose and theoretical framework. For example, while interview data are typically analyzed using content analysis, some researchers have advocated treating interviews as "meaning-making occasions" and analyzing not only *what* interviewees say, but also *how* the process of meaning making develops (Holstein & Gubrium, 2002, p. 113). A researcher adopting this perspective would apply the tools of discourse analysis to the interview data to examine issues such as (a) how the interviewer and interviewee co-construct the interview, (b) how the interviewee presents himself or herself (e.g., as a good teacher), and (c) how the interviewer's identity (e.g., as a person with higher status than the interviewee) might affect the interview (Talmy, 2010; Talmy & Richards, 2011; see also Pavlenko, 2007).

Evaluation

As qualitative analysis inevitably involves interpretation, the question arises as to how well the researcher's interpretations represent the data. Qualitative researchers have responded to this question in different ways. One approach is to take the established criteria of validity and reliability and adapt them to qualitative research. For example, to enhance reliability when coding qualitative data one can use multiple raters, each of whom codes the data separately. The coding schemes are then compared, and differences are negotiated until a consensus is achieved. Similarly, validity can be enhanced through careful sampling and consideration of alternative interpretations.

However, some researchers view this approach as grounded in post-positivism and assert that qualitative research, especially when done within postmodern paradigms, requires a separate set of criteria (Edge & Richards, 1998; Lazaraton, 2003). One alternative framework proposes that *reliability* and *internal validity* be reconceptualized as *dependability* and *credibility*, respectively. For example, rather than use multiple raters, a researcher might aim for dependability by documenting methodology in detail and providing multiple examples of the phenomena being analyzed (i.e., rich description) to allow readers of the research to evaluate the robustness of the coding categories. Methods of achieving credibility (i.e., plausible interpretations of the data) can vary across different research traditions, but may include prolonged engagement, triangulation, and thick description (for ethnography) or rigorous application of analytical method (for CA). Another alternative standard is *authenticity* (e.g., Lincoln & Guba, 2000), which specifies that researchers be honest (both to readers and to themselves) regarding their value systems, possible biases, and stances and how these might affect what they see and how they interpret what they see.

Regardless of the criteria being used, establishing the quality of research is not simply a matter of following a checklist; the fact that there are multiple sources of data or multiple raters does not, in itself, serve to validate claims based on those data. As Edge and Richards (1998, p. 342) point out, the crucial question is "What warrant do you have for the statements that you make?" Qualitative researchers must always be careful not to read more into the data than the data can support; claims that are not firmly grounded are speculation, not analysis.

Project Ideas and Resources

1. Using the guidelines on p. 188, write five questions on a topic of interest and pilot the interview guide by conducting a semi-structured interview with someone you know. After the interview, evaluate how it went. Which questions

worked well and which did not? Were you satisfied with the results? If any problems arose, what was the cause? How would you change the interview guide or your interviewing style in response to these problems?

2.   Select a public site (e.g., a café, library, waiting room) and go there several times to observe for about 15 minutes each time. During your observations take field notes based on the checklist on p. 187. After the final observation, review the field notes and reflect on the experience, considering (a) anything interesting that you observed, (b) issues that arose during the observations, and (c) aspects of your observation skills that you would like to work on.

3.   With permission, record a short piece of interaction (classroom talk, a conversation, etc.). Select a 5-minute segment and transcribe it using transcription conventions of your choice. Compare your transcript with a classmate's and discuss the following questions:

(a)   What differences are there between the transcripts? What accounts for these differences?
(b)   How did you decide what to include in your transcript and what to leave out?
(c)   How did you transcribe features such as intonation, pauses, gestures, etc.?
(d)   What was the most challenging aspect of transcription?

4.   Analyze your transcript from question 3, using either content analysis (p. 191–2) or discourse analysis (p. 192). In your analysis you may consider features such as (a) turn-taking, (b) patterns and recurrent features, (c) unusual occurrences and how they are dealt with, and/or (d) use of gesture.

Further Reading

Handbooks

Holliday, A. (2002). *Doing and writing qualitative research*. London, England: SAGE.
Richards, K. (2003). *Qualitative inquiry in TESOL*. New York, NY: Palgrave Macmillan.

Ethnography

Garcez, P. M. (2008). Microethnography in the classroom. In K. A. King & N. H. Hornberger (Eds.), *Encyclopedia of language and education. Vol. 10: Research methods in language and education* (2nd ed., 257–271). New York, NY: Springer.
Geertz, C. (1973). Thick description: Toward an interpretive theory of culture. In C. Geertz, *Interpretation of cultures* (pp. 4–30). New York, NY: Basic Books.
Toohey, K. (2008). Ethnography and language education. In K. A. King & N. H. Hornberger (Eds.), *Encyclopedia of language and education. Vol. 1: Research methods in language and education* (2nd ed., pp. 177–187). New York, NY: Springer.
Watson-Gegeo, K. A. (1988). Ethnography in ESL: Defining the essentials. *TESOL Quarterly*, 22, 575–592.

Conversation analysis

Kasper, G. (2006). Beyond repair: Conversation analysis as an approach to SLA. *AILA Review*, *19*, 83–99.

Markee, N. (2000). *Conversation analysis*. Mahwah, NJ: Lawrence Erlbaum.

Sacks, H., Schegloff, E. A., & Jefferson, G. (1974). A simplest systematics for the organization of turn-taking for conversation. *Language*, *50*, 696–735.

Schegloff, E. A., Koshik, I., Jacoby, S., & Olsher, D. (2002). Conversation analysis and applied linguistics. *Annual Review of Applied Linguistics*, *22*, 3–31.

ten Have, P. (1999). *Doing conversation analysis: A practical guide*. London, England: SAGE.

Observation

Spada, N., & Lyster, R. (1997). Macroscopic and microscopic views of L2 classrooms. *TESOL Quarterly*, *31*, 787–795.

Spradley, J. P. (1980). *Participant observation*. New York, NY: Holt Rinehart & Winston.

van Lier, L. (1997). Observation from an ecological perspective. *TESOL Quarterly*, *31*, 783–787.

Interviewing

Block, D. (2000). Problematizing interview data: Voices in the mind's machine? *TESOL Quarterly*, *34*, 757–763.

Holstein, J. A., & Gubrium, J. (2002). Active interviewing. In D. Weinberg (Ed.), *Qualitative research methods* (pp. 112–126). Oxford, England: Blackwell.

Talmy, S. (2010). Qualitative interviews in applied linguistics: From research instrument to social practice. *Annual Review of Applied Linguistics*, *30*, 128–148.

Talmy, S., & Richards, K. (Eds.). (2011). Qualitative interviews in applied linguistics: Discursive perspectives [Special issue]. *Applied Linguistics*, *32*(1).

Transcription

Atkinson, J. M., & Heritage, J. (1984). Introduction. In J. M. Atkinson & J. Heritage (Eds.), *Structures of social action* (pp. 1–15). Cambridge, England: Cambridge University Press.

Green, J., Franquiz, M., & Dixon C. (1997). The myth of the objective transcript: Transcribing as a situated act. *TESOL Quarterly*, *31*, 172–176.

Markee, N., & Kasper, G. (2004). Classroom talks: An introduction. *Modern Language Journal*, *88*, 491–500.

Content analysis and grounded theory

Berg, B. L. (2002). An introduction to content analysis. In B. L. Berg, *Qualitative research methods for the social sciences* (pp. 174–199). Boston, MA: Allyn & Bacon.

Glaser, B. G., & Strauss, A. L. (1967). *The discovery of grounded theory: Strategies for qualitative research*. New York, NY: Aldine.

Strauss, A. L., & Corbin, J. (1998). *Basics of qualitative research: Technique and procedures for producing grounded theory* (2nd ed.). London, England: SAGE.

Discourse analysis

Kumaravadivelu, B. (1999). Critical classroom discourse analysis. *TESOL Quarterly, 33,* 453–484.

Martin-Jones, M., de Mejia, A. M., & Hornberger, N. (Eds.). (2008). *Encyclopedia of language and education. Vol. 10: Discourse and education* (2nd ed.). New York, NY: Springer.

Pavlenko, A. (2007). Autobiographic narratives as data in applied linguistics. *Applied Linguistics, 28,* 163–188.

Schiffrin, D. (1994). *Approaches to discourse*. Oxford, England: Blackwell.

Zuengler, J., & Mori, J. (Eds.). (2002). Microanalyses of classroom discourse: A critical consideration of method [Special issue]. *Applied Linguistics, 23*(3).

Evaluating qualitative research

Chapelle, C. A., & Duff, P. A. (Eds.). (2003). Some guidelines for conducting quantitative and qualitative research in TESOL. *TESOL Quarterly, 37,* 163–178.

Duff, P. (2006). Beyond generalizability: Contextualization, complexity, and credibility in applied linguistics research. In M. Chalhoub-Deville, C. A. Chapelle, & P. Duff (Eds.), *Inference and generalizability in applied linguistics* (pp. 65–95). Amsterdam, Netherlands: John Benjamins.

Edge, J., & Richards, K. (1998). May I see your warrant please? Justifying outcomes in qualitative research. *Applied Linguistics, 19,* 334–356.

Lazaraton, A. (2003). Evaluative criteria for qualitative research in applied linguistics: Whose criteria and whose research? *Modern Language Journal, 87,* 1–12.

Lincoln, Y. S., & Guba, E. G. (2000). Paradigmatic controversies, contradictions, and emerging confluences. In N. K. Denzin & Y. S. Lincoln (Eds.), *Handbook of qualitative research* (2nd ed., pp. 163–188). Thousand Oaks, CA: SAGE.

Study Questions

1. Look over the following research questions and discuss (i) their suitability for a qualitative research design, (ii) what qualitative methods might be used to investigate them, and (iii) potential limitations of these methods.

   (a) How does participation on an online social network affect English language learning?

(b) How do L2 learners' motivations change over time?

(c) What is the relationship between pre-task planning and performance of the task in small group work in an L2 classroom?

2. The following comes from an interview with a Ukrainian man (D. Friedman, unpublished data):

> When I was fifteen I moved to [city] and I entered the technical school. And you know, it was in 1994. And at that time, we still had this prejudice in the cities. If you speak Ukrainian, that means you're from the village, from the country. And you know, I saw that, I experienced that, where everyone who came from the country, they would try to speak Russian, you know, to keep popular there. And I felt the pressure as well and I tried to speak Russian. But I never liked it. And so I just switched back to Ukrainian. And I didn't care about what people said about me.

Do some initial coding for this excerpt using the procedures outlined on p. 191 to identify major categories. Compare your coding with a classmate's and discuss similarities and differences.

3. The following excerpt is the same as in question 2, but includes more of the interactional context. (I = Interviewer, R = Interviewee):

I: And you went to school in the village there? Ukrainian school I would assume, in the village

R: Yeah, um-hum

I: Okay. Um

R: Well, maybe I should also tell it might be interesting for you

I: Okay

R: When I was fifteen I ah moved to [city]

I: Um-hum

R: And I entered the technical school

I: Um-hum

R: And you know, it was in 1994 and at that time we still had this prejudice in the cities. If you speak Ukrainian, that means you're from the village

I: Yeah

R: from the country

I: Yeah

R: And you know, I saw that, I experienced that, where everyone who came from the country, they would try to speak Russian

I: Yeah

R: you know, to keep popular there. And I felt the pressure as well

I: Um-hum

R: and I tried to speak Russian. But I I never liked it. And so, I just switched back to Ukrainian.

I: Um-hum

R: and I didn't care about what people said about me.

Using discourse analysis, analyze this excerpt as a "meaning-making occasion" (see p. 193), taking into account factors such as (a) how the interviewee is presenting himself and (b) how the interviewer affects the responses. Point to specific features of the interaction to support your analysis.

4. Discuss the major distinctions between post-positivist and postmodern research paradigms. How might a researcher working in each of these paradigms analyze and interpret the excerpt in question 3?

5. Read one of the research articles summarized in the study boxes in this chapter and critique it based on the following criteria:

    (a) whether the methods used to collect and analyze the data were appropriate to address the purpose of the study and/or the research questions that the study was designed to answer;
    (b) how well the chosen methods were employed; and
    (c) how well the researcher dealt with issues of validity (credibility) and relia-bility (dependability).

References

Atkinson, J. M., & Heritage, J. (1984). Introduction. In J. M. Atkinson & J. Heritage (Eds.), *Structures of social action* (pp. 1–15). Cambridge, England: Cambridge University Press.

Benson, P., Chik, A., Gao, X., Huang, J., & Wang, W. (2009). Qualitative research in language teaching and learning journals, 1997–2006. *Modern Language Journal, 93*, 79–90.

Block, D. (2003). *The social turn in second language acquisition.* Edinburgh, Scotland: Edinburgh University Press.

Cekaite, A. (2007). A child's development of interactional competence in a Swedish L2 class-room. *Modern Language Journal, 91*, 45–62.

Chapelle, C. A., & Duff, P. A. (Eds.). (2003). Some guidelines for conducting quantitative and qualitative research in TESOL. *TESOL Quarterly, 37*, 163–178.

Duff, P. (2006). Beyond generalizability: Contextualization, complexity, and credibility in applied linguistics research. In M. Chalhoub-Deville, C. A. Chapelle, & P. Duff (Eds.), *Inference and generalizability in applied linguistics* (pp. 65–95). Amsterdam, Netherlands: John Benjamins.

Edge, J., & Richards, K. (1998). May I see your warrant please? Justifying outcomes in quali-tative research. *Applied Linguistics, 19*, 334–356.

Gan, Z., Humphreys, G., & Hamp-Lyons, L. (2004). Understanding successful and unsuccess-ful EFL students in Chinese universities. *Modern Language Journal, 88*, 229–244.

Geertz, C. (1973). Thick description: Toward an interpretive theory of culture. In C. Geertz, *Interpretation of cultures* (pp. 4–30). New York, NY: Basic Books.

Glaser, B. G., & Strauss, A. L. (1967). *The discovery of grounded theory: Strategies for qualita-tive research.* New York, NY: Aldine.

Green, J., Franquiz, M., & Dixon C. (1997). The myth of the objective transcript: Transcribing as a situated act. *TESOL Quarterly, 31*, 172–176.

Gullberg, M., & McCafferty, S. G. (Eds.). (2008). Gesture and SLA: Toward an integrated approach [Special issue]. *Studies in Second Language Acquisition, 30*(2).

Haneda, M. (2006). Classrooms as communities of practice: A reevaluation. *TESOL Quarterly, 40*, 807–817.

Holstein, J. A., & Gubrium, J. (2002). Active interviewing. In D. Weinberg (Ed.), *Qualitative research methods* (pp. 112–126). Oxford, England: Blackwell.

Kasper, G. (2006). Beyond repair: Conversation analysis as an approach to SLA. *AILA Review, 19*, 83–99.

Labov, W. (1972). *Sociolinguistic patterns*. Philadelphia: University of Pennsylvania Press.

Lantolf, J. P. (2000). *Sociocultural theory and second language learning*. Oxford, England: Oxford University Press.

Lazaraton, A. (2000). Current trends in research methodology and statistics in applied linguistics. *TESOL Quarterly, 34*, 175–181.

Lazaraton, A. (2003). Evaluative criteria for qualitative research in applied linguistics: Whose criteria and whose research? *Modern Language Journal, 87*, 1–12.

Lincoln, Y. S., & Guba, E. G. (2000). Paradigmatic controversies, contradictions, and emerging confluences. In N. K. Denzin & Y. S. Lincoln (Eds.), *Handbook of qualitative research* (2nd ed., pp. 163–188). Thousand Oaks, CA: SAGE.

Markee, N. (Ed.). (2004). Classroom talks [Special issue]. *Modern Language Journal, 88*(4).

Markee, N., & Kasper, G. (2004). Classroom talks: An introduction. *Modern Language Journal, 88*, 491–500.

Norton, B. (2000). *Identity and language learning: Gender, ethnicity and educational change*. Harlow, England: Longman.

Pavlenko, A. (2007). Autobiographic narratives as data in applied linguistics. *Applied Linguistics, 28*, 163–188.

Richards, K. (2003). *Qualitative inquiry in TESOL*. New York, NY: Palgrave Macmillan.

Sacks, H., Schegloff, E. A., & Jefferson, G. (1974). A simplest systematics for the organization of turn-taking for conversation. *Language, 50*, 696–735.

Schiffrin, D. (1994). *Approaches to discourse*. Oxford, England: Blackwell.

Spada, N., & Lyster, R. (1997). Macroscopic and microscopic views of L2 classrooms. *TESOL Quarterly, 31*, 787–795.

Spradley, J. P. (1980). *Participant observation*. New York, NY: Holt Rinehart & Winston.

Strauss, A. L., & Corbin, J. (1998). *Basics of qualitative research: Technique and procedures for producing grounded theory* (2nd ed.). London, England: SAGE.

Talmy, S. (2010). Qualitative interviews in applied linguistics: From research instrument to social practice. *Annual Review of Applied Linguistics, 30*, 128–148.

Talmy, S., & Richards, K. (Eds.). (2011). Qualitative interviews in applied linguistics: Discursive perspectives [Special issue]. *Applied Linguistics, 32*(1).

ten Have, P. (1999). *Doing conversation analysis: A practical guide*. London, England: Sage.

Watson-Gegeo, K. A. (2004). Mind, language, and epistemology: Toward a language socialization paradigm for SLA. *Modern Language Journal, 88*, 31–350.

Zuengler, J., & Mori, J. (Eds.). (2002). Microanalyses of classroom discourse: A critical consideration of method [Special issue]. *Applied Linguistics, 23*(3).

Part II   Data Coding, Analysis, and Replication

11   Coding Second Language Data Validly and Reliably

Andrea Révész

Background

Data coding is a critical aspect across all areas of second language acquisition (SLA) research. Once data have been collected, it is the first major step in the measurement process. It involves organizing and classifying raw data into categories for the purpose of further analysis and interpretation. For some research, coding is quite straightforward and unambiguous. In other research, coding may be a more complex endeavor, constituting one of the most time-consuming activities in the research project. Regardless of the nature of classification, a central goal is to retain validity and reliability in the coding procedure. The aims of this chapter are to consider the concepts of validity and reliability in relation to coding, to review the various steps involved in coding, and to discuss strategies that can help to increase its validity and reliability. The focus here will be on relatively top-down, theory- and instrument-driven coding methods; qualitative coding, which emerges bottom-up from the data, is the topic of chapter 12.

Validity and Reliability in Coding

In general, *validity* refers to the appropriateness of a procedure for measuring the underlying construct a study intends to investigate. In SLA research, one often needs to measure hypothetical constructs such as acquisition, knowledge, or aptitude – concepts which originate from theory or are inferred from observation but cannot be directly measured. To be measured, constructs need to be operationalized, that is, to be taken from the theoretical level to a more concrete, empirical one. *Validity*

Research Methods in Second Language Acquisition: A Practical Guide, First Edition.
Edited by Alison Mackey and Susan M. Gass.
© 2012 Blackwell Publishing Ltd. Published 2012 by Blackwell Publishing Ltd.

essentially refers to how appropriately and precisely an operationalization matches a construct's theoretical definition. In the context of coding, validity is concerned with the degree to which the coding categories and procedures allow for accurate and meaningful interpretations to be made about the construct in question.

There are two major threats that can jeopardize validity in coding: construct underrepresentation and construct-irrelevant variance (Messick, 1995; Norris & Ortega, 2003). *Construct underrepresentation* occurs when an assessment "fails to capture important aspects of the construct" as a result of being too limited in scope and failing to encapsulate some relevant dimensions associated with its proposed conceptual domain (American Educational Research Association, American Psychological Association, & National Council on Measurement in Education, 1999, p. 10). From the area of interlanguage analysis, an oft-cited example is the use of target-like accuracy scores as a sole criterion for assessing interlanguage development. This approach disregards evidence of improvement which does not yet reach the full target variant (e.g., *bringed*) and, as such, is not sufficient for measuring incremental progress. In this case, construct underrepresentation could be avoided by giving partial credit for interlanguage constructions. *Construct-irrelevant variance* refers to the extent to which assessments are systematically influenced by variables that are not pertinent to the intended construct. That is, the measurement is too broad and includes extraneous factors (Messick, 1995). For example, if a rater, when asked to judge grammatical accuracy, consistently gave higher scores to second language (L2) learners with less foreign-sounding accents, construct-irrelevant variance would arise. This rater's classification would lead to higher than deserved scores for less accented individuals, systematically affecting the validity of interpretations made about the learners' grammatical accuracy level.

Whereas construct underrepresentation and construct-irrelevant variance involve systematic or consistent problems in the fit between theory and coding practices, *reliability* is concerned with random or inconsistent errors of measurement. In the case of coding, reliability involves the extent to which data are categorized consistently. It deals with the question "If a particular dataset were coded repeatedly using the same procedure, would one consistently arrive at the same categorizations?" If a coding protocol is reliable, then another coder following the same procedure, or the same coder categorizing the data on another occasion, would code in a nearly identical way. Reliability in coding is a prerequisite for validity. If a coding process is significantly affected by random errors of measurement, it follows that it will not be accurate or meaningful, and hence will not allow for valid interpretations to be made. Simply put, coding can be reliable without being valid (as in the example of target-like accuracy scoring above), but cannot be valid without being reliable.

There are numerous sources of error, both systematic and random, that can endanger validity and reliability in the coding process. In addition to those already discussed, they include ambiguity in the coding scheme; inadequate coder expertise or training; coder bias, fatigue, or boredom; coder drift; and even simple mistakes such as typing errors. Although it is almost impossible to eliminate errors completely, it is possible to minimize them by carefully designing, piloting, and implementing the coding procedures. The remainder of this chapter considers strategies that can help to reduce and control for error in coding, in relation to the various steps involved in the process. First, we turn to issues of data selection.

Selecting Data for Coding

One of the first decisions to be made is how many of the data will need to be coded. In some research, it may be necessary to code the entire dataset, but in other research it may be sufficient (or desirable) to code only part of it. Decisions about how many and which part of the data to code ultimately depend on the research questions, the resources available, and the requirements of any subsequent analyses. Researchers interested in learners' markings of plurality during relatively spontaneous and unmonitored L2 use, for example, might choose to code only the middle section of each conversation they have recorded. It is likely that, at that point, participants will be less attuned to the fact that they are being recorded. If participants, knowing they are being tested, pay close attention to their grammar, this could muddy the validity of the results since the research is meant to be about relatively unmonitored speech. Researchers sometimes also choose to exclude warm-up and winding-down time when participants may be experiencing anxiety or fatigue, respectively – other possible sources of construct-irrelevant variance (Gass & Mackey, 2000). Regarding available resources and the requirements of the planned statistical procedures, it is important to determine an appropriate sample size for the research questions to be addressed effectively and reliably while staying within the bounds of practicality. Limited availability of research assistants and a short project completion deadline, for example, may prompt the researcher to settle for coding only the data minimally required to address the research questions.

When feasibility is a concern in deciding how to select the data to code, random sampling might be the best choice in many cases. In other cases, another sampling method, such as stratified random sampling, may better fit the purpose. For instance, for a study investigating the relationship between proficiency and oral fluency, stratification based on L2 proficiency level may be desirable, especially if it turns out that various proficiency levels are not comparably represented in the dataset. Note that if only a portion of each participant's data is coded, it is important that the same portion be analyzed across participants. Otherwise, the selections might not be comparable, introducing construct-irrelevant variance.

Preparing Data for Coding

In some types of research, data may come in a format that lends itself to immediate analysis. For example, some types of language tests are scored automatically, and data collected by means of online questionnaires, reaction-time or eye-tracking software, or programs that record computer keystrokes usually yield electronic data that are either instantly or easily transferable to statistical packages. However, if written data are in hard-copy format, like paper questionnaires, handwritten essays, or observation notes, the researcher may wish to convert the raw data into an electronic form before beginning to code. This process often entails tedious manual data entry with great potential for error. It is crucial, therefore, that once the data have been keyed in, the researcher screens the computer file in the case of quantitative data (see Dörnyei, 2007, for a practical guide) or checks the accuracy of the transfer for qualitative data. Alternatively, of course, researchers may decide to mark on the original data sheets. It is important then to make a copy of at least part of the dataset so that the coding procedure can be piloted and coder reliability can be checked, as discussed in more detail below. Oral data, including recordings of classroom interactions, interviews, or communicative tasks, typically need to be transcribed into the written mode for subsequent analysis.

Transcription

When planning the transcription process, two key questions are how much to transcribe and what level of detail to include. These are important considerations because the amount of time and effort invested in transcribing can vary significantly depending on the detail required by the analytical and theoretical framework. Researchers often distinguish between broad transcriptions, entailing relatively little detail, and narrow transcriptions, which are quite precise and can be highly sophisticated, setting off a very time- and labor-intensive enterprise. Transcribing one hour's worth of conversational data can take as long as 20 hours (Markee, 2000) if fine details, like pause length, hesitations, and false starts, are included, as required for conversation or discourse analysis. If the researchers' goal is simply to examine whether learners use a particular L2 construction accurately, however, they may be justified in deciding to transcribe only those utterances that contain this specific construction. When broad or partial transcriptions suffice, the process can be much faster, not lasting longer than one or two hours per hour of recording (Mackey & Gass, 2005).

The next step involves choosing appropriate transcription conventions. There are a variety of conventions available, and it may be best to adopt or adapt one of them, unless existing formats do not seem suitable for the aims of the research. One advantage of using established transcription conventions is that, in general, they have been carefully developed and tested to address the concerns of a particular research domain. For instance, CHAT (http://childes.psy.cmu.edu/manuals/chat.pdf), a format commonly used for transcribing face-to-face conversational interactions, was developed with the express purpose of studying first language (L1) and L2 acquisition. Having transcriptions in a certain format may also ease subsequent data analysis. CHAT transcriptions, for example, can immediately be transferred to a program called CLAN, which facilitates the use of a wide range of analytical and search tools available in the CHILDES system (a corpus developed for sharing and studying language acquisition data; MacWhinney & Snow, 1990). Using an existing system may also promote wider access to the data within the larger research community. Thus, as a first step at the very least, it is useful to explore what conventions are typically used in one's area of research. Nevertheless, researchers at times may need to develop their own transcription conventions to fit the purpose of their research. In such cases, it is essential to include an explanation of the codes or conventions when presenting excerpts of the data.

There are a number of strategies that may help to decrease and control for errors in transcribing. First of all, it is critical that transcribers be adequately trained in using the transcription conventions. With L2 data, familiarity with participants' accents may enhance transcription quality. In some cases, it may be useful to have the transcripts checked by the informants themselves, a procedure often employed by qualitative researchers. Naturally, obtaining high-quality recordings reduces the risk of transcriber error, and, given the tedious and time-consuming nature of the process, factors such as fatigue and boredom need to be taken into account. To verify transcriber reliability, it is important to have the same or another researcher transcribe at least part of the material a second time.

Coding

Once the data have been prepared for coding, the actual process of categorization can begin. Coding may proceed in many ways, but it is helpful to distinguish between three main types: pre-coding, researcher-imposed coding, and coding which emerges from the data (Howitt & Cramer, 2007). The applicability of these procedures depends mainly on whether the data collection methods and intended analyses are quantitative and/or qualitative in nature. Pre-coding is characteristic of research in which the data are both gathered and analyzed quantitatively. Researchers tend to impose coding categories when the data have been collected qualitatively but the intended analysis is quantitative. Researchers typically allow coding categories to emerge from the data when analyzing qualitative data using qualitative approaches. As mentioned above, our concern in this chapter is with pre-coding and researcher-imposed coding.

Pre-Coding

In pre-coding, the researcher designs the elicitation instrument such that a pre-defined coding scheme is built into it. Thus, after the data have been obtained, the researcher's task simply entails assigning the pre-defined codes to the set of possible responses. In a sense, participants "code themselves" at the time of data collection. Pre-coding is typical with highly structured elicitation instruments, such as multiple choice tests, questionnaires, and classroom observation checklists.

In developing any coding scheme, it is important to consider the type(s) of measurement scale that can be used for each variable – nominal, ordinal, interval, or ratio. The nature of the scales determines to a large extent how coding and further statistical analyses can proceed. Only the coding of nominal, ordinal, and interval scales are discussed here, as ratio scales are normally not employed in SLA research. When researchers code *nominal* or *ordinal* variables they usually assign a number to each category so that statistical programs can make use of the information. For example, participants may be categorized as being native speakers of English, Hungarian, or Korean. In this case, native speakers of English may be coded "1," native speakers of Hungarian "2," and native speakers of Korean "3." Naturally, the value 2 does not imply a higher score here than the value 1 in a mathematical sense, given that L1 is a nominal variable. In contrast, the numerical values used to code ordinal variables are not arbitrary. For example, items on a four-point agreement scale are usually coded as: strongly disagree = 1, disagree = 2, agree = 3, strongly agree = 4. Here it is obvious that a value of "4" indicates greater agreement than a value of "3."

Interval data do not need to be coded further; they can be used directly in statistical analyses. Examples of data often treated as interval in SLA research include age, years of language study, and test scores. It is important to note, however, that variables considered as interval data might not truly meet the assumptions of interval scales – namely, that the actual distances between the numbers are equal. As Bond and Fox (2007) explain, for example, a small difference in scores near the test average (e.g., 48 vs. 55, where the average score is 50) often does not reflect the same difference in ability exemplified by a similarly sized gap at the top of the score range (e.g., 88 vs. 95). Certain statistical procedures can establish whether test scores constitute true interval data, and some statistical analyses, such as Rasch measurement, address this issue by transforming raw test data into true interval scores as part of the procedure (see Bachman, 2004; Bond & Fox, 2007).

In relation to levels of measurement, it is also worth noting that in some cases researchers choose to recode data using a lower type of scale by collapsing the data into broader categories and assigning each a numeric code. In general, however, coding categories "should always be as narrow as possible" (Mackey & Gass, 2005, p. 183). Data are easy to collapse into a less precise scale if necessary; however, if they have initially been coded broadly, it can be very time-consuming, difficult, or even impossible to recover more precise values. At times, this may force the researcher to start from scratch and recode the entire dataset. For example, if participants' exact ages are available (on an interval scale), it is advisable to record the actual numbers instead of immediately assigning them to ranges such as 0–9, 10–19, 20–29, 30–39, and so on (on an ordinal scale). Such rougher categorizations might later be used in the analyses – due to theoretical considerations, perhaps, if particular categories are relevant to the testing of a model or hypothesis; or to facilitate a characteristics-based analysis. In general, however, it is important to start out with as much information as possible. In a seminal study of age effects in SLA, for instance, DeKeyser (2000) created high- and low-aptitude groups using a cut-off point derived from the participants' aptitude test scores. By dividing learners into groups, DeKeyser was able to show that aptitude is related to ultimate attainment for adult but not child starters of the L2 learning process, and that age of onset is related to attainment for low- but not high-aptitude learners. However, in order to be able to run correlations between the relevant variables within each group separately, it was necessary to have the data available in more fine-grained form on an interval scale as well.

In pre-coding, apart from these potential problems related to assumptions and choices of measurement scales, a main source of error is simple miscoding due to coder fatigue, boredom, or distraction. One way to minimize this is to double-check all coding for accuracy.

Researcher-Imposed Coding

Researcher-imposed coding entails categorizing data that have been collected in qualitative form, often with the ultimate aim of preparing the data for quantitative analysis. Natural samples of learner language, verbal introspective reports, and interview transcripts may all be subjected to researcher-imposed coding. There are several standard steps involved in the process, such as selecting or developing a valid coding scheme, selecting and training coders, and carrying out appropriate procedures for checking coder reliability.

Selecting or developing a coding scheme

When researchers impose coding categories, they may choose to use an existing coding scheme, with the advantage of enabling comparisons across studies. However, at times, existing frameworks or standard measures may be inadequate for the theoretical models being assessed, not tailored specifically enough to address one's research questions, or not reflective of new research findings. Thus, it may sometimes be necessary to develop a new coding system. A third possibility, of course, is to follow a mixed approach, in which part of a scheme is adopted but refined to suit one's theoretical framework, research purposes, and/or the data obtained.

The studies described in study boxes 11.1 and 11.2 present examples of these various approaches. Study box 11.1 describes a study (Révész, in press) which relied on a combination of standard and specific measures to assess whether task complexity influences the extent to which learners focus on form–meaning connections during task work. The standard indices included global measures of syntactic complexity, accuracy, and lexical diversity. As a specific index, participants' use of conjoined clause types was assessed according to a coding scheme developed particularly for this purpose. The data were also coded for language-related episodes (LRE; Swain & Lapkin, 1998), confirmation checks, clarification requests, recasts, and metalinguistic talk in order to determine the effects of task complexity on interaction-driven language learning opportunities. All of the standard measures had been widely and productively applied to coding data in previous SLA research. Study box 11.2 illustrates how an existing coding framework can be adapted to fit the data obtained. In a study of learners' communication strategies during interactive listening, Vandergrift (1997) based his coding scheme primarily on Rost and Ross's (1991) typology of listener feedback strategies, but needed to adjust the taxonomy to reflect the nature of his dataset by adding new categories and collapsing some of the original categories.

Study Box 11.1

Révész, A. (in press). Task complexity, focus on L2 constructions, and individual differences: A classroom-based study. *The Modern Language Journal.*

Background

There are theoretical proposals in cognitive-interactionist SLA regarding how the characteristics of tasks can influence learners' L2 production. This study, in particular, was motivated by Robinson's (2005) Cognition Hypothesis and Skehan's (2009) Trade-off hypothesis.

Research questions

- Does task complexity affect the accuracy and complexity of L2 speech production?
- Does task complexity affect the quantity and quality of interaction-driven learning opportunities occurring during task work?
- To what extent do individual differences (IDs) in self-perceived communicative competence, linguistic self-confidence, and language use anxiety modulate these relationships?

Method

43 English as a second language (ESL) learners worked in groups during their normal English classes. Each group performed a simple and a complex version of the same argumentative task. Altogether, 23 hours of audio- and videotaped data were collected. Self-report questionnaires were employed to determine the effects of the ID variables.

Coding

The speech production data were coded by two research assistants using several different measures; 10% of the data, randomly selected for each measure, were double-coded by the researcher. A variety of standard general measures of speech production were obtained. To measure syntactic complexity, the number of clauses was divided by the number of AS-units (Foster, Tonkyn, & Wigglesworth, 2000). For lexical diversity, *D*-values were computed using the program *vocd* in CLAN. Accuracy was gauged by the ratio of errors to AS-units and by the ratio of error-free AS-units to the total number of AS-units. An index of error repair was also calculated as the proportion of self-repairs in relation to total number of errors. As a specific measure, participants' use of conjoined clauses was analyzed based on a developmental sequence observed by Diessel (2004); each clause was coded according to its stage in the sequence. Cohen's kappa values indicated strong inter-coder agreement (.91–.96) for all of these measures.

To assess the effects of task complexity on interaction-driven language learning opportunities, the data were analyzed in terms of language-related episodes (LREs; Swain & Lapkin, 1998). The coding was carried out by the researcher and a research assistant, with 20% of the data randomly selected for double-coding. After the LREs had been identified, the exchanges contained in them were coded in terms of four interactional features: confirmation checks, clarification requests, recasts, and metalinguistic talk. Cohen's kappa values showed strong inter-coder agreement (.91 to .94) for all interactional features.

Statistical tools

Paired-samples *t* tests, Wilcoxon Signed Ranks, Sign tests, Pearson correlations.

Results

On the more complex task, participants demonstrated lower syntactic complexity, greater accuracy, and greater lexical diversity (according to the standard general measures), more developmentally advanced clause types (according to the specific measure), and more LREs. Only slight significant effects were detected for IDs.

Study Box 11.2

Vandergrift, L. (1997). The Cinderella of communication strategies: Reception strategies in interactive listening. *The Modern Language Journal, 81*, 494–505.

Background

Skillful use of communication strategies by listeners during interaction can help L2 learners to deal with comprehension problems and promote language development. This study investigated the quality and quantity of reception strategies utilized by L2 learners of French at different proficiency levels during interactive listening.

Research questions

- What types of reception strategies are used by L2 learners while engaged in an interactive listening task and what is the frequency of their use?
- Are there any differences in reception-strategy use by language proficiency level, and if so, what are those differences?

Method

20 high-school learners from four different course levels were interviewed using the ACTFL/ETS Oral Proficiency Interview (OPI). These interviews were video recorded.

Coding

The interviews were independently rated by the investigator and a trained examiner, yielding a proficiency rating for each participant. Inter-rater reliability was high (.85). Disagreements were resolved through discussion and recourse to a third party's independent ratings. Rost and Ross's (1991) taxonomy of listener feedback moves served as a basis for developing a coding scheme to categorize the learners' use of reception strategies. This typology was adapted, however, to include strategies that were observed in the data but not part of the original coding scheme. In addition, some of the original categories were combined because some of the existing, more specific strategies were difficult to apply to the data obtained. The resulting coding scheme included six categories, three of which (*global* reprise, specific reprise, and hypothesis testing) were derived from Rost and Ross's taxonomy, and the rest of which were new, emerging from the data, including kinesics, uptaking, and faking. Using this coding scheme, the investigator and a trained researcher independently coded the interviews for half of the participants at each proficiency level. After differences had been identified and resolved, the researcher finished the rest of the coding.

Results

Learners utilized different reception strategies depending on their proficiency level. Novice students more often used kinesics, global reprises, and hypothesis testing in their L1 (English) in order to seek clarification or request additional input. Intermediate students relied on these strategies as well, but employed them less frequently and in qualitatively distinct ways, while also making more frequent use of uptaking.

Clearly, an essential consideration in deciding whether to adopt, adapt, or create a new researcher-imposed coding scheme is construct validity, to which there are a number of threats. The studies in study boxes 11.1 and 11.2 provide instructive illustrations of how common pitfalls related to construct underrepresentation might be avoided. Révész's (in press) study demonstrates the importance of considering the theoretical models and hypotheses to be tested in a study when making coding decisions. One of the models assessed in that study, Robinson's (2005) cognition hypothesis, makes separate predictions for specific versus global measures of production for the task factor investigated. Thus, if the standard global complexity index of subordination (clauses per AS-unit; Foster et al., 2000) had not been supplemented with a specific measure (use of conjoined clauses), the researcher would have performed a less complete and therefore less valid test of this theoretical framework. Indeed, the specific measures captured task effects which the general measures left undetected. The construct validity of the coding was also strengthened by employing a coding scheme based on a multistage developmental pattern instead of relying on a less sensitive dichotomous coding system (target-like vs. non-target-like). Interestingly, an even fuller picture of task effects might have been obtained had this study included a phrasal complexification measure as well. There is now growing recognition that global syntactic complexity is a multidimensional construct, including at least two unique domains: complexity by subordination and complexity by phrasal elaboration (Norris & Ortega, 2009). Therefore, to obtain even more valid measures of complexity, future researchers will need to refine the standard coding schemes further in light of more recent theoretical developments.

The study by Vandergrift (1997) illustrates how a researcher avoided the threat to validity which can result from adopting a coding system without carefully assessing its suitability for one's research. As mentioned above, although using the same coding system can increase comparability and generalizability across studies, it is not necessarily the case that a coding scheme which proved valid in one study will also be valid in another, even if the constructs under investigation are the same or similar. If Vandergrift had adopted Rost and Ross's typology without amending the framework to fit his dataset, he would have failed to capture important aspects of the construct of listener feedback.

As a prerequisite for validity, it is also key that a coding scheme lend itself to reliable coding. As such, a clear and unambiguous coding protocol should be drawn up (Ortega, 2000). As far as possible, it should include low-inference categories which require little judgment (e.g., supply vs. omission of a grammatical morpheme), rather than high-inference ones which involve evaluation based on less concrete or ambiguous evidence (e.g., learners' noticing or failing to notice errors, based on cross-outs in writing or restatements in speech). Creating categories as low-inference as possible may require a considerable amount of thought and trialing. It is worth the effort, however, as lower-inference categories will tend to result in higher consistency across individuals, since there is less leeway for personal interpretations to play a role.

One way to decrease the amount of inference involved in coding is to break down the procedure into a sequence of simple yes/no decisions. Reliability can also be enhanced by ensuring that definitions of the coding categories are clearly worded and accompanied with examples. After a researcher has developed an initial draft of a coding protocol, it is worthwhile to solicit feedback on it from other researchers with substantive knowledge in the research area. Once the draft has been revised based on this feedback, it can be particularly enlightening to pilot the coding scheme on the actual dataset, trying it out on random subsamples and then addressing any problems that arise. For example, ambiguity in the scheme might be removed by refining categories, providing clearer definitions of coding categories, and/or giving additional examples based on coding decisions that proved difficult during piloting. The researcher may need to repeat several rounds of this procedure until no further adjustments seem necessary. Ortega's (2000) dissertation study of syntactic complexity measures, summarized in study box 11.3, offers an exemplary description of this and the overall coding process.

Study Box 11.3

Ortega, L. (2000). *Understanding syntactic complexity: The measurement of change in the syntax of instructed L2 Spanish learners*. Unpublished doctoral dissertation, University of Hawai'i at Manoa.

Background

The overall goal of this research was to establish guidelines for selecting and interpreting measures of syntactic complexity in instructed SLA research. To help achieve this aim, this study set out to identify indices of syntactic complexity that could provide valid and reliable tools for assessing L2 development and task-related variation.

Research questions (selected)

- What kinds of information about complexification of the linguistic output do measures provide when they tap (a) length, (b) amount of coordination, (c) depth of clause, (d) amount of subordination, and (e) type of subordination?
- How does task affect the syntactic complexity of learners' production?
- What, if any, is the relationship of relative clause development to syntactic complexity measures?

Method

23 L2 Spanish learners from two college classes taught by the researcher participated. The data were collected over a semester and included written and oral narratives, academic papers, and journal entries. Four types of global syntactic complexity measures were employed, including ratios based on length, amount of coordination, amount of subordination, and type of subordination. Learners' use of relative clause types was also subjected to developmental analysis.

Coding

The coding procedure to obtain the global measures included six steps. First, all the oral data were transcribed by two native speakers of Spanish. After the accuracy of all the transcriptions had been checked, they were transformed into CHAT format. Second, coding protocols were developed and pilot tested for each unit of analysis. The piloting entailed trying out the protocols on random subsamples of the data. If any problems arose, the coding schemes were revised and tested on additional random subsamples. This iterative process continued until no further adjustments appeared necessary. Third, the researcher identified and trained a second coder. This coder was a native speaker of Spanish, also fluent in English, who was a doctoral student in a Spanish linguistics program. Each training session began with an informal introduction to the coding scheme, followed by practice on an excerpt judged by the researcher to be easy to code. Next, the researcher and coder read and discussed the coding protocol together. In the rest of the session, the coder engaged in independent coding and worked on difficult excerpts. Additional independent coding and discussion followed until a satisfactory level of inter-coder agreement was achieved. Fourth, the researcher and coder started coding for more formal inter-coder reliability checks. A series of stratified random samples was generated to ensure that the tasks and participants were equally represented in the samples. A new stratified random sample of the corpus was selected for each coding unit, including 10% of the written data and 20% of the oral. Fifth, the researcher and coder met in order to tally and record their agreements and disagreements carefully, then discuss any discrepancies. For all coding units, the level of inter-coder reliability was found to be sufficient, as measured by agreement rate (.87 to .96) and, for two measures, also by Cohen's kappa (.72 and .93). Finally, the researcher coded the rest of the corpus herself, and, with the resulting dataset, obtained the syntactic complexity ratios using the CLAN program in the CHILDES system.

Statistical tools

Pearson correlations, Wilcoxon Matched-Pairs Signed Ranks tests.

Results

In order to obtain a full description of syntactic complexity, at least three subconstructs of complexity need to be tapped: overall length of segmentation unit, amount of phrasal elaboration, and amount of subordination. Interestingly, only the length-based indices and type-of-subordination measures detected task-related variation, and no direct link was found between global syntactic complexity measures and learners' developmental stages in relative clause production.

Coder selection and training

To guarantee an acceptable level of reliability, it is also essential to select and train coders who can apply the coding criteria consistently and accurately. As far as coder selection is concerned, one way to reduce error is by employing coders with substantive expertise. Obviously, the sort of expertise required will depend on the nature of the research and the type of data. For example, in Ortega's (2000) study, which involved analyzing a corpus of L2 Spanish data, it was important that the two coders – the researcher and a second coder – both be fluent in Spanish. Note, however, that while recruiting expert coders can help to reduce error, it is likely to increase the probability of encountering another problem: coder bias. Unless coders are blind to the purpose of the research, the identity of the participants, and/or the participants' group assignments, their expectations may affect their decisions and thereby compromise validity. Researchers therefore often mask this information to reduce the chance of bias. For example, Ortega, in an attempt to minimize threats resulting from being the teacher of her participants, removed identifying information from the transcripts and hired independent raters to score participants' speaking performances.

The exact format of coder training may vary, but there are certain steps that are central to the process. Training sessions typically start with an introduction to the research project, followed by a description, illustration, and discussion of the coding protocol. After this, the coders independently practice coding on the same subset of data, chosen in such a way that it exemplifies both easy and difficult coding decisions. Next, the coders compare their results, and any discrepancies are discussed and resolved. If necessary, the coding protocol is modified to remove any remaining ambiguities or inadequacies, as explained above. Finally, further subsamples are selected, coded, and reviewed until a desirable level of consistency is achieved.

After coder training, it is useful to pilot the coding protocol with the coders on a subset of the data. For one thing, piloting might bring to light further inadequacies of the coding scheme. For another, if coders work with the protocol during the piloting process, the researcher can assess how much additional training might be required, and learning effects while coding the main dataset may be minimized (Orwin & Vevea, 2009). Once the issues that have arisen during piloting have been addressed, reliability statistics (discussed in the next section) should be formally checked, and, if found to be satisfactory, coders may then code the rest of the sample independently. It is a good idea to assess inter-coder reliability early on in the coding process. In this way, error-reduction strategies can be implemented before considerable time and resources have been invested.

Checking coder reliability

Although piloting and coder training are likely to enhance reliability, they do not guarantee that coders will always follow the coding guidelines exactly. It is critical to the validity of the research that independent evidence of reliability be obtained. Both intra- and inter-coder reliability are key. *Intra-coder reliability* is concerned with the extent to which a coder assigns the same coding categories to the same data on different occasions. It can be established by having a coder categorize a dataset once and then recode it a second time, later, in a different, random order. *Inter-coder reliability* refers to the degree to which two or more coders categorize the same data in the same way when they code independently. It is always good practice to employ a second coder when the coding categories are researcher-imposed, but it is crucial when the classification involves making high-inference decisions.

A major threat to intra-coder reliability is coder drift (Mackey & Gass, 2005). As coding proceeds, coders may inadvertently start to apply the coding scheme differently due to factors such as fatigue, boredom, or frustration. The order in which data are coded may also lead to alterations in how the coding criteria are interpreted. For example, when assigning holistic scores, coders may award a higher score than they otherwise might have to a performance which follows very weak samples, given the gap in quality between it and the previous performances. Errors resulting from boredom and fatigue may be reduced by scheduling multiple coding rounds, and frustration might be minimized by setting up regular meetings where difficult coding decisions are discussed. To control for sequencing effects, it is important to recode or double-code samples in a different order.

In determining the procedure for checking inter-coder reliability, a number of decisions need to be made. A key consideration is how many of the data should be double-coded. Ideally, all the data would be independently coded by two or more coders. Given time and cost constraints, however, often only a sample of the dataset can be subjected to inter-coder reliability checks. The appropriate size of the sample depends on the extent to which the coding scheme is likely to generate complex judgments. Ortega (2000), for example, decided to double-code only 10% of her written data, but 20% of her oral data, given the relative difficulty involved. Another key question is which portion of the data the second coder should code. In general, it is desirable to select samples from different sections of the dataset to increase representativeness. Following this principle, Ortega used stratified random sampling to choose data in such a way that every task, participant, and coding unit were included in proportions corresponding to her main dataset.

It is also essential to consider how disagreements between coders are to be dealt with. If the purpose of a second coding is simply to check for and report an acceptable level of inter-coder reliability, disagreements may be left unresolved and the categorizations of the main coder included in the analyses. This procedure was adopted in Ortega's study. When agreement on each decision is deemed crucial, however, consensus might be sought through discussions among coders. This can also be helpful in detecting simple oversights or minor misinterpretations of the protocol. Note, however, that such discussions may risk introducing systematic coder bias, since some of the coders (e.g., more senior ones) might exert more influence than others (Howitt & Cramer, 2007). Therefore, researchers may prefer to choose randomly between the codes assigned to a particular item, or to obtain a third rating and use the principle of majority rule. When multiple ratings are available for a given item, another possibility is to average its ratings. Of course, for nominal variables, averaging is not a viable alternative.

Calculating coder reliability   It is beyond the scope of this chapter to describe all of the numerous statistics available to assess coder reliability, but three types commonly used by SLA researchers are reviewed here: agreement rate, Cohen's kappa, and correlation. Historically, agreement rate has been a widely used coder reliability index for categorical variables. It is calculated by dividing the number of agreements by the total number of decisions made. Although easy to compute, a considerable drawback is that it does not adjust for agreements that may have occurred by chance (Orwin & Vevea, 2009).

Cohen's kappa is another extensively applied coder reliability index for categorical variables. It is considered to be a more robust measure than agreement rate as it takes chance agreement into account. When computing Cohen's kappa, the researcher needs to specify, in relation to each possible combination of categories in the coding scheme, the number of agreements and the number of disagreements. Although Cohen's kappa can be calculated by hand, many statistical programs will perform it, and there are also a number of online kappa calculators available. One limitation of kappa is that it is sensitive to scenarios in which a high proportion of the coding categories are not used or are infrequently employed (Orwin & Vevea, 2009).

For ordered variables, Pearson product-moment or Spearman rank-order correlation coefficients are the two most common measures used to assess coder reliability in SLA research. Rank-order correlations are appropriate for ordinal variables, whereas the Pearson product-moment correlation can be used when the scale is interval. Most statistical packages include a program for calculating these indices. A disadvantage of using correlations is that they do not take into account whether the raters' scores match exactly; they capture only the extent to which they vary in parallel. For example, if one coder awards consistently lower scores than another, the two coders may produce high correlations even if none of their scores is identical. More complex statistical procedures, such as generalizability theory and many-facet Rasch measurement, can address this limitation (see Bachman, 2004), but they require relatively large datasets.

Reporting of Coding Procedures

Finally, it is worth considering what needs to be reported about coding in the write-up of a study. A good rule of thumb is to provide detailed enough information to enable replications of the coding process. With this consideration in mind, it is recommended that researchers report on the following aspects: how many data were coded and, if applicable, how these data were transcribed and selected; a description of the coding scheme, why it was chosen, and how it was piloted; the number of coders, the expertise they possessed, and how they were trained (and blinded); the amount of data double-coded, how these were selected, and how the double-coding was carried out; the type of coder reliability statistic used and the level of reliability reached; and how disagreements in coding were dealt with.

Conclusion

This chapter has reviewed some of the basic steps in coding SLA data, such as preparing the data for coding; transcribing; constructing or modifying coding schemes; selecting and training coders; piloting the coding protocol; and assessing coder reliability. Each and every phase of the coding process entails a number of decisions and many opportunities for error. The aim of this chapter has been to offer guidance on how to reduce and control for such error, with the ultimate goal of enhancing validity and reliability in coding procedures.

Project Ideas and Resources

Ellis and Barkhuizen (2005) provide a hands-on-introduction to a number of ways of analyzing and coding L2 data, considering the theoretical approach underlying each method.

Gass and Mackey (2000) offer useful samples of coding schemes, coding sheets, and coder training protocols, from SLA projects involving stimulated recall methodology. Mackey and Gass (2005) provide a helpful introduction to coding L2 data, supplemented with examples and illustrations of transcription conventions and coding schemes.

Orwin and Vevea (2009) give a detailed overview of the coding issues involved in conducting research syntheses, including an in-depth discussion of the pros and cons of various inter-coder reliability statistics.

Study Questions

1. Obtain a structured elicitation instrument such as a closed-item questionnaire or observation checklist. For example, you could use the questionnaire employed in Borg's (2009) study on teachers' conceptions of research. Determine how the items might have been pre-coded.
2. Choose a study and reflect on the coding system utilized. Did the researcher develop a new coding scheme or use/adapt an existing one? Was the system appropriate for capturing the construct under investigation? Why or why not? If not, how might you modify the coding scheme to better suit the purpose of the research?
3. For a study you plan to carry out, draw up a list of the steps that will be involved in coding the data. Brainstorm potential sources of error at each step of the process. What error-reduction strategies can you implement to increase construct validity and reliability within the practical limitations of your likely resources?
4. Create a coding scheme for the data in the excerpt below. The data come from a study designed to assess L2 development in the use of the English simple past tense.

> I follow the guy yesterday. 8 in the morning he was in the café place. He drink coffee for 20 minutes. And then he left. Then I took the guy at 9 in the park and he's talking with another guy there. I think he give it to him a cell phone. And then 10 o'clock, he was in the swimming pool, he talk with a lady there. He looked for three different person in three hours. And then 11 o'clock, he go to the library. And he taked one book, I'm not sure what was on the book. He take something, some special paper inside the book. After that he take a taxi and then he taked a bus. I think he think somebody is following him.

5. The data below come from a picture narration task. Rate both performances in terms of communicative effectiveness on a scale from 1 (not effective) to 5 (very effective). Compare your ratings with those of a peer. Do you agree? If not, discuss possible sources of disagreement and try to come to an agreement. Based on your discussion, what could be included in a coding protocol to ensure that less inference is required on the part of the coder?

    a. So it's about a lady. She's cooking. She have the pot on the stove. The phone ring. She is going to answer and she forget the food on the stove. And she is speaking on the phone. And she forget the food. She sitting in the seat when I think her husband arrived. He's smoking cigarettes. And there's an explosion because I think there's no more lights on the gas. So there's an explosion.

    b. I see a woman in the picture. She would like to cook something or to heat something. And she is trying to light the gas. And the phone rings. She goes to pick up the phone, and she forget about the gas. She's watching TV. Then she has a guest. The guest is smoking and trying to light a cigarette. I don't know what happens. Bomb? Accident? I don't know.

References

American Educational Research Association, American Psychological Association, & National Council on Measurement in Education. (1999). *Standards for educational and psychological testing.* Washington, DC: Authors.

Bachman, L. (2004). *Statistical analyses for language assessment.* Cambridge, England: Cambridge University Press.

Bond, T. G., & Fox, C. M. (2007). *Applying the Rasch model: Fundamental measurement in the human sciences* (2nd ed.). Mahwah, NJ: Lawrence Erlbaum.

Borg, S. (2009). English language teachers' conceptions of research. *Applied Linguistics, 33,* 358–388.

DeKeyser, R. (2000). The robustness of critical period effects in second language acquisition. *Studies in Second Language Acquisition, 22,* 499–533.

Diessel, H. (2004). *The acquisition of complex sentences.* Cambridge, England: Cambridge University Press.

Dörnyei, Z. (2007). *Research methods in applied linguistics: Qualitative, quantitative and mixed methodologies.* Oxford, England: Oxford University Press.

Ellis, R., & Barkhuizen, G. (2005). *Analysing learner language.* Oxford, England: Oxford University Press.

Foster, P., Tonkyn, A., & Wigglesworth, G. (2000). Measuring spoken language: A unit for all reasons. *Applied Linguistics, 21,* 354–375.

Gass, S., & Mackey, A. (2000). *Stimulated recall methodology in second language research.* Mahwah, NJ: Lawrence Erlbaum.

Howitt, D., & Cramer, D. (2007). *Introduction to research methods in psychology.* Harlow, England: Pearson.

Mackey, A., & Gass, S. (2005). *Second language research methodology and design.* Mahwah, NJ: Lawrence Erlbaum.

MacWhinney, B., & Snow, C. E. (1990). The Child Language Data Exchange System: An update. *Journal of Child Language, 17,* 457–472.

Markee, N. (2000). *Conversation analysis*. Mahwah, NJ: Lawrence Erlbaum.

Messick, S. (1995). Validity of psychological assessment: Validation of inferences from persons' responses and performance as scientific inquiry into scoring meaning. *American Psychologist, 9,* 741–749.

Norris, J. M., & Ortega, L. (2003). Defining and measuring SLA. In C. J. Doughty & M. H. Long (Eds.), *Handbook of second language acquisition* (pp. 717–761). Malden, MA: Blackwell.

Norris, J. M., & Ortega, L. (2009). Towards an organic approach to investigating CAF in instructed SLA: The case of complexity. *Applied Linguistics, 30,* 555–578.

Ortega, L. (2000). *Understanding syntactic complexity: The measurement of change in the syntax of instructed L2 Spanish learners.* Unpublished doctoral dissertation, University of Hawai'i at Manoa.

Orwin, R., & Vevea, J. (2009). Evaluating coding decisions. In H. Cooper, L. Hedges, & J. Valentine (Eds.), *The handbook of research synthesis and meta-analysis* (2nd ed., pp. 177–203). New York, NY: Russell Sage Foundation.

Révész, A. (in press). Task complexity, focus on L2 constructions, and individual differences: A classroom-based study. *The Modern Language Journal.*

Robinson, P. (2005). Cognitive complexity and task sequencing: Studies in a componential framework for second language task design. *International Review of Applied Linguistics, 43,* 1–32.

Rost, M., & Ross, S. (1991). Learner use of strategies in interaction: Typology and teachability. *Language Learning, 41,* 235–273.

Skehan, P. (2009). Modelling second language performance: Integrating complexity, accuracy, fluency, and lexis. *Applied Linguistics, 30,* 510–532.

Swain, M., & Lapkin, S. (1998). Interaction and second language learning: Two adolescent French immersion students working together. *The Modern Language Journal, 82,* 320–337.

Vandergrift, L. (1997). The Cinderella of communication strategies: Reception strategies in interactive listening. *The Modern Language Journal, 81,* 494–505.

12   Coding Qualitative Data

Melissa Baralt

Background

This chapter is about how to code data using NVivo in qualitative research. NVivo is one example of software that assists the researcher in managing data and in carrying out qualitative analysis. In the field of second language acquisition (SLA), qualitative data often includes text, notes, video files, audio files, photos, and/or other forms of media. Increasingly, SLA researchers are using computer-assisted qualitative data analysis software (CAQDAS) to manage of all these data types and to conduct qualitative research, much in part due to the benefits they provide. This chapter introduces the reader to qualitative data analysis software, highlighting how it can facilitate data management, coding, and analysis. The chapter then provides a guide on how to code qualitative data. While coding examples are illustrated with the NVivo software, the basic procedures presented here can be followed with traditional pen-and-paper methods or with other software programs. The chapter concludes with examples of studies in SLA that have used NVivo to code qualitative data, resources to which the reader can refer, and study questions for discussion.

Qualitative versus Quantitative Coding

Coding in qualitative research is the analytical process of organizing raw data into themes that assist in interpreting the data. Coding is thus the activity that the researcher engages in, while *codes* are the "names or symbols used to stand for a group of similar items, ideas, or phenomena that the researcher has noticed in his or

Research Methods in Second Language Acquisition: A Practical Guide, First Edition.
Edited by Alison Mackey and Susan M. Gass.
© 2012 Blackwell Publishing Ltd. Published 2012 by Blackwell Publishing Ltd.

her data set" (LeCompte & Schensul, 1999, p. 55). The main difference between coding in quantitative and in qualitative research is the way in which codes are constructed and then assigned to the data. Qualitative coding is inherently more interpretive. It is a process of delineating the nature of a phenomenon by continuous interaction with and re-reading of the data. By comparing and contrasting themes and stopping often to reflect and ask questions, the researcher discovers patterns in the data. In many cases, qualitative coding is congruous with building explanations and even with generating theory. This is why qualitative analysis is often called "rich" or "deep," because it reveals a much more detailed and complex picture about the human experience of language learning that a mathematical procedure would not be able reveal. For example, say a researcher is interested in the way that teachers' beliefs and prior experience mediate their feedback decisions in the classroom. The researcher triangulates forms of data by collecting questionnaires, interviews, and class observations. Qualitative coding of this data would involve multiple cycles of reading and examining the data. Initial steps of coding would involve extracting themes from the data, comparing themes from one data type (e.g., interviews) to another (e.g., class observations), and between participants. Recursive interaction with the data, reflecting on coding decisions, questioning themes, and bringing out patterns define the qualitative coding process.

Coding data quantitatively is more numerical. Quantitative coding typically involves labeling, counting, tallying, and submitting counts to frequency reports and/ or statistical analyses. A common form of quantitative coding involves assigning a numerical label to data. This might be numbers of value, such as scores on a posttest, or numbers that are arbitrary, such as *0 = women, 1 = men*. With quantitative coding, researchers are able to perform statistical analyses, such as the extent to which a variable is correlated with another. For example, say a researcher is interested in whether or not uptake during task-based interaction predicts second language (L2) development on a posttest. The researcher codes the data by highlighting and counting (1) how many opportunities the participant had to produce uptake, (2) how many times the participant actually produced uptake, and then (3) the participant's overall rate of uptake. The researcher then calculates each participant's gain score on the posttest. With this data, he or she can run a regression analysis and can determine whether there is or is not a statistical relationship between the production of uptake and development. The researcher can also calculate the effect size, thus reporting on the strength of the relationship, and determine how powerful the statistical test was at detecting group differences. These types of calculations are made possible by quantitative coding (see Révész, this volume, chapter 11, on coding quantitative data validly and reliably).

Some aspects of qualitative research can also be quantitative. In addition to coding data qualitatively, a researcher might quantitatively code for demographic data, such as gender (e.g., *0 = women, 1 = men*), age (e.g., *19, 20, 21, 22*), first language (L1; e.g., *1 = English, 2 = Spanish, 3 = Arabic*), and native-speaker (NS) or non-native speaker (NNS) status (e.g., *0 = NNS, 1 = NS*). With this coded data, the researcher can calculate percentages of themes or concepts that came about from a qualitative analysis (e.g., online learner-reported strategies most frequently used by men compared to those used by women). An example of a study that coded data both qualitatively and quantitatively is that by Huang (2010). Huang investigated the effect of modality (individual written reflection, individual spoken reflection, and group spoken reflection) on intermediate-level English as a second language (ESL) learners' awareness of their L2 speaking strategies. Using NVivo to qualitatively code her data, Huang found that there were six categories of strategies that learners reported: *metacognitive, communication, cognitive, social, affective*, and *approach* strategies. Her qualitative analysis provided a definition for each category (e.g., *approach* meant "orienting oneself to the speaking task," p. 251), as well as subcategories that comprised each category (e.g., the subcategories of *approach* were *generating ideas, making choices*, and *developing reasons for choosing what to say*). Huang's quantitative coding of her qualitative findings included counting the frequency of each strategy type. She found that metacognitive strategies for L2 speaking were reported most, at 34.7%. Because of Huang's combination of qualitative and quantitative analyses, this study shed light on the types of strategies learners use for L2 speaking and what strategies learners use most. Furthermore, the modality in which learners were asked to reflect on their strategies seemed to make a difference in what they reported.

Benefits of Using Computer-Assisted Qualitative Data Analysis Software (CAQDAS)

CAQDAS, or simply qualitative data analysis software, refers to all computer programs that assist in carrying out qualitative coding and analysis. There are many options for researchers in SLA who are interested in using qualitative data analysis software. Table 12.1 provides information on some of the better-known software packages used in qualitative research. All provide free, online tutorials that serve as guides on how to get started and how to use the software. Some software is costly; most packages, however, offer reduced student prices and also free trial periods so that researchers can try out the software before purchasing it. So far, NVivo has been the software most used in the field of SLA (e.g., Chiu, 2008; Morrison, 2008; Murday, Ushida, & Chenoweth, 2008; Song & Fox, 2008; Phipps & Borg, 2009; Borg, 2009; Huang, 2010; Xie, 2010), but researchers can use any software to assist in carrying out qualitative coding. Choosing which qualitative data analysis software to use depends on the researcher's preference; the CAQDAS Networking Project at the University of Surrey provides helpful and unbiased descriptions of many different software options to assist researchers in making a decision (see http://caqdas.soc.surrey.ac.uk/).

A significant benefit in using CAQDAS is facilitated data management. Given that qualitative data often involves a plethora of digital, print, and other data materials – to include the researcher's personal notes and memos for coding decisions – it is easy for researchers to get overwhelmed at any point in a qualitative data project due to the sheer extent of data they might have. CAQDAS can manage all of these data and notes in a single data file repository. To illustrate this, consider figures 12.1

Table 12.1 Software packages used in qualitative research.

Qualitative data analysis software	Website	Coding description	Special strengths
ATLAS.ti	http://www.atlasti.com	Coding scheme structure is non-hierarchical; data can be retrieved without being coded (what ATLAS.ti calls quotation independence).	Supports multiple files, to include Google Earth™ kmz files. Particularly strong in establishing and showing links between codes via a network.
HyperRESEARCH	http://www.researchware.com	Coding is done with the code list editor where researcher can add and/or edit codes, or via a drop-down menu.	Mac compatible. Lets the researcher create code maps to graphically represent connections between codes. Also has a tool to facilitate in hypothesis formation, where researcher defines logical connectors (e.g., *IF X THEN Y*).
Ethnograph	http://www.qualisresearch.com	Researcher highlights text and assigns a code name to it; code frequency list is provided during coding.	Visually basic software; for example, all inserted memos on data in this program are shown visually with letter "m." One of the most affordable.
MAXQDA	http://www.maxqda.com	Coding can be done with drop-down menu selection or drag-and-drop. Coded examples can also be weighted to show how strongly they represent that code.	Lets researcher assign different colors to codes and text attributes, which assists in making the coding process more visual.

(*continued*)

Table 12.1 (cont'd)

Qualitative data analysis software	Website	Coding description	Special strengths
NVivo	http://www.qsrinternational.com	System of coding options that includes free nodes, tree nodes (child and nine levels of parent nodes), as well as relationships, classifications, and matrices. Annotations and hyperlinked memos assist in the coding process and note taking.	Strength is in its highly developed search tools and query capabilities for searching through data, nodes, memos, etc. Also has good visualization options with the Model and Chart tool.
Qualrus	http://www.ideaworks.com	As researcher organizes data and makes coding decisions, she or he can stack segments of data as "virtual note cards" to assist in coding.	Has intelligent coding capability which gives term suggestions to the researcher as she or he codes.

Note that, expect for HyperRESEARCH, all of the software described here is designed for PC operating systems. Researchers who use Mac computers can install software to be able to simulate a PC environment on their Mac; they can then run CAQDAS programs in this way. For example, Apple's Boot Camp lets Intel Mac users download the Windows operation system. Other programs, such as VMware or Parallels, let the researcher run Mac and Windows applications at the same time (see http://www.apple.com for more information).

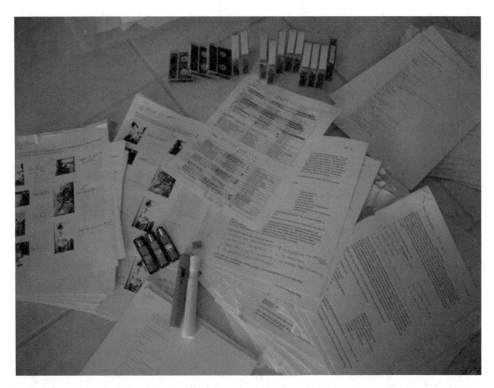

Figure 12.1 Common forms of data for qualitative analysis.

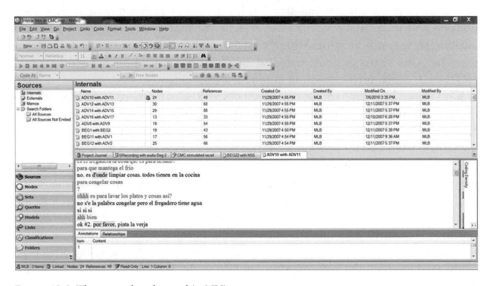

Figure 12.2 The same data housed in NVivo.

and 12.2. Figure 12.1 shows all of the papers, notes, videos, highlighters, and memos involved in a qualitative research project. Figure 12.2 shows the same data, all in NVivo. The use of NVivo or any other program can assist greatly in managing and organizing one's data.

Another benefit afforded by qualitative data analysis software to researchers is the ability to interact with all forms of data in the same workspace. This is because qualitative data analysis software can import and support data of multiple file types, including audio (.mp3, .wma, .wav files), video (e.g., .mpg, .wmv, .avi, .mov, .qt, and .mp4), and other forms of media. In this way, all of the data are housed together, making coding between file types more accessible, more organized, and significantly easier to manage. For example, the researcher can have a project journal, a video, and the transcription of that video open simultaneously. Accessing each is as simple as toggling between tabs or moving the computer mouse around. This obviates the need to have physical papers, digital recorders, a video recorder and television, a journal, and notes in one's workspace, because these same tools to play back or show the data is contained in the software.

A third advantage of CAQDAS is the capacity to do automated searches, similar to online search engines. If the researcher wants to look up words, entire passages, or even varieties of interlanguage forms, the search tools in the software give the results instantaneously. Such a procedure would take hours with manual searching through paper documents. Codes themselves can also be searched, which assists the researcher in examining how a particular theme has manifested itself across partici-pants. A code search will show all text excerpts or data types that had been assigned that code. (This is particularly useful given that text in qualitative coding is often coded for several different ideas, thus being assigned multiple codes!). Say a researcher created a code called "reasons for learning the language." After the first few cycles of coding, being able to examine the search results of all contexts coded as "reasons for learning the language" helps the researcher in fine-tuning a coding decision and in deciding whether a hierarchy for that code is emerging from the analysis, such as subcategories within a category. Most qualitative data analysis soft-ware supports searches constructed of Boolean logic operators (i.e., *AND, OR, NOT*, etc.), which further assist in automated searching.

Some researchers have argued that CAQDAS also helps to improve the credibility of the coding process in qualitative research. The programs are capable of providing an "audit trail" – a kind of accountability for claims made about findings (see Edge and Richards's, 1998, call for providing "warrants" for one's results). This is because most programs support the ability to save queries, creating a record of all searches done by the researcher. Decisions made about coding, relationships, and links are visually pre-sent and accounted for in the project, as are their historical archives (e.g., memos, attributes) that assist the researcher in theme development. As Johnston (2006) explains, qualitative data analysis software allows for a closer examination of the *process*, whereas in manual methods of qualitative research, the focus has often been on the final product. The software thus can help to elucidate steps taken in the proce-dure, which makes the methods and coding decisions more transparent.

Related to the issue of credibility is the shareability of computer-based projects with other researchers. Most qualitative data analysis software supports remote project access. In NVivo, for example, documents, nodes, memos, matrices, and even models can be exported and sent to others who might not have NVivo, or multiple researchers can work together on the same NVivo project from anywhere on the globe. The software MAXQDA supports different functions and coding management for different researchers, as well as project sharing in a read-only format to ensure data is not altered. Being able to share and collaborate on a project assists research teams in consulting together on how different coding decisions were formulated.

Coding Qualitative Data

This section will now focus on how to code qualitative data, with illustrations provided in the NVivo software. Before any coding can begin, however, the researcher needs to organize and prepare the data. This includes naming files as well as grouping files and data together. All of the above can be done electronically if using qualitative data analysis software. If the researcher is doing a qualitative research project with data analysis software for the first time, it is recommended to do some of the online free tutorials and to take time to get acquainted with the software. The researcher then imports all of the data into the program. Just as with traditional pen-and-paper methods, the researcher should name each of the files and organize them in the software before starting to code.

The next step may include data reduction. Data reduction is theoretically informed, so parts (or all) of the data that the researcher chooses to analyze will depend on his or her research question(s). Ethical restrictions can also play a role in selecting what parts of the data will be coded and analyzed. For example, if a researcher collected classroom data and does not have consent from one of the students, she or he must be sure to not include that student's data in the analysis.

Then, once data is set up, data that is comprised of audio or video content usually needs to be transcribed. As with data reduction, the level of detail involved in transcription will also depend on the researcher's theoretical orientation (see Freidman, this volume, chapter 10, on qualitative research and approaches in SLA). Almost all of the qualitative data analysis software have transcription tools that facilitate transcription. For example, NVivo, ATLAS.ti, MAXQDA, and HyperTranscribe have play and pause buttons for audio/video playback and permit media to be synced with transcribed text. This lets the researcher go directly to the original recording while reading through certain parts of the transcript. The transcription tools also allow for further editing of the text, such as cutting and pasting of audio. In NVivo, the researcher can juxtapose any audio or video file with a time span and a space for the transcription, e.g., "[02:32–0:2:41] – Participant 23: I prefer face-to-face because it seems more natural and – ." Playback of the media can be set at slower speeds to facilitate transcription. An example of the NVivo transcriber interface is shown in figure 12.3.

Start a Project Journal

After data preparation, the next step is to start a project journal. Keeping a journal throughout the coding process is imperative so that the researcher records his or her coding decisions, questions, and reflections. Researchers should write about what

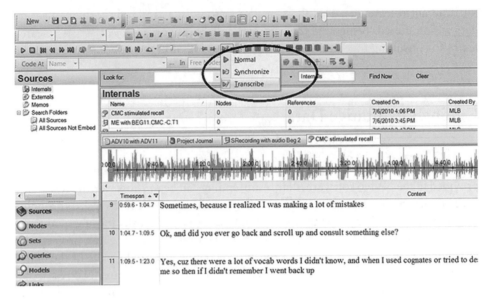

Figure 12.3 Transcribing in NVivo.

they did at the end of every session, so that s/he can see how coding decisions emerge and transform. Bazeley (2007, pp. 29–30) encourages researchers to write in their journals freely, disregarding formality or any notion of correctness. She suggests the following questions to serve as a guide when a researcher writes in the journal:

1. Why are you doing *this* project?
2. What do you think it's about?
3. What are the questions you're asking, and where did they come from?
4. What do you expect to find and why?
5. What have you observed so far?

In NVivo, a project journal can be easily set up by importing a document or creating a new one in the program. The journal can also be written via electronic memo.

First Iteration Followed by Open Coding

Next, the researcher should read through, look at, and watch (in the case of video) all of the data. If the researcher is using a more emergent methodology, she or he will probably start to formulate ideas for codes during this first iteration. The researcher begins to do *open coding*, or the process of assigning a code to represent a concept shown in the data. Corbin and Strauss (2008) define open coding as "breaking data apart and delineating concepts to stand for blocks of raw data ... one is qualifying those concepts in terms of their properties and dimensions" (p. 195). Codes can be single words, phrases, utterances, or even entire sections of highlighted text. These codes can be researcher-denoted or come from the data itself. Researcher-denoted codes are those made when the researcher determines a code name to best represent what the data shows, such as "feedback from peer." A code that comes from the data itself is an *in-vivo* code. In other words, the word or phrase is so descriptive and illuminating that the researcher abstracts the data as its own code. For example, say a participant says the following in a study on anxiety in task-based interaction: "When the teacher was talking, I was so concerned I'd miss something. I was trying to make sense of it all." The researcher might take part of this last statement, "trying to make sense of it all," and use it as one entire code, because it best captures what the participant was saying. This is an example of an in-vivo code, because it is grounded in, or originates from, the actual data. Sometimes, the literature review may inform coding decisions. A researcher may use constructs in the literature, and thus will already have created some codes before s/he starts coding. There is no wrong or right way to code qualitative data; coding can involve researcher-denoted and in vivo codes (e.g., codes that emerged during the analysis), and/or codes that come from previously established constructs.

In traditional pen-and-paper methods of qualitative coding, coding is done manually by physically writing the code on the margin of a paper, right next to the text it represents. Codes done this way are usually in the form of letters that represent a code (e.g., *ANX* for "anxiety"). The researcher may also choose to do color coding with different highlighter pens, and highlight the text to represent a coding decision. Ellis and Barkhuizen (2005) suggest that researchers manage codes by keeping the coding label, its definition, and an example in a separate codebook.

In NVivo, open coding is done electronically by coding for *free nodes*. Nodes in NVivo are analogous to electronic baskets or bins that the researcher labels with an idea or name. Coding data is assigning data to one or more of these nodes. This is illustrated in figure 12.4. The data in figure 12.4 comes from a computer-mediated communication (CMC) task between two learners of Spanish as an L2. After reading through all of the data, the researcher noticed that participants often gave each other praise, and wanted to code this concept. To do this, the researcher highlights the data with the computer mouse (*muy bien* 'very good'), and then writes a name for the code: "giving praise." This code is generated at the free node level (thus creating a 'bin' to which other data can be assigned), and then the researcher clicks the code button. Free nodes can also be assigned to other media content in NVivo, such as video, audio, or pictures. All codes in NVivo are kept in an electronic equivalent of a codebook. In the electronic version, the researcher can quickly edit free nodes, merge and delete nodes, and move them around with the click of a mouse.

Coding all Data and Developing Themes

The next steps are further iterations of interaction with the data. It is very important to continue reflecting on the analytic process in the journal as the researcher generates more codes and carries out additional cycles of reading/watching the data. Say a theme starts to emerge from the data, for example, "negotiation for meaning." The researcher then codes all of the data for this particular theme. That is, each time the data indicates that participants were negotiating the meaning of something, the researcher should code it for "negotiation for meaning."

The auto-code capability of NVivo can further assist in accomplishing this task. With automated searching of text, the researcher can code data automatically. For example, if the researcher is exploring unique features in computer-mediated

Figure 12.4 Coding in NVivo.

discourse, such as emoticons,[1] the researcher can search for all instances of emoticons and code them immediately. Auto-coding typically takes place after some iterations of data analysis have occurred, that is, once the researcher knows what to look for. The combination of auto-coding and automated searching also plays a role in fine-tuning the analysis. NVivo allows the researcher to do a search within codes, and will retrieve all content that has been coded for in a matter of seconds. Searching among codes immediately activates all text or media that had previously been coded for under that code, and shows this in a results window. This greatly facilitates revising the code system because the researcher can browse all content coded for a certain label, and then adjust, merge, move, or delete codes as she or he deems necessary.

After the researcher has coded the data for a major concept (done in some cases in up to three or four iterations of coding), she or he can begin to refine an emerging theme and get a better idea of what makes up that concept. Next it will be necessary to step back and consider all of the data that has been coded for this theme. In order to do this, it is helpful to compare the data that has been coded under the same node. A manual method might involve placing all data coded as "negotiation for meaning" out on a table, and then going back and re-reading that data. In NVivo, the researcher can do a node search with the search tool to be able to compare data. NVivo will immediately retrieve all data coded as "negotiation for meaning" to allow for a visual comparison. The researcher should consider how the data coded for under this node is similar and how it is different. She or he should think about what the characteristics are of a concept, under what conditions this concept seems to occur, and how it relates to other concepts. A good rule of thumb is to always step back after each cycle of coding and write about how a concept is emerging. This further assists in refining and restructuring the coding schema.

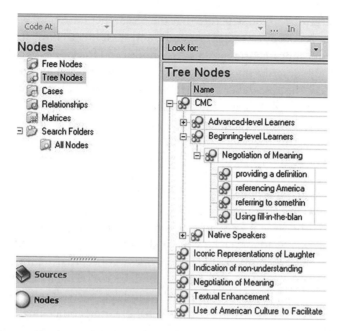

Figure 12.5 Tree nodes: hierarchical way of establishing categories and subcategories in NVivo.

Establishing Relationships

As the researcher progresses to more advanced stages of coding and interpretation, she or he will typically find that some concepts are related to others. In a traditional method, relating concepts can be done by placing folders within a folder, or by making a diagram on a bulletin board. In NVivo, nodes can be hyperlinked to other related nodes and also to memos. A prototypical architecture of coding for relationships in NVivo is coding and then subcoding, done with free nodes and tree nodes. In other words, making connections can be done by organizing free nodes in NVivo hierarchically. This is done with tree nodes, or parent nodes. A tree node serves as a category (e.g., "negotiation for meaning") while a free node is a subcategory (e.g., "providing a definition"). An example is shown in figure 12.5.

Figure 12.5 shows how nodes can be managed in NVivo. Tree nodes can have child nodes, and then under child nodes, free nodes. All categories can be expanded and collapsed to see how the arrangement has been put together. Rearrangement of tree nodes and free nodes is done by moving them around and/or copying and pasting. This is a helpful and visual means of denoting categories and subcategories that have come out of the analysis.

Establishing Patterns

The next step in establishing connections is to examine patterns that are emerging in the codes. Patterns are higher-level concepts or themes, the interconnections of coding decisions. Patterns assist the researcher in reducing and interpreting the data.

They may emerge due to the structure that the researcher has set up with codes, with how much data is coded for under one code, and with hierarchical structures set up via categories and subcategories (such as tree nodes and free nodes in NVivo). Corbin and Strauss (2008) describe this step as moving from description to conceptualization. For example, say the researcher has established multiple subcategories of the tree node "negotiation for meaning." However, she or he notices that the proficiency level of the participants seems to determine the ways in which they negotiate for meaning. Besides establishing further nodes and refining a coding hierarchy, the researcher can start to theorize about how proficiency level mediates strategies for communicating and negotiating meaning.

One way to assist in establishing patterns is to create a visualization of the data. According to Ellis and Barkhuizen (2005), drawing a visualization or model of the data is beneficial because it can facilitate an understanding of the results and also forces the researcher to fine-tune how he or she has interpreted the data. With manual techniques, this may involve sketching out a conceptual figure on a piece of paper. In NVivo, this can be done with the modeler tool. Due to its ability to automatically transfer coding information to the modeler, NVivo (and almost all other qualitative data analysis software) is capable of creating compelling visual displays of the data. The researcher can also create models manually with all or part of the data. He or she is able to insert a symbol that represents data that has been coded for, such as text or codes. Symbol shapes can be changed or assigned colors or pictures, and a visual demonstration of their connection can be created with lines. NVivo can also show the weight or frequency of a coded item in display form, if the researcher instructs it to. The researcher knows if she or he has reached a final stage of qualitative coding when *saturation* is achieved, or the point at which no new themes come out of the analysis. In other words, all concepts are well established and defined, and further analysis does not lead to any new codes or patterns.

Interpreting the Findings

The final stage of qualitative analysis is to present the entire *process* of coding and conceptualization in relation to the original research questions. It is the researcher's opportunity to explain how the research questions were answered, or in some cases, how theory was generated.

Studies that Have Carried Out Qualitative Coding with NVivo

To further illustrate how qualitative coding is done in the field of SLA, this next section describes three studies that carried out qualitative data analysis with the NVivo software. The first (Phipps & Borg, 2009; study box 12.1) investigated tensions between what teachers believe about teaching grammar and what their

Study Box 12.1

Phipps, S., & Borg, S. (2009). Exploring tensions between teachers' grammar teaching beliefs and practices. *System, 37*, 380–390.

Background

Teachers' beliefs about learning and teaching can be mediated by external factors and by their own experiences. In addition, their beliefs can affect how they acquire new knowledge during teacher training. An examination of the relationship between teacher beliefs and what they do in the classroom can lead to a better understanding of the teaching process.

Research questions

- What is the relationship between teachers' grammar teaching beliefs and their actual teaching practices?
- What kinds of tensions does this relationship highlight?

Participants

3 teachers of English as a foreign language.

Method

Data collection consisted of classroom observations and four semi-structured interviews. The researchers used NVivo to code the data, carrying out multiple cycles of reading the data. Coding decisions were informed by the literature review on teaching practices (e.g., incidental/planned focus on form, presentation/practice, correction of grammatical errors), but other codes were also generated as they emerged from the data itself. Each iteration of qualitative coding involved contextualizing and recontextualizing data into themes. The researchers describe their data analysis as three-part: pre-coding (e.g., data preparation and transcription); coding (e.g., data reduction, organizing free nodes and tree nodes into hierarchical categories in NVivo, continued refinement of coding decisions); and theorizing (continued data interpretation, developing conclusions and eventually a theoretical framework).

Results

The researchers found that there were tensions between teachers' beliefs about teaching grammar and their practices. The qualitative analysis shed light on three main concepts that led to this tension: (a) "presenting grammar;" (b) "controlled grammar practice," and (c) "group work for grammar practice." For example, one teacher's stated belief regarding the aspect of "presenting grammar" was that "grammar should be presented in context," but the teacher was observed giving students expository grammar work. Teachers' reasons for the disconnect between their beliefs and practices were: (a) "students' expectations," (b) "ideal ways to promote students' paying attention," and (c) "issues involving classroom management." The researchers conclude by highlighting how discussing differences between beliefs and practices can bring these discrepancies to light for teachers, and argue that they should be addressed in teacher training.

actual practices are. The second study (Song & Fox, 2008; study box 12.2) examined how learners use personal digital assistants (such as cell phones) to assist in incidental vocabulary learning. The third study (Gwyn-Paquette & Tochon, 2002; study box 12.3) explored how feedback and reflective conversation inform preservice teachers' decisions to do communicative teaching tasks in the classroom. These studies serve as an example of how SLA researchers have utilized NVivo to qualitatively code their data. Particular detail is provided on the coding done in each study.

Study Box 12.2

Song, Y., & Fox, R. (2008). Using PDA for undergraduate student incidental vocabulary testing. *ReCALL, 20*, 290–314.

Background

Vocabulary learning is of utmost importance for students of English as a foreign language (EFL), and especially for students who attend universities where English is the language of instruction. With personal digital assistants (PDAs) becoming more advanced in the digital age, it is possible that some students use them for language learning. Having a better understanding of EFL students' perceptions about and use of PDAs will help researchers and teachers alike to understand their needs and learning strategies.

Research questions

- What dictionary use of the PDA did the students make to support their incidental learning of vocabulary?
- How did dictionary use of PDA help the students with their incidental learning of vocabulary?
- What other uses of PDA did the students make to support their incidental vocabulary learning?
- How did these other uses of the PDA help the students with their incidental learning of vocabulary?

Participants

3 first-year undergraduate students at an English as a Medium of Instruction university in Hong Kong.

Method

Each student was given a cell phone with wireless internet capabilities. Data collection consisted of student electronic journals, the collection of artifacts (such as screen captures), and personal interviews over a period of one year. The researchers used NVivo to code and analyze the data. Initial coding of the data involved coding for broad themes that emerged, namely "dictionary use," "other use," and "vocabulary learning." Further iterations of data coding generated subtheme codes. The researchers did a constant analysis of the data to continue to find and refine further subthemes. Excerpts from the data were used to define all coding decisions, and then student artifacts were incorporated into the coding schema. The coding resulted in the following themes and subthemes: "dictionary use," with subthemes "downloaded dictionary use" and "online dictionary use"; "other uses," with subthemes "digital notes," "calls," "email," "messenger," etc.; and "learning use," with subthemes "referential," "data collection," "situated," "constructive," "reflective," "explorative," and "conversing." The second phase of the analysis involved describing and applying this coding scheme to each case (one per participant). For the final phase of the analysis, the researchers created a visual diagram to conceptually represent the complexity and dynamicity of PDA usage to enhance vocabulary learning.

Results

The researchers conclude by reflecting on students' use of technology in language learning as well as their needs, and how this is relevant to FL teaching.

Study Box 12.3

Gwyn-Paquette, C., & Tochon, F. V. (2002). The role of reflective conversations and feedback in helping preservice teachers learn to use cooperative activities in their second language classrooms. *Modern Language Journal, 86*, 204–226.

Background

Research shows that experience with and conscious reflection on teaching practices may help improve teachers' willingness to try new methods. Such practices may improve in the promotion of opportunities to use the L2 in classroom contexts.

Research question

- Can training in and reflecting on experiences with the communicative learning approach positively influence preservice teachers' perception of the approach and also their ability to implement it in the classroom?

Participants

4 preservice language teachers in Canada.

Method

Data collection included classroom observations, audio recordings and filming of lesson planning sessions, journal entries, classroom interventions, and interviews. The researchers used NVivo to code the data, assigning codes to the data electronically. Coding was done over multiple iterations of reading through the data. Each iteration was to further fine-tune codes that were constructed during the previous iteration.

The researchers eventually started to develop patterns and then grouped codes into categories. Every category was informed by specific examples in the data. Further, advanced-level iterations of reading through and analyzing the data in NVivo led to the development of subcategories. Thus, the researchers were able to identify macro-level and micro-level categories.

The researchers then created a table to visually show the hierarchical relationship of their codes. For example, "supporting factors" and "inhibiting factors" were the two macro-level categories. Under these were subcategories (e.g., "need for control" was a subcategory of "inhibiting factors"), and then, further, more fine-grained subcategories (e.g., "disruptive student behavior" and "off-task behavior" were two subcategories of "need for control"). The second part of the analysis, and reporting of the results, were done by applying the subcategories as a framework to describe each case (four in total).

Results

The researchers shed light on how different factors influence a preservice teacher's decision to incorporate communicative-based activities in the classroom. Motivation, moral support, peer support, and even student reactions all played a role. Supportive and reflective feedback that discussed their teaching practices was beneficial to preservice teachers' development. The study concludes by highlighting the types of support that are most beneficial to preservice teachers, what to do if no in-school support is available, and implications for communicative language teaching and education in bilingual Canadian contexts.

Conclusion

The purpose of this chapter has been to introduce the reader to CAQDAS, and to provide a guide on how to code qualitative data in SLA research. Qualitative data analysis software, such as NVivo, affords many benefits to researchers, such as easier data management and organization, automated searching, facilitated code construction, comparison, merging and refinement, and the ability to create models of what the data represents. At the same time, it is also important to point out critiques associated with using the software for qualitative analysis. First, it is a fallacy to assume that qualitative data analysis software is capable of generating theory itself. The software provides powerful tools to the researcher, but the human mind is what drives coding decisions and the analysis. Therefore, it is also important that the researcher have training in SLA qualitative research methodology; the online tutorials for how to code data with qualitative data analysis software cannot replace that training, and the mechanics of any software cannot replace a researcher's qualitative method. Related to this is a concern that software has prompted what Richards (2002) calls "coding fetishism," or getting too close to the data. In other words, coding is so emphasized in the software that it may be difficult for some researchers to progress to further, theory-generating levels of analysis (Séror, 2005). It is critical, therefore, that the researcher step back (keeping an "analytical distance" as argued by Johnston, 2006), visit the original data, and take time to conceptualize the bigger picture. Maintaining a project journal within the qualitative data analysis software will assist the researcher in achieving this goal. As long as it is used correctly, qualitative data analysis software has great potential for qualitative research in the field of SLA.

Project Ideas and Resources

Online Sources and Forums

- The CAQDAS Networking Project (at the University of Surrey) provides excellent and unbiased descriptions of many qualitative data analysis options to help researchers decide on what software is best for them. http://caqdas.soc.surrey.ac.uk/
- The Association for Qualitative Research provides information on upcoming conferences and also publishes the *Qualitative Research Journal*. http://www.aqr.org.au/

Books

Corbin, J., & Strauss, A. (2008). *Basics of qualitative research* (3rd ed.). London, England: Sage. The strength of this book is the extremely detailed example of memo writing that one of the authors conducted in a qualitative analysis. All examples are done with the MAXQDA software.

Gibbs, G. (2002). *Qualitative data analysis: Explorations with NVivo*. Buckingham, England: Open University Press. Simple, easy-to-read manual on coding data and carrying out qualitative analysis with NVivo. The spiral binder makes it easy to handle as well.

Lewis, A., & Silver, C. (2007). *Using software in qualitative research: A step-by-step guide*. London, England: Sage. This book gives examples and exercise options with NVivo, MAXQDA, and ATLAS.ti at every stage of analysis, and also dedicates a section to comparing other programs.

Richards, L. (2010). *Handling qualitative data*. London, England: Sage. Lyn Richards is one of the leading authors on qualitative data analysis. This book provides an excellent introduction on how to carry out a qualitative research project.

Study Questions

1. How is qualitative coding different from quantitative coding? Provide an example.
2. Look up a study in any SLA journal that conducted qualitative research with CAQDAS. What were the steps the researcher(s) took to code their data? Did they employ an emergent methodology to construct codes? Did their literature review inform any coding decisions? What were their main findings?
3. What are the benefits of conducting qualitative research with data analysis software such as NVivo? What are the potential pitfalls?
4. Go online and visit the websites for each of the qualitative data analysis software programs mentioned in this chapter. Which do you prefer? Why? (You might also reference the literature available at the CAQDAS Networking Project on different software options: http://caqdas.soc.surrey.ac.uk.) Download a free trial of the program of your choice and do one of the introductory tutorials for it online.
5. The following data comes from task-based interaction done in iChat, a computer-mediated communication (CMC) mode. The researcher was examining how proficiency level mediates the type of feedback a partner gives to a beginning-level learner when negotiating the meaning of lexical items in CMC. Beginning-level learners of Spanish were paired with either (a) other beginners, (b) advanced-level learners, or (c) native speakers. Read through the data. What stands out to you? What codes can you generate? What is similar and what is different in the way that beginning-level, advanced-level, and native speakers of Spanish explain the same item? Do you see any patterns? Write a brief summary about what you coded for. Compare your coding scheme with another person's coding in class.

Note that each partner is explaining the same chore, to remove the spider webs, to the beginning-level learner (the beginning-level learner's comments are in italics). The original data is first presented in Spanish; an English translation follows.

Original data:

Beginning-level learners

1. quitar las telaranas
teleranas?
es en la casa cuando no limpiar nunca
es un animal?
no, es la casa de animal
la casa?
que tipo de animal
insecto
ocho
ocho brazos

2. quitar las teleranas
ok...qu'e significa las telaranas?
en la pelicula "spiderman"

3. quitar las telerans
que significa telarannas?
no se como se dice
donde son las telarannas?
en la casa?
si o todos las places
los animales hace las telarannas por vivir
y por tener la comida

4. quitar las telaranas
telaranas?
crea: halloween en el EEUU
ahh si si
un animal que tiene ocho algunos
y es asustado
un film, "charlottes web' americano

Advanced-level learners

1. Tienes que quitar las telerannas
las telaranas es lo que hacen las aranas...
ellas
viven alli
que son las aranas
son insectos con ocho piernas
unos ejemplos son "widows negros"

2. Tienes que quitar las telarannas
que es telarrannas

*son**
donde estan

telarannas son insectas con ocho pies

3. quitar las telaranas
que es telaranas
donde viven los aranas
jeje que son aranas?
son insectos con ocho piernas
oh ok
si
usualmente son negros

4. necesitas quitar las telaranas
no se telaranas
es una casa para las aranas
lo siento... no se las aranas
pues.. es un insecto
ok...
como el hombre en la pelicula
un hero super
toby maguire

Native speakers

1. Tienes que quitar las telarannas
Que significa las telarannas?

2. ahora tienes que quitar las telarañas
telarañas son los hilos que hacen las
arañas

las telarannas son la "casa" que hace un animal, la aranna
sabes que es una aranna?
no, no se
es un insecto
que tiene muchas patas
puede ser pequenno o grande
la tarantula es un tipo de aranna, por ejemplo
la telaranna es donde viven las arannas y donde
consiguen comida

que significan los hilos?
lo siento
sabes qué es una araña?
no
es una animal pequeño de 8 patas
del mar?
no
la araña come insectos, que atrapa en una red
hecha con su hilo

hilo es como una pequeña cuerda

3. n2 quitar las telarañas
¿que signifique las telaranas?
son hilos de un insecto con ocho patas

como muchos hilos juntos
hay insectos con ochos patas que habitan en hilos. necesito quitar estos hilos

4. tienes que quitar las telarañas
que significa telaranas
telarañas son los hilos blancos que dejan las
arañas
las arañas son animales pequeños de 8 patas

English translation:

Beginning-level learners

1. to remove the spider webs
spider webs?
it is in the house when no to clean never
it is an animal?
no, it is the house of animal
the house?
what type of animal?
insect
eight
eight arms

2. to remove the spider webs
ok .. what does spider web mean?
in the movie "spiderman"

3. to remove the spdr webs
what does spider webs mean?
I don't know how it's said
where are the spider webs?
in the house?
yes or all of the places
the animals make the spider webs to live and to have the food

4. to remove the spider webs
spider webs?
think: Halloween in the USA
ahh si si
an animal that has eight somethings
a film, "charlottes web' american

Advanced-level learners

1. You have to remove the spider webs
the spider webs are what the spiders make...they live there

2. You have to remove the spider webs
what is spider webs
are[*]

what are spiders
they are insects with eight legs

some examples are "black widows"

where are they
the spiders are the insects with eight legs

3. remove the spider webs
what are spider webs
where the spiders live
haha and what are spiders?
they are insects with eight legs
ok ok
si
usually they are black

4. you need to remove the spider webs
I don't know spider webs
it's a house for the spiders
sorry... I don't know the spiders
well.. it's an insect
ok...
like the man in the movie
a super hero
toby maguire

Native speakers

1. You have to remove the spider webs

What does spider webs mean?

the spider webs are the "house" that an animal
makes,
the spider
Do you know what a spider is?
no, I don't know
it is an insect
that has many legs
it can be small or big
the tarantula is a type of spider, for example
the spider web is where the spiders live and where they find food

2. now you need to remove the spider webs
spider webs are the strings that the spiders
make

what does strings mean?
sorry
do you know what a spider is?
no
it is a small, eight-legged animal
of the sea?
no
the spider eats insects, which it traps in a network made with its string
string is like a small cord

3. Nr. 2 remove the spider webs

what does spider webs mean?
they are strings of an insect with eight legs
as in many strings together
there are insects with eight legs that live in strings. I need to remove the strings.

4. you have to remove the spider webs
what does spider webs mean
spider webs are the white strings that the spiders leave

the spiders are small animals with eight legs

Note

1   Emoticons are textual ways to express emotion, such as smileys, for example, :) :(:/ :-).

References

Bazeley, P. (2007). *Qualitative data analysis with NVivo*. London, England: Sage.

Borg, S. (2009). English language teachers' conceptions of research. *Applied Linguistics, 30,* 358–88.

Chiu, Y. C. (2008). The discourse of an English teacher in a cyber writing course: Roles and autonomy. *Asian EFL Journal, 10,* 79–110.

Corbin, J., & Strauss, A. (2008). *Basics of qualitative research* (3rd ed.). London, England: Sage.

Edge, J., & Richards, K. (1998). May I see your warrant, please? Justifying outcomes in qualitative research. *Applied Linguistics, 19,* 334–356.

Ellis, R., & Barkhuizen, G. (2005). *Analysing learner language*. Oxford, England: Oxford University Press.

Gwyn-Paquette, C., & Tochon, F. V. (2002). The role of reflective conversations and feedback in helping preservice teachers learn to use cooperative activities in their second language classrooms. *Modern Language Journal, 86,* 204–226.

Huang, L-S. (2010). Do different modalities of reflection matter? An exploration of adult second-language learners' reported strategy use and oral language production. *System, 38,* 245–261.

Johnston, L. (2006). Software and method: Reflections on teaching and using QSR NVivo in doctoral research. *International Journal of Social Research Methodology, 9,* 379–391.

LeCompte, M., & Schensul, J. (1999). *Analyzing and interpreting ethnographic data*. Walnut Creek, CA: AltaMira Press.

Morrison, B. (2008). The role of the self-access centre in the tertiary language learning process. *System, 36,* 123–140.

Murday, K., Ushida, E., & Chenoweth, A. (2008). Learners' and teachers' perspectives on language online. *Computer Assisted Language Learning, 21,* 125–142.

Phipps, S., & Borg, S. (2009). Exploring tensions between teachers' grammar teaching beliefs and practices. *System, 37,* 380–390.

Richards, L. (2002). Qualitative computing: A methods revolution? *International Journal of Social Research Methodology, 5,* 236–276.

Séror, J. (2005). Computers and qualitative data analysis: Paper, pens, and highlighters vs. screen, mouse and keyboard. *TESOL Quarterly, 39,* 321–328.

Song, Y., & Fox, R. (2008). Using PDA for undergraduate student incidental vocabulary testing. *ReCALL, 20,* 290–314.

Xie, X. (2010). Why are students quiet? Looking at the Chinese context and beyond. *ELT Journal, 64,* 10–20.

13 How to Run Statistical Analyses

Jenifer Larson-Hall

Background

Inferential statistics are an important part of many research reports and thus research methodology because they let the reader know whether the results that have been found can be generalized to a wider population. This chapter is of necessity a brief survey of how to understand and perform the most basic and frequently used inferential statistical tests in the field of second language acquisition (SLA). This chapter is intended for readers who do not have much experience with statistics; after reading this chapter the interested reader should have some idea of how statistics are used in actual research reports in the field of SLA and also have tools to conduct some basic statistical tests themselves using online resources.

In order to see which tests might be most useful for SLA researchers to understand, I consulted Gass (2009), who conducted a historical survey of statistical procedures used in four SLA journals (*Studies in Second Language Acquisition*, *Language Learning*, *Second Language Research*, and *Applied Linguistics*). Between the years 2001 and 2006, the top five most frequently used statistical procedures in these journals, and thus presumably the wider field of SLA, were ANOVA, correlation and regression, chi-square, t-tests, and repeated-measures ANOVA. This chapter will focus on helping the reader understand the most basic elements of the first four of these statistical procedures: one-way ANOVA, correlation, the chi-square test, and the t-test. In order to help the reader also perform their own statistical analysis, I provide links in this chapter to a number of websites where one can perform basic statistical tests (repeated-measures ANOVA is not treated here because no online resources are available for this more complicated procedure).[1] In each case I will also provide information about the graphics which best summarize and illustrate the data for that particular test.

Research Methods in Second Language Acquisition: A Practical Guide, First Edition.
Edited by Alison Mackey and Susan M. Gass.
© 2012 Blackwell Publishing Ltd. Published 2012 by Blackwell Publishing Ltd.

Statistical Background

In order to understand a statistical report it is important to understand a number of statistical issues. Entire chapters (in Hatch & Lazaraton, 1991; in Larson-Hall, 2010) and even books (Perry, 2005) have been written to help people understand how to interpret statistical reports within the field of SLA, so suffice it to say that this overview cannot be exhaustive. However, this section will try to help orient the reader to the statistical practices used in the field by discussing the issues of hypothesis testing, *p*-values, sample size, effect size, and what data to present in a statistical summary.

Consider the reported results from an empirical study conducted by Abrahamsson and Hyltenstam (2009). The authors investigated whether learners of second language (L2) Swedish who considered themselves near-native or native-like speakers (*N*=195) would also be judged to sound native-like by 10 judges. Native speakers of Swedish were also included as speakers in the experiment. The results (p. 268) showed that:

> The native speakers received a mean PN [perceived nativeness] score of 9.9 ..., the early L2 learners received a score of 7.9, and the late learners received a score of 2.5 ... all differences are statistically significant [one-way ANOVA: $F(2, 215)=111.61, p < .0001$; comparisons of adjacent groups with Fisher's Protected LSD post-hoc test]. Age of onset of acquisition is the variable most strongly associated with perceived nativelikeness, $r=-.72$, $df=193, p < .001$, and can therefore explain more than half of the variation: $r^2=.52$.

Every statistical result is linked to a hypothesis. In the Abrahamsson and Hyltenstam (2009) study (hereafter called A&H2009) the hypothesis is not laid out explicitly, but it clearly examines the question of whether the perceived (phonological) native-likeness of the L2 speakers depends on the age at which they began learning Swedish as an L2, as measured by which of the three groups they are included in (early learner, late learner, or native speaker).

A statistical procedure tests what is called the null hypothesis. The null hypothesis for the one-way ANOVA mentioned for A&H2009 is that there is no difference between the three groups of speakers as to their perceived native-likeness. The null hypothesis for the correlation for A&H2009 (reported with the *r*-statistic) is that there is no relationship between age of onset of learning and perceived native-likeness. Most authors do not lay their null hypothesis bare for the reader to see, but nevertheless such a null hypothesis has been formulated. The null hypothesis for a t-test will say that there is no difference between two groups of scores, and the null hypothesis for a one-way ANOVA will posit no difference between three or more scores. The null hypothesis for a correlation will say there is no relationship between two variables, such as vocabulary size and scores on a reading test. The author may well not believe or anticipate that the null hypothesis is true, but mathematically this is what will be tested.

The results of a statistical test are couched in terms of probabilities. You know that if there's a probability of 80% that it will rain tomorrow, it is likely you will need your umbrella. The *p*-value tells you the probability that you would find the results you did, if the null hypothesis were true. It is thus a truism that statistics can never *prove* a hypothesis, but it can tell you the probability of your results. So for A&H2009 the probability that they would find those results for the one-way ANOVA if there were no difference between the three groups is very small, at less than 1/10,000th of a percentage ($p < .0001$). Likewise, the probability that they would find the results for the correlation if there were no relationship between age of onset and perceived phonological native-likeness is less than 1/1000th of a percentage ($p < .001$). The usual cut-off point in the SLA literature for concluding that a result is statistical (also known as "statistically significant," but I eschew this term following the recommendation of Kline, 2004) is for the *p*-value to be below $\alpha = .05$, where α is a pre-determined cut-off point for establishing statistical significance. If the value is lower than this level, one may conclude the opposite of the null hypothesis; thus, A&H2009 concludes that there is a difference in perceived native-likeness among the three groups of Swedish speakers, and also that there is a relationship between age of onset and perceived native-likeness.[2]

The logic of statistical testing is rather convoluted, so let me summarize it again. First, a null hypothesis is provided. Let's say this time the null hypothesis is that there is no relationship between vocabulary size and scores on a reading test. The statistical procedure then tests the hypothesis mathematically and returns a *p*-value, which is the probability that one would get those same results if the null hypothesis were true. Let's say our correlation test between vocabulary size and scores on a reading test returns a value of $r = .48, p = .03$. If the *p*-value is less than a pre-determined cut-off point, often $\alpha = .05$, then one may reject the null hypothesis, and in this case conclude that there is a relationship between vocabulary size and scores on a reading test. If, however, the correlation tests returned a value of $r = .18, p = .15$, then since the *p*-value is greater than .05, we would accept the null hypothesis and conclude that there was no correlation between the two values.

What is reported in the data report is usually at a minimum the mathematical value of the test (a *t* for a t-test, an *r* for a correlation, an *F* for an ANOVA, a χ for a chi-square test), a number indicating sample size (degrees of freedom or number of participants), and the *p*-value. The convention in using the American Psychological Association (APA) formatting style is also to report any descriptive statistics that support the conclusions such as the mean scores (*M*) and standard deviations (*SDs*). Note that APA style dictates reporting exact *p*-values unless they are smaller than .001 (APA, 2010).

The report for A&H2009 does not include all of these elements because some are included in an adjacent table (namely, the sample size and standard deviations for the mean scores). Note that the prose description does include the statistics of an *F* for the one-way ANOVA and the *r* for the correlation and their associated probabilities (*p*-value). Mean scores for the one-way ANOVA are also given in prose. The numbers 2 and 215 which follow the *F* of the ANOVA are degrees of freedom (*df*). For an ANOVA two numbers representing different degrees of freedom are given. The first number represents the number of degrees of freedom there are in choosing groups (called the between-groups *df*). There are three groups, and you could make a choice for the first two (the third would be left over and thus could not be picked), so there are 2 degrees of freedom for groups. The second number is the degree of freedom within groups, and is the sum of the individual degrees of freedom for each sample minus the number of groups, so a *df* of 215 tells us there were 218 (215=218 – 3 for the groups) participants included in the calculation. Thus if other measures of sample size are not given, the degrees of freedom can provide a rough estimation of the sample size.

Knowing and noticing the sample size is quite important. Sample size means how many people or items were tested (since, in SLA data, most often people are tested, I will refer to sample size as the number of participants in the study). The bigger the number of participants in a study, the more likely it is that the results of a statistical test will be statistical. This is due to the nature of the null hypothesis. The null hypothesis posits that the difference between groups is exactly zero. If you test 10 people and their results are one point away from zero on a 50-point test, then the result would be that the null hypothesis holds because one point away from zero is pretty close to zero. But if you tested 100 people, then the results of the null hypothesis would be that one point away from zero is different from nothing (zero), so you can reject the hypothesis that the difference between groups is exactly zero. Thus a larger sample size is more likely to result in a statistical *p*-value.

One more piece of information that I would like to see reported more often is effect sizes. The APA publication manual states that reporting statistics and *p*-values only is "a starting point" and that "additional reporting elements such as effect sizes, confidence intervals, and extensive description are needed to convey the most complete reporting of the results" (APA, 2010, p. 33). Effect size is a measure of how important the differences between groups are, or how strong the relationship between variables is.

The effect size of a correlation is actually built in to the results – the *r*-value describes how strong the correlation is on a scale of 0–1. So an *r*-value of $r=.5$ means that the correlation is 50% and this explains 25% of the variance in scores (this is calculated by squaring the *r*-value, called the R^2 value). The report from A&H2009 included an *r*-value of –.72, which the authors noted resulted in an R^2 value of .52, explaining a large part of the variance in the relationship between perceived phonological native-likeness and age of onset even among exceptionally gifted L2 speakers.

For effect sizes for t-tests we want to look at the magnitude of differences between two groups. So in the example given previously for sample size, the difference between one and zero is 1/50 (since there are 50 points in the test), or 0.02. The effect size is the same whether there are 10 or 100 people tested. But to compare this effect size to other studies we need to standardize it, since not every study will have a test with 50 points. For a comparison between groups (as is done with a t-test or post-hoc tests from an ANOVA), usually the Cohen's *d* effect size is calculated. Cohen's *d* shows how big the difference between groups is as measured by standard deviations. So a value of $d=1.5$ means the group means differ by 1.5 standard deviations. One standard deviation away from the mean score (in both the negative and positive direction) on a normal curve contains 68% of the participants, so a difference of one standard deviation is considered quite a large one. The A&H2009 report did not contain effect sizes for the comparisons between groups, but since their table 2 reports means and standard deviations, such effect sizes can be easily calculated. The difference between the native speaker and early L2 speakers group is $d=0.97$, between the native speakers and late L2 speakers is $d=3.47$, and between the early and late speakers is $d=1.8$. Note that these are all large effects. This information, more than the p-values, shows us that there are important differences between groups in A&H2009.

Effect sizes for ANOVA results are also of the same type as the correlation but use the Greek letter eta (η) and are called eta-squared or partial eta-squared. A value of $\eta^2=.58$ would mean that the variable dividing groups (say it was treatment type) explained 58% of the variance in scores. In A&H2009 a partial eta-squared could have been given for the effect of group on the one-way ANOVA (but often it turns out to be more interesting and valuable to give effect sizes for comparisons between just two groups with the Cohen's d value, as I showed in the previous paragraph).

There is one last issue I would like to address here. That is the case where the p-value is greater than .05 but the effect size is large. A p-value greater than .05 usually results in the author stating that the results are not statistical, but this can be a misleading practice if the effect size is, in fact, large. One problem is that the $\alpha=.05$ cut-off point is an arbitrary dividing line. The biggest problem, however, is the fact that sample sizes play an outsized role in the determination of p-values (Cohen, 1994; Kline, 2004). If a study has a small sample size but a large effect size then we would expect that if the study were repeated with more participants the p-value would become smaller. In such cases it is perfectly legitimate for an author to put forth their case that with larger sample sizes, the p-value would likely be lower than the cut-off and thus there is at least a case to be made for the importance of the result. Further research needs to be done but a large effect size means that the result should not be summarily dismissed. Effect size is a much better indicator of the importance of a result than the p-value since it does not depend on sample size (Kline, 2004).

t-Tests

What Is a t-Test For?

The first statistical test I will describe, the t-test, compares the mean and standard deviation of one group to another group and asks whether the groups come from the same or different populations. Data consist of sets of numerical scores for two groups. These data should consist of continuous data, which is data with a large range of values (not just a few labeled with names, called categorical data). For example, a study that examines two types of pedagogical practice for pronunciation (production and non-production) will have just two groups of participants. Each group's scores (continuous data) on a sentence repetition task will be compared to the other, and the t-test would indicate whether the groups were statistically different or not. Table 13.1 gives some imagined scores on a 50-point test of pronunciation.

There are actually two commonly used t-tests, and you need to decide which one to use. If your groups contain completely different people (as shown in table 13.1

Table 13.1 Imaginary scores on a pronunciation test.

Pronunciation scores	
Production group	Non-production group
28	36
46	29
37	47
32	33
29	30
33	30
27	41
29	41
31	32
39	40
42	42
45	38
38	36
29	33
26	37
35	30
28	33
27	42
44	45
31	39
30	44
41	40
36	33
33	38

with groups of different people who received different pedagogical approaches), use the independent-samples t-test. Add the Welch procedure if the groups have standard deviations that seem quite different from each other. This adjustment is added when groups have heterogeneous variances, meaning their variances (the square of the standard deviation) are not the same. In general, it is a good idea to use this adjustment even if you think your variances are equal (Dalgaard, 2002). If your groups contain data from the same people, separated by time (like a pretest and a posttest), use a paired-samples t-test.

Conducting a t-Test

Table 13.2 shows a list of websites where you can conduct t-tests. All tests return the mean and standard deviation of your two groups and a *p*-value.

Table 13.2 Websites where you can enter data to conduct a t-test.

Website	Data entry	Types of t-tests	This site additionally gives
http://www.graphpad. com/quickcalcs/ttest1. cfm	Separate entry of data summarized entry (mean, SD, and N)	Independent = "unpaired t-test"; Independent (with adjustment) = "Welch's unpaired t-test"; Paired-samples = "paired t-test"	Difference of means and CIs[a] t-value (statistic) df
http://studentsttest. com/	Separate entry of data	Independent = "groups have equal variance" or "groups have unequal variance"; Paired-samples = "groups are matched"	Choice of 1-tailed or 2-tailed tests (if you don't know which to choose, stick with 2-tailed)
http://faculty.vassar. edu/lowry/ VassarStats. html and then choose "t-Tests & Procedures" along left-hand bar and then first choice on list, "Two-sample t-Test for Independent or Correlated Samples"	Separate entry of data in columns (put in a tab after each number)	Independent = "Independent Samples" button; Paired-samples = "Correlated samples" button	Difference of means and CI of that difference t-value (statistic) df

[a] CIs (confidence intervals) give you the range which the statistic (such as the difference of means) might have with repeated testing; for example, 95% CIs give the range you could expect to find the statistic in 95 times out of 100.

Results of a t-Test

When you report the results, you will need the mean scores and standard deviations of the groups, the number of people (N) in each group, the p-value, and also the t-statistic and degrees of freedom. Now assume that we want to examine whether a treatment with two groups produced any differences between the groups. Using the example mentioned above, assume the treatment was for pronunciation and that it involved one group where the students followed a traditional approach involving production and repetition of sound and sentence, and another group which merely listened to the language but never produced it. The results are listed in table 13.3.

Table 13.3 Results for a t-test.

	Mean (out of 50)	SD	N	p-value	t-statistic	df
Production group	34.0	6.2	24	0.07	1.84	44.7 (using Welch adjustment)
Non-production group	37.0	5.2	24			

Effect Sizes for a t-Test

The following websites will return a Cohen's *d* effect size if you enter mean scores and standard deviations for each group:

- http://www.uccs.edu/~faculty/lbecker
- http://www.cognitiveflexibility.org/effectsize

Oswald and Plonsky (2010) provide one rule of thumb for interpreting Cohen's *d* effect sizes in the SLA field: *d*=.4 is small, *d*=.7 is medium, and *d*=1.0 is large. For my imaginary data I found *d*=1.05, meaning the group means differed by about one standard deviation, and this is a large effect.

Reporting the Results of a t-Test

Using the information in table 13.3, here is an example of a report:

> An independent samples t-test found there was no statistical difference between groups, *t* (44.7)=1.84, *p*=.07, but the Cohen's *d* effect size (*d*=1.05) was large. There are therefore good reasons to think the non-production method (*M*=37.0, *SD*=5.2) is more effective than the traditional method (*M*=34.0, *SD*=6.2), although this should be tested with a larger sample size to increase the power of the t-test.

You would report all of the same information whether the test was statistical or not. Obviously, in this case I have argued in my report that although the *p*-value was not below .05 and the test was thus not statistical, the newer methodology was valuable because the effect size was quite large. Notice how I have included the information about the mean scores and standard deviations of the groups in the report as well.

Graphics for a t-Test

In a t-test you have data from two groups and those data are continuous. A traditional way in SLA to graphically represent these data is by using barplots. However, the barplot usually only gives one piece of information – the mean score of a group. Such a plot is severely lacking in useful substance (Tufte, 2001). Therefore, I

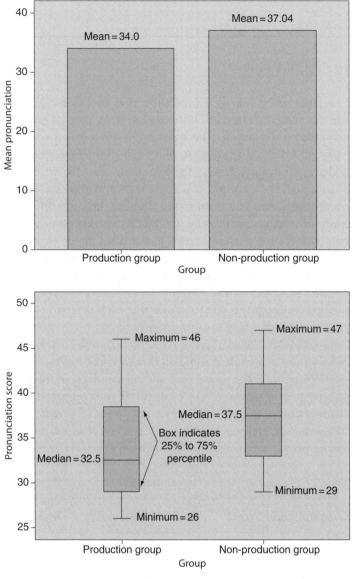

Figure 13.1 Barplot (top) versus boxplot (bottom) for made-up study on pronunciation training. Most graphics in this paper were created using the statistical program R; please request code if you are interested (however, labels on graphs were added using Microsoft Publisher).

recommend using a boxplot to show the range of scores in the two groups you are comparing in a t-test (for more information, see Larson-Hall & Herrington, 2010).

Figure 13.1 shows a comparison of a barplot with a boxplot for the imaginary data on pronunciation that I have discussed in this section. Note that the barplot simply shows the mean score through the height of the bar. The boxplot, on the other hand, indicates the median score by the horizontal black line in the box, and indicates the range of scores of the group as well. In addition, the box contains the middle 50% of scores of the groups. Any outliers (not present here) would be indicated with a circle outside of the range of scores.

ANOVA

What Is an ANOVA For?

Analysis of variance (ANOVA) is a procedure that checks for group differences. When you are checking the effects of only one variable, such as group membership (as was done for the t-test example), this type of ANOVA is called a one-way ANOVA. Thus a one-way ANOVA is an extension of a t-test to the case where you are comparing more than two groups. It tests the hypothesis that the scores from three or more groups are equal. For example, you might have a hypothesis about the effect of topic on writing scores, and you want to see whether there are differences in scores when one group of students writes a compare-and-contrast essay, another group of students writes a narrative personal essay, and a third group of students writes a descriptive essay. Table 13.4 shows imaginary data for such an experiment. The data consist of scores on a piece of writing that has been graded by two independent graders and represent a score out of 100.

Be careful when choosing this test to ensure that each person belongs to only one of the groups. In situations where the same person has scores in more than one of the groups, the one-way ANOVA is inappropriate. For example, if you wanted to compare the scores of the same student using all three writing topics, this would not be a one-way ANOVA because the groups are not independent. In this case you would need to use a repeated-measures ANOVA instead. If you compared scores over time such as a situation where you looked at scores on a piece of writing at the beginning and end of the semester, you would also need to use a repeated measures ANOVA because the same people are being sampled. Also, if you were comparing how well

Table 13.4 Imaginary scores on a writing test.

Compare-and-contrast	Narrative personal	Descriptive
50	85	85
73	73	79
49	69	93
62	90	88
84	77	93
70	80	75
62	82	83
55	80	83
67	73	100
60	66	94
58	80	79
70	72	82
63	78	85
68	88	94

listeners were able to perceive different types of phonemic distinctions (such as [b] vs. [v] as one contrast and [b] vs. [p] as another), where the same people would be involved in the scoring of each contrast, the repeated-measures ANOVA would be the appropriate test.

Study box 13.1 summarizes data from a real SLA study that used a one-way ANOVA in research on the effectiveness of a teaching approach.

Study Box 13.1

Jalilifar, A. (2009). The effect of cooperative learning techniques on college students' reading comprehension. *System, 38*(1), 96–108.

Research question

- Could different cooperative learning approaches to teaching reading comprehension affect scores on a semester-final reading comprehension test at the university level?

Participants

90 female Iranian learners of English who attended 16 sessions of 45 minutes each during a college semester.

Method

There were three groups: those who received a cooperative learning approach to reading labeled "Student team achievement divisions" (STAD); another group who received a different cooperative learning approach called "Group Investigation" (GI); and a third control group who practiced reading through "Conventional instruction" (CI). STAD involves having students tutor each other on course material, work together to prepare for quizzes, and have team goals. GI involves teams who work together to synthesize information to produce a final product which is presented to the whole class. In both of the two cooperative learning approaches, student teams were formed. Each team had three participants and they were grouped so that students of differing English proficiency level were together.

Results

Mean scores and standard deviations on a semester-final reading comprehension test showed the highest scores went to the STAD group ($M=12.3, SD=3.3$), the next highest was the GI group ($M=11, SD=3.14$), and the lowest scores went to the control group ($M=10.23, SD=2.76$). A one-way ANOVA was performed, $F(2, 87)=3.46, p=.036$, indicating that not all of the groups performed the same way on the reading comprehension task. Post-hoc tests found a statistical difference between the STAD and control groups only.

(Note that because means and standard deviations are included, I can calculate effect sizes. Cohen's d effect sizes for comparisons between groups are: STAD vs. GI, $d=.40$, effect size is small; STAD vs. control, $d=.68$, effect size is medium; GI vs. control, $d=.26$.)

Conclusion

It appears that using cooperative learning approaches is an effective way to increase reading comprehension in this population of learners, with the best approach being the STAD approach, and the GI approach being somewhat less effective.

Conducting an ANOVA

As in the t-test, mean scores and standard deviations will be used in a calculation of a statistic for the one-way ANOVA, this time an F-statistic. Table 13.5 shows websites that can be used to enter your data and conduct a one-way ANOVA. All websites return an ANOVA summary with the sum of squares (SS), degrees of freedom, mean squares (MS), Anova F-statistic, and associated p-value of that F-statistic.

One of the assumptions for this test, as for the t-test, is that your groups have homogeneous variances (in other words, their variances are the same). However, unlike the t-test, the one-way ANOVA does not have an adjustment if variances are not the same. Unequal variances make it more likely that you will not find differences between groups even though they may actually exist (Wilcox, 2001).

Results of an ANOVA

Table 13.6 shows the results of a one-way ANOVA calculation. Using our fictional data, we are trying to decide whether the writers who wrote about different topics differed in their scores on the writing test. We can see that numerically their mean values are different. However, using the statistics we are able to get at the question as to whether these are just random fluctuations in scores that should be expected (after all, if you took a standard admissions test once and then again another time, you might get slightly different scores) or whether they mean that the groups come from different populations (in which case, we would conclude that the topic treated in the writing is important to holistic scores).

Notice that there are two numbers for degrees of freedom in any ANOVA; one is the *df* between groups, and one is the *df* within groups. You need to report both these degrees of freedom. All of the websites will return other numbers that are used to calculate the F-statistic, such as the sum of squares and mean squares. Reporting these numbers is not necessary, however, according to the APA publication manual (APA, 2010).

Table 13.5 Websites where you can enter data to conduct a one-way ANOVA.

Website	Data entry	This site additionally gives
http://faculty.vassar.edu/lowry/anova1u.html (note that the final part of this address involves the number "1," not the letter "l," so it is anova + the number 1 + the letter u)	In the window marked "Data entry" enter the data for each group as a different "sample." Thus, if you have three groups, you will use windows for "Sample 1," "Sample 2," and "Sample 3." As you enter data for your groups, put the score of one individual on a line and then press the return button (enter the data for each person on a separate line within the "Sample X" window)	Summary data for each group: N, M, SD, etc. Post-hocs for all group comparisons
Use "Independent Samples" button (scroll down to it) http://www.danielsoper.com/statcalc/calc43.aspx	Uses summary data only; you need to know the N, M, and SD for each group previous to using this website	N/A
http://www.physics.csbsju.edu/stats/anova_NGROUP_NMAX_form.html	First enter the number of groups and the number of participants in your largest group. Then you will have separate boxes for each entry of each individual data point within each group	Summary data for each group: N, M, SD, range, 95% CI for mean, median

Table 13.6 Results for a one-way ANOVA.

Group	M	SD	N	p-value	F-statistic	df
Compare-and-contrast	63.6	9.4	14	.000	30.14	Between groups=2 (sometimes labeled "treatment" df)
Narrative personal	78.1	7.0	14			Within groups=39 (sometimes labeled "error" df)
Descriptive	86.6	7.2	14			

There is one more issue we need to consider before reporting the data. From table 13.6 we understand that not all of the groups performed equally, and that there is a difference among the groups (since our p-value is very low; however, don't report that the p-value is equal to zero, since the probability will never be zero – instead, report that $p<.001$). However, we have three groups so we don't know which groups exactly are different from the other groups. In this case, we can conduct post-hoc tests, which are basically t-tests pairing up each group against the other with statistical adjustments for conducting multiple tests. If you find a statistically significant result for the one-way ANOVA, you could in fact go back and conduct t-tests on the groups to see which are different from each other. The first website listed in table 13.5 will also automatically perform post-hocs if your p-value is less than .05. Post-hoc comparisons (using the least significant difference (LSD) method, which does not adjust the p-values and which Howell, 2002, recommends for comparisons with only three groups) on these data show that scores on the compare-and-contrast essay are different from the personal essay ($p<.005$) and descriptive essay ($p<.005$), and that the personal essay and descriptive essay scores are also different ($p=.007$).

Effect Sizes for an ANOVA

The same websites as noted for the t-test will return Cohen's d effect size for comparisons between two groups at a time. Entering the mean scores and standard deviations from table 13.6 returns an effect size of $d=1.75$ for the comparison between the compare-and contrast essay and the narrative personal essay, $d=2.75$ for the comparison between the compareandcontrast and the descriptive essay, and $d=1.20$ between the narrative and the descriptive essay (you can just ignore a negative sign in the calculation of the effect size). These are all very large effect sizes.

As noted under "Statistical Background" above, effect sizes for ANOVAs may also be reported using the eta-squared effect size. This type of effect size ranges from zero to one and indicates the percentage of the variance that is explained by the independent variable with the effect of the other variables factored out.

Reporting the Results of an ANOVA

Here is a sample report for the fictional data being considered in this section, using the data in table 13.6 and the section on effect sizes:

> A study on the results of essay topic on writing scores found large differences between topics. Mean scores and standard deviations for a compare-and-contrast essay were $M=63.6, SD=9.4$; for a personal narrative $M=78.1, SD=7.0$; and for a descriptive essay $M=86.6, SD=7.2$. A one-way ANOVA testing for differences in writing topic found a statistical difference between topics, $F(2, 39)=30.14, p<.001$. LSD post-hoc tests found that all of the writing topic scores were statistically different from each other ($p<.05$) and the effect size for each contrast was large (Cohen's $d=1.75$ for compare-and-contrast essay vs. narrative personal essay, $d=2.75$ for compare-and-contrast essay vs. descriptive essay, and $d=1.20$ for narrative personal vs. descriptive essay), showing that the writing topic played a large role in the scores students received on the writing sample.

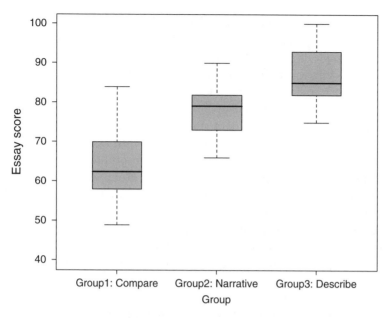

Figure 13.2 Boxplots of the made-up data regarding influence of essay type on writing scores.

Graphics for an ANOVA

The best graphic representation for a one-way ANOVA would be boxplots for each group. Figure 13.2 shows boxplots of the data from table 13.4. This graphic clearly shows how the median scores of each group are quite different (medians are different from means in that they represent the point at which 50% of the data is above and 50% is below). They also show that there is a limited range of variation in each group around the median. In other words, we don't see large amounts of variation in each group, but instead, scores are fairly neatly clustered around the median. I created the data this way, but actual data would probably be far more messy with lots of variation in each group, meaning that even if the median scores were different, it might be difficult to find statistical differences between groups.[3] The boxplots make it easy to examine the range of variation at the same time as median scores.

Correlations

What Is a Correlation For?

A correlation is used to test the strength of the relationship between the two variables. In the SLA field, say you would like to know whether students with higher working memory scores more quickly learn a set of vocabulary words than a group with lower working memory scores. In this case an appropriate statistical test would be the correlation between working memory and how many vocabulary words were learned. Sometimes researchers are more familiar with ANOVA-type tests, and inadvertently waste data by using an ANOVA instead of a correlation for this type of data. For example, if a researcher gathered the data I have described here, but then divided students into those who had high working memory and low working memory, the researcher could perform a one-way ANOVA to examine whether the two working memory groups differed in how many vocabulary words they learned. However, this would be wasting data since persons near the cut-off line (between high and low working memory) would be viewed as just as different as those whose scores were quite different. In other words, if the cut-off line were 50, then the participant with a score of 49 and placed in the "low" group would be considered just as different from a person with a score of 51 as the person with a score of 2. In a case like this it is wiser to keep all your data and calculate a correlation.

A correlation is calculated with two variables that consist of continuous data. Table 13.7 shows two continuous variables with made-up data from a working memory test and a vocabulary learning test, where both tests have a maximum score of 100.

Table 13.7 Imaginary scores for a working memory (WM) and vocabulary learning (Voc) test.

ID	Working memory score	Vocabulary score
1	53	70
2	74	66
3	98	63
4	47	70
5	37	71
6	59	53
7	75	59
8	66	68
9	42	70
10	68	58
11	18	59
12	29	60
13	70	63
14	73	69
15	72	73
16	50	57
17	36	75
18	57	58
19	54	58
20	73	60
21	46	55
22	29	53
23	79	68
24	80	71

Table 13.7 (cont)

ID	Working memory score	Vocabulary score
25	47	74
26	86	48
27	68	58
28	95	56
29	83	66
30	58	72
31	33	60
32	85	53
33	68	59
34	69	62
35	52	72
36	60	70
37	77	73
38	69	69
39	47	58
40	78	58
41	50	66
42	55	64
43	52	68
44	79	70
45	80	70
46	68	71
47	58	65
48	27	50
49	38	62
50	79	70

Conducting a Correlation

Table 13.8 lists some websites where you can run a correlation. All sites return a correlation coefficient (a Pearson r), an associated p-value, and the number of participants in the correlation (the N). The effect size for correlation is already found in the size of the r-statistic you will see. As a starting point, Cohen (1988) suggests that $r=.1$ is small, $r=.3$ is medium, and $r=.5$ is a large effect size; however, what is considered a large effect size will depend on the particular area of study. Note that correlations may be positive or negative, but will always range between 0 and ±1.

One of the important assumptions for a correlation is that the data are linear. In other words, if you looked at a scatterplot of the data points, the best way to describe the data would be by a line or random scattering of points, but not a curve or some other figure.

Table 13.8 Websites where you can enter data to conduct a correlation.

Website	Data entry	This site additionally gives
http://faculty.vassar. edu/ lowry/corr_big. html or	Scroll down to see the "Data Entry" box; at this site, paste data already formatted (separated by spaces)	Summary statistics for each group: M, variance, SD, standard error
http://faculty.vassar. edu/ lowry/corr_stats. html	At this site, enter data points separately in each box (you will be prompted to enter the N first); scroll down to see "Data Entry" box	Slope, standard error CI for the r-statistic
http://www.wessa.net/ rwasp_correlation. wasp	Enter data points with each individual's data separated by a return	Summary statistics: M, SD, variance scatterplot
http://easycalculation. com/statistics/ correlation.php	Enter data points (click "Add More" button to add more boxes for data entry)	N/A
http://www. stattucino.com/ calculate/correlations. html	Delete previous data (Cherry Tree) and add own data in rows; change variable names if desired	Multiple calculations at the same time (note: does not return p-value)

Results and Reporting a Correlation

Entering the data in table 13.7 into one of the sites in table 13.8, a correlation coefficient of $r=0.06$ and a p-value of $p=.66$ was returned. Notice that I could report on this statistic as follows:

> A Pearson correlation coefficient of $r=.06$, $p=.66$ ($N=50$) was found between scores on the memory test and a timed vocabulary recall test that students took. This means that scores on the memory test explained $R^2=4\%$ of the variance in the vocabulary test, a very small effect size.

Effect Sizes for a Correlation

As noted under '"Statistical Background" above, the effect size for a correlation is inherent in the r-value that is returned when calculating correlations. In order to understand what these statistics mean, I have created figure 13.3.

Notice that figure 13.3a has an r-statistic that is close to the maximum of 1 (the first line above the graph says "$r=0.98$". The line is almost a perfect fit to the data points, and thus the effect size of R^2 (written as "r^2" above the graph) shows that the

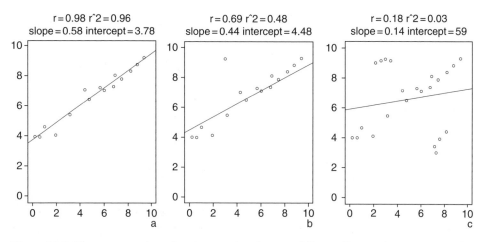

Figure 13.3 Three scatterplots showing varying degrees of fit to a line.

x variable explains most of the variance in the y variable (96%). In figure 13.3b, I inserted only one more data point, but this is far from the line, which considerably reduces the r-statistic (to $r=.69$) and the effect size. Now, the x variable explains only about 50% (48% to be exact) of what is happening in the y variable, but actually this is still a sizeable amount. For figure 13.3c I began inserting more data points close to two points far away from the line. Now there is very little slope in the fit line, the r-statistic is quite small ($r=.18$), and the x variable explains only 3% of the variance in the y variable. Thus, figure 13.3 graphically shows that the larger the r and R^2 statistics, the more closely the data points fit a line drawn over the data.

Study box 13.2 illustrates the use of correlation in recent SLA empirical research.

Study Box 13.2

Harrington, M., & Carey, M. (2009). The on-line yes/no test as a placement tool. *System, 37*, 614–626.

Research question

- Can determination of ESL proficiency level be speeded by use of a yes/no online test where students indicate whether they know a word or not? If separate analyses of proficiency level correlate highly with scores on the yes/no test then placement can be speeded up by using the online tool instead of the more labor-intensive tests that are currently in use in the Milton College English as a second language (ESL) program.

Participants

88 learners entering the Milton College ESL program. Placement was into one of five levels: Beginner, Elementary, Lower Intermediate, Upper Intermediate, and Advanced.

Method

The yes/no test was administered first. Students saw 200 words and had to indicate simply whether they knew the word or not. A score was calculated that subtracted points for guessing (pseudowords were included in the test). Then students took the four exams that were traditionally given to determine placement into the program. These included listening, grammar, writing, and speaking tests.

Results

Table 6 of the article gives Spearman's rho correlations between yes/no test accuracy, scores on the four Milton test scores, and placement. (Note that Spearman's *rho* is a non-parametric alternative to the Pearson's *r* correlation I examined above, but its results can be interpreted in the same way as the Pearson's *r*.)

"The Milton tests have a stronger correlation with the placement level decisions (.72–.80) than the Yes/No accuracy scores (.54–.64). Although not as strong as the Milton program correlations, the Yes/No test results are nonetheless notable ... recognition vocabulary knowledge is a basic foundation for performance across all domains ..., and a dimension that can be effectively measured for placement purposes" (p. 262).

Conclusion

All correlations were very strong, above the .50 level, indicating that there was a very strong relationship between how well students did on the yes/no test and how accurate their placement in the program was (as compared to their placement using the traditional way of testing previously in place). The authors conclude that this online test would be an effective way to conduct placement testing.

Graphics for a Correlation

The best graphic for understanding a correlation is the scatterplot. The scatterplot is an excellent graphic because it displays all of the data included in the analysis. A look at the scatterplot can also help you understand the *r*-statistic because you can see how tightly clustered around a regression line the data are (the regression line is the straight line drawn over the data which best fits all of the points). The scatterplot also is a visual way to identify whether the data satisfy the statistical assumption of linearity as well. Figure 13.4 shows a scatterplot of the fictional data from table 13.7.

A scatterplot will be more informative if you include a straight regression line and a Loess line on the graphic as well (a Loess line gives the best fit to the data for just small

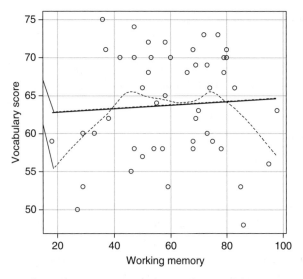

Figure 13.4 A scatterplot with a regression and Loess line.

chunks of data at a time, resulting in a line that may not be straight). In figure 13.4 the Loess line is the dotted line while the regression line is solid. The Loess line follows the fit of the data whereas the regression line tries to make the best fit over the entire data set. If these lines match fairly well this means the data are linear. The Loess line in figure 13.4 is not a good fit to the regression line and indicates that there may be something different going on with participants whose working memory is either extremely high or extremely low.

Chi-Square

What Is a Chi-Square Test For?

When you have data with two variables, both of which are categorical, and you want to know whether these variables are related, you should use a chi-square test to analyze your data. Categorical data are those whose categories hold no intrinsic numerical value, such as first language or experimental group, or data where there may be a ranking involved but the small number of levels means it cannot be treated as a continuous variable. For example, let's imagine a study which examined whether students learning German at the university level who had studied abroad had lower levels of anxiety in their third-year German class. Participating in study abroad is clearly an either/or category (and, thus, categorical), and let's say anxiety was measured by asking students whether they had a low, moderate, or high level of anxiety throughout the semester (here, the number of levels is quite small and we will also call this categorical in spite of the fact that there is some ranking of anxiety involved).

Table 13.9 Contingency tables of categorical data.

German	Anxiety			Teaching method	Relative clauses	No relative clauses
	Low	Mid	High			
Study abroad	14	38	4	A	12	18
No study abroad	44	58	21	B	0	16

The chi-square test will answer the question of whether anxiety levels are related to having studied abroad. Another example of an imaginary analysis that would use chi-square is a study design that used two teaching methods and looked at whether students produced relative clauses or not during the classroom period. Both of these variables – teaching method and whether relative clauses were produced – are categorical and in this case have only two levels. This design would answer the question of whether teaching method was related to increased production of relative clauses.

Data for a chi-square test are different from all of the data seen previously in this chapter (in tables 13.1, 13.4, and 13.7). Previous datasets consisted of individual scores. Of course, individuals are involved in collecting the data for this test as well, but for the calculation of the chi-square test online, contingency tables that summarize the counts in each category are needed. Table 13.9 consists of summary counts and not individual data points for both of the examples outlined in the previous paragraph.

To understand the data in table 13.9, consider the following points. One thing that table 13.9 shows is that of the German students who did not study abroad, 58 of them said they had a mid or moderate level of anxiety. However, of those who did study abroad, 38 had mid or moderate levels of anxiety. Notice that each person will fit into only one cell of the count. That is, for the German study, a person either attended study abroad or they did not, and then their anxiety level was measured. For the teaching method study, the chart shows the number of people who produced relative clauses for each teaching method. There were a total of (12 + 18 + 0 + 16=) 46 participants in the study. In other words, what was counted was not the number of relative clauses, but the number of students who produced them. Chi-square is not appropriate for data where one person's data are summarized and counted in more than one of the cells of the contingency table. The data for the German study is called a 2 × 3 table, because there are 2 rows and 3 columns, while the data for the teaching method study is called a 2 × 2 table.

Conducting a Chi-Square Test

You should be aware that you need to enter data for a chi-square online in the form of a contingency table, which is a summary of counts of each category. Table 13.10 lists websites which can run a chi-square analysis on data. Some of the sites in

Table 13.10 Websites where you can enter data to conduct a chi-square test.

Website	Data entry	This site additionally gives
http://www.physics.csbsju. edu/stats/contingency_ NROW_NCOLUMN_form. html	Lets you choose number of rows (conditions) and number of columns (outcomes) (can be larger than 2×2)	Contingency table with expected values
http://faculty.vassar.edu/ lowry/odds2x2.html (for more choices, go to the home page (scroll to bottom of page to find) and click on "Frequency Data" on left-hand bar; from this page, scroll down to "Fisher Exact Probability Test for Tables Larger than 2×2" and choose $2 \times 3, 2 \times 4$ or 3×3 configurations)	This page is 2×2 only but see website instructions to get larger tables	Odds ratio, risk ratio, *phi* (all effect sizes)
http://www.graphpad.com/ quickcalcs/contingency1.cfm	2×2 only	

table 13.10 will perform chi-square only on data for a 2×2 table. All of the sites will give you the chi-square statistic (χ^2), associated *p*-value, and the degrees of freedom (*df*) if you use the chi-square test. However, you cannot use the chi-square if there are cells in your contingency table that have a count of less than 5. Therefore, the data for teaching method could not be used with the chi-square calculation (because one cell's count is zero). Some of the sites give you a choice of other types of tests you can use in this situation, such as Fisher's exact *p*-value, which does not return a chi-square statistic, but can give you a *p*-value indicating whether the variables are related or not.

Results of a Chi-Square Test

In looking at table 13.9 we see that numerically, more students who did not study abroad have high levels of anxiety than students who did study abroad. However, numerically there are also many more students who did not study abroad (123) versus those who did study abroad (56). A chi-square tests asks whether the proportion of respondents in one cell of the table is what we would expect given an equal distribution in all of the cells. If the distribution is not equal across the variables, we can conclude there is some type of relationship between the variables.

Conducting a chi-square test on the German data using the Vassar site, I get a result of $\chi^2=7.17$, $df=2$, $p=.03$. This means we can reject the null hypothesis that there is no relationship between the variables of study abroad and anxiety level. In other words, students in this data set who study abroad are different in their reported levels of anxiety in third-year German from students who do not study abroad. For the teaching method data, the Vassar site returns a Fisher exact p-value of $p=.004$ (it notes that the chi-square can only be calculated if all cells have at least a count of 5). This means we can reject the null hypothesis that there is no relationship between variables and thus conclude the groups are different. In other words, teaching method definitely played a role in whether participants produced relative clauses or not.

Effect Sizes for a Chi-Square Test

The Vassar website also gives an effect size of $phi=.43$ for the teaching method data. *Phi* is an effect size used for the chi-square test and can be squared to refer to the percentage of variance explained, just like the *r* of the correlation test. Thus, the teaching method accounted for $.43^2=18\%$ of the variance in whether relative clauses were produced. Note that effect sizes for a chi-square test can be calculated only for a 2×2 contingency table. Tables larger than 2×2 may be split into 2×2 tables in order to obtain effect sizes (this would be conceptually similar to doing a post-hoc test on just two groups in a one-way ANOVA), but explaining how to do this is beyond the scope of this chapter (see Larson-Hall, 2010, for more details).

Reporting the Results of a Chi-Square Test

I could report on the results of these two studies in the following way:

> A chi-square test investigating the relationship of study abroad time on anxiety in third-year German students (as measured by a categorical "low," "mid," or "high" scale) found these two variables were related ($\chi^2=7.17$, $df=2$, $p=.03$).
>
> A Fisher's exact test was used to evaluate the relationship between teaching method and whether or not students produced any relative clauses. The Fisher's exact p-value was $p=.004$, indicating that these two variables are related. The effect size of the relationship is $phi=.43$, meaning the effect of teaching method has a medium-to-large effect size on whether relative clauses are produced.

For descriptive statistics, make sure to include the contingency table somewhere in your report. Study box 13.3 illustrates the research question and results found in a real SLA research study that used a chi-square analysis.

Study Box 13.3

Kondo-Brown, K. (2006). How do English L1 learners of advanced Japanese infer unknown *kanji* words in authentic texts? *Language Learning, 56*(1), 109–153.

Research question

- How do several aspects of students who enroll in the less-commonly taught language (LCTL) classes compare to those of students who take the more commonly taught languages (CTL)? Kondo-Brown noted that in a time when speakers of LCTLs may be more needed than ever, little is known about the demographics of students who enroll in language classes like Arabic or Chinese.

Participants

1,502 students at a large public university in the southwest USA were surveyed in their first or second year of language study. Students who were taking Spanish, French, or German were classified as CTL students while those taking Arabic, Hebrew, Japanese, Turkish, Greek, or Italian were classified as LCTL students.

Method

The participants took a questionnaire that asked for demographic data (gender, age), academic data (grade point average, reason for taking the course), and foreign/second language data (exposure to language as children, length of study abroad, amount of third language study, etc.).

Results

Each question asked in the questionnaire was analyzed with a separate chi-square analysis (resulting in a correct application of this statistical procedure). I will focus here on reporting on just one question: "Have you studied another language other than this language and your native language?" Kondo-Brown gives the following contingency table for this question:

Third language	Yes	No	Total
CTL (Spanish, French, German)	510 (24%)	717 (58%)	1,227 (100%)
LCTL (others)	254 (92%)	21 (8%)	275 (100%)

The chi-square result is $\chi^2 = 231.956$, $df = 1$, $p < .001$. This means there was indeed a relationship between choice of an LCTL and study of additional languages. The contingency table makes clear that most of the LCTL students had studied another language while a much smaller percentage of those taking CTLs had.

Conclusion

Kondo-Brown concludes that because most students taking LCTLs have experience with learning languages (and were also found to have higher motivation and expected to get higher grades), instructors might increase the difficulty of the courses and adjust instructional techniques in the classroom.

Graphics for a Chi-Square Test

The most common graphic for understanding categorical data is a barplot. As noted previously, this type of graphic is not as informative as other possible graphs, and I suggest the use of a newer graphic called the association plot. To illustrate the usefulness of the association plot I will compare a barplot of the teaching method data with an association plot in figure 13.5.

The barplot in figure 13.5a shows graphically that teaching method B did not result in *any* students who could produce relative clauses but does not give much information beyond what was already found in the contingency table summary. But the association plot in figure 13.5b graphs the data in a way that indicates where the data deviate from the expected (idealized) distribution (Zeileis, Meyer, & Hornik, 2007). In this way, this graphic differs from a barplot by not showing the actual count of the data, but by giving information about the ways that variables might be interacting that would not be expected if there were no relationship between the variables. The association plot in figure 13.5b displays the distribution of counts for the two groups crossed by the two categories of teaching methods, resulting in four areas of interest. Basically, if the data were distributed in a perfectly balanced way across both groups and teaching methods (meaning there was no effect of group and no effect of teaching method), the association plot would just consist of two horizontal lines with no boxes. The presence of a box means that either the count is more than is expected (and the box will be above the horizontal line) or less than expected (and the box is below the horizontal line). The boxes shown with solid lines above the black midpoint line indicate that the count is more than what would be expected if the variables were independent of each other (so there are more people who produce relative clauses with method A than is expected, and more people who do not produce relative clauses than would be expected for method B). The boxes shown with dashed lines below the midpoint line indicate that the count is less than what would be expected if the variables were independent. However, it is not until the square becomes deeply shaded that the difference becomes a statistical difference. In figure 13.5b one box is shaded, but not deeply so, and this indicates a larger difference between the expected count and the reality than the unshaded boxes. However, it is not until the Pearson residuals get larger than +4 that the difference becomes statistical.

At this time, SPSS cannot create association plots. The interested reader could use the *R* statistical program, and might like to consult the appropriate section from the online *R* companion to Larson-Hall (2010).

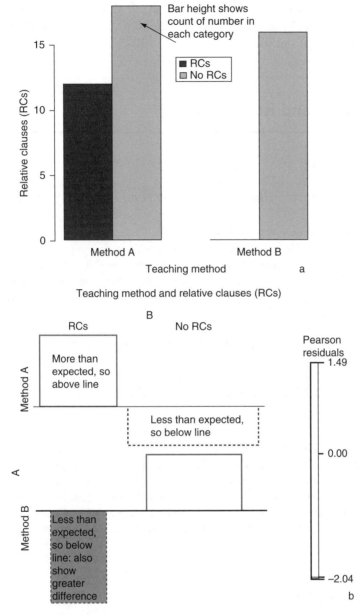

Figure 13.5 Comparing barplot (a) to association plot (b) for categorical data.

Conclusion

This chapter has of necessity cut down on some levels of complexity about statistical analysis which are important. However, for conducting statistical analyses that are some of the most commonly seen in SLA, this chapter should provide some quick help for getting data analyzed and reported (please see "Further Reading" below for ideas about books with more detail to consult). It should also provide the reader with the understanding of which types of graphs are the most useful for reporting data for each type of statistical test.

Project Ideas and Resources

Further Reading

Statistics books with illustrations from the field of psychology

Field, A. (2009). *Discovering statistics using SPSS*. Thousand Oaks, CA: Sage. Large and detailed, with a lot of information on using the SPSS statistical program.

Howell, D. C. (2009). *Statistical methods for psychology* (7th ed.). Pacific Grove, CA: Duxbury/Thomson Learning. Large and detailed, with a moderate amount of information on how to perform analyses by computer using various statistical programs (my favorite textbook from this field).

Pallant, J. (2007). *SPSS survival manual*. Maidenhead, England: Open University Press. Compact, with a large amount of information on using the SPSS statistical program.

Statistics books with illustrations from the field of second language acquisition

Hatch, E. M., & Lazaraton, A. (1991). *The research manual: Design and statistics for applied linguistics*. New York, NY: Newbury House. Large and detailed, but with no information about how to perform analyses by computer, and currently out of print.

Larson-Hall, J. (2010). *A guide to doing statistics in second language research using SPSS*. New York, NY: Routledge. Medium-size, with a large amount of information on using the SPSS statistical program (and website links for using the R statistical program).

Study Questions

1. What are the five most frequently used statistical tests in the reported SLA research literature, and why does this chapter not cover all of these tests?
2. Assume that a study reports that a t-test is statistical, with $p = .03$. What does this mean? (Use the word "probability" in your answer.)
3. Does every author have a null hypothesis? If they do, do they always give their null hypothesis explicitly in their research paper? If they don't, what hypothesis is tested in a statistical test?
4. Why do you think APA guidelines say that exact p-values (unless smaller than .001) should be reported?

5. Assume that a study trying to find a correlation between age and performance on a test found a correlation of $r=.48$. Explain what this means about the relationship between age and test performance.

6. Assume that a study trying to see how three different types of teaching methods affected grammatical accuracy found a difference between method 1 and method 2 with an effect size of $d=2.4$, and the numerical scores for method 2 were higher than for method 1. What would you conclude about how important the difference between these teaching methods was?

7. Assume that you ran a study with 10 participants in each of two groups. You wanted to see whether providing subtitles to movies (or not) would affect vocabulary acquisition in a group of French L2 learners. Assume that a t-test found $t=1.79$, $p=.08$, Cohen's $d=1.3$. What conclusions would you draw about the effect of subtitles on vocabulary acquisition?

Notes

1　As of the writing of this chapter, all of the links worked. However, because websites can change, I have listed at least three websites which will perform each test.

2　Although the level that is usually set in the field is an alpha level$=.05$, I have argued elsewhere (Larson-Hall, 2010) that setting it higher, say, to .10, would result in higher power and would be appropriate for our field. Such a level means we would admit a 10% possibility that we would find a statistic that large or larger just by chance, but the trade-off is that we would gain more power to find the situation that truly exists.

3　This is because increased variation increases the measurement of standard deviation, and the statistical calculations for tests use the standard deviation in the denominator of the calculation equation. This means that the larger the standard deviation, the smaller the statistical test number (such as the t-test value, or the ANOVA F-value) will become, resulting in a higher p-value. For more information, see Larson-Hall and Herrington (2010) and Wilcox (2003).

References

Abrahamsson, N., & Hyltenstam, K. (2009). Age of onset and nativelikeness in a second language: Listener perception versus linguistic scrutiny. *Language Learning, 59*(2), 249–306.

American Psychological Association. (2010). *Publication manual of the American Psychological Association* (6th ed.). Washington, DC: American Psychological Association.

Cohen, J. (1988). *Statistical power analysis for the behavioral sciences*. Newbury Park, CA: Sage.

Cohen, J. (1994). The earth is round (p<.05). *American Psychologist, 49*(12), 997–1003.

Dalgaard, P. (2002). *Introductory statistics with R*. New York, NY: Springer.

Gass, S. (2009). A historical survey of SLA research. In T. K. Bhatia & W. C. Ritchie (Eds.), *The new handbook of second language acquisition* (pp. 3–27). Bingley, England: Emerald.

Harrington, M., & Carey, M. (2009). The on-line yes/no test as a placement tool. *System, 37*, 614–626.

Hatch, E. M., & Lazaraton, A. (1991). *The research manual: Design and statistics for applied linguistics*. New York, NY: Newbury House.

Howell, D. C. (2002). *Statistical methods for psychology* (6th ed.). Pacific Grove, CA: Duxbury/Thomson Learning.

Jalilifar, A. (2009). The effect of cooperative learning techniques on college students' reading comprehension. *System, 38*(1), 96–108.

Kline, R. (2004). *Beyond significance testing: Reforming data analysis methods in behavioral research.* Washington, DC: American Psychological Association.

Kondo-Brown, K. (2006). How do English L1 learners of advanced Japanese infer unknown *kanji* words in authentic texts? *Language Learning, 56*(1), 109–153.

Larson-Hall, J. (2010). *A guide to doing statistics in second language research using SPSS.* New York, NY: Routledge.

Larson-Hall, J., & Herrington, R. (2010). Examining the difference that robust statistics can make to studies in language acquisition. *Applied Linguistics, 31*(3), 368–390.

Oswald, F. L., & Plonsky, L. (2010). Meta-analysis in second language research: Choices and challenges. *Annual Review of Applied Linguistics, 30*, 85–110.

Perry, F. L. (2005). *Research in applied linguistics: Becoming a discerning consumer.* Mahwah, NJ: Lawrence Erlbaum.

Tufte, E. R. (2001). *The visual display of quantitative information* (2nd ed.). Cheshire, CT: Graphics Press.

Wilcox, R. (2001). *Fundamentals of modern statistical methods: Substantially improving power and accuracy.* New York, NY: Springer.

Wilcox, R. (2003). *Applying contemporary statistical techniques.* San Diego, CA: Elsevier.

Zeileis, A., Meyer, D., & Hornik, K. (2007). Residual-based shadings for visualizing (conditional) independence. *Journal of Computational and Graphical Statistics, 16*(3), 507–525.

14   How to Do a Meta-Analysis

Luke Plonsky and Frederick L. Oswald

Background

Before we outline the major steps and key considerations when conducting a meta-analysis, the term will be defined in both a narrow and broad sense. The narrower definition of meta-analysis refers to a statistical method for calculating the mean and the variance of a collection of effect sizes across studies, usually correlations (r) or standardized mean differences (d). The broader definition of meta-analysis includes not only these statistical computations, but the conceptual integration that gives the meta-analysis its substantive meaning. This integration involves the expert's understanding, translation, and communication of the research studies and samples involved, along with the best that theory has to offer across studies and beyond those studies. The current chapter will focus primarily on the practical aspects of meta-analysis more broadly conceived, where meta-analysis addresses (if not solves) three major problems with narrative or qualitative reviews in second language acquisition (SLA) research.

Why Meta-Analysis

The first problem is that narrative reviews often do not account for sampling error variance when interpreting variation in research findings. Small samples alone can contribute to fluctuations in study effects, no matter what the particular theories, samples, measures, or settings are that gave rise to those effects. Rather than treating effect sizes and the accompanying study narrative in a qualitative manner, a meta-analysis is an objective method where study effects with large sample sizes contribute more to meta-analytic results. The second problem with narrative reviews is their general over-reliance on the ritual of null hypothesis significance testing (NHST). If a narrative review focuses narrowly on the results of NHST, two dangers are likely

Research Methods in Second Language Acquisition: A Practical Guide, First Edition.
Edited by Alison Mackey and Susan M. Gass.
© 2012 Blackwell Publishing Ltd. Published 2012 by Blackwell Publishing Ltd.

to arise: some statistically significant results will be given too much attention (i.e., when the actual effect is negligible but significant because it is based on large samples) and non-significant results may be ignored (i.e., whenever many non-significant results would be suggestive of a practically and statistically significant effect if combined in a meta-analysis). The third problem with narrative reviews is that although experts in SLA have a vast storehouse of discipline-specific knowledge, as humans, they are fallible and subject to the foibles of human memory and emotion, making imperfect or inconsistent decisions about a body of research. To be sure, the judgment of SLA researchers remains essential to any literature review process, yet meta-analysis serves as one critical tool that is objective and systematic in nature; meta-analysis can invaluably assist and complement the skills of an expert when interpreting a body of SLA research. Without such tools, they may pay greater attention to empirical findings that are accompanied with more compelling verbal rationale or are published in prestigious journals. It may be obvious that researchers conducting their own individual studies ought to rely on statistics to summarize their data, but it is no less important to use statistical methods to summarize data across studies, and meta-analysis is one such method.

In addition to addressing these three problems with a more comprehensive and systematic approach to synthesizing primary research, meta-analysis can answer focused substantive research questions that cannot be answered in any individual study, such as "What is the overall effect of a particular treatment or intervention (e.g., reading strategy instruction on second language (L2) reading ability; Taylor, Stevens, & Asher, 2006)?" and "How strong is the relationship between two or more constructs (e.g., motivation and L2 achievement; Masgoret & Gardner, 2003)?"

The Prominence of Meta-Analysis

As found in the work of Pearson and his eponymous correlation coefficient over a century ago (Pearson, 1904), scientific researchers have long since engaged in the practice of averaging effects found across a set of studies or observations; however, meta-analysis has developed relatively recently as a formalized statistical method for doing so. Over the past 35 years, meta-analysis has become essential to those disciplines that were first introduced to it: psychology, education, and medicine. Literally thousands of meta-analyses have been published since the inception of the method (Dalton & Dalton, 2008), and they often end up as canonical citations in the literature.

In the field of SLA, meta-analysis was not formally introduced until much more recently (Ross, 1998, and then Norris & Ortega, 2000), yet its application in the discipline has expanded dramatically since then (see figure 14.1). Numerous methodological papers on meta-analysis in SLA provide further evidence for the interest in the topic (e.g., Norris & Ortega, 2007, 2010; In'nami, & Koizumi, 2010; Oswald & Plonsky, 2010; Plonsky, 2011), as well as an explicitly stated preference for meta-analyses in the Call for Papers of the 2009 and 2010 Second Language Research Forum.

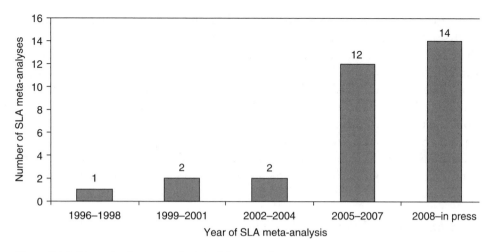

Figure 14.1 Growth of meta-analysis in L2 research.

How to Do a Meta-Analysis

Meta-analysis has many parallels with the primary studies it attempts to summarize. In both cases, the researcher must define the domain of interest, develop measures, collect and analyze data, and interpret the theoretical and practical significance of those findings.

Defining the Research Domain

Defining the research domain of a meta-analysis is the critical first step that impacts all subsequent steps. This often involves bridging the territory that a particular theory (or theories) has staked out with what has been covered empirically and is available. Such a task can be deceptively challenging. To illustrate this point, consider several SLA meta-analyses that have looked at the effects of corrective feedback. Li's (2010) meta-analysis cast the net somewhat broadly by including primary studies that measured the effects of oral or computer-mediated feedback on any type of L2 feature. By contrast, Russell and Spada (2006) restricted their meta-analysis to grammatical forms, while others pursued an even narrower focus by examining feedback effects in classroom contexts (Lyster & Saito, 2010) or on L2 writing (Truscott, 2007; Poltavtchenko & Johnson, 2009). Still others have meta-analyzed the effects of different types of error correction as subsets of larger syntheses on L2 instruction (Norris & Ortega, 2000) and L2 interaction (Mackey & Goo, 2007). Although the effects of corrective feedback were meta-analyzed on several occasions, each study defined the domain uniquely and, consequently, arrived at a unique result.

The scope of research covered is sometimes guided by the statistical question regarding the minimum number of primary studies required for an appropriate meta-analysis. As with primary research, a larger sample provides the researcher with greater statistical power, more general results, and more refined moderator analyses (Cohn & Becker, 2003; Valentine, Pigott, & Rothstein, 2010). Nevertheless, there is also value in conducting a *local* meta-analysis on a smaller set of narrow replications (Oswald & McCloy, 2003), which can be easier to interpret when the goal is to understand relationships dealing with the same measure, setting, and research question. We recommend that meta-analyses find a balance between these two endpoints: meta-analyses can take a broader approach in the literature search and the analysis, followed by narrower and more focused subgroup analyses. In this way, the meta-analysis can have the conceptual and statistical breadth that reflects the literature, along with more refined hypotheses and analyses as the study data allow.

Conducting the Literature Search

Specifying the breadth of the SLA research domain to be meta-analyzed requires balancing the researcher's a priori goals with whatever research literature is actually available. Even a task as routine as searching an academic database requires the meta-analyst to choose which databases and keywords to search, both of which will influence the studies that ultimately are found. The most popular databases among L2 meta-analysts have been the Education Resources Information Center (ERIC; http://www.eric.ed.gov), Linguistics and Language Behavior Abstracts (LLBA; http://www.csa.com/factsheets/llba-set-c.php), and PsycINFO (http://www.apa.org/pubs/databases/psycinfo/index.aspx) (In'nami & Koizumi, 2010; Oswald & Plonsky, 2010). In addition to these and other databases (e.g., Academic Search Premier and ProQuest Dissertations and Theses), we also recommend databases that show who has cited a particular article, such as Web of Science and Google Scholar (see White, 2009, for additional search strategies).

Despite their convenience and accessibility, databases and other computer resources can be incomplete and should always be used in concert with other literature-searching strategies (see McManus et al., 1998). Eligible studies might also be found by "manually" searching book chapters, journal archives, conference programs, technical reports, websites of government and non-government agencies (e.g., Center for Applied Linguistics, Title VI Language Research Centers), as well as more personal and/or interactive venues that Cooper (1998) refers to collectively as the "invisible college" (p. 49), such as academic listservs, professional websites of well-known scholars in a particular area, and individual researchers who may be contacted for manuscripts that would otherwise be inaccessible.

Filtering the Literature: Inclusion and Exclusion Criteria

At a minimum, a meta-analyst should catalog and report steps that would allow someone to replicate the literature search: the databases and keywords that were used, other sources that were searched (conference programs, technical reports), researchers who were contacted, the steps that were taken either to broaden or to refine the literature search as it proceeded, and the standards that were applied that led to a study being either included or excluded from the meta-analysis. The methods and criteria that are developed and applied during the literature search may seem somewhat mechanical in nature but can affect the study outcome dramatically. Truscott (2007) used 548 words to describe very specific inclusion criteria for his meta-analysis of corrective feedback on L2 writing ($d = -0.16$). A similar meta-analysis by Poltavtchenko and Johnson (2009) used 42 words to describe their broader inclusion criteria and obtained a result that differed in both size and direction ($d = 0.33$).

Generally, we suggest that it is much better to over-search the literature than to under-search it. A thorough search will likely result in a number of studies that appear relevant initially but fail to meet one or more of the search criteria. These studies may be useful because their reference sections may contain citations to additional useful literature. Although it can be somewhat laborious, these and all other procedures involved in the literature search should be documented as the search is conducted by maintaining, at a minimum, a log of which databases, websites, and so forth have been searched and which search terms and keywords have been used. This helps keep a record of the process and avoid repeat searches, document the proportion of studies that were retained after inclusion criteria were applied, and inform readers' assessments of comprehensiveness. This is one area where many meta-analyses fall short. (Ross's, 1998, meta-analysis of the validity of L2 self-assessment, for instance, listed only the inclusion criteria and provided no details of how or where the search for primary studies was carried out. See In'nami & Koizumi, 2009, pp. 223–225, for their detailed description of the process by which primary reports were searched for and culled.)

Designing a Coding Sheet

In most meta-analyses, a coding sheet serves as the data collection instrument. As such, it requires a careful and thorough design with categories broad enough to absorb data from a set of studies with potentially mixed conceptual and methodological approaches, but narrow enough to allow for subgroup analyses wherever enough study data have accumulated. Perhaps more than any other, this stage of the meta-analysis depends on the meta-analyst's substantive expertise and creativity in determining study characteristics to be coded. And as with previous steps, we recommend tending toward an inclusive approach, coding for more variables predicted by the theoretical and empirical literature rather than fewer.

Lipsey and Wilson (2001) categorize the items in a meta-analysis coding sheet into two general categories: study descriptors and study outcomes. Four types of study descriptors are usually coded: (a) study identifiers, (b) study sample and context, (c) research design, and (d) measures. Study quality is a fifth category that can be coded for and used during the analysis phase to weight studies, so that those of higher quality contribute more to the meta-analytic average or to assess the relationship between measured research quality and study outcomes (see Plonsky & Gass, 2011, Plonsky, 2011, and Plonsky, in press, for assessments of primary study quality in SLA). Study outcomes are effect sizes (d values and correlations) or the descriptive statistics that

Table 14.1 Suggested categories for coding within meta-analyses of L2 research

Coding category	Items
Identification	Author, Year, Source/venue, Journal, Title
Study context	Second language/foreign language (SL/FL), Classroom/laboratory, Type of institution (e.g., elementary, university), Age, Target language(s), first language (L1), L2 proficiency level, Location of study
Design and treatment	Observational vs. (quasi-)experimental; Pretest (Y/N); Delayed posttest (Y/N); Number of delayed posttests; Interval(s) between treatment and delayed posttest(s); Comparison group (Y/N); Random assignment by classroom or group (Y/N); Random assignment by individual (Y/N); Number (N): comparison group(s); N: treatment group(s); Length of intervention: minutes/hours; Length of intervention: days/weeks; Teacher-, researcher-, or teacher/researcher-led intervention; Pre-treatment equivalence of groups
Measures	Dependent variable(s), Type(s) of outcomes measures (e.g., open-ended, Likert scale, recall, grammaticality judgment task), Reliability (alpha, test–retest, inter-rater)
Outcomes	Means and standard deviations for both control and experimental groups, Effect sizes (*d*-value, correlation, eta-squared, partial eta-squared), Frequencies, Percentages, *p*-values, Statistical test results (e.g., *t*- or *F*-values)

allow for their computation (e.g., group means, standard deviations, regression weights).

Although no one coding sheet will work for everyone, certain information will be common to almost all meta-analyses (see table 14.1; see Lipsey & Wilson, 2001, for a non-domain-specific example, and Abraham, 2008, for an example from the L2 literature). Other information particular to the domain being meta-analyzed will also need to be coded. For example, a meta-analysis of reading comprehension intervention studies might code for variables such as the study's text length and genre, learners' L2 vocabulary knowledge, and first language (L1) reading ability. A coding manual that defines each variable and its associated values is also needed in order to train coders, resolve inter-coder ambiguities, and generally ensure that the coding stage leads to a reliable and justifiable dataset. (See Wilson, 2009, for a thorough discussion of decision points and procedures related to developing a valid and reliable coding scheme for meta-analysis.)

Finally, "the first draft of a coding sheet should never be the last" (Cooper, 1998, p. 30). The meta-analyst should be prepared to pilot, revise, and re-pilot the coding sheet before and even during the coding process.

The Coding Process

If meta-analytic results are the meal that readers feast upon, coding is what happens back in the kitchen to prepare the food for the meal. Coding is the essential process of meta-analysis, whereby information from a variety of formats—graphs, tables, text, and so forth—from each study is translated into a standardized format on the coding sheet previously described. It is also the most time-consuming process involved. Each study may have its own coding sheet, which then gets input into a spreadsheet; alternatively, the meta-analyst may code studies directly into a spreadsheet.

During the coding process, expert knowledge will prove especially useful as the meta-analyst discovers important study characteristics that were not anticipated. Sometimes this means going back and recoding an initial set of studies. In this sense, the coding process is often an iterative one. Furthermore, as primary studies are coded, it will be apparent that some variables will be coded in a very straightforward manner (e.g., target language) and others will require more judgment (e.g., task complexity). Still other variables may appear straightforward with explicitly stated values reported in primary studies, but the coding for these variables may actually be much more complex. For example, consider how L2 proficiency might be coded in a meta-analysis. Should coding be based on months of exposure to the language, number of semesters of target language instruction, vocabulary knowledge scores, class grades, or some combination of these? And what if this information is reported unevenly across studies? This is one example of why it is good practice to keep a log (paper or electronic) to record all decisions that had to be made during the coding process, and particularly whenever a value recorded in the coding sheet was not stated explicitly in the study and had to be inferred (cf. Orwin & Cordray, 1985). By keeping a log, the meta-analyst can then report the extent to which data for certain variables were inferred, imputed, or left out.

At least one additional rater should be trained and then asked to code as many of the studies being meta-analyzed as possible. Lipsey (2001) recommends double-coding at least 20 but ideally 50 or more studies. However, with a median sample of only 16 studies in the 27 L2 meta-analyses reviewed by Oswald and Plonsky (2010), it may be possible to double-code all of the studies involved in the meta-analysis. It is then very important to report some measure of inter-rater agreement to determine coding accuracy (e.g., intra-class correlation, Cohen's kappa, percent agreement), along with some description of the number and nature of rating discrepancies and how their resolution was achieved and how any disagreements were handled. Additionally, we also urge SLA meta-analysts to make their coding procedure and all coding sheets directly accessible to their readership available as supplementary material (e.g., Excel sheets, scanned PDF files). These documents can be made available through journals' or individual researchers' websites by providing a link in the written report or a footnote such as that in Plonsky (in press) that states "In order to facilitate replication and/or re-analysis, the data set used in this study will be made available upon request."

Analysis

As we stated at the outset of this chapter, meta-analysis essentially involves calculating a mean effect size and its corresponding variance from a particular body of SLA research. Whereas the literature searching and coding stages help ensure the body of research is appropriate, the analysis stage is where the meta-analyst decides how best to aggregate those data to estimate this overall mean and variance.

There can be some challenges in the aggregation process. A single study, for example, may report multiple effect sizes on the same relationship, based on multiple settings, multiple groups, multiple measures, and/or multiple time points. It may be justifiable merely to average them prior to the meta-analysis. But often, the data dependencies in studies like these are more complex. For instance, caution must be exercised when handling a set of studies where some are pretest–posttest designs and others are between-groups designs. Although most SLA meta-analyses have treated effects from both types of studies as comparable, they should generally be treated separately, because pretest–posttest designs tend to produce larger effects (see Morris, 2008). A related issue is how SLA meta-analyses have mistakenly applied the between-groups formula for the *d* value to pretest–posttest designs. This is a mistake because in the latter case, calculation of an appropriate *d* value requires the correlation between pre- and posttests. This correlation is almost never reported in primary studies but without its value (or some reasonable estimate), the effect size will be biased (Cheung & Chan, 2004; Gleser & Olkin, 2009).

Another common issue in the analysis phase is how to deal with missing data. Studies often lack information critical to meta-analysis. Sometimes the only option is to remove them, and most SLA meta-analyses have had to do this with some of the studies under consideration. However, if the number of available studies for meta-analysis itself is preciously small, then a second option might be to estimate unreported values (cf. Higgins, White, & Wood, 2008). A meta-analyst must weigh the benefits of retaining studies that at least provide partial information by estimating the data that they lack, with the potential drawbacks of estimating or assuming too much out of the missing data. A third option is to request missing data directly from the study's researchers (two SLA meta-analyses have reported this approach resulting in a modest increase in available data). Although this last decision may be the ideal solution, it may be a challenge to contact researchers successfully and have them comply with data requests (see Orwin, 1994; McManus et al., 1998).

Weighting Effect Sizes

Once all effect sizes have been compiled, calculated, or converted into the same metric (e.g., correlations to *d* values), it is time to compute the meta-analytic mean and variance, both of which require weighting the effect sizes. One could merely average the effect sizes, but this would be inappropriate because some effect sizes are more accurate than others. At the very least, an SLA meta-analysis should weight effect sizes by their corresponding sample size. This operationalizes the assumption that larger samples have greater statistical power and therefore should contribute more to the meta-analytic estimates of the mean and variance. The meta-analytic mean in this case is simply each effect size multiplied by its corresponding sample size, divided by the total sample size across studies. Other techniques for weighting effect sizes are much more complex, such as those that attempt to account for the attenuating effects of measurement unreliability and range restriction: studies that are more reliable or with less range restriction contribute more to the meta-analysis than those effects that are less reliable or with more range restriction (Hunter & Schmidt, 2004; for an example in SLA, see Masgoret & Gardner, 2003). A meta-analyst can also create a weight that multiplies together the individual weights for sampling error variance, reliability, possibly incorporating other factors such as rated study quality (see Hunter & Schmidt, 2004, and Schmidt, Le, & Oh, 2009, for detailed information on this approach). This is a more complex method that should be pursued but perhaps in the future, once the use of meta-analysis in SLA has matured and studies routinely report information on measurement reliability. In general, it is the meta-analyst's responsibility to strike a balance between choosing a meta-analysis method that is too simple versus one that is too complex in order to summarize the data in a reliable and maximally informative manner.

Choice of Meta-Analysis Model

The choice of meta-analysis model that an SLA researcher decides to use is what determines the approach to estimating the meta-analytic mean and variance. A *fixed effects* (FE) model assumes that there is only one population effect size, and all effect sizes are sample realizations of that population effect. Therefore, under the FE model, any observed variation in effects across studies is assumed to be predictable, from either sampling error variance, statistical artifacts (e.g., differences in measurement reliability), or moderator variables. The Q-test for homogeneity of effect sizes is a post-hoc test of this assumption. When this test is statistically significant, that provides evidence that the FE model is not strictly true due to unmodeled variance. A *random effects* (RE) meta-analysis model, on the other hand, directly estimates the meta-analytic variance in effect sizes rather than assume it is zero. This variance estimate can be used to determine the practical significance heterogeneity: take the square root to get the standard deviation, then create a 90% or 95% *credibility interval* to estimate the range of effects across study populations.

The RE model is preferred over the FE model because it is more flexible (Schmidt, Oh, & Hayes, 2009). Specifically, if the RE model arrives at a variance estimate that is zero, the RE model becomes the FE model. By contrast, a statistically significant Q-test in the FE model does not indicate practically significant variance as the variance estimate and credibility interval in the RE model does. We felt the need to introduce FE and RE models briefly, because these are now entrenched in the meta-analysis literature. In terms of practical benefit, however, we believe that SLA meta-analysis is much more productive and useful for computing weighted averages within and across subgroups, and the choice of meta-analysis model generally does not change this average very much. Despite the conceptual appeal of RE models, the variance estimates they produce are notoriously inaccurate, meaning that if we trust them, we may often

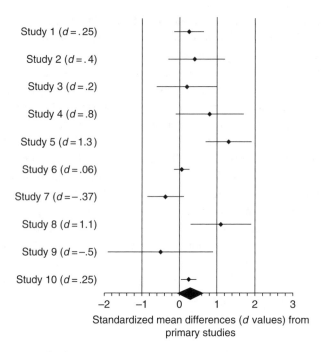

Study 1 ($d = .25$)

Study 2 ($d = .4$)

Study 3 ($d = .2$)

Study 4 ($d = .8$)

Study 5 ($d = 1.3$)

Study 6 ($d = .06$)

Study 7 ($d = -.37$)

Study 8 ($d = 1.1$)

Study 9 ($d = -.5$)

Study 10 ($d = .25$)

Standardized mean differences (d values) from primary studies

Figure 14.2 Example of a forest plot.

make the mistaken inference that homogeneity exists when it does not, or that study effects are heterogeneous when they are not (Oswald & Johnson, 1998; Hedges & Pigott, 2001; although see Sutton & Higgins, 2008). It is much better to take an a priori approach to understanding variance in effect sizes by dividing study effects into a priori subgroups determined by theory and/or coded variables, meta-analyzing the subgroups, and comparing the meta-analytically weighted average effects. This approach is far superior to the post-hoc approaches of estimating effect sizes in the RE model or testing for effect size heterogeneity with the Q-test.

Finally, in line with the saying "a picture is worth a thousand words," graphs and plots of data serve as critical tools in any data analysis (Wilkinson & Task Force on Statistical Inference, 1999), and the forest plot and funnel plot are the primary visualization tools used in meta-analysis (Borenstein, Hedges, Higgins, & Rothstein, 2009). A *forest plot* presents the size of the effect on the x axis with the names of the studies being ordered (alphabetically or by the magnitude of the effect) on the y axis (see figure 14.2). The plotted points usually bisect a symmetric horizontal bar that shows the 95% confidence interval (CI), and in the bottom row is the meta-analytic mean and its 95% CI. A *funnel plot* provides similar information to a forest plot: It is a scatterplot of the effect size on the x axis, with some function of measurement precision associated with the effect on the y axis (e.g., the sample size, the inverse of the sampling error variance). If the level of imprecision in some studies is much larger than the variance in the effects of the underlying study populations (as is usually the case), then this plot will tend to show a funnel shape, hence the name (see figure 14.3). Asymmetries in the funnel plot can serve as an indicator of publication bias, such as when authors, editors, and reviewers suppress small or statistically non-significant

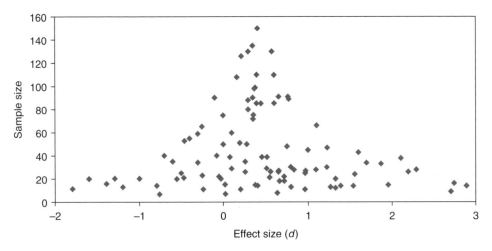

Figure 14.3 Example of a funnel plot without the presence of publication bias.

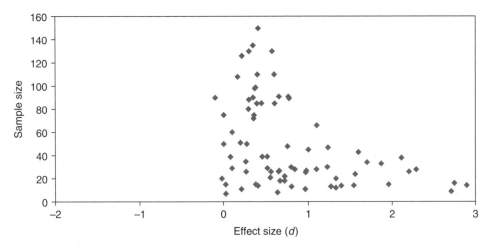

Figure 14.4 Example of a funnel plot with the presence of publication bias.

effects (see figure 14.4). Asymmetries can also indicate the need to examine modera-tor effects (subgroup analyses) or other anomalies, such as the question of whether effect sizes from one research team tend to be much larger than the rest. In short, the forest plot and funnel plot for publication bias are indispensible visualization tools that can indicate meaningful patterns in the meta-analytic database.

In closing this section on the analysis stage in meta-analysis, we want to point out our bottom-line intent. Our goal is for SLA researchers to understand how studies are weighted in meta-analysis and how FE and RE meta-analytic models assume or estimate the variance across study effect sizes. However, we ultimately recommend that meta-analytic estimates be considered in combination with graphs of the effects (forest or funnel plots), and of course, a solid knowledge of the research associated with the effects under study. Only then can meta-analysts attempt to give partial insight into three fundamental questions: (a) Are all studies similar enough to be considered replicates of one another? (b) Do subgroups of effect sizes differ in meaningful ways (e.g., lab vs. classroom studies)?, or (c) Are there effect sizes that are outliers or that otherwise show unique characteristics (e.g., a single large-sample military language-learning study within a sample of college-classroom studies)?

Interpreting the Results

Once the analysis is complete, the numerical results must be presented in a meaningful way. Meaningfulness is distinct from the size of the effect: not all large effects are meaningful, and not all small effects are meaningless; it depends critically on the research context (Prentice & Miller, 1992; Kirk, 1996; Volker, 2006).

The d value is the effect size metric used most often in meta-analyses of L2 research (Oswald & Plonsky, 2010), and is most literally interpreted as the meta-analytic average difference between control-group means and experimental-group means in terms of standard deviation units. Several meta-analyses of L2 research have taken this literal approach to interpreting their results (e.g., Taylor et al., 2006). However, it has been the convention—if not the default—across the social sciences to interpret the magnitude of d values according to Cohen's (1988) benchmarks for standardized mean differences (i.e., .20 for small, .50 for medium, and .80 for large; Cohen provides a similar set of benchmarks for other effect size indices such as correlation coefficients and eta-squared). Although these benchmarks serve as a useful starting point for discussing practical significance as opposed to focusing solely on statistical significance, they were never intended to be applied universally. In fact, Cohen (1988) and others (e.g., Hedges, 2008) have argued for years against such a one-size-fits-all approach. Responding to the need for field-specific standards for effect sizes, Oswald and Plonsky (2010) summarized the quantitative results of 27 meta-analyses of L2 research and suggested a preliminary set of benchmarks for interpreting d values in SLA, with .40 representing a generally small effect, .70 medium, and 1.00 large. We are not suggesting that this new set of benchmarks should be applied universally to the breadth of SLA research. Instead we offered this as a single step away from Cohen toward a more specific interpretation of the practical significance of effect sizes from L2 meta-analyses. We hope that many more steps will be taken in the future, as the issue of practical significance becomes increasingly important in SLA research.

For example, the findings of previous syntheses can provide additional sources of comparison for interpreting the relative magnitude of effect sizes in L2 research. Plonsky (in press), for example, discussed the findings of his meta-analysis of L2 strategy instruction in relation to meta-analyses of strategy instruction in L1 educational contexts (e.g., Hattie, Biggs, & Purdie, 1996). Another way to refine these benchmarks is to examine the historical trajectory of effects in the area being investigated. Effect sizes that decrease over time may indicate that the variables of interest are being examined at an increasingly nuanced level (Kline, 2004), in light of theoretical refinements and as research shifts from the laboratory setting (where independent variables are strongly manipulated) to the classroom setting (where independent variables are more naturalistic). Plonsky and Gass (2011), for example, reviewed 174 studies of L2 interaction, finding that average d values tended to decrease steadily over time (1980–1989, $d = 1.62$; 1990–1999, $d = 0.82$; 2000–2009, $d = 0.52$). This finding was attributed in part to increasingly subtle models of interaction that have been introduced, developed, and tested over the last 30 years. In a similar vein, Mackey and Goo (2007) and Plonsky (in press) calculated effects for subgroups based on research context, and substantially larger *d* values were found in both meta-analyses for lab over classroom studies (.96 vs. .57 and .79 vs. .43, respectively; see study box 14.1).

Study Box 14.1

Plonsky, L. (in press). The effectiveness of second language strategy instruction: A meta-analysis. *Language Learning*.

Background

Research on L2 strategy instruction has been extensive, but methods and results in this area have been inconsistent. The goals of this study were to summarize current findings and examine theoretical moderators of the effects of strategy instruction (SI).

Research questions

- How effective is L2 strategy instruction?
- How is SI affected by different learning contexts, treatments, outcome variables, and research methods?

Method

Conventional database searches, Web of Science, and Google Scholar were used to locate a total of 95 unique samples from 61 studies (*N* = 6,791) that met all the inclusion criteria. Each study was then coded on 37 variables. Five of fifteen authors who were contacted provided missing data for studies reporting insufficient information to calculate an effect size.

Statistical tools

Effect sizes (Cohen's *d*) were weighted by sample size and combined to calculate the meta-analytic average, standard error, and confidence intervals. Publication bias was examined using a funnel plot. Summary effects were also calculated for subgroups based on study characteristics.

Results

The meta-analytic *d* value for the effects of L2 strategy instruction was .49, smaller than most effects in the L2 domain but comparable to the results of similar syntheses in L1 educational contexts. Results indicated clear relationships between the effects of SI and research contexts, type and number of strategies taught, length of intervention, skill areas, and several indicators of methodological quality.

In an alternative scenario of how effect sizes may change over time, improvements to design and measurement in a particular research area might overcome the flaws of past research and lead to larger effect sizes (Fern & Monroe, 1996). Meta-analyses by Spada and Tomita (2010) and Mackey and Goo (2007) found that more recent studies prefer using open-ended test formats, which were found to produce larger effect sizes than more constrained test formats in Li (2010; see study box 14.2) and Lyster and Saito (2010) (but larger effects were not found for open-ended formats in Mackey & Goo, 2007, or Norris & Ortega, 2000). It should be noted that

Study Box 14.2

Li, S. (2010). The effectiveness of corrective feedback in SLA: A meta-analysis. *Language Learning*, 60(2), 309–365.

Background

The theoretical and practical centrality of corrective feedback has led to extensive research testing its effects, yet disagreement remains over how empirical findings can inform SLA theory and practice. It is also unclear how different types of feedback, learning contexts, and L2 features might relate to its effectiveness.

Research questions

- What is the overall effect of corrective feedback on L2 learning?
- Do different feedback types impact L2 learning differently?
- Does the effectiveness of corrective feedback persist over time?
- What are the moderator variables for the effectiveness of corrective feedback?

Method

Primarily, Li searched two academic databases, manually searched the archives of over a dozen journals of L2 research, and scanned the references of review articles. This study also included 11 dissertations for a total of 33 unique study reports.

Statistical tools

The Comprehensive Meta-Analysis software program enabled a relatively sophisticated meta-analysis, statistically speaking. All results were calculated and presented using both RE and FE models, and availability and publication bias were addressed using a funnel plot and a trim-and-fill analysis. (Trim-and-fill is a non-parametric statistical technique that adjusts the meta-analytic mean. It does so by estimating effects that appear to be missing if a fixed-effects model and no systematic bias are assumed.) Additionally, Li tested for several subgroup differences between studies.

Results

The overall d value for CF according to the FE model was .61 (RE = .64). Moderator results were also found for feedback types, delayed effects, and different contexts (e.g., classroom vs. lab; see also Lyster & Saito, 2010). There was some evidence of publication bias, yet the effect sizes from the 11 non-published dissertations in this study were larger on average than in published studies.

the two trends described here may occur simultaneously and either cancel each other out or lead to increased variation in effects over time. To be sure, locating and explaining patterns related to the maturity of a domain is complex, and the data will not speak for themselves, once again necessitating the substantive knowledge and perspective of the expert reviewer.

One final consideration with respect to interpreting meta-analytic effect sizes is the degree to which independent variables in primary research are manipulated. From a practical standpoint, a particular intervention may not be feasible, despite producing a large effect, if it is excessively involved or laborious. Conversely, an instructional treatment leading to small effects may be well worth integrating into L2 pedagogy when the effort in applying it is minimal. Lee and Huang (2008), for instance, found a meta-analytic d value of .22 for the effect of input enhancement on L2 grammar learning. Although this effect is small by most standards, the benefits of enhanced input may justify the minimal cost required to achieve them.

Conclusion

Meta-analysis has immense potential to summarize SLA research in a systematic manner, adding clarity to the current status of its theoretical claims while providing critical research insights and research directions. Along with the benefits, however, taking on a meta-analytic approach introduces a set of challenges, those inherent to the method as well as particular to the field of SLA. In light of these challenges, we close with suggestions that summarize the approach and perspective that we have presented throughout this chapter. First, despite what this chapter's title might suggest, there is no single best way to do a meta-analysis. Each step involves multiple decisions that must be made in accordance with the researcher's goals, the substantive domain being synthesized, and the practical constraints of the available data. As a principle, we believe that better decisions are usually the simpler ones, such as analyses that are clear and understandable as opposed to more sophisticated analyses that are technically correct but confusing and without practical benefit. Second, as each of these important decisions is made, it is essential that the SLA meta-analyst maintain precise records so the results are understood appropriately in the context of the entire process that led to them. Third and last, we have attempted to identify and translate some of the general insights that other disciplines have gained through decades of experience with meta-analysis, and we hope that other SLA researchers will do the same in these critical formative years for meta-analysis in SLA. With some confidence, we can predict for SLA what has happened in all other major disciplines that have been exposed to meta-analysis: the coming years will show an exponential gain in the publication of meta-analytic results. Meta-analysis will begin to be the microscope through which past SLA research is interpreted as well as the telescope through which theoretical developments and future research efforts in SLA will be directed. Exciting times lie ahead as meta-analysis becomes an essential tool in the SLA researcher's toolbox.

Project Ideas and Resources

Further Reading

History

- Introduction of meta-analysis to the field of education: Glass (1976).
- Introduction of meta-analysis to industrial/organizational psychology: Schmidt and Hunter (1977).
- Early work on combining quantitative results across studies: Rosenthal (1978).
- Meta-analysis as an alternative to qualitative reviews: Cooper and Rosenthal (1980).
- One of the first book-length treatments of meta-analysis: Hedges and Olkin (1985).

Current methods

- Accessible introduction to meta-analysis: Lipsey and Wilson (2001).
- Advanced meta-analytic techniques (e.g., correcting for measurement error and range restriction): Hunter and Schmidt (2004).
- Publication bias in meta-analysis: Rothstein, Sutton, and Borenstein (2005).
- APA reporting standards for primary studies and meta-analyses: APA Publications and Communications Board Working Group on Journal Article Reporting Standards (2008).
- Current, thorough coverage of meta-analytic techniques: Borenstein et al. (2009).
- Specialized handbook on meta-analysis: Cooper, Hedges, and Valentine (2009).

Meta-analytic methods in L2 research

- First edited volume of meta-analyses in SLA: Norris and Ortega (2006a).
- Introduction to meta-analysis and research synthesis in SLA: Norris and Ortega (2006b, 2007).
- Database searches for meta-analysis: In'nami and Koizumi (2010).
- Introduction to research synthesis: Ortega (2010).
- Timeline of research synthesis and meta-analysis: Norris and Ortega (2010).
- Review of meta-analysis in L2 research: Oswald and Plonsky (2010).
- Meta-analysis and replication: Plonsky (in press).
- Plonsky's online bibliography of meta-analysis in applied linguistics.

Software and Resources

- David B. Wilson's "Meta-analysis stuff": http://mason.gmu.edu/~dwilsonb/ma.html.
- Borenstein's Comprehensive Meta-Analysis commercial software program: http://www.meta-analysis.com.
- Meta-analysis in Excel using MIX 2.0: http://www.meta-analysis-made-easy.com.
- Windows-based meta-analysis software, developed in the medical field: http://tuftscaes.org/meta_analyst.

Study Questions

Specific

1. *Defining the domain*: Consider two or three of the meta-analyses of corrective feedback (CF). How do the studies differ in terms of their domain of interest and inclusion/exclusion criteria? And how did their different operationalizations of CF relate to their research questions and results?
2. *Locating primary studies*: Examine the search strategies used in any three SLA meta-analyses. Are they the same? Are they different? Does one search appear more exhaustive than the others?
3. *Designing a coding sheet*: Choose an area of SLA research that you are very familiar with. Make a list of the substantive and methodological variables you would code for if you were going to meta-analyze the body of research in that area.
4. *Coding*: Using the list of codes from question 3, which items would you consider to be *high-inference* and *low-inference*? Try to write a definition for each of the high-inference items, then try coding a study in that area according to your coding sheet and reflect on the precision and usefulness of your definitions.

5. *Analyses*: Examine and compare the funnel plots in Norris and Ortega (2000, p. 452), Li (2010, p. 331), and Plonsky (in press). Do you see any evidence for publication bias in those plots? If so, which one(s)? Do you see any other irregularities? How might they be explained?

6. *Interpreting the results*: The overall findings in Plonsky's (in press) meta-analysis of strategy instruction are interpreted in a variety of ways (e.g., compared to a meta-analysis of LI strategy instruction, Cohen's benchmarks, Oswald & Plonsky's, 2010, benchmarks, standard deviation units). Which one(s) do you find most informative or relevant to the discussion? Why?

General

7. Which steps in carrying out a meta-analysis are the most/least objective and subjective? How might each step of a meta-analysis affect the results that are obtained.

8. With whom would you want to collaborate on a meta-analysis (faculty in other disciplines, graduate students)? Explain your answer.

9. Which areas of SLA research do you think might be good candidates for meta-analysis?

10. Describe the most important similarities between primary research and meta-analysis.

11. Meta-analyses depend entirely on past research, but they can also be used to direct future research. Select an SLA meta-analysis and consider its implications for future research.

12. Imagine that you were carrying out a meta-analysis in a particular area of L2 research and wanted to investigate the quality of studies in your sample. How would you operationalize and measure study quality in that area? What would you do with these data on study quality?

13. What are some of the benefits and drawbacks of using benchmarks such as Cohen's (1988) or Oswald and Plonsky's (2010) to explain the magnitude of effects found in a meta-analysis?

References

Abraham, L. B. (2008). Computer-mediated glosses in second language reading comprehension and vocabulary learning: A meta-analysis. *Computer Assisted Language Learning, 21*(3), 199–226.

APA Publications and Communications Board Working Group on Journal Article Reporting Standards. (2008). Reporting standards for research in psychology: Why do we need them? What might they be? *American Psychologist, 63*, 839–851.

Borenstein, M., Hedges, L. V., Higgins, J. P. T., & Rothstein, H. R. (2009). *Introduction to meta-analysis*. Chichester, England: Wiley.

Cheung, S. F., & Chan, D. K-S. (2004). Dependent effect sizes in meta-analysis: Incorporating the degree of interdependence. *Journal of Applied Psychology, 89*(5), 780–791.

Cohen, J. (1988). *Statistical power analysis for the behavioral sciences* (2nd ed.). Hillsdale, NJ: Lawrence Erlbaum.

Cohn, L. D., & Becker, B. J. (2003). How meta-analysis increases statistical power. *Psychological Methods, 8*(3), 243–253.

Cooper, H. (1998). *Synthesizing research: A guide for literature reviews.* Thousand Oaks, CA: Sage.

Cooper, H., Hedges, L. V., & Valentine, J. C. (Eds.). (2009). *The handbook of research synthesis and meta-analysis* (2nd ed.). New York, NY: Russell Sage Foundation.

Cooper, H. M., & Rosenthal, R. (1980). Statistical versus traditional procedures for summarizing research findings. *Psychological Bulletin, 87*(3), 442–449.

Dalton, D. R., & Dalton, C. M. (2008). Meta-analyses: Some very good steps toward a bit longer journey. *Organizational Research Methods, 11*(1), 127–147.

Fern, E. F., & Monroe, K. B. (1996). Effect-size estimates: Issues and problems in interpretation. *Journal of Consumer Research, 23*(2), 89–105.

Glass, G. V. (1976). Primary, secondary, and meta-analysis of research. *Educational Researcher, 5*, 3–8.

Gleser, L. J., & Olkin, I. (2009). Stochastically dependent effect sizes. In H. Cooper, L. V. Hedges, & J. C. Valentine (Eds.), *The handbook of research synthesis and meta-analysis* (2nd ed., pp. 357–376). New York, NY: Sage.

Hattie, J. A., Biggs, J., & Purdie, N. (1996). Effects of learning skills interventions on student learning: A meta-analysis. *Review of Educational Research, 66*(2), 99–136.

Hedges, L. V. (2008). What are effect sizes and why do we need them? *Child Development Perspectives, 2*(3), 167–171.

Hedges, L. V., & Olkin, I. (1985). *Statistical methods for meta-analysis.* Orlando, FL: Academic Press.

Hedges, L. V., & Pigott, T. D. (2001). The power of statistical tests in meta-analysis. *Psychological Methods, 6*(3), 203–217.

Higgins, J. P. T., White, I. R., & Wood, A. M. (2008). Imputation methods for missing outcome data in meta-analysis of clinical trials. *Clinical Trials, 5*(3), 225–239.

Hunter, J. E., & Schmidt, F. L. (2004). *Methods of meta-analysis: Correcting error and bias in research findings.* Thousand Oaks, CA: Sage.

In'nami, Y., & Koizumi, R. (2009). A meta-analysis of test format effects on reading and listening test performance: Focus on multiple-choice and open-ended formats. *Language Testing, 26*(2), 219–244.

In'nami, Y., & Koizumi, R. (2010). Database selection guidelines for meta-analysis in applied linguistics. *TESOL Quarterly, 44*(1), 169–184.

Kirk, R. E. (1996). Practical significance: A concept whose time has come. *Educational and Psychological Measurement, 56*(5), 746–759.

Kline, R. B. (2004). *Beyond significance testing: Reforming data analysis methods in behavioral research.* Washington, DC: American Psychological Association.

Lee, S-K., & Huang, H-T. (2008). Visual input enhancement and grammar learning: A meta-analytic review. *Studies in Second Language Acquisition, 30*(3), 307–331.

Li, S. (2010). The effectiveness of corrective feedback in SLA: A meta-analysis. *Language Learning, 60*(2), 309–365.

Lipsey, M. W., & Wilson, D. B. (2001). *Practical meta-analysis.* Thousand Oaks, CA: Sage.

Lyster, R., & Saito, K. (2010). Oral feedback in classroom SLA: A meta-analysis. *Studies in Second Language Acquisition, 32*(2), 265–302.

Mackey, A., & Goo, J. (2007). Interaction research in SLA: A meta-analysis and research synthesis. In A. Mackey (Ed.), *Conversational interaction in second language acquisition: A collection of empirical studies* (pp. 407–451). New York, NY: Oxford University Press.

Masgoret, A-M., & Gardner, R. C. (2003). Attitudes, motivation, and second language learning: A meta-analysis of studies conducted by Gardner and associates. *Language Learning, 53*(1), 123–163.

McManus, R. J., Wilson, S., Delaney, B. C., Fitzmaurice, D. A., Hyde, C. J., Tobias, R. S., Jowett, S., & Hobbs, F. D. R. (1998). Review of the usefulness of contacting other experts when conducting a literature search for systematic reviews. *British Medical Journal, 317*, 1562–1563.

Morris, S. B. (2008). Estimating effect sizes from pretest–posttest-control group designs. *Organizational Research Methods, 11*(2), 364–386.

Norris, J. M., & Ortega, L. (2000). Effectiveness of L2 instruction: A research synthesis and quantitative meta-analysis. *Language Learning, 50*(3), 417–528.

Norris, J. M., & Ortega, L. (2006a). *Synthesizing research on language learning and teaching.* Philadelphia, PA: John Benjamins.

Norris, J. M., & Ortega, L. (2006b). The value and practice of research synthesis for language learning and teaching. In J. M. Norris & L. Ortega (Eds.), *Synthesizing research on language learning and teaching* (pp. 3–50). Philadelphia, PA: John Benjamins.

Norris, J. M., & Ortega, L. (2007). The future of research synthesis in applied linguistics: Beyond art or science. *TESOL Quarterly, 41*(4), 805–815.

Norris, J. M., & Ortega, L. (2010). Research timeline: Research synthesis. *Language Teaching, 43*, 461–479.

Ortega, L. (2010). Research synthesis. In B. Paltridge & A. Phakiti (Eds.), *Companion to research methods in applied linguistics* (pp. 111–126). London, England: Continuum.

Orwin, R. G. (1994). Evaluating coding decisions. In H. Cooper & L. V. Hedges (Eds.), *Handbook of research synthesis* (pp. 139–162). New York, NY: Russell Sage Foundation.

Orwin, R., & Cordray, D. S. (1985). Effects of deficient reporting on meta-analysis: A conceptual framework and reanalysis. *Psychological Bulletin, 97*(1), 134–147.

Oswald, F. L., & Johnson, J. W. (1998). On the robustness, bias, and stability of statistics from meta-analysis of correlation coefficients: Some initial Monte Carlo findings. *Journal of Applied Psychology, 83*(2), 164–178.

Oswald, F. L., & McCloy, R. A. (2003). Meta-analysis and the art of the average. In K. R. Murphy (Ed.), *Validity generalization: A critical review* (pp. 311–338). Mahwah, NJ: Lawrence Erlbaum.

Oswald, F. L., & Plonsky, L. (2010). Meta-analysis in second language research: Choices and challenges. *Annual Review of Applied Linguistics, 30*, 85–110.

Pearson, K. (1904). Report on certain enteric fever inoculation statistics. *British Medical Journal, 3*, 1243–1246.

Plonsky, L. (2011). *Study quality in SLA: A cumulative and developmental assessment of designs, analyses, reporting practices, and outcomes in quantitative L2 research.* Unpublished doctoral dissertation, Michigan State University, East Lansing, MI.

Plonsky, L. (2011). Replication, meta-analysis, and generalizability. In G. Porte (Ed.), *A guide to replication in applied linguistics.* New York, NY: Cambridge University Press.

Plonsky, L. (in press). The effectiveness of second language strategy instruction: A meta-analysis. *Language Learning.*

Plonsky, L., & Gass, S. M. (2011). Quantitative research methods, study quality, and outcomes: The case of interaction research. *Language Learning, 61*, 325–366.

Poltavtchenko, E., & Johnson, M. D. (2009, March). *Feedback and second language writing: A meta-analysis.* Poster session presented at the annual meeting of TESOL, Denver, CO.

Prentice, D. A., & Miller, D. T. (1992). When small effects are impressive. *Psychological Bulletin, 112*(1), 160–164.

Rosenthal, R. (1978). Combining results of independent studies. *Psychological Bulletin, 85*(1), 185–193.

Ross, S. (1998). Self-assessment in second language testing: A meta-analysis and analysis of experiential factors. *Language Testing, 15*(1), 1–20.

Rothstein, H. R., Sutton, A. J., & Borenstein, M. (Eds.). (2005). *Publication bias in meta-analysis: Prevention, assessment and adjustments.* Chichester, England: Wiley.

Russell, J., & Spada, N. (2006). The effectiveness of corrective feedback for the acquisition of L2 grammar: A meta-analysis of the research. In J. M. Norris & L. Ortega (Eds.), *Synthesizing research on language learning and teaching* (pp. 133–164). Philadelphia, PA: John Benjamins.

Schmidt, F. L., & Hunter, J. E. (1977). Development of a general solution to the problem of validity generalization. *Journal of Applied Psychology, 62*(5), 529–540.

Schmidt, F. L., Le, H., & Oh, I-S. (2009). Correcting for the distorting effects of study artifacts in meta-analysis. In H. Cooper, L. V. Hedges, & J. C. Valentine (Eds.), *The handbook of research synthesis and meta-analysis* (2nd ed., pp. 317–333). New York, NY: Russell Sage Foundation.

Schmidt, F. L., Oh, I-S., & Hayes, T. (2009). Fixed versus random effects models in meta-analysis: Model properties and an empirical comparison of differences in results. *British Journal of Mathematical and Statistical Psychology, 62*(1), 97–128.

Spada, N., & Tomita, Y. (2010). Interactions between type of instruction and type of language feature: A meta-analysis. *Language Learning, 60*(2), 263–308.

Sutton, A. J., & Higgins, J. P. T. (2008). Recent development in meta-analysis. *Statistics in Medicine, 27*(5), 625–650.

Taylor, A., Stevens, J. R., & Asher, J. W. (2006). The effects of explicit reading strategy training on L2 reading comprehension: A meta-analysis. In J. M. Norris & L. Ortega (Eds.), *Synthesizing research on language learning and teaching* (pp. 213–244). Philadelphia, PA: John Benjamins.

Truscott, J. (2007). The effect of error correction on learners' ability to write accurately. *Journal of Second Language Writing, 16*(4), 255–272.

Valentine, J. C., Pigott, T. D., & Rothstein, H. R. (2010). How many studies do you need?: A primer on statistical power for meta-analysis. *Journal of Educational and Behavioral Statistics, 35*(2), 215–247.

Volker, M. A. (2006). Reporting effect size estimates in school psychology research. *Psychology in the Schools, 43*(6), 653–672.

White, H. D. (2009). Scientific communication and literature retrieval. In H. Cooper, L. V. Hedges, & J. C. Valentine (Eds.), *The handbook of research synthesis* (2nd ed., pp. 51–71). New York, NY: Russell Sage Foundation.

Wilkinson, L., & Task Force on Statistical Inference. (1999). Statistical methods in psychology journals: Guidelines and explanations. *American Psychologist, 54*(8), 594–604.

Wilson, D. B. (2009). Systematic coding. In H. Cooper, L. V. Hedges, & J. C. Valentine (Eds.), *The handbook of research synthesis* (2nd ed., pp. 159–176). New York, NY: Russell Sage Foundation.

15 Why, When, and How to Replicate Research

Rebekha Abbuhl

Background

Let's begin with a fictional study. Last year a team of researchers investigated the impact of a particular type of instruction on second language (L2) writing skills. Employing a carefully thought-out research design, appropriate statistics and a decent sample size ($N = 20$), the researchers found that their treatment group made significantly greater gains in writing skills than did a control group. The study went through a rigorous peer review process and was published in one of the top journals of the field. Some might conclude at this point that the issue is settled and that no further research is necessary. In particular, some might believe that *replicating* the study – broadly speaking, repeating it to test whether the same findings are obtained – would be a waste of research time, an insult to the original team of researchers, and, in general, a step unlikely to advance the field. However, nothing could be further from the truth. As Epstein (1980) notes, "there is no more fundamental requirement in science than that the replicability of findings be established" (p. 796).

Replicability is one of the cornerstones of the scientific method in part because it helps prevent Type I and Type II errors (the incorrect rejection or acceptance of the null hypothesis, respectively; Schmidt, 2009). Statistically significant results from a single study are often viewed as "real" and "replicable" (i.e., that similar studies would find the same result; Goodman, 1992; Hubbard & Armstrong, 1994). However, it needs to be kept in mind that even in a study with a statistically significant finding, there is a risk, albeit small, that the results were due to chance. As Lindsay and Ehrenberg (1993) note, "a test of significance tells us no more than that the observed result is in fact *probably* real – as if the whole population in question had been measured – and that it is unlikely to have been the result of a sampling error" (p. 218, italics added). In order to have greater confidence that the results of

Research Methods in Second Language Acquisition: A Practical Guide, First Edition.
Edited by Alison Mackey and Susan M. Gass.
© 2012 Blackwell Publishing Ltd. Published 2012 by Blackwell Publishing Ltd.

the original study were in fact not due to chance or sampling error, replication studies are essential (Levin, 1998; Kelly, 2006).

Replications also help evaluate the validity (both external and internal) of the original study. External validity refers to the extent to which findings can be generalized to a wider population; internal validity refers to the extent to which potential confounds have been controlled for in a study (Abbuhl & Mackey, 2008). If a replication supports the results of the original study, we can have greater confidence that the original results possess external validity and thus are not simply the result of local experimental conditions. Strenuous review processes, sophisticated designs, and/or significant findings cannot by themselves guarantee external validity; it is only when replications are conducted that we can have confidence in the generalizability of our results (Lindsay & Ehrenberg, 1993; Ottenbacher, 1996; Schmidt, 2009). With respect to internal validity, many researchers have noted that the potential for "contaminating" variables is great in any research dealing with human behavior (such as L2 acquisition; Valdman, 1993; Easley, Madden, & Dunn, 2000). Replications, with their potential to tease apart confounding variables, may help us gain a greater understanding of when and under what conditions a particular generalization can be made (Amir & Sharon, 1990).

Given the importance of replication to the scientific method, one might assume that replications were commonly conducted and well represented on the pages of the top journals in our field. Unfortunately, this is not the case. For over twenty years, second language acquisition (SLA) researchers have been commenting on the need for (and lack of) replications (see, for example, Santos, 1989; Polio & Gass, 1997; Language Teaching Review Panel, 2008). The tide is slowly changing – as witnessed, for example, by explicit calls in journals such as *Studies in Second Language Acquisition* and *Language Teaching* for replication studies, by book-length treatments of replication work in our field (Porte, in press), and by conference panels on the topic (Porte et al., 2009) – but work still needs to be done to educate both pre-service and in-service researchers about what replications are and how (and why) they should be conducted.

Types of Replications

Over the years and across disciplines, a variety of labels have been used to refer to different types of replication studies. One may come across such terms as *literal replications, strict replications, conceptual replications, systematic replications, virtual replications*, and so on and wonder how (and whether) each of these differ. Confusing matters, terms are not always used consistently, even within a single discipline. The present discussion draws upon the classification proposed by the Language Teaching Review Panel (LTRP) (2008) and Abbuhl (2009) and used in Porte (in press).

The first point to keep in mind is that replications exist along a continuum, depending on how closely they follow the original study (Hendrick, 1990; Polio & Gass, 1997). *Exact replications* (also known as literal, strict, or virtual replications) involve taking a previous methodologically sound study and repeating it – as the name suggests – exactly (or as exactly as possible; Beck, 1994). This type of replication is virtually non-existent in applied linguistics and other social sciences due to the fact that no subject population, with all of its idiosyncratic characteristics and experiences, can be duplicated exactly. The closest we can come in our field to an exact replication is to have the original researcher(s) conduct the same study again with all or most of the original participants (however, it needs to be kept in mind that time lag between the original and replication studies would almost guarantee that the participants would not have the same level of knowledge or L2 experience as they did in the original study, thus rendering comparisons problematic). An alternative would be to have different researcher(s) adhere to the methods of the original study as closely as possible for the primary purpose of verification (e.g., Birdsong & Molis, 2001, in study box 15.1 below).

A more common type of replication in the social sciences is the *approximate* (also known as partial or systematic) replication. This type of study involves repeating the original study exactly in most respects, but changing one of the non-major variables (so as to allow for comparability between the original and replication studies). For example, researchers may investigate a different population (e.g., a different age or proficiency level of student), perhaps in different setting (English as a second language (ESL) vs. English as a foreign language (EFL), for example), or perhaps using a different task (e.g., a written one instead of an oral one). The purpose of this kind of replication "with changes" is to see whether the results of the original study are generalizable, for example, to a new population, setting, or modality. Examples of this type of replication in the field of SLA include Edge (1991), Leow (1995), Kupferberg (1999), Wong (2001), Mackey and Oliver (2002), Bigelow, Delmas, Hansen and Tarone (2006), Tremblay (2006), Crossley and McNamara (2008), and Eckerth (2009).

Conceptual (also known as constructive) replications are the least similar to the original study. Conceptual replications begin with a similar problem statement as the original study but employ a new research design to verify the original findings. For example, a conceptual replication might use different, but related data collection procedures, such as observation instead of self-report, or use qualitative methods in addition to the quantitative methods relied on in the original study. If successful, conceptual replications provide stronger support for the original findings as they provide evidence that the outcomes were not just artifacts of the original methods. Example SLA studies that may be considered conceptual replications include Allen (2000), Gass and Lewis (2007), and Henry, Culman, and VanPatten (2009). As Polio and Gass (1997) point out, however, "many more studies than claim to be are actually some type of replication … clearly, a fine line exists between replication and extending research" (p. 501).

How to Conduct Replications

The following section will provide information on the key steps involved in choosing a study to replicate, selecting a replication type, and interpreting (and writing up) results.

Study Box 15.1

Birdsong, D., & Molis, M. (2001). On the evidence for maturational constraints in second-language acquisition. *Journal of Memory and Language, 44,* 235–249.

Background

Birdsong and Molis (2001) conducted an exact replication of Johnson and Newport (1989). The original study examined the relationship between age of arrival (AoA) and English grammaticality judgment test (GJT) scores. The original finding – that AoA was a significant predictor of the performance of the early arrivals (native speakers (NSs) of Korean or Chinese who arrived in the USA prior to the age of 15) but not of the late arrivals (after age 17) – was controversial but at the same time widely cited as evidence for a neurobiologically based "critical period" in SLA.

While acknowledging the contributions made by previous partial replications of Johnson and Newport's study, Birdsong and Molis (2001) noted that "because of procedural differences, or because of use of subsets or variations of the original stimuli, these findings cannot be compared directly to those of [Johnson & Newport, 1989]" (p. 237).

Research question

- To facilitate a comparison with the original study, Birdsong and Molis investigated the same research question concerning the effects of age on L2 grammar learning, using the same methods as the original study.

Method

The participants in Birdsong and Molis's study were 61 NS of Spanish (29 who arrived before the age of 16 and 32 who arrived after the age of 17) who had similar levels of education to Johnson and Newport's participants. The participants were given the original test used in Johnson and Newport's study and the same procedures were followed.

Results

Birdsong and Molis found *inter alia* that (a) AoA was not a significant predictor of the early arrivals' performance (due to ceiling effects) and (b) AoA was a significant predictor of the late arrivals' performance, leading the researchers to suggest that the critical period hypothesis may need to be modified or rejected.

Step 1: Critically Review and Choose a Study

While it has been said that, in theory, any study could be replicated, there are in fact certain key questions to keep in mind when choosing a candidate study.

Is the original research question still relevant to the concerns and issues of the field?

As scientific research is less a matter of pursuing personal interests and more a matter of helping a larger discipline gain a greater understanding of an issue, you need to determine whether the issue investigated by the original study is still current (Kugler, Fischer, & Russell, 2006). As the LTRP (2008) states, "what has to be stated is the projected significance *for the field*, apart from simply repeating the experiment, in terms of what we are likely to gain from the new (replication) research" (p. 4, italics added). Replications of trivial studies, articles published in non-refereed journals, or investigations that are not germane to the field's current debates will do little to move the field forward (Kelly, 2006).

Let's say, for example, you are considering replicating a particular study, Guiora, Acton, Erard, and Strickland (1980; a study published in the refereed journal *Language Learning* that dealt with the effect of valium on L2 pronunciation). To see whether the issue (the relationship between drugs and L2 pronunciation) is current, you could go to Google Scholar (www.scholar.google.com) and enter the title ("The effects of benzodiazepine (valium) on permeability of language ego boundaries"). You see that the study has been cited only 34 times in the past 30 years, mostly by authors of non-empirical articles. Additional searches through some relevant peer-reviewed journals in the field (e.g., *Studies in Second Language Acquisition, Journal of Phonetics, Language Teaching Research, Modern Language Journal*) reveal that no authors have either cited this study or investigated the same issue, leading you to conclude that perhaps the effect of imbibed substances on L2 pronunciation is a dead-end line of research. Thus, you might conclude that replicating this particular study (at least at this point in time) is unlikely to inform a current controversy in the field.

Have researchers called for replications of certain studies?

At the end of their studies, researchers commonly discuss the limitations of their work, including sample size, duration of treatment, and confounding variables. They may also make specific recommendations for future replication studies (see, for example, Mackey, 1999; Nassaji & Swain, 2000; Sasaki, 2000; Carpenter, Jeon, MacGregor, & Mackey, 2006; Sheen, Wright, & Moldawa, 2009; to name just a very few). If the original research question is still current (see the preceding subsection), then their commentary could serve as a source of inspiration. Recent meta-analyses and review articles (see, for example, Norris & Ortega, 2000; Ferris, 2004; LTRP, 2008) may also point out specific research areas in need of replication.

What are the strengths and weaknesses of the study?

In addition to carefully reading the comments that researchers typically provide on the limitations of their studies, it is also important to critically evaluate the strengths and weaknesses of the original study (see, for example, Porte, 2002). Are there any threats to the internal or external validity of the study? Is there reason to suspect that the results would not be generalizable to another language, population of learners, or setting? Have important variables been controlled? Does the original study employ a small sample size? Are there significant findings but small effect sizes? In asking yourself questions such as these, you can make informed decisions about which, if any, aspects of the study to modify and what kind of replication to conduct. As noted by LTRP (2008), "all studies have weaknesses or otherwise make compromises, and replication inevitably helps to expose and remedy any weaknesses" (p. 6).

Is conducting a replication of a particular study feasible?

In order to conduct a replication study, a researcher needs to have detailed information on the participants, materials, and procedures of the original study (Santos, 1989). Due in part to space constraints, however, full methodological details are often not reported, making it difficult to reconstruct the original study (Polio & Gass, 1997). Digital databases, access to materials on journal websites (see, for example, the supplementary materials available at the website for *Applied Linguistics*), and stricter reporting standards are all helping to increase the feasibility of replications, but you may also wish to consider contacting the author(s) directly for more information.

Step 2: Decide on the Replication Type

The next step is to decide on the type of replication that is most appropriate for the study you've chosen and the gaps you've identified. If you are interested in "checking" the results of a previous methodologically sound study (especially one that is often cited in the literature or is among a small number of studies being used to support a central theory in the field) *and* have access to the same materials and procedures used in the original study, then an exact replication may be the most appropriate choice (Lindsay & Ehrenberg, 1993; LTRP, 2008). Exact replications can also be useful for checking the results of studies that produce unexpected findings (LTRP, 2008). Study box 15.1 presents information on Birdsong and Molis (2001), a study that may be considered an example of an exact replication.

Whereas exact replications are used primarily for checking the results of an original study, approximate replications are typically used to determine whether earlier results can be generalized to a new population (e.g., Bigelow et al., 2006; see study box 15.2) or setting (e.g., Loewen & Erlam, 2006; see study box 15.3). This type of research is particularly useful when the majority of studies on a topic have

Study Box 15.2

Bigelow, M., Delmas, R., Hansen, K., & Tarone, E. (2006). Literacy and the processing of oral recasts in SLA. *TESOL Quarterly, 40*, 665–689.

Background

Bigelow et al. (2006) conducted an approximate replication of Philp's (2003) study on learners' recall of oral recasts (target-like reformulations of non-target-like learner utterances).

Research question

Noting that Philp's study had been conducted with literate learners and drawing upon research providing evidence that literate and illiterate individuals process oral cognitive tasks differently, Bigelow et al. wanted to determine whether the results of Philp's study (which showed that short recasts with few changes had the greatest rate of recall) would be generalizable to the little-studied population of illiterate learners. In particular, their research question (p. 65) was:

- Is the ability to recall a recast related to the learner's alphabetic print literacy level?

Method

Eight native speakers of Somali (four with moderate levels of literacy and four with low) were recruited to participate in the same tasks given to Philp's (2003) learners: four spot-the-difference tasks and six story-completion tasks. When learners made an error with question formation, they heard a non-verbal auditory prompt (a knock on the table) and the recast, which they were then asked to repeat. Following Philp's method of analysis, Bigelow et al. examined the learners' degree of accuracy in recast recall and the mediating role of recast length and number of changes.

Given the small sample size, the researchers used exact permutation tests to determine whether there were significant differences between the low literate and moderately literate groups in terms of their ability to recall recasts with different characteristics.

Results

Bigelow et al. found that the more literate group recalled significantly more recasts than the less literate group. In contrast to Philp's study, Bigelow et al. also found that neither the length of the recast nor the number of changes in the recast was a significant predictor of recast recall, leading the researchers to conclude that "conscious noticing during oral interaction may be only one of many roads to SLA and of substantially more use for literate populations than for illiterate ones" (p. 685).

Study Box 15.3

Loewen, S., & Erlam, R. (2006). Corrective feedback in the chatroom: An experimental study. *Computer Assisted Language Learning, 19*, 1–14.

Background

Loewen and Erlam (2006) conducted an approximate replication of Ellis, Loewen, and Erlam (2006). Ellis et al. (2006) compared the impact of two types of oral feedback moves (recasts and metalinguistic information) on 34 ESL learners' accuracy with the past tense form, finding that the metalinguistic group outperformed the recast and control groups on an oral elicited imitation test and on the untimed GJT.

Research questions

Highlighting the scarcity of research on computer-mediated communication (CMC) and L2 learning, Loewen and Erlam (2006) sought to determine whether the results of the original study would generalize to this new learning context. Their specific research questions (p. 4) were:

- Does corrective feedback on English regular past tense during online meaning-focused tasks lead to an increase in learners' performance on timed and untimed grammaticality judgment tests?
- Is there a difference in the effectiveness of more implicit and more explicit types of feedback?

Method

Thirty-one ESL learners were recruited to participate in a pretest/posttest/delayed posttest study involving online chat sessions. In these sessions, the learners completed story-retelling tasks and received no feedback (control group), recasts, or metalinguistic feedback from the teacher on all errors with the simple past tense form. Repeated-measures ANOVAs were used to determine whether there were significant group differences on the measures of proficiency (a timed GJT and an untimed GJT).

Results

In contrast to Ellis et al. (2006), Loewen and Erlam (2006) found no significant group differences on either measure of performance and no significant pretest–posttest gains. While not discounting the possibility that their learners were not developmentally ready to acquire the past tense form, the authors suggested that the context itself may have made the feedback less salient to the learners (in chat, contributions to a conversation are posted in the order in which they are received, leading to a lack of adjacency between non-target-like utterances and teacher feedback).

been conducted in only one setting or with only one subject population (LTRP, 2008). As noted by Lindsay and Ehrenberg (1993), approximate replications are "a search for *exceptions*, a route towards establishing the conditions under which the generalization does *not* hold" (p. 221).

In conceptual replications, researchers typically start with the findings from the original study and, from there, develop their own sampling, measurement, and data analysis methods (Kelly, 2006). As Connelly (1986) notes, "in constructive replication, investigators deliberately avoid imitation of the original investigators' methodology" (p. 75); as such, this method is particularly useful for determining whether the original results were an artifact of the particular methodology used. An example of a study that falls more toward the conceptual end of the replication continuum is provided in study box 15.4.

However, although the use of new methods in a conceptual replication helps separate method-specific results from those that can serve as the basis of generalization, there needs to be comparability between the replication and the original study. As more and more variables are changed, the replication "becomes a development from the original rather than an investigation into the latter's validity, reliability, and generalizability" (LTRP, 2008, p. 5). In such a case, the conceptual replication may be deemed uninterpretable if it obtains different results from the original (see, for example, Sanz and VanPatten's, 1998, criticism of Salaberry's, 1997, replication of VanPatten and Cadierno, 1993).

Step 3: Formulate the Research Question

Formulating the research question is a step that you can conduct either before or after you decide on a replication type. In either case, make sure that your question(s) is/are based on your analysis of the strengths and weaknesses of the original study and that the dependent and independent variables are clearly specified. If you are undertaking an exact replication, make sure that your research question(s) is/are not substantially different from the one(s) in the original study. For an approximate replication, be certain that the new element you are introducing (e.g., a new population, target structure, or setting) is clear and well motivated (Gass & Mackey, 2005). Likewise, for a conceptual replication, strive for comparability between the replication and original research questions and clearly motivate all changes made.

Step 4: Interpret the Results

After carrying out the study (following guidelines for methodologically sound research, cf. Porte, 2002; Mackey & Gass, 2005; Dörnyei, 2007), the next step is to interpret the results. If a replication, regardless of the type, supports the findings of the original study, then we can have greater confidence in both the external and internal validity of the original study. As noted earlier, one statistically significant finding cannot be accepted as "the truth"; only when results are repeated in other studies can we have greater confidence that our decision to accept or reject a hypothesis is correct.

Study Box 15.4

Allen, L. (2000). Form–meaning connections and the French causative: An experiment in processing instruction. *Studies in Second Language Acquisition*, 22, 69–84.

Background

Allen (2000) conducted a conceptual replication of VanPatten and Cadierno (1993). VanPatten and Cadierno compared the effect of traditional instruction (TI, operationalized as explicit grammar information plus opportunities for production of the target structure), processing instruction (PI, instruction which alerted learners to faulty input processing strategies, such as interpreting the first noun of a sentence as the agent, but did not involve production of the target structure), and a control group. Using six intact SSL (Spanish as a second language) classes at the university level, the researchers found that the PI group significantly outperformed both the TI and control groups on interpretation tasks, and that the PI and TI groups outperformed the control group on the production tasks (although there was no significant differences between the PI and TI groups on this latter assessment).

Allen (2000) sought to replicate this study using a different language and structure (the French causative), a modified production task (open-ended vs. sentence completion in the original), and larger sample size of high school students. The assessment procedures were similar to those of the original study.

Research question

- Allen also addressed the same research questions as the original study, comparing the different forms of instruction on learners' ability to interpret and produce sentences containing the French causative immediately, one week after, and one month after instruction.

Method

Pretest, posttest, and delayed posttest scores on the production and interpretation tasks were submitted to one-way ANOVAs.

Results

In contrast to the original study, Allen found that there was no significant difference between the PI and TI groups on the interpretation tasks, with both outperforming the control group. On the production task, the TI group significantly outperformed both the PI and control groups. While acknowledging the need for further replication studies, Allen suggested that "processing instruction [may be] effective only for certain grammatical structures" (p. 80).

With respect to the different types of replications, it has sometimes been claimed that exact replications that confirm the results of an original study (so-called "confirming replications") have no "novelty value" (e.g., Kelly, 2006). However, the field of SLA has reached a point where a concern for "novelty" must be balanced with a concern for science. As Polio and Gass (1997, p. 500) note:

> Discussions of replication have received little attention in the field of second language acquisition and, one might venture to say, have been considered relatively unimportant. To some extent, this may have been an acceptable state of affairs in the early years when our field was attempting to identify itself as a valid discipline and valid area of study ... [However], we are now at the point where it seems appropriate and necessary to consider issues surrounding replication more carefully. Replication is, of course, crucial in order to distinguish the spurious from the real and will, undoubtedly, become even more central to our field as we attempt to push our theories forward.

Confirming approximate replications are also important, as they provide evidence that a result is not restricted to a certain population, language, setting, or modality. Likewise, confirming conceptual replications give us more confidence that a finding was not method-specific or due to sampling error.

Although "confirming replications" help increase confidence in findings, this is not to say that disconfirming replications (those that do not support the results of the original study) are "failures" or "worthless" (as has been suggested occasionally in the literature, e.g., Hendrick, 1990). If we view research as a conversation, disconfirming replications suggest that there is a need to continue discussing an issue (Hubbard & Armstrong, 1994; Eden, 2002). So-called "unsuccessful" exact replications, for example, can help the field reassess its acceptance of previous findings, ultimately helping us forge more solid foundations for our theories. Disconfirming approximate replications can provide valuable information as to whether findings can be generalized to new populations, languages, and settings. The approximate replications reviewed in study boxes 15.1 and 15.2 above, for example, provided evidence that the results of previous studies of corrective feedback in L2 learning may not be generalizable to illiterate learners (Bigelow et al., 2006) or to computer-mediated communication (Loewen & Erlam, 2006). Though further studies will obviously be needed before firm conclusions can be reached, these studies, far from being failures, help the field reach a deeper understanding of the multifaceted and complex nature of L2 development.

Disconfirming conceptual replications, however, are potentially more difficult to interpret. A conceptual replication is the least similar to the original study, differing potentially in methodology, target language, subject population, and so on. Thus, when a conceptual replication fails to duplicate the results of the original study (e.g., see study box 15.4 above), it is difficult to determine whether the original results were "merely spurious" or whether there is "something in the methodology or subject population that differed significantly" between the two studies (Polio & Gass, 1997, p. 502). By itself, then, a disconfirming conceptual replication perhaps raises more questions than it answers.

If, however, we return to the analogy of research as a conversation, a disconfirming conceptual replication can be seen as an opportunity for further dialogue and response. VanPatten and Wong (2004), for example, responded to Allen's (2000) replication by conducting a replication of their own. Seeking to determine the exact source of the differences in findings between Allen (2000) and VanPatten and Cadierno (1993) (and noting that full details on both methodology and materials are not always provided in articles), VanPatten and Wong asked Allen for her materials. Inspecting those materials, VanPattern and Wong found some notable differences between VanPatten and Cadierno (1993) and Allen (2000), including (a) the replication materials not addressing event probabilities (i.e., the fact that participants could have relied on real-world knowledge to interpret sentences rather than on their knowledge of the French causative); (b) the replication's use of the third person singular in the interpretation task but the first person singular object pronoun in the production task (making comparison between the two tasks difficult, as the former structure is more difficult than the latter); and (c) the replication's blurring of processing and traditional instruction. In their own replication of VanPatten and Cadierno (1993), using Allen's target structure (the French causative) but addressing Allen's methodological problems, VanPatten and Wong (2004) found that the PI group outperformed the TI and control groups on both the interpretation and production tasks. This finding supported VanPatten and Cadierno's (1993) results. As the methodological discrepancies between the studies were clearly discussed, VanPatten and Wong (2004) were able not only to explain the differences in findings, but also help readers understand how certain methodological changes could impact research results. This sequence of original study, replication, and response is a good example of how replication research can play a role in enhancing the knowledge base of the field.

Step 5: Write Up the Results

When writing up a replication study, the researcher needs to clearly explain why the original study needs replication. The objectives of the particular type of replication chosen should be clearly articulated and theoretically or methodologically motivated. In the literature review, enough detail on the original study needs to provided so that differences, if they arise, between the replication and original can be interpreted. In the method section, the researcher needs to clearly explain what (if any) changes were made (and why they were made) and also cover the methods of his or her own study in sufficient detail to permit comparisons and replications (Polio & Gass, 1997). If space limitations are an issue, details of the questionnaires, survey instruments, and assessment tools can be placed in footnotes, appendices, or external websites; alternatively, note can be made that materials are available upon request from the author(s). In the discussion and conclusion sections, comparisons should be made to the original study "focusing on how and why they are similar or different" (LTRP, 2008, p. 6). In this way, the results of the replication, whether confirming or disconfirming, can be better contextualized and interpreted.

Project Ideas and Resources

Although replications have not received much attention within the field of SLA, there are a few articles and books that focus specifically on replications and can provide useful information for the interested researcher, including Porte (in press), LTRP (2008), and Polio and Gass (1997). In addition, there are book-length treatments of methodology and design issues in SLA research that can help you critically evaluate studies, one of the key steps in identifying studies worthy of replication and determining replication strategies. These include Porte's (2002) book, *Appraising Research in Second Language Learning: A Practical Approach to Critical Analysis of Quantitative Research*, and Mackey and Gass (2005), *Second Language Research: Methodology and Design*.

While these (and hopefully in the future more) resources will benefit researchers interested in conducting replications, resources alone will not help end the field's treatment of replications as poor cousins of original research. As mentioned earlier, replications are ascribed little importance by journal editors, conference organizers, and members of hiring, promotion, and tenure committees. In order to change this situation, both researchers *and* stakeholders need to recognize the critical role that replications play in any field claiming to be a science.

Study Questions

1. Imagine that a team of researchers investigated the impact of written feedback on ESL learners' accuracy with relative clauses in English. In our fictional study, 15 learners were assigned to a treatment group where they received written recasts of all errors with the relative clause; 15 learners were assigned to a control group that received no grammatical feedback (but rather only feedback on content). Using a pretest/posttest/delayed posttest design, the researchers found that the treatment group, over the course of three months, improved their accuracy with relative clauses by 40%. The accuracy rate of the control group also improved, but only by 25%. Which of the following would you consider more convincing evidence of the effectiveness of the treatment? Why?

    (a) The researchers employed statistical tests and found that the difference between the treatment and control groups were significantly different on both the posttest and delayed posttest (but not on the pretest).
    (b) A different team of researchers, employing the same methodology, but with a larger sample size and different target structure (the French passé composé), found the same results.

2. Still taking a look at the fictional study in question 1, what might you conclude if the replication researchers employed the same methodology, a larger sample size, and a different target structure (the French passé composé) and found *different* results (namely that there was no significant difference between the treatment and control groups on their accuracy with the target structure)?

3. It has been sometimes claimed that replication is "uninventively verifying someone else's empirical research [and] is not a completely respectable use of one's time. Choosing such a task is widely regarded as *prima facie* evidence of intellectual mediocrity, revealing a lack of creativity and perhaps even a bullying spirit" (Kane, 1984, p. 3). How would you respond to such a claim? What do you think the field of SLA can do to help promote a more positive view of replication?

4. The focus of the discussion in this chapter has been on quantitative research, and in particular, the role of replications in promoting generalizability. With respect to qualitative research, "it is often said that [such] research is neither interested in nor able to achieve generalizability" but rather "provides access to rich data about others' experience that can facilitate understandings of one's own as well as others' contexts and lives, both through similarities and differences across settings or cases" (Duff, 2006, pp. 73, 75). In your mind, would it be either possible or desirable to conduct replications of qualitative research, such as case studies? Why or why not?

5. Imagine that you are interested in replicating Mackey (1999), a laboratory-based study that examined the impact of different forms of interaction on the development of ESL questions. Participants included 7 beginners and 27 lower-intermediate ESL learners from a variety of L1 backgrounds. (Due to a limited participant pool and attrition, a larger sample size was not possible.) Participants were assigned to one of the following groups:

*   interactors (low-intermediate non-native speakers (NNSs) given interactionally modified input when necessary to complete the tasks) (7 subjects);
*   interactor unreadies (beginning NNSs given interactionally modified input when necessary to complete the tasks) (7 subjects);
*   observers (given copies of tasks and asked to observe interaction; not allowed to interact in any way) (7 subjects, lower-intermediate level);
*   scripteds (given simplified directions rendering interactionally modified input unnecessary) (6 subjects, lower-intermediate level);
*   control (7 subjects, lower-intermediate level).

The researcher found that participants in the Interactor and Interactor unready groups experienced the greatest gains in ESL question formation, a finding that has been often cited as support for the value of interaction in SLA.

(a) If you were going to conduct an approximate replication of this study, what changes would you make and why? What would be the purpose of making these changes?

(b) If you were going to conduct a conceptual replication of this study, what changes would you make and why? What would be the purpose of making these changes?

References

Abbuhl, R. (2009). *Practical methods of integrating replications into linguistic graduate programs.* Paper presented at the invited colloquium "Encouraging replication research in the field of AL and SLA" (Convener G. Porte), American Association for Applied Linguistics Annual Conference, Denver CO.

Abbuhl, R., & Mackey, A. (2008). Second language acquisition research methods. In K. King & N. Hornberger (Eds.), *Encyclopedia of language and education. Vol. 10: Research methods in language and education* (2nd ed., pp. 99–111). London, England: Kluwer.

Allen, L. (2000). Form–meaning connections and the French causative: An experiment in processing instruction. *Studies in Second Language Acquisition, 22,* 69–84.

Amir, Y., & Sharon, I. (1990). Replication research: A "must" for the scientific advancement of psychology. *Journal of Social Behavior and Personality, 5,* 51–69.

Beck, C. (1994). Replication strategies for nursing research. *IMAGE: Journal of Nursing Scholarship, 26,* 191–194.

Bigelow, M., Delmas, R., Hansen, K., & Tarone, E. (2006). Literacy and the processing of oral recasts in SLA. *TESOL Quarterly, 40,* 665–689.

Birdsong, D., & Molis, M. (2001). On the evidence for maturational constraints in second-language acquisition. *Journal of Memory and Language, 44,* 235–249.

Carpenter, H., Jeon, K., MacGregor, D., & Mackey, A. (2006). Learners' interpretations of recasts. *Studies in Second Language Acquisition, 28,* 209–236.

Connelly, C. (1986). Replication research in nursing. *International Journal of Nursing Studies, 23,* 71–77.

Crossley, S., & McNamara, D. (2008). Assessing L2 reading texts at the intermediate level: An approximate replication of Crossley, Louwerse, McCarthy & McNamara (2007). *Language Teaching, 41,* 409–429.

Dörnyei, Z. (2007). *Research methods in applied linguistics.* Oxford, England: Oxford University Press.

Duff, P. (2006). Beyond generalizability: Contextualization, complexity, and credibility in applied linguistics research. In M. Chalhoub-Deville, C. Chapelle, & P. Duff (Eds.), *Inference and generalizability in applied linguistics: Multiple perspectives* (pp. 65–95). Amsterdam, Netherlands: John Benjamins.

Easley, R., Madden, C., & Dunn, M. (2000). Conducting marketing science: The role of replication in the research process. *Journal of Business Research, 48,* 83–92.

Eckerth, J. (2009). Negotiated interaction in the L2 classroom. *Language Teaching, 42,* 109–130.

Eden, D. (2002). From the editors: Replication, meta-analysis, scientific progress, and AMJ's publication policy. *Academy of Management Journal, 45,* 841–846.

Edge, B. (1991). The production of word-final voiced obstruents in English by L1 speakers of Japanese and Cantonese. *Studies in Second Language Acquisition, 13,* 377–393.

Ellis, R., Loewen, S., & Erlam, R. (2006). Implicit and explicit corrective feedback and the acquisition of L2 grammar. *Studies in Second Language Acquisition, 28,* 339–368.

Epstein, S. (1980). The stability of behavior: II. Implications for psychological research. *American Psychologist, 35,* 790–806.

Ferris, D. (2004). The "grammar correction" debate in L2 writing: Where are we, and where do we go from here? (And what do we do in the meantime ... ?) *Journal of Second Language Writing, 13,* 40–62.

Gass, S., & Lewis, K. (2007). Perceptions of interactional feedback: Differences between heritage language learners and non-heritage language learners. In A. Mackey (Ed.), *Conversational interaction and second language acquisition: A series of empirical studies* (pp. 173–196). Oxford, England: Oxford University Press.

Gass, S., & Mackey, A. (2005). *Second language research: Methodology and design.* Mahwah, NJ: Lawrence Erlbaum.

Goodman, S. (1992). A comment on replication, *p*-values and evidence. *Statistics in Medicine, 11,* 875–879.

Guiora, A., Acton, W., Erard, R., & Strickland, F. (1980). The effects of benzodiazepine (valium) on permeability of language ego boundaries. *Language Learning, 30,* 351–363.

Hendrick, C. (1990). Replications, strict replications, and conceptual replications: Are they important? *Journal of Social Behavior and Personality, 5,* 41–49.

Henry, N., Culman, H., & VanPatten, B. (2009). More on the effects of explicit information in instructed SLA: A partial replication and a response to Fernández (2008). *Studies in Second Language Acquisition, 31,* 559–575.

Hubbard, R., & Armstrong, J. (1994). Replications and extensions in marketing: Rarely published but quite contrary. *International Journal of Research in Marketing, 11,* 233–248.

Johnson, J., & Newport, E. (1989). Critical period effects in second language acquisition: The influence of maturational state on the acquisition of English as a second language. *Cognitive Psychology, 21,* 60–99.

Kane, E. (1984). Why journal editors should encourage the replication of applied econometric research. *Quarterly Journal of Business and Economics, 23,* 3–8.

Kelly, C. (2006). Replicating empirical research in behavioral ecology: How and why it should be done but rarely ever is. *Quarterly Review of Biology, 81,* 221–236.

Kugler, C., Fischer, S., & Russell, C. (2006). Preparing a replication study. *Progress in Transplantation, 16,* 15–16.

Kupferberg, I. (1999). The cognitive turn of contrastive analysis: Empirical evidence. *Language Awareness, 8,* 210–222.

Language Teaching Review Panel. (2008). Replication studies in language learning and teaching: Questions and answers. *Language Teaching, 41,* 1–14.

Leow, R. (1995). Modality and intake in second language acquisition. *Studies in Second Language Acquisition, 17,* 79–89.

Levin, J. (1998). What if there were no more bickering about statistical significance tests? *Research in the Schools, 5,* 43–53.

Lindsay, R., & Ehrenberg, A. (1993). The design of replicated studies. *American Statistician, 47,* 217–228.

Loewen, S., & Erlam, R. (2006). Corrective feedback in the chatroom: An experimental study. *Computer Assisted Language Learning, 19,* 1–14.

Mackey, A. (1999). Input, interaction, and second language development: An empirical study of question formation in ESL. *Studies in Second Language Acquisition, 21,* 557–587.

Mackey, A., & Gass, S. (2005). *Second language research: Methodology and design.* Mahwah, NJ: Lawrence Erlbaum.

Mackey, A., & Oliver, R. (2002). Interactional feedback and children's L2 development. *System, 20,* 459–477.

Nassaji, H., & Swain, M. (2000). A Vygotskian perspective on corrective feedback in L2: The effect of random versus negotiated help on the learning of English articles. *Language Awareness, 9,* 34–51.

Norris, J., & Ortega, L. (2000). Effectiveness of L2 instruction: A research synthesis and quantitative meta-analysis. *Language Learning, 50,* 417–528.

Ottenbacher, K. (1996). The power of replications and replications of power. *American Statistician, 50,* 271–275.

Philp, J. (2003). Constraints on "noticing the gap": Nonnative speakers' noticing of recasts in NS–NNS interaction. *Studies in Second Language Acquisition, 25,* 99–126.

Polio, C., & Gass, S. (1997). Replication and reporting: A commentary. *Studies in Second Language Acquisition, 19,* 499–508.

Porte, G. (2002). *Appraising research in second language learning: A practical approach to critical analysis of quantitative research.* Amsterdam, Netherlands: John Benjamins.

Porte, G. (Ed.). (in press). *Replication studies in applied linguistics and second language acquisition.* Cambridge, England: Cambridge University Press.

Porte, G. (Chair), Abbuhl, R., Fitzpatrick, T., Mackey, A., Robinson, R., Nassaji, H., & Ortega, L. (2009, May). *Encouraging replication research in the field of applied linguistics and second language acquisition.* Colloquium conducted at the American Association of Applied Linguistics, Denver, CO.

Salaberry, M. (1997). The role of input and output practice in second language acquisition. *Canadian Modern Language Review, 53,* 422–451.

Santos, T. (1989). Replication in applied linguistics research. *TESOL Quarterly, 23,* 699–702.

Sanz, C., & VanPatten, B. (1998). On input processing, processing instruction, and the nature of replication tasks: A response to Salaberry. *Canadian Modern Language Review, 54,* 263–273.

Sasaki, M. (2000). Toward an empirical model of EFL writing processes: An exploratory study. *Journal of Second Language Writing, 9,* 259–291.

Schmidt, S. (2009). Shall we really do it again? The powerful concept of replication is neglected in the social sciences. *Review of General Psychology, 13,* 90–100.

Sheen, Y., Wright, D., & Moldawa, A. (2009). Differential effects of focused and unfocused written correction on the accurate use of grammatical forms by adult ESL learners. *System, 37,* 556–569.

Tremblay, A. (2006). On the second language acquisition of Spanish reflexive passives and reflexive impersonals by French- and English-speaking adults. *Second Language Research, 22,* 30–63.

Valdman, A. (1993). Replication study. *Studies in Second Language Acquisition, 15,* 505.

VanPatten, B., & Cadierno, T. (1993). Explicit instruction and input processing. *Studies in Second Language Acquisition, 15,* 225–243.

VanPatten, B., & Wong, W. (2004). Processing instruction and the French causative: Another replication. In B. VanPatten (Ed.), *Processing instruction: Theory, research, and commentary* (pp. 97–118). Mahwah, NJ: Lawrence Erlbaum.

Wong, W. (2001). Modality and attention to meaning and form in the input. *Studies in Second Language Acquisition, 23,* 345–368.

Index

Tables, figures and notes are identified as, respectively, 168*t*, 168*f* or 168n.

Research Methods in Second Language Acquisition: A Practical Guide, First Edition.
Edited by Alison Mackey and Susan M. Gass.
© 2012 Blackwell Publishing Ltd. Published 2012 by Blackwell Publishing Ltd.